AN INTRODUCTION TO

Christianity

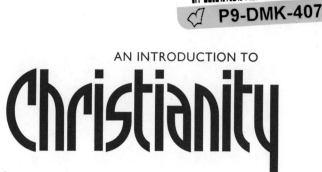

AN INTRODUCTION TO

Christianity

ALISTER E. McGRATH
Wycliffe Hall, Oxford

First published 1997
Reprinted 1997 (twice), 1998

Blackwell Publishers Inc
350 Main Street
Malden, Massachusetts 02148, USA

Blackwell Publishers Ltd
108 Cowley Road
Oxford OX4 1JF, UK

Library of Congress Cataloging in Publication Data
McGrath, Alister E., 1953–
An introduction to Christianity / Alister E. McGrath
p. cm.
Includes bibliographical references and index.
ISBN 0–631–20195–5 (hbk: alk. paper)
ISBN 0–631–20196–3 (pbk: alk. paper)
1. Christianity. I. Title.
BR121.2.M387 1996 96–23776
200—dc20 CIP

British Library Cataloguing in Publication Data
A CIP catalogue record for this book is available from the British Library

Commissioning Editor: Alison Mudditt
Desk Editor: Tony Grahame
Production Controller: Lisa Eaton
Text Designer: Lisa Eaton
Picture Researcher: Sandra Assersohn

Typeset in 10.5 on 12.5pt Galliard
by Best-set Typesetter Ltd, Hong Kong
Printed and bound in Great Britain
by T. J. International Limited, Padstow, Cornwall

This book is printed on acid-free paper

Contents

Contents

Contents

Study Panels

Maps, Diagrams and Tables

Why Study Christianity?

Anyone interested in understanding the modern world, or the process by which it came into existence, needs to understand something about the Christian faith. Christianity is by far the largest religion in the world, with somewhere between 1,250 and 1,750 million adherents (depending on the criteria employed). To understand the modern world, it is important to understand why Christianity continues to be such an important presence in, for example, the United States, and a growing presence in China. A basic understanding of the beliefs of Christianity is therefore essential to a person's basic education, particularly in western cultures whose traditions and values have been deeply shaped by Christianity.

There is also a fascination with Christianity, particularly with the person of Jesus, on the part of many who would not consider themselves to be Christians. In April 1996, the American evangelist Billy Graham spoke for an hour on the subject of the Christian gospel and its relevance for today. The talk was relayed by video and other links to a worldwide audience now known to have been in the region of 2.5 *billion* people. In western culture, a decline in church attendance has often been understood to imply a loss of interest in religion in general, or Christianity in particular. However, this represents a serious misreading of a complex situation. There has been a growing drift away from traditional institutions – whether these are social, political or religious – in the west, as people have opted for more individual-orientated activities. Christianity, which offers personal spiritual consolation as well as a community-based ethos, continues to have a considerable appeal, which it is important to understand.

There are, however, other reasons for acquiring a basic understanding of Christianity in the modern world. Some examples will bring out the points at issue.

As the recent history of the United States makes clear, Christianity is in the process of reasserting its integrity and distinctiveness, and especially its right to be represented fully in the public arena. The idea that Christianity simply has to do with private beliefs is no longer valid. Christianity, especially in its Catholic and evangelical forms, is part of the political as much as the religious landscape of modern America. The same pattern is emerging elsewhere. Anyone involved in public life needs to know about Christianity, including the distinctiveness of at least some of its forms (Catholicism, Orthodoxy, and evangelicalism being of supreme importance).

Christians represent an enormously important market in the modern world. Anyone engaged in marketing or advertising therefore needs to be aware of Christian sensitivities. Certain types of advertising will be regarded as offensive by Christians, and will thus act as a significant purchasing disincentive for this numerically and economically important group. Understanding Christianity will help you avoid giving offense needlessly to this enormously important constituency.

Those engaged in any form of counselling are increasingly becoming aware of the need to respect the integrity of the belief and value systems of those they are dealing with. Many of those seeking counselling will be Christians. It is important, in respecting the integrity of all concerned, to ensure that their beliefs are respected and understood. In particular, Christians who are suffering from low self-esteem need particularly sensitive handling, as the classic Rogerian approach involves implicit acceptance of a set of beliefs and values unacceptable to many Christians.

Numerically, Christianity is the most important of the world's religions. It is estimated that there are up to 1.7 billion Christians in today's world. While such statistics are potentially misleading, they nevertheless indicate the enormous importance of an understanding of Christianity. Anyone concerned with the modern world will have to come to terms with its leading religious faith. Yet understanding the Christian faith, in all its richness and diversity, represents one of the most rewarding topics anyone can hope to study. The present work aims to give as much help as possible within the space available.

Christianity continues to play a major role in shaping the lives, beliefs, and hopes of ordinary people. It has had a major impact on the shaping of western culture, and is a growing presence in the Pacific Rim, currently regarded as the most important region of global economic expansion. It is impossible to understand such major issues as medieval European history, modern American politics, the development of capitalism, the history of the natural sciences, or modern social tensions within Ireland or the Balkans without some understanding of the distinctive ideas and the historical development of Christianity.

But how is such a basic understanding of the beliefs and history of Christianity to be gained? It has been known for some considerable time that there is a need for a basic introduction to Christianity, which sets out and explains such fundamental matters clearly and simply. The present work aims to meet this need, by providing an entry-level introduction to Christianity, understood both as a system of beliefs and as a social reality. It is an introduction in the proper sense of the term, in that it has been written on the basis of the assumption that its readers know little or nothing about its history, practices and beliefs. Every idea and development is introduced and explained; wherever possible, the reader is given information about suitable access points for further study of all the themes dealt with in this volume. Every effort has been made to keep the language and style of this book as simple as possible.

This volume follows on from two highly successful introductions to aspects of Christian thought by the present author, also published by Blackwell Publishers – *Christian Theology: An Introduction* and *The Christian Theology Reader*. Wherever possible, the structure of the companion volumes to this work has been followed, to allow readers to progress on to them with the minimum of difficulty.

How to Use this Book

Christianity is one of the most fascinating subjects it is possible to study. This book aims to make that study as simple and rewarding as possible. It has been written assuming that you know nothing about Christianity. Obviously, the more you already know, the easier you will find this volume to handle. By the time you have finished this work, you will know enough to be able to follow most technical theological discussions and arguments, benefit from specialist lectures, and get the most from further reading.

This book aims to be a comprehensive introduction. For this reason, it includes a lot of material – considerably more than is included in many introductions of this kind. Do not be frightened by the amount of material the volume includes; you do not need to master it all. Considerable thought has been given to the best way of organizing the material. Mastering the structure of the work – which is quite simple – will allow it to be used more effectively by both teachers and students.

The work is divided into four major sections. The first part deals with the person of Jesus. It is impossible to understand Christianity without engaging with the figure of Jesus, and the sources through which we know him. The work thus opens with a major analysis of the Christian understanding of the identity and significance of Jesus, including a detailed discussion of the contents and themes of the Bible. This section includes a presentation of the New Testament portrayal of the person of Jesus, as well as the subsequent development of this material in the Christian tradition. You are strongly recommended to read this material first; without it, many later sections of this work will not make sense.

The second part of the book is an introduction to the basic teachings of Christianity. This opens with a discussion of the role of creeds in relation to Christian beliefs, and continues with an exploration of the sources and contents of Christian theology. The section dealing with Christian beliefs focuses on the Apostles' Creed, on account of its importance in relation to Christian instruction. As the Christian understanding of the identity and significance of Jesus has already been discussed at length in the first part of this work, this material is not duplicated in the second.

The third part of the work deals with the historical development of Christianity. It explores the way in which Christianity expanded from its origins in Palestine to become by far the largest global religion. The story of this expansion is fascinating. The five chapters in this part of the work present the story of this development. To understand the nature of Christianity in the world today, you need to understand its history. It is particularly important to understand the historical origins of the distinction between Catholic, Orthodox, and Protestant Christianity.

The final part of the work introduces Christianity as a way of life, rather than just a set of ideas. It will allow you to understand something of the way in which Christians worship, and especially the events lying behind the major Christian festivals. It also explains in more detail the distinctions between Catholic, Orthodox, and Protestant Christianity.

Each chapter is provided with study questions to allow you to test how well you have understood the material. If you are not a Christian, you will find it helpful to discuss some of the questions with your Christian friends. They will be able to give fuller answers to the questions, and help you with other questions you may have as you read the book.

Finally, the work includes a glossary of Christian terms and a list of suggestions for further reading. The Internet is now firmly established as a major source of information. A concluding section provides you with details of major Web sites which will offer you access to an astonishing amount of information on every aspect of Christianity. If you have access to the Internet, you will find this an invaluable source of up-to-date information on Christian meetings, debates, beliefs, prayers, people and liturgies. Enjoy surfing!

Exploring Christianity from the Outside

Many of those using this book will be Christians. Others will be using it to try to gain some kind of understanding of the Christian faith from outside. If you are not a Christian, you may find the following comments helpful in getting the most out of your study of the Christian faith. The most important thing to understand is that Christianity is a way of living. It is not just ideas or values – it is about an entire mode of life, which involves beliefs, hopes, values, goals, and commitment.

It is therefore important to realize that Christianity can never be understood or appreciated simply by reading a book about it! It is often difficult to understand or appreciate the inner dynamics of Christianity if you are looking in from the outside. At times, it is like looking into a lighted room from outside, being able to see people moving and talking, yet without understanding what is being said or done. This book will be of some use to you. It will certainly provide you with invaluable information about what Christians believe, and why. But it cannot do justice to Christianity as a way of living. For this reason, you will find it helpful to get to know some Christians, and ask them to take you to their meetings, or talk about their faith. A book can never convey adequately the full richness and diversity of the Christian faith.

It is helpful to think of Christianity as having three components.

1   *A set of beliefs.* Although there are differences between Christians on a number of doctrinal matters, it is relatively easy to show that a common core of beliefs lies behind the different versions of Christianity you are likely to encounter. A book such as this will be useful as an introduction to the beliefs of Christians, and help you to understand the central themes of the Christian faith.
2   *A set of values.* Christianity is a strongly ethical faith. This does not,

however, mean that Christianity is about a set of rules, in which Christians mechanically conform to a set of instructions. Rather, it is about a set of values which arises from being redeemed. Christian values are what result from being a Christian. This book will help you understand something of those values, and how they arise.

3   *A way of life.* Being a Christian is not just about beliefs and values; it is about a definite way of living which involves everyday life being affected in certain ways by your faith. At its most obvious, this is reflected in going to a church or other form of Christian community which meets for prayer and worship. While this book will attempt to describe at least some aspects of Christian living, you need to be aware that the best way of understanding Christianity at this point is to get involved in a local Christian church or community. There are enormous variations in the ways in which Christianity expresses itself, reflecting differences of climate, geography, culture, tradition, and theology. Exploring Christianity is thus something of a challenge – but it is an enormously rewarding and satisfying challenge!

Acknowledgments

All Scripture quotations, unless otherwise indicated, are taken from the Holy Bible, New International Version®, © 1973, 1978, 1984 by International Bible Society, used by permission of Zondervan Publishing House and published in Great Britain by Hodder & Stoughton Ltd. All rights reserved. Quotations identified RSV are from the Revised Standard Version of the Bible, copyright 1946, 1952, 1971 by the Division of Christian Education of the National Council of the Churches of Christ in the USA, and used by permission.

We are grateful to the following for permission to reproduce the pictures:

Christie's Images–pp. 118, 196, 379, 393, 404;
Sonia Halliday Photographs–pp. 245 (F.H.C. Birch), 392, 408;
Hutchison Library–pp. 23, 266 (M. Harvey), 403 (V. Juleva), 409 (I. Tree);
Popperfoto–pp. 97, 325, 334, 381, 400;
Sotheby's London–pp. 86, 88, 102, 104

Introduction

At some point around the year 60, the Roman authorities woke up to the fact that there seemed to be a new secret society in the heart of their city, which was rapidly gaining recruits. They had not the slightest idea what it was all about, although it was clearly due to some agitator. The reports that filtered back spoke of some mysterious and dark figure called "Chrestus" or "Christus" being the cause of all the trouble. But who was he? And what was it all about?

The authorities had little hesitation in blaming this new religious movement for the great fire which swept through Rome in 64. The Roman historian Cornelius Tacitus gave a full account of this event some fifty years later. In this account, he refers to "the Christians," a group who took their name from someone called "Christus," who had been executed by Pontius Pilate back in the reign of Tiberius. This "pernicious superstitition" had found its way to Rome, where it had gained a huge following. It is clear that the term "Christian" has its origins as a term of abuse. Yet, muddled and confused though the official Roman accounts of this movement may be, they were clear that it centered, in some way, on the figure of "Christus." It was not regarded as being of any permanent significance, being seen as something of a minor irritation. At worst, it was a threat to the cult of emperor worship.

Yet three hundred years later, this new religion had become the official religion of the Roman empire. Where once Roman historians dated events from the founding of the city of Rome, those events would now be dated from the coming of Jesus Christ.

So what was this new religion? What did it teach? Where did it come from? Why was it so attractive? How did it come to be so influential in its first few centuries? What happened after it had achieved such success at Rome? And how has it shaped the lives of individuals and the history of the human race? It is these questions which this book will attempt to answer. The study of Christianity is one of the most fascinating, stimulating and intellectually and spiritually rewarding undertakings available to anyone. This book aims to lay the foundations for such a study, opening doors to discovering more about the world's leading religion.

This introductory book is divided into four parts. The first part focuses on the founder of Christianity, Jesus of Nazareth. This part explores both the sources of our knowledge of Jesus in the Bible, and the Christian understanding of the importance of Jesus. The second part offers an overview of Christian doctrines, aiming to bring out the main themes of Christian thinking. Particular care will be taken to ensure that the doctrinal differences between Christians are identified and discussed. The third part provides a survey of Christian history, exploring the way in which Christianity expanded and developed during the first two thousand years of its existence. Finally, the fourth part explores Christian life, focusing on the way in which Christianity impacts on everyday living. This part will focus on everyday church life – such as worship and church architecture. It will also trace the way in which Christianity has shaped, and been shaped by, the cultures into which it has expanded and found a home.

Finally, an apology must be offered to readers. There is so much more that needs to be included in this volume. To introduce Christianity properly would take at least three times the amount of material than is presented in this book. By definition, an "introduction" can do little more than whet the appetite for more. The reader of this volume will find plenty of advice about where to turn next for further reading, contacts with Christian organizations, or exploring the vast network of Christian resources available on the Internet.

PART 1

Jesus of Nazareth: the Founder and the Sources

The figure of Jesus Christ is central to Christianity. Indeed, there is a sense in which Christianity *is* Jesus Christ. The gospel of Mark, widely regarded as the first of the gospels to be committed to writing, opens with the following words: "The beginning of the gospel of Jesus Christ, the Son of God" (Mark 1:1). It is all too easy to assume that the word "gospel" refers to the book which Mark wrote. Yet Mark is not referring to his book with these words. He is declaring that the "gospel" – that is, the "good news" – *is* Jesus Christ. After two thousand years or so, people have become accustomed to referring to the first four books of the New Testament as "gospels." Yet the reason that the books are called "gospels" is that they deal with the central figure of the Christian gospel – Jesus Christ, or, to use a title often encountered in the gospels and the Acts of the Apostles, Jesus of Nazareth.

So what does this important word "gospel" mean? As we have seen, it has come to refer to one particular type of writing – a book which deals with the life of Jesus. Its real meaning, however, is "good news." The New Testament was written in the everyday Greek of the first century (a particular form of Greek which is often referred to as *koine*, meaning "common" or "everyday"). The Greek word which is translated as "gospel" is *evangelion*, which comes from two Greek roots meaning "good" and "news" or "message." The term refers to something having happened with positive implications for its hearers. The gospels are thus books which relate "the good news of Jesus Christ."

So what are the sources for our understanding of the identity and importance of Jesus? He is certainly referred to in the writings of those Roman historians who deal with events of the first century. However, our main source of knowledge of Jesus is the New Testament in particular, and the Bible in general. For this reason, we shall begin our discussion of Jesus with an exploration of the Christian Bible.

The Christian Bible: an Introduction

Anyone beginning to study Christianity soon realizes how central the Bible is. If you attend a Christian service of worship, you will hear the Bible read publicly as an essential part of that worship. You will probably hear a sermon preached on one of the biblical passages read during the service. If you join a small group of Christians meeting for study and prayer, you will probably find that "Bible Study" – that is, reflection on the meaning and relevance of a short passage from the Bible – is an important part of their time together. Millions of Christians begin the day with a personal study of a short biblical passage. Countless commentaries on the Bible as a whole, or individual books of the Bible, are available in bookstores, and are part of the staple diet of many active Christians.

So what is the Bible? And why is it so important? In this part of this introduction, we shall begin to explore what the Christian Bible is, and the role it plays for Christians.

The Bible: the Origin of the Term

The term "the Bible" is used to refer to the collection of writings regarded as authoritative by Christians. Other terms are also used: for example, the terms "Sacred Scripture" or "Holy Scripture" will be encountered regularly in Christian writings. However, the term "Bible" is widely regarded as the most acceptable way to refer to this collection of writings. The unusual word "Bible" needs explanation. Like many words in modern English, it derives from a Greek original. The Greek phrase which has been rendered into English is *ta biblia* – literally, "the books." The Greek phrase is plural, and refers to the collection of books, or writings, regarded as authoritative by Christians.

The Bible is divided into two major sections, referred to as the *Old*

Testament and the *New Testament*. A brief overview of the contents of each of these testaments will be provided below; a more detailed analysis can be found in later sections (p. 20, p. 55). The Old Testament consists of 39 books, beginning with Genesis and ending with Malachi. It is almost entirely written in Hebrew, the language of Israel; however, some short sections are written in Aramaic, an international language widely used in the diplomacy of the ancient near east. The Old Testament itself includes a number of different kinds of writings, of which the most important are the following:

1 The *Five Books of the Law* are sometimes also referred to as *The Five Books of Moses*, reflecting a traditional belief that they were largely written by Moses. In more scholarly works, they are sometimes referred to as *The Pentateuch*, from the Greek words for "five" and "books". These are: Genesis, Exodus, Leviticus, Numbers, and Deuteronomy. These deal with the creation of the world, the calling of Israel as a people, and its early history, including the Exodus from Egypt. The story which they tell ends with the people of Israel being about to cross over the Jordan, and enter the promised land. One of the most important themes of these books is the giving of the Law to Moses, and its implications for the life of Israel.

2 The *Historical Books*: Joshua, Judges, Ruth, 1 and 2 Samuel, 1 and 2 Kings, 1 and 2 Chronicles, Ezra, Nehemiah and Esther. These books deal with various aspects of the history of the people of God from their entry into the promised land of Canaan to the return of the people of Jerusalem from exile in the city of Babylon. It includes detailed accounts of the conquest of Canaan, the establishment of a monarchy in Israel, the great reigns of kings David and Solomon, the break-up of the single nation of Israel into two parts (the northern kingdom of Israel and and the southern kingdom of Judah), the destruction of Israel by the Assyrians, the defeat of Judah and exile of her people by the Babylonians, and the final return from exile and the rebuilding of the temple. The books are arranged in historical order.

3 The *Prophets*. This major section of the Old Testament contains the writings of a group of individuals, inspired by the Holy Spirit, who sought to make the will of God known to their people over a period of time. There are sixteen prophetic writings in the Old Testament, which are usually divided into two categories. First, there are the four *major prophets*: Isaiah, Jeremiah, Ezekiel and Daniel. These are followed by the twelve *minor prophets*: Hosea, Joel, Amos, Obadiah, Jonah, Micah, Nahum, Habakkuk, Zephaniah, Haggai, Zechariah, and Malachi. The use of the words "major" and "minor" does not imply any judgment about the relative importance of the prophets. It refers simply to the

length of the books in question. The prophetic writings are arranged roughly in historical order.

Other types of book can be noted, including the *Wisdom Writings*: Job, Proverbs, Ecclesiastes. These works deal with the question of how true wisdom may be found, and often provide some practical examples of wisdom. Another category of writings which lies outside the Old Testament should also be noted – the *Apocrypha*. This small collection of seven books (which is roughly 15 percent of the length of the Old Testament) is also sometimes referred to as the "deuterocanonical writings." It includes a number of later writings from Old Testament times which, although informative, has not been regarded as of binding importance by Christians. Some Bibles include this section of writings; others do not (see pp. 15–17).

The *New Testament* is of particular importance to Christians, as it sets out the basic events and beliefs of the Christian gospel. The New Testament, which consists of 27 books, is considerably shorter than the Old Testament. It is entirely written in Greek. It is strongly recommended that new readers of the Bible begin by reading one of the four *gospels*: Matthew, Mark, Luke, and John. The word "gospel" basically means "good news." Each of the four gospel writers – or "evangelists," as they are sometimes known – sets out the basic events lying behind the good news. These four books describe the life of Jesus Christ, which reaches its climax in his resurrection, as well as presenting his teachings.

The four gospels have distinctive characteristics (see pp. 60–64) – for example, Matthew is concerned to present Jesus' teaching, whereas Mark is more interested in focusing on the last week of his earthly life. Taken together, all four build up to give a comprehensive account of the life, death, and resurrection of Jesus Christ. They provide the main building blocks of the Christian faith, allowing readers to understand why Christians have believed that Jesus Christ is indeed the Lord and Saviour of the world. The term *synoptic gospels* is often used to refer to the first three gospels (Matthew, Mark, and Luke). This term refers to their similar literary structure.

This is followed by an account of the expansion of Christianity. How were events described in the gospels received at the time? How did the gospel spread from Palestine to Europe? These questions are addressed in the fifth work to be found in the New Testament, the full title of which is "the Acts of the Apostles," but which is more usually referred to simply as "Acts." The gospel of Luke and Acts are widely agreed to have been written by the same person – Luke.

The next major section of material in the New Testament are the *letters*, sometimes still referred to by the older English word *epistles*. These letters provide teaching concerning both Christian beliefs and behaviour, as important today as they were when they were first written. Some of the false teachings which arose in the early period of the church's history are in circulation once more, and these letters provide important resources for defending the integrity of the Christian faith today.

Most of the letters were written by Paul, whose conversion to the Christian faith led him to undertake a major program of evangelism and church planting. Many of his letters were written to churches he had planted, giving them advice. Other letter-writers include the apostles Peter and John. The letters should not be thought of primarily as doctrinal textbooks, but living testimonies to every aspect of the Christian faith, which include doctrinal teaching along with moral guidance and spiritual encouragement. The term *Pastoral Letters* is sometimes used to refer to the two letters addressed to Timothy and his letter to Titus, which deal particularly with issues of pastoral importance.

The New Testament then ends with the book of Revelation, which stands in a class of its own. It represents a vision of the end of history, in which the writer is allowed to see into heaven, and gain a glimpse of the new Jerusalem which is prepared for believers.

STUDY PANEL 1

Referring to Passages in the Bible

How do you identify the biblical passage you want to study or talk about? To make this as easy as possible, a kind of shorthand way of referring to biblical passages has evolved over the years. To locate a verse in the Bible you need to identify three things: the *book* of the Bible; the *chapter* of that book, and the *verse* of that chapter. To make sure you understand this, turn to the Acts of the Apostles, chapter 27, verse 1. What is the name of the centurion mentioned in this verse? If your answer is not "Julius," check your reference again. Now try turning to Paul's letter to the Romans, chapter 16, verse 5. Who was the first convert to Christ in Asia? If your answer was not "Epenetus," check it again.

The above system is potentially quite cumbersome. Writing out everything – as in Paul's letter to the Romans, chapter 16, verse 5 – takes up too much space. So it is abbreviated, as follows: Rom 16:5. This is the standard form of reference, with the following features:

1 An abbreviation of the book of the Bible being referred to, usually two or three letters in length (such as 1Ki for "1 Kings," Mt for "Matthew," and 1Co for "1 Corinthians").
2 The number of the chapter of that book, usually followed by a colon (:);
3 The number of the verse in that chapter.

Study Panel 1 Continued

A full list of the books of the Bible, and their standard abbreviations, will be found on page 10. There is no need to identify the writer of the book (such as Paul), or state whether it is found in the Old or New Testament. All that is needed are these three parameters.

Having got used to referring to individual verses, we now need to explore how to refer to a passage of more than one verse. This is very simple. The reference "Mt 3:13–17" is to the passage which begins with Mt 3:13, and ends at Mt 3:17. To indicate a passage within a single chapter of a biblical book, you need only identify the opening and closing verse in this way. Sometimes the passage will include material from two or more chapters. The following reference is of this kind: 1Th 4:13–5:11. This refers to a passage which begins at 1Th 4:13, and ends at 1Th 5:11.

Now that you are familiar with the basic aspects of this system, there are some minor points that need qualifying. First, some biblical books are so brief that they consist only of one chapter (Obadiah; Philemon; 2 John; 3 John; Jude). In this case, only the verse number is cited. Thus Phm 2 is a reference to the second verse of Philemon. Second, individual Psalms are treated as chapters of the Psalter. Thus a reference to Ps 23:1 is a reference to the first verse of the twenty-third Psalm.

Finally, in older books, you will find that this system is not always followed. Roman numerals, superscript numbers, and all kinds of punctuation may be used. To give you an idea of the variety, the following are all ways of referring to Paul's second letter to the Corinthians, chapter thirteen, verse fourteen.

2Co 13:14   II Cor. xiii.14   2 Cor 13.14   *II Cor* 13.14

The Continuity Between Old and New Testaments

The Christian terms "Old Testament" and "New Testament" are strongly theological in nature. These Christian terms rest upon the belief that the contents of the Old Testament belong to a period of God's dealings with the world which has in some way been superseded or relativized by the coming of Christ in the New Testament. Roughly the same collection of texts is referred to by Jewish writers as "the law, prophets and writings," and by Christian writers as "the Old Testament." There is thus no particular reason why someone who is not a Christian should feel obliged to refer to this collection of books as the "Old Testament," apart from custom of use.

The Books of the Bible and Their Abbreviations

Old Testament

Genesis	Ge	Zephaniah	Zep
Exodus	Ex	Haggai	Hag
Leviticus	Lev	Zechariah	Zec
Numbers	Nu	Malachi	Mal
Deuteronomy	Dt		
Joshua	Jos		
Judges	Jdg	*New Testament*	
Ruth	Ru	Matthew	Mt
1 Samuel	1 Sa	Mark	Mk
2 Samuel	2 Sa	Luke	Lk
1 Kings	1 Ki	John	Jn
2 Kings	2 Ki	Acts	Ac
1 Chronicles	1 Ch	Romans	Rom
2 Chronicles	2 Ch	1 Corinthians	1 Co
Ezra	Ezr	2 Corinthians	2 Co
Nehemiah	Ne	Galatians	Gal
Esther	Est	Ephesians	Eph
Job	Job	Philippians	Php
Psalms	Ps	Colossians	Col
Proverbs	Pr	1 Thessalonians	1 Th
Ecclesiastes	Ecc	2 Thessalonians	2 Th
Song of Songs	SS	1 Timothy	1 Ti
Isaiah	Isa	2 Timothy	2 Ti
Jeremiah	Jer	Titus	Tit
Lamentations	La	Philemon	Phm
Ezekiel	Eze	Hebrews	Heb
Daniel	Da	James	Jas
Hosea	Hos	1 Peter	1 Pe
Joel	Joel	2 Peter	2 Pe
Amos	Am	1 John	1 Jn
Obadiah	Ob	2 John	2 Jn
Jonah	Jnh	3 John	3 Jn
Micah	Mic	Jude	Jude
Nahum	Na	Revelation	Rev
Habakkuk	Hab		

The Christian theological framework which leads to this distinction is that of "covenants" or "dispensations." The basic Christian belief that the coming of Christ inaugurates something new expresses itself in a distinctive attitude toward the Old Testament, which could basically be summarized thus: religious principles and ideas (such as the notion of a sovereign God who is active in human history) are appropriated; religious practices (such as dietary laws and sacrificial routines) are not.

How, then, are the Old and New Testaments related to one another according to Christian theology? One option was to treat the Old Testament as the writings of a religion which had nothing to do with Christianity. This approach is especially associated with the second-century writer Marcion, who was excommunicated in the year 144. According to Marcion, Christianity was a religion of love, which had no place whatsoever for law. The Old Testament relates to a different god than the New; the Old Testament God, who merely created the world, was obsessed with the idea of law. The New Testament God, however, redeemed the world, and was concerned with love. According to Marcion, the purpose of Christ was to depose the Old Testament God (who bears a considerable resemblance to the Gnostic "demiurge," a semi-divine figure responsible for fashioning the world), and usher in the worship of the true God of grace. A similar teaching was associated with the Manicheans, who had a significant influence on the leading Christian writer Augustine of Hippo during his younger period. In refuting the Manichean view of the Old Testament as an irrelevance, Augustine argued that it was necessary to see the Old Testament in the light of the New to appreciate its full significance and importance for Christians. Augustine's views are conveniently summarized in his famous dictum: "The New Testament lies hidden in the Old, and the Old Testament is unveiled in the New."

There are faint echoes of this Manichean idea in the writings of the German reformer Martin Luther. Although Luther insists that both Old and New Testaments relate to the actions of the same God, he nevertheless insists upon the total opposition of law and grace. Judaism, according to Luther, was totally preoccupied with the idea of justification by works, believing that it was possible to merit favor in the sight of God by one's achievements. The gospel, in contrast, emphasized that justification was completely gratuitous, resting only on the grace of God. Although grace could be detected in the Old Testament (e.g., Isaiah 40–55), and law in the New (e.g., the Sermon on the Mount, Matthew 5–7), Luther often seemed to suggest that the Old Testament was primarily a religion of law, contrasted with the New Testament faith in grace.

The majority position within Christian theology has on the one hand emphasized the continuity between the two testaments, while at the same time noted the distinction between them. This seems to be the approach found within the New Testament itself. Thus New Testament writers clearly saw themselves as continuing the great history of salvation, narrated in the Old Testament. Matthew's gospel, for example, brings out the continuity between Jesus and Moses, the gospel and the law, and the church and Israel. Paul's letters often focus on the continuity between the faith of Christians and that of Abraham. The letter to the Hebrews provides what is virtually a point by point comparison between Christianity and Judaism, stressing both the continuity between them, and the way in which Christianity brings to perfection the themes of the Old Testament. Several strands can be seen in the New Testament affirmation of continuity with the Old Testament; we shall consider two of particular interest.

In the first place, there is a continuity of divine action, purpose and identity between the testaments. The New Testament writers stress the fact that the God to whom the New Testament bears witness is the same God who is present and active in the history of Israel, and who may be read about in the Old Testament.

In the second place, there is a continuity of institutions between the testaments. This is a more complex idea, and requires a little explanation. In the sixteenth century, what is usually referred to as the "threefold office of Christ" became of major importance within Protestant circles as a means of highlighting the continuity between the Old and New Testaments. We have already noted the importance of three major institutions in the Old Testament: prophecy, the priesthood, and the monarchy. Jesus' identity and relevance can be summed up in the threefold formula "prophet, priest and king." The prophetic aspects of Jesus' identity relate to his teaching and his miracles; the priestly aspects of his identity concern his offering made for the sin of humanity upon the cross, and the continued intercession of the risen Christ for his people; the kingly aspects of his identity concern the rule of the risen Christ over his people.

These three categories were seen as a convenient summary of all that Jesus Christ had achieved in order to redeem his people. Jesus is prophet (Matthew 21:11; Luke 7:16), priest (Hebrews 2:17; 3:1) and king (Matthew 21:5; 27:11), bringing together in his one person the three great offices of the Old Testament. Jesus is the prophet who, like Moses, would see God face to face (Deuteronomy 17:15); he is the king who, like David, will establish and reign over the people of God (2 Samuel 7:12–16); he is the priest who will cleanse God's people from their sins. Thus the three gifts brought to Jesus by the Magi (or Wise Men, Matthew 2:1–12) were seen as reflecting these three functions.

A more rigorous analysis of this understanding of the relation between the Old and New Testaments can be found in the works of John Calvin. Calvin argues that there exist a fundamental similarity and continuity between Old and New Testaments on the basis of three considerations. First, Calvin stresses the immutability of the divine will. God cannot do one thing in the Old Testament, and follow it by doing something totally different in the New. There must be a fundamental continuity of action and intention between the two. Second, both celebrate and proclaim the grace of God manifested in Jesus Christ. The Old Testament may only be able to witness to Jesus Christ "from a distance and darkly"; nevertheless, its witness to the coming of Christ is real. In the third place, both testaments possess the "same signs and sacraments," bearing witness to the same grace of God.

Calvin thus argues that the two testaments are identical. In terms of their substance and content, there is no radical discontinuity between them. The Old Testament happens to occupy a different chronological position in the divine plan of salvation than the New; its content (rightly understood), however, is the same. Calvin proceeds to identify five points of difference between Old and New Testaments, relating to form, rather than substance.

1   The New Testament possesses greater clarity than the Old, particularly in relation to invisible things. The Old Testament tends to be pervaded by a certain preoccupation with things visible and tangible, which might obscure the invisible goals, hopes and values which lie behind them. Calvin illustrates this point with reference to the land of Canaan; the Old Testament tends to treat this earthly possession as an end in itself, whereas the New Testament regards it as a reflection of the future inheritance reserved for believers in heaven.

2   The Old and New Testaments adopt significantly different approaches to imagery. The Old Testament employs a mode of representation of reality which Calvin suggests leads to an indirect encounter with the truth, through various figures of speech and visual images; the New Testament, however, allows an immediate experience of truth. The Old Testament presents "only the image of truth, . . . the shadow instead of the substance," giving a "foretaste of that wisdom which would one day be clearly revealed"; the New Testament presents the truth directly in all its fulness.

3   A third difference between the two testaments centers on the distinction between law and gospel, or the letter and the spirit. The Old Testament lacks the empowering activity of the Holy Spirit, whereas the New is able to deliver this power. The law can thus command, forbid and promise, but lacks the necessary resources to effect any fundamental change within human nature which renders such commands necessary in the first place. The gospel is able to "change or correct the perversity which naturally exists in all humans." It is interesting to note that the radical antithesis between law and gospel, so characteristic of Luther (and Marcion before him), is quite lacking. Law and gospel are continuous with each other, and do not stand in diametrical opposition.

4   Developing this previous distinction, Calvin argues that a fourth distinction can be discerned in the differing emotions evoked by the law and the gospel. The Old Testament evokes fear and trembling, and holds the conscience in bondage, whereas the New produces a response of freedom and joy.

5   The Old Testament revelation was confined to the Jewish nation; the New Testament revelation is universal in its scope. Calvin restricts the sphere of the old covenant to Israel; with the coming of Jesus Christ, this partition was broken down, as the distinction between Jew and Greek, between those who were circumcised and those who were not, was abolished. The calling of the Gentiles thus distinguishes the New from the Old Testaments.

Throughout this discussion of the distinction between the Old and New Testaments, and the superiority of the latter over the former, Calvin is careful to allow that certain individuals within the old covenant – for example, the patriarchs – were able to discern hints of the new covenant. At no point do the divine purposes or nature alter; they are merely made clearer, in accordance with the limitations imposed upon human understanding. Thus, to give but one example, it was not as if God had originally determined to restrict grace to the Jewish nation alone, and then decided to make it available to everyone else as well; rather, the evolutionary thrust of the divine plan was only made clear with the coming of Jesus Christ. Calvin summarizes this general principle with the assertion that "where the entire law is concerned, the gospel differs from it only in clarity of presentation." Christ is shown forth and the grace of the Holy Spirit is offered in both Old and New Testaments – but more clearly and more fully in the latter.

The Contents of the Bible

The Christian Bible is a collection of 66 books, of which 39 are found in the Old Testament, and 27 in the New Testament. But how were the contents of the Bible decided? By what process were the 66 books of the Bible selected? At a fairly early stage in its history, the Christian church had to make some important decisions as to what the term "Scripture" actually designated. The patristic period witnessed a process of decision making, in which limits were laid down to the New Testament – a process usually known as "the fixing of the canon."

The word "canon" derives from the Greek word *kanon*, meaning "a rule" or "a fixed reference point." The phrase "the canon of Scripture" thus refers to a limited and defined group of writings, which are accepted as authoritative within the Christian church. The term "canonical" is used to refer to scriptural writings accepted to be within the canon. Thus the Gospel of Luke is referred to as "canonical," whereas the Gospel of Thomas is "extra-canonical" (that is, lying outside the canon of Scripture).

For the writers of the New Testament, the term "Scripture" meant primarily a writing of the Old Testament. This can be seen particularly clearly in Paul's insistence that "All Scripture is God-breathed and is useful for teaching, rebuking, correcting and training in righteousness" (2 Timothy 3:16), which is a specific affirmation of the inspiration and authority of the writings of the Old Testament. (The phrase here translated as "all Scripture" could equally well be translated as "every Scripture" or "every writing".) However, within a short period, early Christian writers (such as Justin Martyr) were referring to the "New Testament" (to be contrasted with the "Old Testament"), and insisting that both were to be treated with equal authority. By the time of Irenaeus, writing in the late second century, it was generally accepted that there were four canonical gospels; by the late second century there was a widespread consensus that the four gospels, Acts, and letters had the status of inspired Scripture. Thus Clement of Alexandria recognized four gospels, Acts, fourteen letters of Paul (the letter to the Hebrews being regarded as Pauline), and Revelation. Tertullian, writing in the early second century, declared that alongside the "law and the prophets" were the "evangelical and apostolic writings (*evangelicae et apostolicae litterae*)," which were both to be regarded as authoritative within the church. Gradually, agreement was reached on the list of books which were recognized as inspired Scripture, and the order in which they were to be arranged. In 367, the influential Greek Christian writer Athanasius circulated a letter which identified the 27 books of the New Testament, as we now know it, as being canonical.

Debate centered especially on a number of books. The western church had hesitations about including the letter to the Hebrews, in that it was not specifically attributed to an apostle; the eastern church had reservations about the book of Revelation (sometimes also referred to as "the Apocalypse"). Four of the smaller books (2 Peter, 2 and 3 John, and Jude) were often omitted from early lists of New Testament writings. Some writings now outside the canon were regarded with favor in parts of the church, although they ultimately failed to gain universal acceptance as canonical. Examples of these include the first letter of Clement (an early bishop of Rome, who wrote around 96) and the *Didache*, a short early Christian manual on morals and church practices, probably dating from the first quarter of the second century.

The arrangement of the material was also subject to considerable variation. Agreement was reached at an early stage that the gospels should have the place of honor within the canon, followed by the Acts of the Apostles. The eastern church tended to place the seven "catholic epistles" or "general letters" (that is, James; 1 and 2 Peter; 1, 2 and 3 John; and Jude) before the fourteen Pauline letters (Hebrews being accepted as Pauline), whereas the western church placed Paul's letters immediately after Acts, and followed them with the catholic letters. Revelation ended the canon in both east and west, although its status was subject to debate for some time within the eastern church.

What criteria were used in drawing up the canon? The basic principle appears to have been that of the *recognition* rather than the *imposition* of authority. In other words, the works in question were recognized by Christians as already possessing authority, rather than having an arbitrary authority imposed upon them. For Irenaeus, the church does not create the canon of Scripture; it acknowledges, conserves, and receives canonical Scripture on the basis of the authority which is already inherent in it. Some early Christians appear to have regarded apostolic authorship as of decisive importance; others were prepared to accept books which did not appear to have apostolic credentials. However, although the precise details of how the selection was made remain unclear, it is certain that the canon was closed within the western church by the beginning of the fifth century. The issue of the canon would not be raised again until the time of the Reformation.

At the time of the Reformation, a major debate broke out over whether some works accepted by the medieval church as canonical really deserved this status. It must be emphasized that debate centered on the Old Testament; the canon of the New Testament was never seriously questioned, despite Martin Luther's musings about the letter of James. While all the New Testament works were accepted as canonical – Luther's misgivings concerning four of them gaining little support – doubts were raised concerning the canonicity of a group of Old Testament works. A comparison of the contents of the Old Testament in the Hebrew Bible on the one hand, and the Greek and Latin versions (such as the Vulgate) on the other, shows that the latter contain a number of works not found in the former. Following the lead of Jerome, the reformers argued that the only Old Testament writings which could be regarded as belonging to the canon of Scripture were those originally included in the Hebrew Bible.

A distinction was thus drawn between the "Old Testament" and the "Apocrypha": the former consisted of works found in the Hebrew Bible, while the latter consisted of works found in the Greek and Latin Bibles (such as the Vulgate), but *not* in the Hebrew Bible. While some reformers allowed that the apocryphal works were edifying reading, there was general agreement that these works could not be used as the basis of doctrine. Medieval theologians, however, to be followed by the Council of Trent in 1546, defined the Old Testament as "those Old Testament works contained in the Greek and Latin bibles," thus eliminating any distinction between "Old Testament" and "Apocrypha."

The Deuterocanonical Books

The following works are regarded as "deuterocanonical." Note that they are also referred to as "apocryphal," in that the collection of books is also known as "the Apocrypha."

Tobit (sometimes spelled "Tobias")
Judith
Wisdom
Ecclesiasticus
1 Maccabees
2 Maccabees
Baruch

A fundamental distinction thus developed between Catholic and Protestant understandings of what the term "Scripture" actually meant. This distinction persists to the present day. A comparison of Protestant versions of the Bible – the two most important being the *Revised Standard Version* (RSV) and *New International Version* (NIV) – with a Catholic Bible, such as the Jerusalem Bible, will reveal these differences. But what is the relevance of this difference?

The difference in question has no major importance, although it is of relevance to one debate which broke out at the time of the Reformation. One Catholic practice to which the reformers took particular exception was that of praying for the dead. To the reformers, this practice rested upon a non-biblical foundation (the doctrine of purgatory), and encouraged popular superstition and ecclesiastical exploitation. Their Catholic opponents, however, were able to meet this objection by pointing out that the practice of praying for the dead was explicitly mentioned in Scripture, at 2 Maccabees 12:40–6. The reformers, however, having declared that this book was apocryphal (and hence not part of the Bible), were able to respond that, in their view at least, the practice was not scriptural. This merited the obvious riposte from the Catholic side – that the reformers based their theology on Scripture, only after having excluded from the canon of Scripture any works which happened to contradict this theology.

One outcome of this debate was the production and circulation of authorized lists of books which were to be regarded as "scriptural." The fourth session of the Council of Trent (1546) produced a detailed list, which included the works of the Apocrypha as authentically scriptural, while Protestant congregations in Switzerland, France and elsewhere produced lists which deliberately omitted reference to these works, or else indicated that they were of no importance in matters of doctrine. The 1559 Gallic Confession is an excellent example of this kind of work.

The Gallic Confession on the Canon of Scripture

The "Gallic Confession" is a French Protestant confession of faith which was originally published in French in 1559. It sets out clearly the characteristic Protestant understanding of the Canon of Scripture. Note how each book is specified by name, with variants of the name being noted – for example, in the case of Proverbs and Revelation.

Holy Scripture is contained in the canonical books of the Old and New Testaments, as follows: the five books of Moses, namely Genesis, Exodus, Leviticus, Numbers, Deuteronomy; then Joshua, Judges, Ruth, the first and second books of Samuel, the first and second books of the Kings, the first and second books of the Chronicles, otherwise called Paralipomenon, the first book of Ezra; then Nehemiah, the book of Esther, Job, the Psalms of David, the Proverbs or Maxims of Solomon; the book of Ecclesiastes, called the Preacher, the Song of Solomon; then the books of Isaiah, Jeremiah, Lamentations of Jeremiah, Ezekiel, Daniel, Hosea, Joel, Amos, Obadiah, Jonah, Micah, Nahum, Habakkuk, Zephaniah, Haggai, Zechariah, Malachi; then the holy gospel according to St Matthew, according to St Mark, according to St Luke, and according to St John; then the second book of St Luke, otherwise called the Acts of the Apostles; then the letters of St Paul: one to the Romans, two to the Corinthians, one to the Galatians, one to the Ephesians, one to the Philippians, one to the Colossians, two to the Thessalonians, two to Timothy, one to Titus, one to Philemon; then the letter to the Hebrews, the letter of St James, the first and second letters of St Peter, the first, second, and third letters of St John, the letter of St Jude; and then the Apocalypse, or Revelation of St John.

STUDY PANEL 3

Having considered some general issues concerning the Bible, we may now turn to examine its contents in more detail. We begin our exploration by turning to the Old Testament.

1   Why do Christians refer to their faith in terms of "good news"?
2   Why is the word "testament" used to refer to the two main components of the Christian Bible?
3   In what way is there continuity between the Old and New Testaments? You will find it interesting to read the first two chapters of Matthew's gospel; note the way in which Matthew clearly supposes continuity between Jesus and the Old Testament.
4   The Bible "is the swaddling clothes and manger in which Christ is laid" (Martin Luther). What does Luther mean by this? Is he right?
5   Saint Paul speaks of Jesus as "the end (Greek: *telos*) of the law" (Romans 10:4). The Greek word *telos* can mean either "termination" or "objective or goal"; the word "law" refers to the revelation of God in Israel, under the Old Testament. Try out the meaning of Paul's statement using both senses of the word. What is the meaning of his statement in each case? And which do you think corresponds more to what Paul himself thought?

STUDY QUESTIONS

The Old Testament

We open our exploration of the contents and themes of the Christian Bible by focusing on the Old Testament. In classic Christian thought, the Old Testament is regarded as preparing the way for the coming of Jesus Christ.

The Contents of the Old Testament

The Old Testament consists of 39 books, which can be broken down into four broad categories, as follows:

The Five Books of the Law
Genesis	Numbers
Exodus	Deuteronomy
Leviticus	

The Historical Books
Joshua	1 and 2 Samuel	Ezra
Judges	1 and 2 Kings	Nehemiah
Ruth	1 and 2 Chronicles	Esther

The Writings
Job	Ecclesiastes
Psalms	Song of Solomon
Proverbs	

The Prophets
Isaiah	Joel	Habakkuk
Jeremiah	Amos	Zephaniah

(Lamentations)	Obadiah	Haggai
Ezekiel	Jonah	Zechariah
Daniel	Micah	Malachi
Hosea	Nahum	

The Five Books of the Law

The first five books of the Old Testament are usually referred to as "the five books of the law," or "the Pentateuch" (from the Greek words for "five scrolls"). The Pentateuch describes the origins of the people of Israel, and especially the revelation of the God who called that people into being. It provides the foundations for a proper understanding of the both distinctive calling and identity of Israel as the people of God, and the nature and character of the "God of Israel." Above all, it sets out the specific form of law which would give and safeguard the distinctive identity and ethos of Israel as the people of God. The five books of the law were thus of considerable importance to Israel in its later period, as it sought to maintain its unique character. In many ways, the narrative which is set out in the Pentateuch sets the scene for the remainder of the Bible, which can be seen as an outworking of some of the major themes introduced in its five constituent books.

It is not clear when the Pentateuch was written. The most helpful way of understanding the distinctive nature of the work is to see it as a collection of documents, some of which are extremely old, which were brought together at a definite moment in Israel's history, possibly during the period of the exile in Babylon in the sixth century BC. This was a particularly important period in the history of the Jewish people. Cut off from their homeland, the Jewish exiles made strenuous efforts to preserve and safeguard their distinctive identity through preserving and affirming their religious roots. All the available information concerning Israel's history was gathered together and, where possible, committed to writing. The past history of the people of God was seen as a major controlling influence over its future, whenever restoration to the Jewish homeland took place. However, our understanding of the chronology of the compilation of the Pentateuch remains uncertain, and it is quite possible that we shall never know the exact circumstances of its compilation.

The Pentateuch opens with the book of Genesis. The book takes its name from the Greek word for "origins," reflecting the book's characteristic concern to explain the origin of the world in general, and the people of God in particular. In contrast to other accounts of creation found in the ancient near east (in which a series of minor gods, goddesses and heroes is involved in the creation of the world), Genesis affirms that the creation is the work of one, and only one, god. There are two accounts of the creation of the world, each told from different perspectives and with different points of focus. The first creation account in Genesis (Genesis 1:1–2:3) opens with its famous declaration that God created the heavens and the earth. Everything has its origins from God. During the six days of creation, everything that is now a familiar part of the world is surveyed, and declared to owe its existence to a sovereign act of creation on the part of God.

The account of the creation of the sun, moon, and stars is of especial interest. For many ancient peoples, these heavenly bodies represented divine or supernatural powers, and were the object of worship and superstition. Genesis puts them firmly in their place: they are parts of God's creation, and are thus subject to God's authority. They should not be worshipped, and need not be feared. God has authority and dominion over them. No part of God's creation is to be worshipped. The entire creation is the work of the creator God, who alone is to be worshipped.

The creation of humanity is of especial importance. The first creation account places the creation of humanity at the end of God's work of creation (1:26–27). This is the high point of creation, in which the only creature to bear the image of the creator God is introduced. The passage just cited is unusual in that it opens with something like a fanfare, a declaration that something major is about to take place. It is clear that humanity is meant to be seen as the zenith of God's creative action and power. The Hebrew word often translated as "man" is here to be understood as "humanity" in general, rather than as "a male human being" in particular.

The second creation account (Genesis 2:4–25) takes a different form from the first account, yet makes many of the same points. The second account opens with the creation of humanity (2:7), affirming that humanity is the most important aspect of the creation. It is made absolutely clear that human life is totally dependent upon God. The reference to God breathing the "breath of life" into humanity (2:7) is of particular importance, in that it both emphasizes the God-given origins of life, and also anticipates the important life-giving role of the Holy Spirit. (The Hebrew term *ruach* can mean "spirit," "wind" or "breath," pointing to the close connections between these ideas.) It is only when God breathes upon humanity that it comes to life.

With the book of Genesis, the curtain thus lifts over the stage of world history. As the book unfolds, its readers will begin to learn about the great story of God's calling of Israel to be the people of God. Just as an operatic overture will introduce the themes of the opera to its awaiting audience, so Genesis introduces its readers to the great themes which will dominate Scripture. We learn of God's creation of the world, and of that world's rebellion against its creator. We learn of God's decision to restore the creation to fellowship, and the calling of a people to serve God and bring this good news to the ends of the earth. In short, Genesis sets the scene for the great drama of redemption which forms the subject of Scripture. Particular attention is focused on the person of Abraham, who is seen as the origin of a people who will inherit Canaan as their promised land, and share in the blessings promised to them by God. By the end of the book of Genesis, the people of Israel have settled in Egypt.

The narrative is then continued in the book of *Exodus*, which derives its name from the Greek term for "way out." (In modern Greek airports, the word "exodus" bears the meaning of "a departure gate"). It tells of how the people of Israel fell into slavery in Egypt, and of the way in which Moses emerged as their deliverer. A particularly important theme is that of God calling Moses, and appointing him as the deliverer of the people of God. Exodus tells of how the oppressive Egyptian monarch was forced to allow the captive people of Israel to go free, before changing his mind and pursuing them into the desert. The account of the crossing of the Red Sea is one of the high points in this dramatic narrative.

Yet Exodus tells of more than the deliverance of Israel from bondage in Egypt. It begins to narrate the way in which Israel's identity as the people of God was impressed upon her. Of central importance here is the giving of the Law, or the Ten Commandments, at Mount Sinai. This code of law provided a distinctive way of living which was to be characteristic of the people of God, shaping their identity and ethos.

The book of *Leviticus* develops this further. It sets out the characteristic religious and cultural practices and beliefs which marked Israel off from all

Mount Sinai, the traditional site of the giving of the Law to Moses. Hutchison Library.

other nations, and safeguarded her distinctive identity as the people of God. Leviticus gives specific guidance for the forms of worship to be adopted by Israel, and particularly the sacrifices which ensured individual and corporate purity before God. Of particular importance is the ritual associated with the Day of Atonement, which was ordained as an annual event for the removal of sin from the people of God. The full ritual is complex (see Leviticus 16:1–34), involving the High Priest ritually cleansing himself, and then offering a bull as a sacrifice for himself and the other priests. After this, two goats would be brought forward. One would be selected by lot as a sacrifice, while the other would become the scapegoat. The first goat would then be sacrificed as an offering for the sins of the people. Afterwards, the dead bull and goat were taken outside the camp, and burned. The high priest would then lay his hands upon the head of the second goat, and transfer all the sins of the people to the unfortunate animal. The scapegoat would then be driven out into the wilderness, carrying the guilt of the sins of Israel with it.

The Day of Atonement is of major importance as a background to understanding the significance of the death of Christ for New Testament writers, a point brought out especially clearly in the letter to the Hebrews. Christ is seen as the perfect high priest, who makes a perfect sacrifice once and for all (instead of the annual ritual of the Day of Atonement). The sacrifice which he offers is himself; by his death, the sins of the people are transferred to him, and removed from his people. Note especially the fact that Jesus is put to death outside the walls of Jerusalem, just as the bull and goat were finally burned outside the camp of the Israelites. The Levitical ritual sets the scene for the greater and perfect sacrifice which is yet to come, and which brings about what the Old Testament sacrifices could merely point to, yet not deliver (see pp. 48–9).

The book of *Numbers* picks up the account of Israel's wanderings in the wilderness, as it moves from Egypt to the borders of the promised land of Canaan. Much of the book is taken up with details of the preparations being made to invade Canaan. The books ends with Israel poised on the eastern side of the River Jordan, waiting to enter the promised land.

The final book in the Pentateuch is *Deuteronomy*. This unusual word derives from the Greek words for "the second law," or perhaps "a copy of the law." This name refers to one of the distinctive features of the work, which is its repetition of the main themes of the law to Israel before she is permitted to enter Canaan. The book emphasizes the distinct identity of Israel as the people of God, and the vitally important role of the law as a means by which this unique identity and role can be safeguarded. Once Israel is established in Canaan she is to keep the law of the Lord, not the customs of the Canaanites. Only in this way can Israel's identity and mission be preserved. As will become clear from the later historical writings, one of the most persistent features of Israel's history after the entry into the promised land is the compromise of her distinctive religious ideas and practices. Assimilation to Canaanite beliefs and rituals was a constant threat to Israel.

All this lies in the future, however. The Pentateuch ends with the death of Moses, who had led the people of Israel to the brink of Canaan, but would not himself be allowed to enter it. A new period in the history of Israel is about to dawn.

The Historical Books

The Old Testament places considerable emphasis on the importance of the acts of God in history. The deliverance of Israel from captivity in Egypt is often referred to by Old Testament writers as an illustration of God's power and faithfulness. The historical books serve a major purpose in relation to the Old Testament: they provide a historical narrative and theological commentary, providing its readers with an understanding of God's intentions for Israel.

Deuteronomy ended with the people of Israel waiting to cross into the promised land. The narrative of Israel is now taken up in the book of *Joshua*, named after Moses' successor as the leader of Israel. The book deals with the conquest of Canaan. One issue of particular interest concerns the dating of the conquest of Canaan. A range of dates for the conquest has been suggested, based on a variety of considerations, including archaeological evidence and the internal evidence of the biblical documents. Some factors point to an early date for the events in question, perhaps around 1400 BC; others point to a later date, perhaps in the region of 1250–1200 BC. The precise date is not, however, of major importance to understanding the theological and cultural importance of the events.

After the crossing of the River Jordan, three major campaigns of conquest are described, focusing on the central, southern, and northern regions of Canaan. The first campaign was directed against the Gibeonites (Joshua 9:1–27), a group of peoples to the north of Jerusalem. The second campaign involved a coalition of kings from the southern regions of Canaan, including the cities of Jerusalem and Hebron (Joshua 10:1–43). Finally, Joshua dealt with a coalition of city-states in the northern region of Canaan (Joshua 11:1–23). Armies drawn from the Galilean hill country assembled at a site referred to as Merom, which is thought to be some 12 kilometers to the north-west of Lake Galilee. Joshua defeated the armies, pursuing them to the north, and eventually turning south again to take and destroy the important city of Hazor. Joshua completed his subjugation of the region by defeating the Anakites. With this, the military campaigns ended, and "the land had rest from war" (Joshua 11:23). Joshua could now divide the land amongst the tribes of Israel. This action was understood in terms of the fulfillment of the promises made to Abraham, and confirmation of God's covenant with Israel.

The history of Israel in Canaan is then taken a stage further in the book of *Judges*, which describes the consolidation of Israel's presence in the region. The book of Judges deals with the history of Israel from the death of Joshua to the rise of Samuel, before there was any permanent centralized administration (in, for example, the form of a monarchy) in the land. It chronicles the decline in religious faith and obedience in the land after the death of Joshua, especially its lapse into idolatry and pagan practices. One of the most noticeable differences between the books of Joshua and Judges concerns the situations that confront Israel. In Judges, Israel has to occupy and subdue Canaan, facing threats from the various peoples already living in Canaan. Israel is portrayed as a people acting and working together against these threats from within Canaan. In Judges, however, the main threats come from outside Canaan – from peoples from the east side of the Jordan, such as the Ammonites, Midianites and Moabites. Only on one occasion is there any reference to a threat from within Canaan itself. Israel is no longer a single centralized body of people, but a settled group of tribes who have now established themselves in various regions of Canaan. Although they share a common faith and a common story, they increasingly tend to think of their identities in terms of individual tribes and clans, rather than being a member of Israel as a whole. For example, there was no national standing army; whenever a national emergency arose, volunteers had to be recruited locally to meet the challenge. The general theme of the book is the internal decline of Israel into a collection of self-serving groups, without any sense of national identity. The need for a national leader was clear.

The word "judge" needs a little explanation. During this period a number of individuals, such as Deborah and Samuel, are referred to as "judges." In modern days this would be understood to mean something like "an impartial arbitrator in legal debates," or "someone who passes judgment." The word is, however, used in a very different sense in this book. Its basic meaning is "a charismatic leader raised up by God to deliver Israel from danger." The emphasis is upon deliverance from danger rather than impartial legal administration. The "judges" are actually figures of salvation, rather than judgment. It is against this background that the book of *Ruth* is set, documenting a love affair which illustrates the issues and concerns of the period.

The book of Judges documented the inner decay of Israel through a lack of national identity. So what was to happen? The book of Judges offers a graphic account of Israel's degeneration into political, religious, and moral corruption after the golden period of Joshua. The closing chapters of the book of Judges frequently reiterates that "in those days Israel had no king" (Judges 17:6; 19:1; 21:25). It is clear that the establishment of the monarchy is envisaged. So how did the kingship come to be established? The two books we now know as 1 and 2 Samuel were originally one larger book, which was divided into two halves by early translators. The division is not entirely helpful, and disrupts the flow of the work. The two works together document the development of kingship in Israel, eventually leading to the recognition of Saul as the first king of Israel, and his subsequent death and replacement by David. Although David was the most significant and successful of Israel's kings, the books of Samuel offer a sympathetic yet realistic assessment of his character and achievements.

One of the developments which should be noted in this narrative is the emergence of the terms "Israel" and "Judah" to refer to the northern and southern regions of the land which was originally Canaan. The term "Israel" was originally used to refer to this, up to and during the reign of Saul. However, after the death of Saul open warfare resulted between the supporters of Saul in the north, and the supporters of David in the south of the country. As David was himself a member of the tribe of Judah, it was probably only to be expected that the term "Judah" came to refer to both the southern tribes of Simeon and Judah (Joshua 19:1–9), who backed David against the house of Saul.

The house of Saul regarded itself as continuing the rule of Saul over all Israel, and thus retained the term "Israel" to refer to its sphere of influence, despite the fact that this now referred only to the northern region of the country. David is initially proclaimed king of Judah at the southern city of Hebron; it is only as a result of his military campaigns that he becomes king of all Israel. Up to the time of Saul's death, there had been a non-Israelite corridor separating the northern tribes from the southern tribes. This corridor included the city of Jerusalem, which was held by the Jebusites, and the city of Gezer, which was under Egyptian control. David's conquest of Jerusalem united the two halves, a process which was finally completed when Gezer was given to Solomon as a wedding present by Pharaoh (see 1 Kings 9:16–17). When the united kingdom was divided into two after the death of Solomon (930 BC) it was natural that the northern kingdom should retain the name "Israel," and the southern kingdom, centering on Jerusalem, the name "Judah."

As with 1 and 2 Samuel, the two *books of Kings* were originally one long work, which was divided into two for convenience by translators. The two books of Kings follow on directly from the two books of Samuel, with the result that the four books together provide a continuous account of the development and history of the kingdom of Israel (and subsequently of Israel and Judah) from the establishment of the monarchy until the exile in Babylon. This continuity is brought out more clearly in the title which is given to the books in the Greek translation of the Old Testament, usually referred to as the "Septuagint." In that translation, 1 and 2 Samuel are referred to as "1 and 2 Kingdoms," while 1 and 2 Kings are given the titles "3 and 4 Kingdoms."

1 Kings opens with a description of the monarchy of Israel at its high point under David, and subsequently under Solomon (970–930 BC). The description of the building of the temple is clearly seen as the climax of David and Solomon's great achievement of establishing Israel as a military, political and religious entity. Yet Solomon's flirtations with paganism are chronicled, along with their implications for the life of the nation. Shortly after Solomon's death, the nation of Israel split apart into the northern region (still known as "Israel," but severely reduced in territory), and the southern kingdom of Judah, with Jerusalem as the capital city of the southern kingdom.

The story of decline which follows links historical narration with theological comment. The destruction of the northern kingdom by Assyria in 722 BC is clearly interpreted as a sign of God's disfavor, resulting from the paganism introduced into the region by successive kings of Israel. Among those pagan practices, Canaanite fertility cults made their reappearance. The southern kingdom survived the collapse of its northern neighbor. However, it was only a matter of time before it too collapsed. In 587 BC Jerusalem was sacked by invading Babylonian armies, and many of the inhabitants of the city were deported to exile in Babylon.

This event marks a watershed in the Old Testament, and is widely interpreted as God's punishment of Jerusalem for her sins, offering her a period of exile in which to repent and renew her identity as the people of God. Eventually the community would be restored to Jerusalem, and would work to renew the faith and institutions of pre-exilic Israel. That would involve a major process of retrieval and renewal, which is described in the books of Ezra and Nehemiah.

The two *books of Chronicles* are clearly written with the needs of this restored community in mind. They demonstrate the continuity between the past and the present, and reassure their readers of the continuing validity of God's covenant promises to the people of Jerusalem. In many ways the books of Chronicles can be regarded as bringing together material which is spread out across the books of Samuel and Kings. However, additional material is provided in many cases, probably from archive resources. Part of the additional material relates to a much earlier period in Israel's history; its inclusion stresses the continuity of God's presence and promises throughout the history of God's people.

It is also noticeable that Chronicles tends to portray both David and Solomon in a much more favorable light than that found in the books of Samuel and Kings. The incidents which highlight David's weaker side (such as his adulterous relationship with Bathsheba) are passed over. Similarly,

Solomon is portrayed in a very flattering manner. No mention is made of his foreign wives or the pagan practices or beliefs which they encouraged.

It is clear that one of the purposes of Chronicles is to stress the importance of David and Solomon, and the example and encouragement they provide for the restored community which has now returned from exile in Babylon. They are also seen as pointing ahead to the coming of the Messiah, the ideal king of Israel, who will bring to final fulfillment all that David and Solomon tried to achieve. The work aims to encourage and inspire the nation at a time when its fortunes were often low, and reassure Israel that the God who entered into a covenant with David and Solomon remains faithful to that covenant to this very day. The temple is seen as a major focus for Israel's hope and faith, and particular attention is paid to this theme throughout the works. Thus the account of Solomon's reign is dominated by the building of the temple, which is seen as his major contribution to the well-being of his people.

The books of *Ezra* and *Nehemiah* document the events which resulted from the overthrow of the Babylonian empire by the Persian monarch Cyrus in 538 BC. Cyrus liberated the exiled Jewish population from Babylon, and granted them permission to return to Jerusalem and to rebuild their temple. The books document various aspects of the resettlement of Jerusalem, the slow rebuilding of the temple, and the problems encountered by the returning exiles. A theme which becomes of considerable significance is the renewal of Israel's religious life, and the need for the exiles to maintain their cultural and religious identities, particularly through refusing to marry with other local peoples in the region. Finally, the book of *Esther* documents the way in which a Jewish community in the later Persian empire was spared from destruction.

The Writings

One of the most important themes in the Old Testament is that of "wisdom." A number of Old Testament writings focus on this theme of wisdom, noting in particular how this wisdom is linked with a knowledge of God. Of the four major writings of the Old Testament, three (Job, Proverbs and Ecclesiastes) are regarded as belonging to this specific category of "wisdom" literature. The fourth book (the Psalter) has its natural context in the worship of Israel in the temple. A fifth book is also usually included in this collection – the love poem widely known as the Song of Solomon.

The theme of "wisdom" is of considerable importance within the Old Testament. The term can refer to a form of commonsense wisdom, which notices certain patterns in human behavior. More fundamentally, however, it refers to a profound understanding of the mysteries of life, which is ultimately due to God. This can be seen illustrated in the history of Solomon, widely regarded as Israel's wisest king, who petitioned God to give him wisdom. This request was granted on the condition that he remains faithful to God during his reign (1 Kings 3:2–15). The wisdom for which Solomon thus became famous is to be seen as a gift from God, rather than a natural endowment. That wisdom is immediately shown in action in the famous case of the two women who claimed to be the mother of the same infant (3:16–28). We later learn that, on account of his wisdom, Solomon was sought out by rulers throughout the world (4:29–34). The fundamental lesson to the reader of the Old Testament is clear: true wisdom is a gift from God, and cannot be had from any other source.

The Wisdom of the Old Testament

STUDY PANEL 4

According to biblical tradition, Solomon was a man of outstanding wisdom. He is credited with having "spoken" some three thousand proverbs (1 Kings 4:32); the sayings collected together in the main body of the work would amount to less than one-seventh of these. This suggests that the bulk of Proverbs was written in the tenth century BC, at a time of relative peace and stability suitable for the production of literary works. However, there are indications that not all the material collected in Proverbs may be due directly to Solomon. For example, there is reference to the sayings of two unknown writers, "Agur son of Jakeh" and "King Lemuel."

The proverbs are not intended to be treated as laws which must be adhered to strictly. They are intended to provide practical guidance as to how someone might act in a particular situation. The complexities of human relationships are such that true discernment and wisdom is required to deal with them. Most of the proverbs consist of only two lines, although slightly longer sayings are also encountered occasionally. Frequent use is made of comparisons, often centering on pictures drawn from everyday life. Their basic theme could be summarized as follows: act wisely, and you will prosper; act foolishly, and you will fail.

Proverbs 10:12–16
A man who lacks judgment derides his neighbor, but a man of understanding holds his tongue.
A gossip betrays a confidence, but a trustworthy man keeps a secret.
For lack of guidance a nation falls, but many advisers make victory sure.

The book of *Job* is one of the most remarkable writings in the Old Testament. It focuses on a question of continuing interest and importance. Why does God allow suffering? Or, more precisely, does the fact that someone is suffering mean that he or she has fallen out of God's favor? Is suffering the direct result of sin?

The book of Job has a distinctive structure, which needs to be understood before it can be fully appreciated. The book opens by setting the scene for Job's sufferings, allowing us to overhear Job's own understanding of his situation. We are then introduced to his three well-meaning friends, Elphaz, Bildad, and Zophar. As the well-known phrase "Job's comforters" implies, these end up causing Job more misery and confusion than he had in the first place. Their basic assumption is that Job's suffering results from sin – an assumption that the reader of Job knows to be incorrect, on account of the information supplied in the opening chapters of the work. The first part of the work consists of three cycles of speeches by the comforters, to which Job replies. This is then followed by some comments by Elihu, who seems to have been an onlooker who wished to contribute to the discussion at this point. Finally God responds, clearing up the confusion which has been generated by the theological ramblings of the disputants.

The Book of *Psalms* (sometimes also known as "the Psalter") is composed of a series of collections of psalms, which was probably arranged in its final form in the third century BC. The Psalter as we now have it includes a number of smaller collections, including the "Psalms of Asaph" (Psalms 73–83), the "Psalms of the Sons of Korah" (Psalms 84–85; 87–88), and the "Psalms of David" (Psalms 138–145). The 150 psalms brought together in this collection of collections are arranged in five books, as follows:

Book 1: Psalms 1–41
Book 2: Psalms 42–72
Book 3: Psalms 73–89
Book 4: Psalms 90–106
Book 5: Psalms 107–150

Although the book probably took its final form in the third century BC, most of the material brought together dates from much earlier, generally in the region 1000–500 BC. The task of dating some individual Psalms can be difficult, although some can be assigned to dates with a reasonable degree of certainty.

Many Psalms have titles attached to them. For example, Psalm 30 is entitled "A psalm. A song. For the dedication of the temple. Of David." This would naturally suggest that the Psalm in question was written by David for the occasion of the dedication of the property and building materials for the temple, as recorded at 1 Chronicles 21:1–22:6. Although the reliability of the individual psalm titles have often been challenged, there are good reasons for believing that they are original and authentic. For example, psalms recorded outside the Psalter are generally given titles (such as those found at 2 Samuel 22:1, Isaiah 38:9 and Habakkuk 3:1). Furthermore, the historical information preserved in the titles accords well with the content of the psalm in question.

The book of *Proverbs* consists mainly of a collection of short proverbial sayings, attributed to Solomon, famed for his wisdom. The Hebrew word here translated as "proverbs" has a much broader range of meaning than the corresponding English word, and can also have the meaning of "parable" or "oracle" (both of which suggest God's involvement in the gathering of human wisdom). According to biblical tradition, Solomon was credited with having "spoken" some three thousand proverbs (1 Kings 4:32); the sayings collected together in the main body of the work would amount to less than one-seventh of these. This suggests that the bulk of Proverbs was written in the tenth century BC, at a time of relative peace and stability suitable for the production of literary works. However, there are indications that not all the material collected in Proverbs may be due directly to Solomon. Although the work gives every indication of having been written in the tenth century

BC, there are indications in the text itself that it may have received its final form at some point during the reign of Hezekiah (*c*.715–686 BC).

The book of *Ecclesiastes* is perhaps the most pessimistic in the Old Testament. Like Proverbs and Job, it belongs to the category of wisdom literature. The book takes the form of a collection of proverbs and observations, some long and some very brief. The book is best understood as a powerful and convincing commentary on the meaninglessness of life without God, and the utter despair and cynicism which will inevitably result from lacking a biblical faith. It represents a graphic portrayal of the misery and futility of human life without God, and the inability of human wisdom to discover God fully.

The author of this work introduces himself as "the teacher" (*Ekklesiastes* in the Greek translation of the Old Testament), and is traditionally identified as Solomon on account of the reference to "son of David, king of Jerusalem" (Ecclesiastes 1:1). This designation could, however, be used of any descendant of David. The book itself occasionally indicates that it was written by a subject rather than a ruler, and the style of Hebrew used suggests that the book dates from later than the time of Solomon. There is no general consensus on any particular date, and it is probable that we shall never know with certainty when the book was written.

Finally, this collection of writings ends with a brief work, sometimes referred to as the *Song of Solomon*. This is generally regarded as an outstanding love poem. The work is also known as the "Song of Songs," which literally means "the greatest of songs." The work is traditionally understood to have been written by Solomon, although there is insufficient evidence within the text of the work itself to confirm this with certainty. The book is loosely structured around five meetings between the lover and the beloved, with reflection on the periods during which they are obliged to be apart.

The Prophets

The theme of prophecy is of major importance within the Old Testament (see pp. 50–7). The prophets were understood to be individuals inspired by God, who spoke on behalf of God to Israel. Prophecy is found in the historical books, which relate the careers and prophecies of Elijah and Elisha. However, a major section of the Old Testament is specifically devoted to collections of the prophecies of individual prophets. The Old Testament indicates that the prophets were often highly critical of the establishment. The themes which often recur in their writings include the need for national and individual repentance, a turning away from pagan beliefs and practices, and a rejection of dependence on military and political power. Jeremiah appears to have been particularly unpopular. Nevertheless, despite this unpopularity, the prophets were seen as maintaining a vital link between God and Israel. While the prophets were active, God continued to speak to Israel. When prophecy died out, it seemed to many that God no longer communicated with the nation.

The book of the prophet *Isaiah* is the first of the four "major prophets" (the other three books being Jeremiah, Ezekiel, and Daniel). Isaiah lived and worked in Jerusalem in the latter part of the eighth century BC. His call to prophesy came in 640 BC, the year of King Uzziah's death (6:1), and he is known to have prophesied up to at least 701 BC, when the northern kingdom of Israel fell to Assyria. At this stage, Judah and Israel were both moving out of a longer period of peace and prosperity into one of uncertainty and danger. Assyria was becoming aggressive in the region, and Israel, Judah and Syria were uncertain as to how to react to this threat. It is against this context of political and military uncertainty that Isaiah's ministry is set. However, the prophecy is not restricted to this period in the history of Jerusalem. The later parts of the book concern prophecies of hope and restoration for the Babylonian exiles. The early parts of the prophecy cover the period between the fall of the northern kingdom of Israel in 722, and the extreme danger to Judah from Assyria in 702 BC. An important section of the work (chapters 36–39) deals with Judah's survival of this threat. A major later section (chapters 40–55) goes on to prophesy Judah's later enslavement to Babylon and its eventual deliverance from exile in that land. The final perspective of the book looks beyond events in Judah's immediate future to a glorified Jerusalem, set amidst "new heavens and a new earth."

The prophecy of *Jeremiah* is the longest book in the whole Bible. Jeremiah was called to be a prophet to Jerusalem in the year 626 BC. He would continue his ministry during the remainder of the reign of Josiah (who died in battle against the Egyptians in 609 BC), and during the reigns of Jehoahaz (609), Jehoiakim (609–598), Jehoiachin (598–597), and Zedekiah (597–586 BC). These were turbulent years. The basic sequence of events during the period of Jeremiah's ministry can be summarized as follows. Josiah, who had instigated a series of religious reforms which led to a purification and refining of Judah's religious life, died in 609, attempting to oppose an Egyptian advance to aid the ailing Assyrian forces, who were about to fall to the sustained attacks of the Babylonians and their allies the Medes. The capital city of Assyria, Ninevah, fell to their armies in 612; it was just a matter of time before Babylon established itself as supreme in the region. The death of Josiah was something of a personal tragedy for Jeremiah, as it is clear that the king was sympathetic to both the prophet and his message from the Lord. Josiah's successors were consistently hostile towards him, and often openly contemptuous of his prophetic message. In 605, during the reign of Jehoiakim, the Babylonians laid siege to Jerusalem, and subdued it for a while. Following further unrest within the city, the Babylonians attacked it again in 598–597 BC, taking off Jehoiakin, who had succeeded the king of similar name at that time. The Babylonians attacked Jerusalem again in 588 BC, and took full possession of the city two years later. Gedaliah was appointed governor. Jeremiah found himself within the circle of the governor, which was shattered by his assassination shortly afterwards. Jeremiah sought refuge in Egypt, where he is believed to have died.

The basic themes of Jeremiah's prophecies focus on Jerusalem's need to remain faithful to God, rather than rely on military alliances with her neighbors. This theme can be found in many of the prophets of this dangerous period. A short work which is linked with the name of Jeremiah immediately follows this prophecy. The book of *Lamentations* consists of five poems or "laments" over the destruction of Jerusalem by the Babylonians in 586 BC. According to an ancient tradition, they were written by Jeremiah himself. While this cannot be proved, the book certainly seems to have been written at some point between 586 and 538 BC. The fact that the book provides such a graphic portrayal of the destruction of Jerusalem suggests that most of the material is to be dated shortly after the fall of the city in 586 BC, when the events described would still have been vivid in the memory of those who lived through them.

The book of *Ezekiel* centers on the great issues of apostasy, sin, and exile – which also dominated both Isaiah and Jeremiah. Ezekiel deals with the period in the history of Judah in which the threat of exile became both real and urgent. Following the Babylonian defeat of the Egyptians at the battle of Carcemish (605 BC), the way was clear for the Babylonians to dominate the entire region (which included Judah). This development is the background to some of Jeremiah's major prophecies concerning the threat of exile. That threat would be fulfilled in its totality in 586 BC, when the besieging Babylonian army would finally conquer Jerusalem, and deport its population. However, an earlier deportation took place in 597 BC, when Jehoiachin and a group of about 10,000 of the population were deported. This group included Ezekiel.

Ezekiel thus prophesies about the state of affairs in Jerusalem from his exile near Babylon. There is no evidence that Ezekiel himself ever left Babylon. The exiles settled in Babylon along the "Kebar river" (Ezekiel 1:1), which was actually an irrigation canal. We learn that Ezekiel had been born into a priestly family, and would thus normally have expected to serve in the temple at Jerusalem. In 593, when he would normally have begun his priestly duties in the temple, Ezekiel was called to be a prophet to the exiles. This prophetic ministry was carried out entirely in Babylon, and covers the period 593–573 BC.

The fourth of the "major prophets" is the book of *Daniel*. This unusual work is possibly better described as an apocalyptic rather than a prophetic work, on account of the importance attached to visions of the end-times.

The book of Daniel emphasizes the importance of remaining faithful to God, even under difficult circumstances, and illustrates this from the story of Daniel and his three companions in Babylon. The later part of the book consists of visions of coming judgment and retribution, which often include symbols of peoples and nations, emphasizing God's sovereign control over history, and God's ultimate victory over forces which may seem to have gained the upper hand for the time being.

The twelve books collectively known as the "minor prophets" follow, arranged generally in terms of their dates of activity. Some of the prophets, such as Amos and Hosea, were active in the northern kingdom of Israel prior to its destruction by Assyria in 722 BC; most, including Isaiah and Micah, prophesied to the southern kingdom of Judah, and particularly its capital city, Jerusalem.

Hosea dates from the middle of the eighth century BC. It is clear that Hosea, like Amos, came from the northern kingdom of Israel, and prophesied to it during its final days before it was destroyed by the Assyrians, and its peoples taken off into exile. Despite this, however, the book itself appears to have been written in the southern kingdom of Judah, suggesting that Hosea may have fled to the safety of this region after the fall of Israel. Hosea focuses on the unfaithfulness of Israel to God.

Little is known about *Joel*, apart from the name of his father. The prophecy contained in this book is difficult to date, as there are no clear references to any historical events which would allow even a provisional date to be assigned to this work. Some have suggested that the work may date from as early as the ninth century; others point to a later date, suggesting that the work may have been written after the return from exile. The central theme of the work is the coming of the "Day of the Lord." A day of darkness is at hand, in which destruction will come to Zion. Although the reference is primarily to the coming of a vast cloud of locusts, it is clear that Joel sees in this catastrophe a sign of God's judgment. This disaster is intended to move a complacent people to repentance. Joel looks forward to a coming day when the "Spirit of the Lord" will be poured out on the people of God – a prophecy which Christians regard as being fulfilled in the Day of Pentecost.

The book of *Amos* focuses on the failures of the northern kingdom of Israel. Although born in the southern kingdom of Judah, Amos appears to have ministered primarily to the northern kingdom of Israel during the reigns of Uzziah, king of Judah 792–40 BC, and Jeroboam II, king of Israel 793–53. While little is known about Amos for certain, we know that the main part of his ministry was probably carried out over a two-year period at some point during the years 767–53, centering on the shrine at Bethel. The prophecy takes the form of judgment against both the pagan nations and Israel for their sins. Israel is declared to be no better than the surrounding nations; in fact, she bears an even greater responsibility for her sins, on account of being God's chosen people. It is clear from several references in the prophecy that this was a time of national prosperity. There were few indications of the disaster that Israel would suffer at the hands of Assyria in 722–1, which would lead to the fall of the northern kingdom. The prophecy particularly complains about the lack of social justice in Israel, and her failure to remain faithful to the covenant.

The prophecy of *Obadiah* is one of the briefest works in the Old Testament, and is difficult to date. Also difficult to date is the book of *Jonah*, which describes the missionary journey of a prophet to the city of Ninevah at some point during the eighth century BC. The work is unusual in several respects, not least of which is its emphasis on the actions, rather than the words, of its central character. The book includes the famous story of "Jonah and the whale."

Micah prophesied in the southern kingdom of Judah at some point during the period 750–686 BC. The work is a powerful and spirited attack on the corruption of life in the great cities of the two kingdoms. For Micah, both Judah and Israel are guilty of a series of unacceptable offenses, including the oppression of the weak by the strong, the dispossession of people from their lands by powerful landowners, and the enslavement of helpless children. The priests and prophets, who ought to have been speaking out against these events, have totally failed to do so. Micah offers a vigorous criticism of these trends, and looks forward to the coming of a king from Bethlehem in Judea who will put things right. Christians see this prophecy as being fulfilled in the birth of Jesus at Bethlehem.

Relatively little is known about *Nahum* and *Habakkuk*. Both operated in the southern kingdom of Judah. *Zephaniah* prophesied during the reign of Josiah (640–609 BC), which was one of the most important periods of religious reform in Judah. The rediscovery of the "Book of the Law" led to a major religious reformation, and a corporate renewal of the covenant with the Lord which had been violated by the paganism which had flourished under earlier monarchs. It would seem that Zephaniah's prophecies were delivered before these reforms. It is quite clear from their general tone that the religious life of Judah has reached an all-time low, and that the threat of imminent divine judgment was required to spur the King and nation into any kind of reform and renewal. The great warning of destruction in Judah (Zephaniah 1:2–13) speaks of a continuing legacy of Baal worship, worship of the stars, and devotion to the god Molech, who was chiefly noted for the cult of child sacrifice associated with his name. Zephaniah demands that these practices should end.

The prophecies of *Haggai* and *Zechariah* are both to be dated to the period when the deported population of Jerusalem was returned from exile in Babylon to rebuild their city and temple. Haggai's calling can be dated to

August 520 BC; Zechariah's calling took place a few months later, in October or November of the same year. Haggai's prophecy focuses on the need to rebuild the temple as an act of honor to God. Why, he asks, are the people of Jerusalem building expensive houses for themselves, while failing to build a house for their God. Is it any wonder that Jerusalem is in such a miserable state, when they treat their God in such a way? Until the temple is rebuilt, Jerusalem will remain a wilderness. It is clear that this message has its desired effect. The rebuilding of the temple begins under Zerubbabel (Haggai 1:12). Like Haggai, Zechariah wishes to encourage the people of Jerusalem to rebuild the temple. Alongside these messages of encouragement and rebuke for inaction there are to be found a series of strongly messianic prophecies, including the famous prophecy (Zechariah 9:9–13) of the great messianic king, the descendant of David, entering into the city of Jerusalem in triumph, seated on a donkey. For Christians. this would reach its ultimate fulfillment in the triumphant entry of Jesus Christ into Jerusalem (Matthew 21:1–11).

It is generally thought that *Malachi* (whose name literally means "my messenger") was the final prophet of the Old Testament period. If this is the case, the work represents an important point of transition between the Old Testament and the New. Like Haggai and Zechariah, Malachi appears to have prophesied in the post-exilic period, at some point soon after the return of the exiles from Babylon to Jerusalem. This is suggested by a number of considerations, including the close similarity between the sins condemned in this book, and those singled out for condemnation by Nehemiah. Yet a promise of forgiveness and restoration remains open. Malachi proclaims the future coming of the "Day of the Lord" (Malachi 4:1).

But when will this great day be? When will God come? Malachi declares that God will send the prophet Elijah before that day comes, to prepare the way for his coming (Malachi 4:5–6). The importance of this point in connection with the relation between the Old and New Testaments cannot be overlooked. When John the Baptist appeared by the Jordan, dressed in the kind of clothes that Elijah was known to have worn, people began to get very excited. John the Baptist declared that he had only come to prepare the way for the coming of someone greater than himself – Jesus Christ. It is clear that the New Testament can be seen as picking up where the Old Testament left off, and continuing the same story of God's involvement with Israel and the world.

Major Themes of the Old Testament

The Old Testament is a remarkably complex work, which merits much fuller study than is possible in this overview. If you have the time to take the study of the Old Testament further, you are strongly recommended to make use of one of the excellent introductions which are currently available, and which are noted in the "further reading" section of this book. What follows can only serve as a very elementary introduction to some of the themes of the Old Testament, and will therefore probably tantalize and frustrate as much as inform. However, it is important to have at least some idea of some of its major themes, making the inclusion of this present section, in however brief a form, imperative.

From a Christian standpoint, the collection of writings referred to as "the Old Testament" refers to the history of God's actions in the world in preparation for the coming of Jesus Christ. Christians regard the New Testament as an extension of the same pattern of divine activity and presence as that declared in the Old, so that the New Testament both *continues* and *extends* the witness to the words and deeds of the God of Israel. Christians thus see the Old Testament as a preparation for the good news of Jesus Christ, in that it witnesses to the laying of the ground for the coming of Christ to fulfill the hopes and expectations of the prophets. The use made by New Testament writers of Old Testament prophecy is of particular interest in this respect. The Old Testament describes the history of the people of Israel, which is seen from a Christian perspective as an anticipation of the Christian church. We have already (see pp. 20–38) indicated the contents of the Old Testament, identifying some of its main books. In what follows, we shall give a very brief description of the main themes of the Old Testament, and indicate some of the ways in which they link up with the New Testament.

The Old Testament Fulfilled in the New Testament

At many points, New Testament writers see the words and actions of Jesus as fulfilling Old Testament prophecy, thus affirming the continuity of the mission of Jesus with the people of Israel.

The Birth of Jesus: Matthew 1:18–23
This is how the birth of Jesus Christ came about: His mother Mary was pledged to be married to Joseph, but before they came together, she was found to be with child through the Holy Spirit. Because Joseph her husband was a righteous man and did not want to expose her to public disgrace, he had in mind to divorce her quietly. But after he had considered this, an angel of the Lord appeared to him in a dream and said, "Joseph son of David, do not be afraid to take Mary home as your wife, because what is conceived in her is from the

STUDY PANEL 5

Study Panel 5 Continued

Holy Spirit. She will give birth to a son, and you are to give him the name Jesus, because he will save his people from their sins." All this took place to fulfill what the Lord had said through the prophet: "The virgin will be with child and will give birth to a son, and they will call him Immanuel" – which means, "God with us."

The Birthplace of Jesus: Matthew 2:1–6

After Jesus was born in Bethlehem in Judea, during the time of King Herod, magi from the east came to Jerusalem and asked, "Where is the one who has been born king of the Jews? We saw his star in the east and have come to worship him." When King Herod heard this he was disturbed, and all Jerusalem with him. When he had called together all the people's chief priests and teachers of the law, he asked them where the Christ was to be born. "In Bethlehem in Judea," they replied, "for this is what the prophet has written: 'But you, Bethlehem, in the land of Judah, are by no means least among the rulers of Judah; for out of you will come a ruler who will be the shepherd of my people Israel.'"

The Ministry of John the Baptist: Mark 1:1–3

The beginning of the gospel about Jesus Christ, the Son of God. It is written in Isaiah the prophet: "I will send my messenger ahead of you, who will prepare your way" – "a voice of one calling in the desert, 'Prepare the way for the Lord, make straight paths for him.'" And so John came, baptizing in the desert region and preaching a baptism of repentance for the forgiveness of sins.

The Creation

The Old Testament opens with an affirmation that God created the world. The fundamental theme which is affirmed in the opening chapters of the book of Genesis is that God is the originator of all that is in the world. No created thing can compare with God. This point is of particular importance, given the importance of worship of, for example, the sun or the stars, among other religions of the Ancient Near East. For the Old Testament, God is superior to everything in creation. The height of God's creation is declared to be humanity, which alone is created in the image and likeness of God. Humanity is understood to be the steward (not the possessor!) of God's creation, and is entrusted with its care.

The account of the creation is followed by an account of the nature and origins of sin. One of the fundamental points made in Genesis 3 is that sin enters the world against God's intentions. Sin disrupts the close relationship between God and the creation, and leads to humanity rebelling against God, and asserting its autonomy. This theme recurs throughout the Bible. For example, the story of the Tower of Babel (Genesis 11:1–9) is basically about human attempts at self-assertion in the face of God. God's hostility toward sin is depicted in a number of ways, including both the expulsion of Adam and Eve from the Garden of Eden, and Noah's flood.

Abraham: Calling and Covenant

The calling of Abraham is seen as being of foundational importance to the emergence of Israel, both as a nation and as the people of God. The central theme of God's calling of Abraham (Genesis 12:1–4) is that God has chosen an individual, whose descendants will possess the land of Canaan and become a great nation. The theme of the fulfillment of this promise is of major importance throughout the Pentateuch. It is also of importance to Paul in the New Testament, who sees Abraham's willingness to trust in the promises of God as a prototype of Christian faith.

The idea of a "covenant" between God and Abraham and his descendants is introduced at this point. The ritual of circumcision is seen as the external sign of belonging to the covenant people of God. For Paul, it is of particular importance that God's promise to Abraham precedes the external sign of this covenant; this, according to Paul, implies that the promise takes precedence over the sign. As a result, Gentiles (that is, those who are not ethnic Jews) do not require to be circumcised when they convert to Christianity.

The book of Genesis traces the fortunes of Abraham and his descendants, showing the manner in which the covenant between God and Abraham is realized. The book ends with an account of the way in which Abraham's descendants settle in the land of Egypt, thus setting the scene for the next major theme of the Old Testament.

The Exodus from Egypt and the Giving of the Law

A major theme which now appears is that of captivity and deliverance. The story of the Exodus (a Greek word which literally means "exit" or "way out") is well known. A new ruler arises in Egypt (referred to by the term "pharaoh"), who regards the descendants of Abraham as a potential threat. The identity of this pharaoh is unknown, although there are good reasons for suggesting that it may have been Rameses II (who ruled during the period 1279–1212 BC). He subjected the Hebrews to a series of oppressive measures, designed to limit their numbers and influence. The book of Exodus describes God's call of Moses to be a liberator of Israel from its bondage in Egypt.

STUDY PANEL 6

The Passover and the Exodus

One of the most important Old Testament festivals is closely linked with the Exodus from Egypt. The *Passover* festival had its origins in the period before the exodus. The origins and purpose of the festival are described at Exodus 11:1–12:30. It marks an act of divine judgment against Egypt. The regulations for the marking of the festival are laid down with some precision. Each household or group of households in Israel is to sacrifice a perfect lamb or goat, and daub its blood across the sides and tops of their doorframes. This will mark them off as God's own people, and distinguish them from their Egyptian oppressors. They are then to eat a meal, to remind them of their time in Egypt. Part of the meal consists of "bitter herbs," which symbolize the bitterness of their bondage. Another major part of the meal is unleavened bread. This "bread made without yeast" points to the haste with which the people were asked to prepare to leave Egypt. There was not even enough time for dough to rise, through the action of the yeast. The festival is named "the Lord's Passover," which refers to the fact that God will "pass over" the houses of his own people as he brings vengeance against the first-born sons of the Egyptians. In commemoration of this act of deliverance, the Passover is to be celebrated every year as a "lasting ordinance." Further regulations concerning its celebration are mentioned later (Exodus 12:43–49).

The Passover festival thus has strong associations of divine deliverance. It is no accident that the "Last Supper" of Jesus was a Passover meal. In celebrating God's great act of deliverance in the past, Jesus was preparing for the great act of deliverance which would take place through his death upon the cross.

The theme of liberation comes to dominate the book of Exodus. While considerable attention is devoted to the fine details of how this liberation or redemption is accomplished (the accounts of the Ten Plagues and the crossing of the Red Sea being particularly important), the most important point is that God acts to redeem Israel from its bondage. This theme of "God as liberator" is frequently taken up in later Old Testament writings, such as the Psalms, which recall the great act of deliverance from Egypt as an assurance of God's power and faithfulness.

Earlier, we noted how circumcision was seen as a physical or external sign of the covenant between God and Israel. The theme of the covenant between God and Israel is developed significantly in the book of Exodus. Two particular points should be noted. First, a specific name is now used to refer to God. This is the term "Lord," which is the English term used to translate a cypher of four letters used to name God in this way. This group of four letters, often referred to as the "Tetragrammaton" (from the Greek words for "four" and "letters"), is sometimes represented as "Yahweh" or "Jehovah" in English versions of the Bible. Other Hebrew words could be used to refer to gods in general; this specific name "Lord" was used to refer only to the "God of Abraham, Isaac, and Jacob." It is never used to refer to any other divine or angelic being, unlike other Hebrew words for "god." These latter words act as common nouns, referring to "god" or "gods" in general, and can be used to refer to Israel's own God, or to other gods (such as the pagan gods of other nations). But the Tetragrammaton is used only to name the specific God which Israel knew and worshipped.

Second, the obligations which being the covenant people of God impose on Israel are made clear. This is the series of specific unconditional demands which are now usually referred to as the "Ten Commandments," which Moses received at Mount Sinai. These commandments continue to be of major importance within Judaism and Christianity alike.

The Ten Commandments

This important text, which is of major importance to both Christians and Jews, opens with an affirmation of the identity and achievements of God, followed by the ten requirements imposed on Israel as a result of the covenant between them and God.

Exodus 20:1–17
I am the Lord your God, who brought you out of Egypt, out of the land of slavery.

1 You shall have no other gods before me.
2 You shall not make for yourself an idol in the form of anything in heaven above or on the earth beneath or in the waters below. You shall not bow down to them or worship them; for I, the Lord your God, am a jealous God, punishing the children for the sin of the fathers to the third and fourth generation of those who hate me, but showing love to a thousand generations of those who love me and keep my commandments.

STUDY PANEL 7

Study Panel 7 Continued

3 You shall not misuse the name of the Lord your God, for the Lord will not hold anyone guiltless who misuses his name.

4 Remember the Sabbath day by keeping it holy. Six days you shall labor and do all your work, but the seventh day is a Sabbath to the Lord your God. On it you shall not do any work, neither you, nor your son or daughter, nor your manservant or maidservant, nor your animals, nor the alien within your gates. For in six days the Lord made the heavens and the earth, the sea, and all that is in them, but he rested on the seventh day. Therefore the Lord blessed the Sabbath day and made it holy.

5 Honor your father and your mother, so that you may live long in the land the Lord your God is giving you.

6 You shall not murder.

7 You shall not commit adultery.

8 You shall not steal.

9 You shall not give false testimony against your neighbor.

10 You shall not covet your neighbor's house. You shall not covet your neighbor's wife, or his manservant or maidservant, his ox or donkey, or anything that belongs to your neighbor.

The Entry into the Promised Land

One of the central themes of the book of Genesis is the promise that the descendants of Abraham will settle and dwell in the land of Canaan. The story of the wanderings of the people of Israel in the wilderness, and their final entry into the land of Canaan, takes up the remainder of the Pentateuch. Israel's period of wandering in the wilderness for forty years is seen as a time of purification, in which all traces of the influence of the pagan religions of Egypt are removed. After the period of forty years, only two people to have left Egypt in the Exodus remain alive – Moses and Joshua. Moses himself dies before the entry into the promised land of Canaan, although he is allowed to view it from a mountain peak on the far side of the Jordan.

Broadly speaking, "Canaan" refers to the territory to the west of the River Jordan, including both the Sea of Galilee to the north, and the Dead Sea to the south. The occupation of Canaan is described in some detail in the book of Joshua. The initial crossing of the River Jordan into Canaan is clearly understood to parallel the earlier crossing of the Red Sea, during the Exodus from Egypt. The book of Joshua brings together accounts of three major

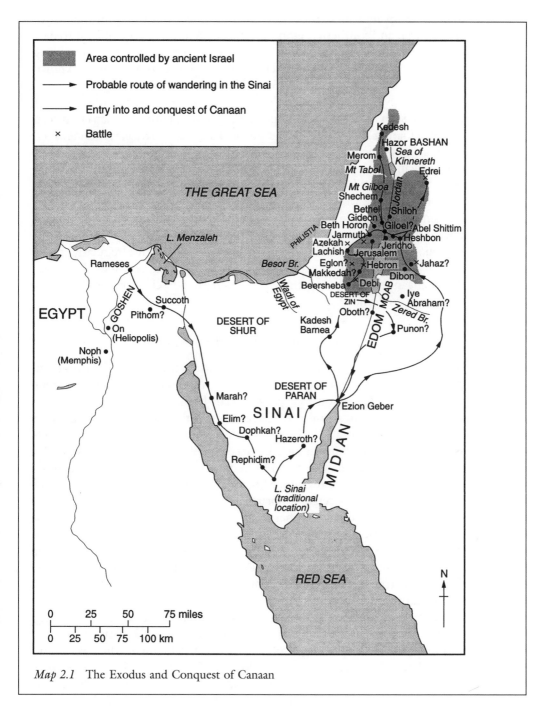

Map 2.1 The Exodus and Conquest of Canaan

military campaigns, undertaken by different groups of tribes, in the northern, central, and southern regions of Canaan. While it is very difficult to date the occupation of Canaan with any degree of certainty, there are strong parallels between the biblical descriptions of the events and what is known of the territory in the period 1450–1350 BC.

It is, however, the religious rather than the historical aspects of the matter which are seen as being more important. The occupation of Canaan is seen as consolidating the distinctive identity of Israel. In particular, it established the worship of the Lord, and obedience to the covenant established between the Lord and Israel, as of central importance to the identity and well-being of the people. The book of Joshua describes elaborate measures being taken to ensure that the worship of the Lord was not in any way compromised by indigenous Canaanite religions. Canaanite religion was strongly orientated toward fertility issues – such as the fertility of the land, animals, and humans. Its major deities – including Baal and Ashtaroth – feature regularly in the biblical accounts of the history of Israel over the next centuries. It is clear that Canaanite religion continued to exercise a fascination for Israel for some time to come.

The Establishment of the Monarchy

In its early period, Israel had no king. During the period following the conquest of Canaan, the region was ruled by a series of charismatic religious and political leaders, known as "judges." The book of Judges documents the serious threats to the unity of Israel at the time (partly from internal disunity, partly from external threats), and notes the role of "judges" such as Gideon, Samson, and Samuel. Under Samuel, the last of the "judges," a series of moves was made which resulted in the establishment of the monarchy. The first king was Saul, who probably reigned during the period 1020–1000 BC. Saul's reign is portrayed as divisive and tragic. One of his most significant internal opponents was David. Following Saul's death in a battle against the Philistines, David launched a military campaign which eventually led to the restoration of the unity of Israel, and the expansion of its territory. Although opposition to David continued throughout his reign, particularly from the supporters of Saul, David was able to maintain his hold on the nation until the final years of his reign.

The reign of David (*c*.1000–961 BC) saw significant developments taking place in Israel's religion. David's conquest of the city of Jerusalem led to it becoming the center of Israel's religious life, a development which would be consolidated during the reign of Solomon. The role of the king became important religiously, with the king being seen as a son of God. The theme of a future successor to David, who would rule over a renewed people of

God, became a significant element of messianic hopes within Israel, and explains the importance of the "David" theme within parts of the New Testament. For New Testament writers (especially Matthew and Paul), Jesus of Nazareth is to be seen as the successor to David as king of Israel. Many Old Testament writings, particularly within the Psalter, extol the greatness of the king, the temple, and the city of Jerusalem (often referred to as "Zion"). All three are seen as tokens of God's favor toward Israel.

A Psalm Celebrating Jerusalem and its King

Psalm 48:1–8

Great is the Lord, and most worthy of praise, in the city of our God, his holy mountain.

It is beautiful in its loftiness, the joy of the whole earth. Like the utmost heights of Zaphon is Mount Zion, the city of the Great King.

God is in her citadels; he has shown himself to be her fortress.

When the kings joined forces, when they advanced together, they saw her and were astounded; they fled in terror.

Trembling seized them there, pain like that of a woman in labor.

You destroyed them like ships of Tarshish shattered by an east wind. As we have heard, so have we seen in the city of the Lord Almighty, in the city of our God: God makes her secure forever.

STUDY PANEL 8

David was succeeded as king by Solomon, who reigned during the period 961–922 BC. During his reign, the temple was constructed as a permanent place of worship of the Lord. A strongly centralized administrative system was set in place, and extensive trading agreements negotiated with neighboring countries. Solomon's extensive harem caused disquiet to some, on account of the pagan religious beliefs of some of his wives. Solomon was famed for his wisdom, and some collections of proverbs in the Old Testament are attributed to him.

With the death of Solomon, the nation of Israel proved unstable. Eventually, the nation split into two sections, each with its own king. The northern kingdom, which would now be known as "Israel," would eventually cease to exist under the Assyrian invasions of the eighth century. The southern kingdom of Judah, which retained Jerusalem as its capital city, continued to exist until the Babylonian invasions of the sixth century. At this point, the monarchy ended. The Jewish hopes of restoration increasingly came to focus on the restoration of the monarchy, and the rise of a new figure like David. From a Christian perspective, these expectations could be directly related to the coming of Jesus of Nazareth.

The Kings of Israel and Judah

It is difficult to assign precise dates to the kings of Israel or Judah. What follows is a good scholarly estimate of the likely dates for the reigns of the kings of the kingdoms of Israel and Judah.

THE UNITED KINGDOM		RULERS OF JUDAH		RULERS OF ISRAEL	
Saul	1020–1000	Rehoboam	922–915	Jeroboam	922–901
David	1000–961	Abijam	915–913	Nadab	901–900
Solomon	961–922	Asa	913–873	Baasha	900–877
		Jehoshaphat	873–849	Elah	877–876
		J(eh)oram	849–842	Zimri	876
		Ahaziah	842	Omri	876–869
		Athaliah	842–837	Ahab	869–850
		J(eh)oash	837–800	Ahaziah	850–849
		Amaziah	800–783	J(eh)oram	849–842
		Uzziah	783–742	Jehu	842–815
		Jotham	742–735	Jehoahaz	815–801
		Ahaz	735–715	J(eh)oash	801–786
		Hezekiah	715–687	Jeroboam II	786–746
		Manasseh	687–642	Zechariah	746–745
		Amon	642–640	Shallum	745
		Josiah	640–609	Menahem	745–738
		Jehoahaz	609	Pekahiah	738–737
		Jehoiakim	609–598	Pekah	737–732
		Jehoiachin	598–597	Hoshea	732–721
		Zedekiah	597–587/6		

STUDY PANEL 9

The Priesthood

The centrality of religion to the identity of Israel gave the guardians of its religious traditions a particularly significant role. The emergence of the priesthood is a major theme in its own right. One of the most significant functions of the priesthood related to the cultic purity of Israel. This purity could be defiled (often referred to as "being made unclean") by various forms of pollution. The priesthood was responsible for ensuring the cleanliness of the people, which was seen as being vital for the proper worship of the Lord. More importantly, the priesthood was responsible for the maintenance of the sacrificial system, and particularly the Day of Atonement ritual, in which sacrifices were offered for the sins of the people. A distinction is to be drawn between "uncleanliness" (which arises from natural bodily functions), and "sin" (which has strongly ethical overtones). Sin was seen as something which created a barrier between Israel and God. It is significant that most of the Old Testament images or analogies for sin take the form of images of separation. In order to safeguard the continuing relationship between the Lord and Israel, the priesthood was responsible for ensuring that the proper sacrifices were offered for sin.

One Old Testament ordinance is of particular importance, both to a full understanding of the role of the priesthood in Israel, and also to the meaning of the death of Jesus Christ within Christianity. This is the Day of Atonement, described in detail at Leviticus 16:1–34, which was ordained as an annual event for the removal of sin from the people of God. The full ritual is complex, involving the High Priest ritually cleansing himself, and then offering a sacrifice for himself and the other priests. After this, two goats would be brought forward. One would be selected by lot as a sacrifice, while the other would become the scapegoat. The first goat would then be sacrificed as an offering for the sins of the people. Afterwards, the dead bull and goat were taken outside the camp, and burned. The high priest would then lay his hands upon the head of the second goat, and transfer all the sins of the people to the unfortunate animal. The scapegoat would then be driven out into the wilderness, carrying the guilt of the sins of Israel with it.

The Day of Atonement is of major importance as a background to understanding the death of Christ, a point brought out especially clearly in the letter to the Hebrews. Christ is seen as the perfect high priest, who makes a perfect sacrifice once and for all (instead of the annual ritual of the Day of Atonement). The sacrifice which he offers is himself; by his death, the sins of the people are transferred to him, and removed from his people. Note especially the fact that Jesus is put to death outside the walls of Jerusalem, just as the bull and goat were finally burned outside the camp of the Israelites. For the New Testament, the Levitical ritual sets the scene for the greater and perfect sacrifice which is yet to come, and which brings about what the Old Testament sacrifices could merely point to, yet not deliver.

There is ample evidence that many Jews were expecting the coming of a new priest, who would have a close personal relationship with God. An example of a text which bears witness to this hope is the *Testament of Levi*, which probably dates from about 108 BC:

Then the Lord shall raise up a new priest, and to him all the words of the Lord shall be revealed. The heavens shall be opened, and sanctification shall come

> upon him from the temple of glory, with the Father's voice, as from Abraham to Isaac. And the glory of the Most High shall be spoken over him, and the spirit of understanding shall rest upon him.

The accounts of the baptism of Jesus of Nazareth (for example, see Mark 1:10–11) clearly indicate that such expectations were understood to be fulfilled in him.

A related theme is that of the Temple. During the first period of its history, Israel used a moveable tent or tabernacle for its religious rites. However, when David captured the Jebusite city of Jerusalem and made it his capital, he declared his intention to build a permanent place of worship for the Lord. This was actually carried out under the direction of his successor, Solomon. The splendor of the building is a frequent theme of Old Testament writings dating from around this period. The temple was destroyed by the Babylonians in 586 BC, and rebuilt after the return from exile, half a century later. The Second Temple (as the building erected by the returned exiles is known) appears to have been rather less magnificent. However, with the end of the monarchy, the temple came to have increased civil significance, in that the temple authorities were responsible for both religious and civil matters.

A more splendid temple was constructed under Herod. Although work on this project appears to have begun in the decades immediately prior to the birth of Christ, the work was only completed in 64 AD. It was destroyed, never to be rebuilt, during the suppression of a Jewish revolt against the Romans in the city in 70 AD. The western wall of the temple largely survived; this is now widely referred to as "the wailing wall," and is an important place of prayer for Jews to this day.

Prophecy

The English word "prophet" is generally used to translate the Hebrew word *nabi*, which probably is best understood as "someone who speaks for another" or perhaps "a representative." The phenomenon of prophecy was widespread in the Ancient Near East, and not restricted to the "prophets of the Lord." The Old Testament refers to a number of "prophets of Baal," meaning charismatic individuals who claimed to act or speak on behalf of the Canaanite deity, Baal. Early prophets of importance include Elijah and Elisha, both of whom were active during the ninth century BC. However, the most important period of prophetic activity focuses on the eighth to the sixth centuries BC, and deals with the will of the Lord for Israel during a period of enormous political turbluence, arising from the increasing power of Assyria and Babylonia. Prophets such as Jeremiah proclaimed a coming period of exile, which would be both a punishment for the past sins of the people, and an opportunity for them to renew their religious practices and beliefs. After the period of exile in Babylon, post-exilic prophets such as Haggai and Malachi address some of the the issues which became of importance as the returning exiles attempted to restore Jerusalem and its temple.

The prophets of Israel were seen as affirming the Lord's continued commitment to and presence within Israel. Yet with the ending of the classic period of prophecy, the Holy Spirit seemed to have ceased to operate. God became viewed in distant and remote terms. God had been active in the past, and would be active again in the future; in the present, however, there was no real sense of the presence or power of God. With the ending of the phenomenon, a period of questioning thus appears to have set in within Judaism. No longer was the "voice of God" heard within Israel. Even the most senior rabbis (or "teachers") could expect to catch nothing more than an echo of the voice of God – an idea which was expressed in the technical term *bath qol* (literally, "the daughter of the voice"). The enormous interest in both John the Baptist and Jesus of Nazareth partly reflects this concern. Might the coming of these two figures signal the renewal of prophecy, and the restoration of Israel? The account of the baptism of Jesus (see Mark 1:10–11) clearly indicates that the coming of Jesus marks an inauguration of a period of renewed divine activity and presence.

The Exile

One of the most important events recounted in the Old Testament is the exile of Jerusalem to Babylon in 586 BC. Jerusalem thus shared the earlier fate of its northern neighbor, Israel. The events which led to the exile of the northern and southern kingdom of Judah are set out in 2 Kings. In 740 BC, Pekah ascended the throne of Israel. At this time, the Assyrian king Tiglath-Pilesar invaded part of the territory of the northern kingdom, and deported its inhabitants to Assyria. The policy of deportation was designed to minimize the risk of rebellion on the part of conquered peoples by resettling them far from their homelands. Pekah was assassinated by Hoshea, who took the throne in his stead in the year 732. In 725 BC, Tiglath-Pilesar was succeeded by Shalmanesar, who proceeded to invade the region of Samaria in 725 BC, and laid siege to it for three years. When the fighting was over, a substantial section of the population of the region was deported to regions deep with the Assyrian empire. Israel existed no longer as a nation in its own right.

Israel, then, ceased to exist as a nation in 722 BC. But what of the southern kingdom of Judah? It is clear that a new era in Judah's history opens with the reign of Hezekiah in 729 BC. Initially reigning alongside his father Ahaz, Hezekiah took full control in 715. Hezekiah introduced a major program of religious reform. This was continued under Josiah, who began to reign in 640 BC. In the course of some work on the temple, a work referred to as the "Book of the Law" is rediscovered. It is thought that this is a reference to the book of Deuteronomy, or at least to its central chapters. On hearing it read, Josiah set in place a program of reform, including the renewal of the covenant – the declaration on the part of kind and people that they will remain faithful to the law of the Lord. The Passover, which had been neglected since the days of the judges, was reinstated, and celebrated at Jerusalem.

After Josiah's death in battle, he was succeeded by Jehohaz and Jehoiakim. During the reign of Jehoiakim, an ominous series of events which will eventually lead to the end of Judah takes place. In 605 BC, the Babylonian emperor Nebuchadnezzar defeated the massed Egyptian armies at Carchemish, establishing Babylon as the leading military and political power in the region. Along with many other territories in this region, the land of Judah became subject to Babylonian rule, possibly in 604. Jehoiakim decided to rebel against Babylon. It is possible that he may have been encouraged in this move by a successful Egyptian counter-attack against Babylon in 601, which may have seemed to suggest that Babylon's power was on the wane. It was to prove to be a terrible misjudgment. Judah was invaded by Babylonian forces, which was clearly interpreted by writers of the time as the execution of the promised judgment of the Lord against his faithless people and king. Egypt, once the hope of Judah, was also defeated, and neutralized as a military power. (These same events are also vividly described and analyzed by Jeremiah, the later chapters of whose prophecy should be read in the light of this historical narrative.)

Jehoiakim was succeeded by Jehoiakin (the close similarity of these names being a constant source of confusion to readers) toward the end of 598 BC, shortly before the Babylonians finally laid siege to the city. Early the following year, the king, the royal family, and the circle of royal advisors gave themselves up to the besieging forces. They were deported to Babylon, along with several thousand captives. The Babylonians placed Zedekiah, a relative of Jehoiakin, on the throne as their vassal, and seemed happy to leave things like that for the present. Yet Zedekiah attempted to rebel against Babylon. The Babylonian response was massive and decisive. In January 588, they laid siege to the city; in July 586, they broke through its walls, and took the city. The defending army attempted to flee, but was routed. The next month, a Babylonian offical arrived in Jerusalem to supervise the destruction of the defenses of the city and its chief buildings, and the deportation of its people. The furnishings of the temple were dismantled, and taken to Babylon as booty. Any hope of a quick end to the exile soon passed. Anyone capable of leading a revolt or taking charge of a government was taken and executed. Ishmael's assassination of Gedaliah, the governor appointed by the Babylonians, caused dismay among the remaining inhabitants of the city. Fearing Babylonian reprisals, many fled to Egypt.

It is the interpretation of these events which is of particular interest to New Testament writers. The period of exile is interpreted as, in the first place, a judgment against Judah for its lapse into pagan religious beliefs and practices; and in the second, a period of national repentance and renewal, which will lead to the restoration of a resurgent people of God. It is this theme which we may consider in the final part of this section.

The Restoration

The Babylonian empire finally fell. Cyrus the Great, king of Persia (559–530 BC), conquered Babylon in 539 BC. As part of his policy of religious toleration, Cyrus permitted the exiled inhabitants of Judea to return to their homeland. The restoration of the deported inhabitants of Jerusalem to their home city after decades of exile is seen by Old Testament writers as a demonstration of the faithfulness of the Lord, and an affirmation of the repentance of the people of God. The most important Old Testament works to deal with the restoration include the historical works of Ezra and Nehemiah, and the prophet Haggai. Although we are told little of what happened to the people of Jerusalem during their time in exile, we can nevertheless gain at least some understanding of the difficulties which they faced, and their longing to return home. The book of Ezra opens by publishing the proclamation of Cyrus, the founder of the Persian empire, which set the exiles free (Ezra 1:1–4). The proclamation dates from 538 BC, and shows a spirit of generosity and tolerance towards the religion of Israel which had been conspicuously absent from the Babylonians.

As a result, many of the inhabitants of Jerusalem and Judah prepared to return home, taking the captured treasures of the temple at Jerusalem with them. By September or October 537, the returning exiles had settled down in their home towns, and had begun to renew their old patterns of worship. Not all the exiles returned to Jerusalem; other towns in Judah received returning exiles. The Feast of Tabernacles was celebrated with an altar built specially for that purpose, depsite the risk of alienating peoples in the region around them. There was still no temple at Jerusalem; however, by building an altar dedicated to the Lord, the returning exiles could begin the process of restoring worship to what it had been before the exile.

But sooner or later, the temple would have to be rebuilt, The ruins of Solomon's temple, which had been razed to the ground by the Babylonians, would act as the foundations of the new building. Under the direction of Zerubbabel, who emerges as the natural leader in Jerusalem during this period, preparations are made to rebuild the temple in the spring of 536 BC. While many were overjoyed when the foundations were laid, older people (who could remember the great edifice built by Solomon) were distressed. It is clear that the new temple would not be on the same scale as its predecessor. On 12 March 516, the temple was finally completed and dedicated. The first major festival to be celebrated in the new building was the Passover, a festival with strong associations of deliverance from bondage and the commemoration of the faithfulness of the Lord. Although this "second temple" lacked the physical grandeur of Solomon's edifice, it nevertheless was of enormous significance. It pointed to the centrality of religious concerns to the newly restored people of God. The measures taken by Ezra to prevent foreign religious influence within Jerusalem (such as the total prohibition of intermarriage) is an indication of the seriousness of the returning exiles in this respect. The post-exilic portions of the Old Testament are notable for their emphasis on the need to maintain racial and religious purity, and the importance attached to religious festivals as national events. Jerusalem had no king; the temple and its priests gradually came to assume most of the roles of the monarchy, including responsibility for civil matters.

One point that is worth commenting on here is the use of the term "Jews" to refer to the returned exiles (see, for example, Ezra 4:23; 5:1). Up to this time, the people of God had been referred to as "Israelites" or "Judahites." The term "Jew" comes to be used in the post-exilic period to designate the people of God, and would be used regularly in later writings for this purpose.

Our attention now turns to the development of the themes of the Old Testament to be found in the New Testament.

STUDY QUESTIONS

1 You should try to learn the basic order of the books of the Old Testament. You will find it helpful to break them down into categories – for example, you might like to learn the five works in the Pentateuch, then the historical works, and then the major prophets.
2 Why is it important to affirm that God created the world?
3 What major religious themes are linked with the exodus of the people of Israel from captivity in Egypt, and their entry into the Promised Land?
4 What interpretations did Israel place upon the exile in Babylon?
5 Why was prophecy so important to Israel?

The New Testament

The New Testament consists of 26 books, which can be broken down into a number of different categories – such as the gospels and the letters. Their common theme is the identity and significance of Jesus. It must be stressed that Christians were proclaiming the words and actions of Jesus from shortly after his death. Christian churches were being established in the eastern Mediterranean within a matter of years. The earliest written documents within the New Testament take the form of letters written by prominent Christians to these churches. Yet the preaching of the words and deeds of Jesus went on in the background. It was only at a later stage, probably in the early 60s, that the words and deeds of Jesus were committed to writing, in the form that we now know as the gospels. We shall begin our study of the New Testament by examining these works.

The Gospels

The first four books of the New Testament are collectively known as "gospels." They are best understood as four portraits of Jesus, seen from different angles, and drawing on various sources. The first three have many features in common, and are widely regarded as drawing on common sources in circulation within early Christian circles. Each of the gospels has its own distinctive character, which needs to be appreciated. The following sections will aim to explore the distinctive features of each of the gospels. Before this, however, it is important to appreciate some features of the gospels in general.

10

STUDY PANEL

The Gospel

The English word "gospel" comes from an Old English word *godspel*, meaning "good news," used to translate the Greek word *evangelion*. The word "gospel" is used in two different senses within Christianity. First, it refers to the events which center on Jesus of Nazareth, which are seen as being good news for the world. The gospel is primarily the "good news" of the coming of Jesus of Nazareth, with all that this has to offer humanity. The term is also used in a secondary and derivative sense to refer to the four books in the New Testament which focus on the life, death, and resurrection of Jesus of Nazareth. Strictly speaking, these books should be referred to as "the gospel according to Matthew," "the gospel according to Luke," and so on. This makes it clear that it is the same gospel which is being described, despite the different styles and approaches of the compilers of each of these four works.

Two related words should also be noted, deriving from the Greek word *evangelion* (which also means "good news"). The word "evangelism" refers to the bringing of the good news to people. The related word "evangelist" refers primarily to a person who brings the good news to people (such as Billy Graham). It can also, however, be used in a derivative way, to refer to the compilers of each of the four gospels. Thus commentaries on, for example, Mark's gospel, may refer to Mark as an "evangelist" with this meaning in mind.

The gospel writers were not biographers, or even historians, by our standards, nor were they interested in providing an account of absolutely everything that Jesus said and did. For example, occasionally it does not seem to have mattered to them exactly at what point in his ministry Jesus told a particular parable. The important thing was that he *did* tell it, and that it was realized to be relevant to the preaching of the early church. The gospel writers seem to have been concerned to remain as faithful as possible to the accounts of the life, death, and resurrection of Jesus which had been handed down to them.

There can be no doubt whatsoever that the gospel accounts of Jesus contain a solid base of historical information. Nevertheless, this is linked with an interpretation of this information. Biography and theology are interwoven to such an extent that they cannot be separated any more. The early Christians were convinced that Jesus was the Messiah, the Son of God, and their Saviour, and naturally felt that these conclusions should be passed on to their readers, along with any biographical details which helped cast light on them. It is for this reason that fact and interpretation are so thoroughly intermingled in the gospels. The first Christians had no doubt that their theological interpretation of Jesus was right, and that it was therefore an important fact which should be included in their "biographies." To tell the story of Jesus involved explaining who he was, and why he was so important. Interpretation of the significance of Jesus is therefore found alongside the material which leads to this conclusion.

From what has just been said, it will be clear that the New Testament documents, especially the gospels, are strongly committed to their subject. They do not offer us a dispassionate account of the history of Jesus, but speak of him as Lord and Savior. For example, toward the end of John's gospel, we read the following words from the author of the gospel, as he apologizes for having had so much material concerning Jesus that he has had to omit some of it (John 20:30–1):

> Jesus did many other miraculous signs in the presence of his disciples, which are not recorded in this book. But these are written that you may believe that Jesus is the Christ, the Son of God, and that by believing you may have life in his name.

This clear commitment to faith in Jesus on the part of the gospel writer might seem to raise a serious problem. It is pointed out, with reason, that the gospel writers were committed to Jesus. Is there not a danger that this commitment leads to them being prejudiced, and thus incapable of providing an objective picture of Jesus?

The potential bias of any historical source is of major importance, and cannot be ignored. A Christian source of the period is likely to show pro-Christian bias, just as a Jewish source might well be expected to be anti-Christian. Identification of possible bias is important in assessing possible variations in weight to be given to different sources. Yet it must be stressed that a source can be committed and correct at one and the same time. An example will make this clear. During the Second World War, the German Nazi leader, Adolf Hitler, initiated an extermination program directed against Jews and others in areas of Europe occupied by the Nazis. A program of mass murder was undertaken. Gradually, news of this campaign of genocide (often referred to as "the Holocaust") filtered through to the outside world, especially the United States of America.

However, the initial reports of what was going on at the Nazi extermination camps came from Jews, who were regarded as having vested interests in the matter. Their reports were often dismissed as "biased." As a result, the recognition of the horrifying facts of the Holocaust was delayed in the United States. It was not appreciated that committed witnesses, caught up in and involved in the events in question, could nevertheless be reliable witnesses. A witness to a particularly horrifying or thrilling event is bound to be affected by what he or she has seen. Yet that does not diminish the potential reliability of his or her witness to what has happened.

Precisely the same point needs to be made in relation to the New Testament writings. They are indeed written from the standpoint of faith, and with the object of bringing their readers to faith. But it does not follow that they are unreliable for that reason.

The gospels are not arranged in chronological order. As we shall see, there are reasons for thinking that Mark's gospel may have been the first to have been written, with Matthew's gospel dating from slightly later. Scholars have suggested that the reason why Matthew is placed before Mark in the canonical ordering of the New Testament has to do with the great value which the early church placed upon that gospel as a teaching resource. However, it must be appreciated that the materials which are incorporated into the gospel represent a series of recollected sayings and actions of Jesus, which were widely used for teaching purposes in the early church. These were eventually committed to writing in the gospels. The period of "oral tradition," during which the sayings and actions of Jesus were committed to memory by the disciples, probably dates from about 30–65.

It is thus important to appreciate that the gospels were not written by Jesus himself, nor do they date from his lifetime. It is generally thought that Jesus was crucified around the years 30–33, and that the earliest gospel (probably Mark) dates from about 65. There is probably a gap of about thirty years between the events described in the gospels taking place, and subsequently being written down in the form of a gospel. By classical standards, this was an incredibly short time. The Buddha, for example, had one thing in common with Jesus: he wrote nothing down. Yet the definitive collection of his sayings (the "Tripitaka") is thought to date from around four centuries after his death – more than ten times the interval between the death of Jesus and the appearance of the first gospel.

In any case, Christians were committed to writing down their understanding of the importance of Jesus long before Mark's gospel was written. The New Testament letters (still sometimes referred to as the "epistles") date mainly from the period 49–69, and provide confirmation of the importance and interpretations of Jesus in this formative period. It is now becoming clear that Paul's letters include many references to the teaching of Jesus, providing an important link between the epistles and the gospels.

Yet despite these comments, some readers may find this gap of thirty years distressing. Why were these things not written down immediately? Might people not forget what Jesus said and did, and what happened at the crucifixion and resurrection? Yet this overlooks the fact that Christians were preaching the good news of Jesus to the world from within weeks of his resurrection, making full use of this material. There was no danger of forgetting about Jesus; his words and deeds were constantly being recalled by Christian preachers and evangelists.

This process is hinted at by Luke. After relating the early part of Jesus' life, to which his mother Mary was a central witness, Luke remarks that "his mother treasured all these things in her heart" (Luke 2:51). Is Luke hinting that Mary was his source for this part of the history of Jesus? We shall never know. But it is clear that what Jesus said and did was remembered by those around him. There are no reasons for thinking that Jesus, for example, told each parable only once. The parables were probably told numerous times, with slight variations.

It is difficult for twentieth-century readers, who are so used to information being recorded in written or other visual form, to appreciate that the classical world communicated by means of the spoken word. The great Homeric epics are good examples of the way in which stories were passed on with remarkable accuracy from one generation to another. If there is one ability which modern westerners have probably lost, it is the ability to remember a story or narrative as it is told, and then to pass it on to others afterwards.

As one study of primitive culture after another confirms, the passing down of stories from one generation to another was characteristic of the pre-modern era, including the time of the New Testament itself. Indeed, there are excellent grounds for arguing that early educational systems were based upon learning by rote. The fact that most people in the West today find it difficult to commit even a short story or narrative to memory naturally tends to prejudice them against believing that anyone else could do it; yet it is evident that it was done, and was done remarkably well. Yet this ability has not been completely lost. There is also evidence that a form of writing known as "tachygraphy" (literally, "speed writing") was used during the first century. This way of writing, which corresponds roughly to modern short-hand, would have allowed aspects of Jesus' life or teaching to be committed to writing at an early stage. We possess, however, no evidence that this actually happened.

The period between the death of Jesus and the writing of the first gospel is usually referred to as the "period of oral tradition," meaning the period in which accounts of Jesus' birth, life and death, as well as his teaching, were passed down with remarkable accuracy from one generation to another. In this period, it seems that certain of Jesus' sayings, and certain aspects of his life, especially his death and resurrection, were singled out as being of particular importance, and were passed down from the first Christians to those who followed them. Others were not passed down, and have been lost forever. The early Christians seem to have identified what was essential, and what was not so important, of Jesus' words, deeds and fate, and passed down only the former to us.

An excellent example of this process of oral transmission may be found in Paul's first letter to the Christians at Corinth, almost certainly dating from the period of oral transmission:

> For I received from the Lord what I also passed on to you: The Lord Jesus, on the night he was betrayed, took bread, and when he had given thanks, he broke it and said, "This is my body, which is for you; do this in remembrance of me." In the same way, after supper he took the cup, saying, "This cup is the new covenant in my blood; do this, whenever you drink it, in remembrance of me." (1 Corinthians 11:23–5)

Paul is here passing something on to the Corinthian Christians which had been passed on to him, presumably by word of mouth. It is interesting to compare these verses with their equivalents in the synoptic gospels (Matthew 26:26–28; Mark 14:22–24; Luke 22:17–19).

The "period of oral tradition" may thus be regarded as a period of "sifting," in which the first Christians assessed what was necessary to pass down to those who followed them. Thus Jesus' sayings may have become detached from their original context, and perhaps on occasion even given a new one, simply through the use to which the first Christians put them – proclaiming the gospel to those outside the early community of faith, and deepening and informing the faith of those inside it.

Matthew

The first of the gospels is traditionally attributed to Matthew, the tax-collector who left everything to follow Jesus (Matthew 9:9–13). The same person is referred to as "Levi" in the gospels of Mark and Luke. Matthew's gospel is perhaps the most Jewish of the gospels, showing a particular interest in the relation of Jesus to the Jewish nation and its religious laws and institutions. It is of particular importance for Matthew that Jesus fulfills the great prophecies of the Old Testament. Matthew regards it as being particularly important that Jesus was a direct descendant of David, the great hero king of Israel, and that Jesus was born in the city of David, Bethlehem. Phrases such as "this took place to fulfill what the Lord said through the prophet" can be found regularly in Matthew's presentation of the gospel, as he points out how aspects of Jesus' ministry bring to fulfillment the great expectations of the Old Testament (see the frequent use of the phrase in the first two chapters, dealing with the birth of Jesus: Matthew 1:22—23; 2:15; 2:17–18; 2:23). Similarly, Matthew brings out how Jesus does not come to abolish the Old Testament law or prophets, but to bring them to their proper fulfillment (Matthew 5:17).

Matthew brings out clearly the continuity between Jesus and Israel. The careful reader of the "Sermon on the Mount" (the traditional way of referring to the body of teaching presented at Matthew 5–7) will notice that Jesus seems to be being portrayed as the new Moses delivering the new law to the new Israel on a new mountain. Similarly, Matthew allows us to see a connection between the synagogue and the church, and particularly between the Twelve Tribes of Israel and the twelve disciples or apostles. The continuity between Judaism and Christianity is thus made clear.

It is not clear when Matthew was written. As noted above, the sources on which Matthew drew in compiling his gospel go back to the 30s. Matthew may have gathered his collections of material together and committed them to writing in the 70s. In part, the dating of Matthew's gospel depends on how one understands the relation of Matthew and Mark (see pp. 64–6), and it is possible that we shall never know for certain precisely when Matthew's gospel was written.

Mark

Mark is widely regarded as having been the first of the gospels to have been written down. The gospel is generally accepted to have been written by the "John Mark" who is known to have accompanied both Peter (1 Peter 1:14) and Paul (Acts 12:12, 25). The gospel is thought to have been written in Rome, drawing extensively on the memories of Peter. The vivid details which are such a distinctive feature of this gospel (such as the specific reference to the "pillow" in the boat at 4:38), and the occasionally critical portrayal of the disciples (as at 8:14–21) are best understood if Peter was the source of the stories in question. For these and other reasons, scholars tend to regard Mark's gospel as the first of the gospels to be written down, with Matthew and Luke expanding his accounts of the life of Jesus on the basis of additional sources available to them. Peter was executed during the Roman emperor Nero's persecution of the Christians during the period 64–67, and it is possible that the death of Peter was the stimulus Mark needed to ensure that the gospel was committed to writing. This would suggest a date in the early 60s for the composition of the gospel.

It is widely thought that Mark's gospel was written at Rome (note, for example, the reference to the "Praetorium" at 15:16). Mark also draws his readers' attention to the testimony of the Roman centurion, who declared that Jesus was the "Son of God" (15:39) – a vitally important testimony, coming from a Gentile. The testimony of this Roman officer would have been of especial importance to Mark's intended readership in Rome. The reference to the "cock crowing" is also important in this respect. The Romans divided the night into four "watches": "evening" 6:00–9:00 p.m.; "midnight" 9:00–12:00 midnight; "when the cock crows" 12:00 midnight–3:00 a.m.; and "dawn" 3:00–6:00 a.m. The "cock crowing" may in fact be a reference to the trumpet blast which marked the end of the third watch of the night, rather than to the cry of a cockerel. Although some versions of the text of Mark make reference to the cock crowing twice, many early manuscripts refer to it only as crowing once.

One of the most noticeable features of this gospel is its emphasis upon the deeds of Jesus, rather than his teaching. Mark's focus on the cross, rather than the teaching, of Jesus gives his gospel a distinctive emphasis. Nevertheless, Mark passes down some major parables and sayings of Jesus. Matthew includes some major sections of teaching (such as the "Sermon on the Mount") which are not found in Mark. This is widely assumed to be due to Matthew having access to sources which Mark did not use (whether this was because he did not have access to them, or because he did not regard them as relevant to his purposes).

Luke

Luke is the third of the synoptic gospels. Luke's gospel is actually the first part of a two-part work, the second being the Acts of the Apostles. Taken together, these two works constitute the largest piece of writing in the New Testament. Both works are dedicated to a man named Theophilus (the Greek word literally meaning "a lover of God"), who may well have been a wealthy and influential Christian sympathizer at Rome. Luke himself was probably a Gentile by birth, with an outstanding command of written Greek. He was a physician, and the travelling companion of Paul at various points during his career.

Luke's gospel has clearly been written with the interests and needs of non-Jewish readers in mind, apparently with a special concern to bring out the relevance of the "good news" for the poor, oppressed and needy. He uses the word "savior" (which would already have been familiar to Greek-speaking readers) to help his readers understand the identity and significance of Jesus, and does not place as much emphasis on the messiahship of Jesus as Matthew. It includes two of the best-loved parables of Jesus: the parable of the Good Samaritan (10:30–37), and the parable of the Prodigal Son (Luke 15:11–32).

It is not clear when Luke's gospel was written. The abrupt ending of the account of Paul's imprisonment in the Acts of the Apostles suggests an early date for the two-part work, such as some time in the period 59–63. However, many scholars argue that Luke draws upon Mark's gospel at points, suggesting that the third gospel is to be dated later than the second, and pointing to the 70s as a possible time of writing.

John

John's gospel differs significantly in style from the first three gospels. It is sometimes referred to as "the Fourth Gospel," to bring out this difference. One of the most distinctive features of this gospel is the "I am" sayings, by which the full significance of Jesus is brought out.

The "I am" Sayings

John's Gospel is noted for a number of reasons, including the seven "I am" sayings, which are found on the lips of Jesus in this gospel alone. The first of these sayings is found at John 6:35, in which Jesus speaks the following words: "I am the bread of life." Each of the sayings picks up some major themes from the Old Testament (such as Israel as a vine, Moses as the giver of the bread from heaven, and God as the shepherd of Israel), and applies them directly to Jesus. The form of these sayings is grammatically unusual; making them stand out from the remainder of the text. This point is probably a little difficult for readers not familiar with Greek to appreciate; however, the importance of the point is that there is a direct similarity between these sayings and Exodus 3:14, in which God reveals himself to Moses as "I am who I am." There thus seems to be an implicit declaration of divinity on the part of Jesus within each of these sayings. The seven "I am" sayings can be listed as follows:

6:35	The Bread of Life
8:12, 9:5	The Light of the World
10:7, 9	The Gate for the Sheep
10:11	The Good Shepherd
11:25	The Resurrection and the Life
14:6	The Way, the Truth and the Life
15:1, 5	The True Vine

STUDY PANEL 11

Who wrote the gospel according to John? The text of the gospel itself indicates that its author was "the disciple whom Jesus loved" (e.g., 13:23–26; 18:15–16). Tradition has identified this as the apostle John, although it should be noted that the text of the gospel itself does not make this statement explicitly. There are reasons for thinking that the gospel may have been written with the special needs of the churches in the region of Ephesus in mind. The date of writing of the gospel remains unclear. The gospel text itself suggests that both Peter and the "beloved disciple" are dead (see 21:19, 22–23), thus pointing to a date at some point after 70. This is also suggested by other factors. Most scholars suggest a date towards the end of the first century (perhaps around 85), although the possibility of an earlier date remains open.

The Synoptic Problem

The first three gospels include a lot of material in common. The same material is sometimes presented in one setting in Mark, another in Matthew, and perhaps even a third in Luke. The same story may be told from different perspectives in different gospels. Sometimes a story is told at greater length in one gospel than in another. This is widely believed to be due to the fact that all three draw on several common sources, such as collections of the sayings of Jesus which were committed to memory at a very early stage. The opening of Luke's gospel (Luke 1:1–4) makes it clear that a number of accounts of the life and sayings of Jesus were in circulation at an early stage, also indicating that he has composed his own account of Jesus on the basis of eyewitness reports which had been made available to him. Some of this material is common to all three gospels; some is common to Matthew and Luke (which are much longer than Mark); and some is found only in Matthew or Luke. In each case, the evangelist (as the gospel writers are known) has drawn on his own set of historical sources to allow his readers access to the details of the central figure of the Christian faith. The overlap between the first three gospels is reflected in the name that is sometimes given to them: the "synoptic gospels," from the Greek word *synopsis*, or "summary."

The academic discipline of "source criticism" attempts to clarify the sources on which the gospels are based. In general terms, it is clear that all three synoptic gospels contain common material, often reporting the same incident or teaching in exactly the same words. Much of Mark's gospel is found in other synoptic gospels. Matthew and Luke also include some material common to each, as well as some material which is found only in one of them. Of particular importance is the observation that the material common to all three gospels follows the same order. This has led scholars to the universal conclusion that the synoptic gospels are interdependent. But how is this dependence to be explained?

The general consensus within New Testament scholarship is that four sources can be discerned for the synoptic gospels:

1   Mark's gospel itself, which seems to be used as a source by Matthew and Luke. Thus 90 percent of the contents of Mark's gospel is included in Matthew; 53 percent of Mark can be found in Luke. Mark's material is written in a style which suggests that it is older than the style found in the corresponding passages in Matthew or Luke, using many semitic phrases. It is very difficult to explain this observation on the basis of any hypothesis other than that Matthew and Luke both based themselves on Mark, and "tidied up" his style.

2   Material common to both Matthew and Luke. This section of material, which is about two hundred verses in length, is generally referred to as "Q." These is no evidence that Q was a complete gospel in itself, or that it existed as an independent written source.

3   Material found only in Matthew (usually known as "M").

4   Material found only in Luke (usually known as "L").

The most widely accepted explanation of this theory was developed in detail in its current form at the University of Oxford in the opening decade of the twentieth century. Its most celebrated statements can be found in B. H. Streeter's *Four Gospels* (1924) and W. Sanday's *Studies in the Synoptic Problem* (1911). Streeter's work represented a collection of papers reflecting the work of the Oxford gospel seminar, which met nine times a year over a period of fifteen years. Although this theory is sometimes known as "the Oxford hypothesis," it is more commonly referred to as "the two source theory." Its basic features can be set out as follows.

Mark was the first gospel to be written down. It was available to both Matthew and Luke, who used it as a source, altering the style of the language as appropriate, but retaining Mark's ordering of the material. Matthew was written after Mark, but before Luke. Both Matthew and Luke had access to the source known as Q. In addition, Matthew had access to another source known as M; Luke had access to a different source, known as L. Although this theory acknowledges four sources (Mark, Q, M and L), it is known as the "two source" theory on account of the importance of Mark and Q in relation to its approach.

This theory is the most widely accepted in modern New Testament scholarship. Other approaches exist, but are not widely supported. For example, Augustine of Hippo argued that Matthew was written first, and that Mark abbreviated Matthew. J. J. Griesbach developed an influential hypothesis, according to which Matthew was written first, followed by Luke (who used Matthew). Finally, Mark was written, making use of both Matthew and Luke.

It must also be stressed that the "synoptic problem" concerns our understanding of the way in which the oral traditions concerning Jesus were passed down to us. It does not call their historical accuracy or theological reliability into question, but allows a deeper understanding of the formative period of the gospel traditions, in which the words and deeds of Jesus were passed down and handed over during the period *c.*30–60.

Acts

The "Acts of the Apostles," to give this work its full title, is the second installment of Luke's account of the origins of the Christian church, and follows on from the gospel which is attributed to him (see p. 62). Taken together, Luke's gospel and history of the early church is the largest single document in the New Testament. In his gospel, Luke informed one "Theophilus" (probably a well-placed Roman official who had become interested in Christianity) of the basic details of the life, death, and resurrection of Jesus. However, by the time that Luke was writing, Christianity was well on the way to becoming a major force in the Roman empire. So how did Christianity progress from its humble origins in Palestine to the hub of the Roman Empire? How did it come to wield such influence in so short a time? Luke's task was to explain this development to his (presumably Roman) reader, and particularly to show that Rome had nothing to fear from Christianity.

Luke sets out to document the rapid expansion of Christianity throughout the Roman Empire. The first twelve chapters focus on Peter, and the series of events which led to the Christian gospel becoming firmly rooted in Jerusalem and the surrounding regions. Having shown how the gospel became rooted in Palestine, Luke moves on to show how it gradually became established in much of the Roman Empire. The remainder of the work focuses on Paul – a figure familiar to readers of the New Testament, who was initially a law-abiding Jew named "Saul." Luke explains Paul's background, and shows how he became first a Christian, and then the "apostle to the Gentiles." He gives a vivid account of the impact that Paul had upon the expansion of the Christian church from Palestine into the regions of modern-day Turkey and Greece. It gives details of the three missionary journeys he undertook in the eastern Mediterranean, and ends with a description of his final voyage as a prisoner to Rome itself. At several points, Luke uses the term "we" to refer to events (e.g., Acts 16:10–17; 20:5–21:18; 27:1–28:16). This clearly implies that Luke was present on these occasions, and is writing as an eyewitness.

It is not clear when the work was written. The last event to be recorded in the work dates from immediately before the outbreak of serious persecution of Christians at Rome in 64. There is no reference of any kind to the burning of Rome and the subsequent suppression of the Christian community at Rome under Nero, which began in 64, and continued on and off for several years. Nor is there any hint of the destruction of Jerusalem by Roman armies in 70. Both these events would be of relevance to Luke's narrative; the fact that neither is mentioned strongly suggests that the work predates them.

The Letters

The New Testament includes a series of letters written to individuals or churches by leading figures within the early church. These letters often clarify points of Christian doctrine and practice, and offer encouragement to Christians in the face of hostility from other religious groupings or from the secular authorities. It is clear, for example, that Christianity was subject to various forms of harassment by Jews in the first decades of its existence. It must be remembered that Christianity was very weak numerically for much of the first century, and was often forced to hold its meetings in secret for fear of persecution from the local Roman authorities. In particular, the reigns of Nero and Domitian witnessed concerted efforts to eliminate the growing Christian church; some documents within the New Testament are written in the face of this kind of situation.

The Letters of Paul

By far the largest collection of letters within the New Testament is due to Paul. During the course of his missionary efforts, Paul established a number of small Christian groups in Asia Minor, Macedonia, and Greece. He remained in touch with some of them subsequently by letter. Not all these letters have survived; Paul himself makes reference to additional letters to the church at Corinth, and to a letter to the church at Laodicea. The use of the word "church" is potentially misleading; the early Christians did not meet in buildings designated as "churches," but gathered in secret in small groups. The word "church" is probably better translated as "congregation" or "gathering" in this context. Paul's early letters are often concerned with matters of doctrine, particularly concerning the second coming of Christ and the relation between Jews and Gentiles. The later letters reflect the increasing importance of church order and structure, as Christianity increasingly becomes a permanent presence in the eastern mediterranean region.

The dating of Paul's letters is very difficult, for a number of reasons. In what follows, we shall consider the letters in "canonical order" – that is, in the order in which they appear in the New Testament. It must, however, be appreciated that this does not necessarily represent the order in which they were written. In general terms, the New Testament seems to arrange letters according to their length, grouping letters to the same churches or individuals together.

The first letter to be encountered is *Romans*. Paul probably wrote his letter to the Christian community at Rome in the early spring of 57 AD, during his time at Corinth in the course of his third missionary journey (see p. 246). No apostle had ever visited Rome before; the letter therefore provides the church at Rome with the basic elements of Christian teaching. Most of Paul's letters were written to churches which he had personally established and taught. Romans is an exception.

The letter is of major importance in many ways. It sets out clearly Paul's understanding of the relation between Israel and the Christian church. In particular, it sets out Paul's doctrine of justification by faith, rather than by the works of the law. According to this teaching, both Jews and Gentiles can be justified (a word which is probably best paraphrased as "made right with God" or "put in a right relationship with God") by faith. It is not necessary to be circumcised, be a Jew, or observe the Old Testament law. What matters is faith in God. The letter is also of interest historically, in that it bears witness to the growth of the Christian church at Rome.

This is followed by the two letters to the *Corinthians*. Corinth was one of the most important cities of Greece, often being estimated as having a population of more than 500,000 people. It was a leading seaport and commercial centre, and was evangelized by Paul during his third missionary journey (see p. 246). The letter is written from Ephesus, a leading city in Asia Minor, and probably dates from some point before the feast of Pentecost in 55 AD. Paul's second letter to this church was written at some point late that same year, before winter had finally set in. The letter was written from Macedonia, the region to the north of the Roman province of Achaia (in which both Corinth and Athens were located).

The first of the two letters focuses on a number of questions. It is clear that the question of how Christians should relate to their pagan environment was of particular concern. Should Christians eat meat which had been offered to pagan idols? In addition, the church was embroiled in controversy over a number of issues relating to its worship. Were some members more important than others? What was the role of spiritual gifts? It seems that the Christians at Corinth experienced something like the kind of experience now associated with the charismatic movement, and were anxious to know what to make of the phenomenon. Alongside this, we find Paul dealing with some matters of theology, including a major discussion of the nature of the resurrection.

The second letter is notable for its dark tone. Paul was obliged to cancel a planned visit to Corinth, and caused considerable resentment by doing so. The letter sets out his credentials as a minister and apostle, in the face of those who criticize him. Alongside this affirmation of his ministry, we find

Paul stressing the compassion and graciousness of God. This is expressed in what is probably the best-known statement in Paul's writings, which has passed into general Christian use as "the grace."

The Grace

The ending of one of Paul's early letters is widely used in Christian public meetings as a way of bringing it to an end by commending those present to God's care. It is widely referred to simply as "The Grace." Note the strongly Trinitarian form of the prayer.

2 Corinthians 13:14
May the grace of the Lord Jesus Christ, and the love of God, and the fellowship of the Holy Spirit be with you all.

STUDY PANEL 12

Paul's letter to the *Galatians* is generally thought to date from around 53. Another possibility is that the letter dates from shortly after the Council of Jerusalem (Acts 15), which raised questions very similar to those which Paul addresses in this letter. This would point to an earlier date, possibly around 49. The leading theme of the letter is the freedom of Christians from the letter of the Old Testament law. Christians, according to Paul, are justified by faith, not by the works of the law. There is thus no reason for Christians to be circumcised. It seems that there were "Judaizers" (that is, people who wished to see Christians remaining faithful to the Old Testament law) within the church in Galatia.

The letter to the *Ephesians* poses some difficulties. Ephesus was the chief city of the region of Asia Minor, and the scene of some of Paul's most difficult evangelist work. This letter does not have the usual specific greetings which are customary in Paul's letters, which has led some scholars to conclude that the letter was meant to be circulated throughout the churches of the region, rather than addressed to any one specific congregation. Even the specific reference to Ephesus (Ephesians 1:1) is omitted by many manuscript versions of the text. The letter does not deal directly with any specific false teaching. This further suggests that the letter was intended to circulate throughout the churches of Asia Minor, rather than focus on the specific problems of any one congregation. It is difficult to date the letter precisely.

The letter to the *Philippians* was addressed to the Christians in the city of Philippi, an important Roman colony in Macedonia, which had been evangelized by Paul during his second missionary journey (Acts 16:11–40). It was the first European city in which Paul proclaimed the gospel. There were so few Jews in the region that there was no synagogue (Acts 16:16 refers only to a "place of prayer," not a synagogue). This may explain both why Paul does not cite the Old Testament at all during this letter, and also why the letter is virtually free of argument. Paul's letter to the church at Philippi is generally thought to have been written during a period of imprisonment, probably in Rome, around 61. The circumstances of the letter fit in well with those described in Acts 28:14–31, when Paul was under house arrest, but was still permitted to see visitors and enjoy at least some degree of freedom.

The letter to the Colossians is difficult to date, and gives some indications of being a later letter. The city of Colossae (also spelled Colosse) was located on the River Lycus in Asia Minor. Paul himself had not evangelized this city during any of his missionary journeys; however, Epaphras, one of Paul's converts during his Ephesian ministry (Acts 19:10), had travelled to the city in order to preach the gospel there. The letter is particularly concerned to deal with a false teaching which has arisen within this young church. Although this false teaching is never specifically identified, its basic features appear to have included an emphasis upon some secret or mystical knowledge (a theme which would become a major theme of the movement known as Gnosticism, which became especially influential in the second century); a strict set of rules concerning what it was legitimate to eat and drink, linked with an emphasis on asceticism; and a tendency to play down the importance of Jesus Christ, and worship angels. In many ways, the ideas seem to represent a mingling of Jewish and Greek ideas. Paul counters the teaching by emphasizing that all that needs to be known about God and his purposes has been revealed supremely, uniquely, and adequately in Jesus Christ.

The two letters to the *Thessalonians* are probably the earliest of Paul's letters. As noted above, there is a possibility that Galatians may have been written as early as 49; however, the majority view among scholars remains that the Thessalonian letters are the earliest of Paul's writings. Paul's first letter to the Christians at Thessalonica was written from Corinth, probably at some point in 51, although the date cannot be fixed with certainty. Thessalonica was the largest city in Macedonia, and was evangelized by Paul during his second missionary journey (Acts 17:1–14). Paul was only able to stay in the city briefly, being obliged to flee from the city and seek refuge in nearby Berea, before moving on to Athens and then Corinth. While in Corinth, Paul wrote to the Christian church at Thessalonica, to offer it encouragement and guidance. The second letter to the region probably dates from about six months after the first. Both letters focus on the issue of the second coming of Christ, and the need for Christians to remain watchful. The letters indicate a concern within the very early church over the fate of Christians who have died before Christ's return.

Paul's two letters to Timothy and the letter to Titus form a special group. They are distinguished by the fact that they are written to specific individuals, rather than to churches, and also by their strongly pastoral tone. This latter is seen in their concern with issues of church government and practical Christian living. For this reason, these three letters are often referred to collectively as "The Pastoral Letters." The pastoral letters date from a time after the events described in Acts 28. The most obvious explanation is that Paul was released from his house arrest in Rome at some point around 63 AD, and that these letters were written after this release.

The first two such letters are written to Timothy, who had played a significant role in Paul's missionary work (especially in Achaia and Macedonia: see Acts 17:14–15; 18:5), and is referred to with great affection in several of Paul's letters (Philippians 2:19–22). In addition, no fewer than six of Paul's letters name him in their opening greetings (2 Corinthians, Philippians, Colossians, 1 Thessalonians, 2 Thessalonians, and Philemon). Titus was one of Paul's many Gentile converts, and is known to have served him well and faithfully at several major stages in his ministry. Luke does not mention Titus at any point during Acts; however, there are frequent references to him elsewhere in the New Testament, indicating his importance to the early churches.

These letters differ from the earlier Pauline letters in a number of ways. They are written to individuals, rather than to churches; they focus primarily on issues of church order and ministry, rather than matters of belief and conduct; all three letters are written with a style and vocabulary which differs from those of earlier letters, such as Galatians or Romans. These observations have led some to conclude that the letters were not written by Paul; others, however, argue that Paul was simply responding to the situation which developed in the 60s.

The final letter to be grouped in this collection is the letter to *Philemon*. This short letter was written by Paul from Rome, probably during the period in which he was held under house arrest (around 60). It is a highly unusual letter, in that it deals with a purely practical matter – the fate of a runaway slave – rather than with theology.

The Letters of Peter

The New Testament includes two letters attributed to *Peter*, widely regarded as the pre-eminent of the disciples of Jesus. The first letter is addressed to Christians scattered throughout the general region of Asia Minor, who are facing the threat of persecution. Although that persecution has yet to begin, it is clearly seen as a major threat by those to whom Peter was writing. The situation which the letter presupposes could easily fit in with what we know of the difficulties faced by Christians in the reign of

Nero (54–68 AD). Peter indicates that he was in "Babylon" when he wrote the letter (1 Peter 5:13). The letter aims to encourage Christians facing hardship and persecution, reminding them that Christ suffered for them. For the writer, suffering is an inevitable part of being a Christian in a hostile environment. Peter acknowledges the assistance of Silas in writing the letter (5:12). It is highly likely that Silas did more than transcribe Peter's words; secretaries were often given the task of putting a writer's thought into better Greek than the writer himself could manage. The letter is written in excellent Greek – much better than might be expected from a former Galilean fisherman! The second letter, in contrast, is written in much poorer Greek (there is no reference to Silas!), and seems to envisage a situation which arose at a later stage in the history of the early church.

The Letters of John

The three letters of John are very similar in content and style. Their common author is the apostle John, also regarded as the author of the fourth gospel. There are very clear similarities between the style of writing and the vocabulary, particularly in the case of John's gospel and the first letter of John. It is generally thought that the letters date from the end of the first century, perhaps having been written from the city of Ephesus around 85–90. The identity of the readership of the first two letters is not clear; they are addressed to believers in general, and may have been intended as circular letters for the use of traveling evangelists. The third letter is specifically addressed to "Gaius," although his identity is not clear.

It is clear that the threat posed by some form of Gnosticism is seen as particularly important. It seems that some Gnostic ideas had found their way into the communities for which John was writing. The first letter clearly addresses at least two Gnostic teachings – that Jesus' human nature was apparent rather than real, and that a radical distinction existed between the "spiritual" and the "material." The consequence of this second idea was that sins committed in the physical nature had no negative implications for someone's spiritual nature. The first letter emphasizes the reality of Christ's human nature, and affirms that Christians should not sin.

Other Letters

The letter to the *Hebrews* is one of the most fascinating letters in the New Testament, stressing how Jesus Christ represents the fulfillment of the Old Testament sacrificial system. The author of the letter is unknown. Some older translations suggest that the author is Paul. However, the text makes no such claim; in any case, the style of the writing is very different from that of Paul. The two people who are most likely to have written the work are

Barnabas and Apollos, both of whom are noted appreciatively in the Acts of the Apostles. Either would have had the deep familiarity with the Old Testament and the excellent command of the Greek language which this book demonstrates. It is not clear who the intended readers of the letter would have been. The most appropriate readers would have been Greek-speaking Jewish converts to Christianity, who wanted to know the relationship between their new faith and the old ways and ideas of Judaism; neither is it clear when the letter was written.

The letter of *James* is the first of a group of letters sometimes referred to as the "catholic letters" or "epistles general," in that the letters in question are not written to specific individuals, or specific churches, but seem to be intended to be read by a wide range of people. (The word "catholic" basically means "universal" or "general.") The letter of James was probably not written by James the apostle, but by James the brother of Jesus, who played an important role in the Council of Jerusalem (Acts 15:13). This council was especially concerned with clarifying whether Christian believers would be under any obligation to respect the law of Moses, especially its requirement that males should be circumcised. In the end, the council decided that this should not be a requirement (see p. 236). However, no reference is made to this controversy in the letter. The absence of any such reference to this controversy points to an early date for the letter. However, James appears to be concerned to correct a possible misunderstanding of Paul's doctrine of justification by faith, which would suggest a date at some point in the late 50s or early 60s.

The letter of *Jude* is one of the shortest books in the New Testament. The precise identity of the author of the letter remains unclear. The main concern of the letter is to counter a false teaching which appears to have become widespread. The teaching in question seems similar to that noted in 2 Peter, and seems to represent a form of Gnosticism, tinged with elements drawn from popular Jewish superstition.

The Book of Revelation

The book of *Revelation*, which brings the New Testament to its close, is traditionally regarded as having been written by John the apostle, who was also responsible for the gospel and three letters bearing his name in the New Testament. The book seems to have been written at a late date, probably during the later part of the reign of the Roman emperor Domitian (81–96), when the Roman authorities were attempting to suppress Christianity in certain regions of their empire, particularly Asia Minor. The book is apocalyptic in its outlook, resembling the second half of the book of Daniel in the Old Testament. It takes the form largely of visions, making extensive use of symbolism and highly figurative language. In some cases, it is reasonably clear what the symbols represent; there are clear allusions to the city of Rome, the Roman empire and the Roman emperor at several points. In many cases, however, the interpretation of the visions is difficult and speculative. The clear purpose of the book is to encourage Christians in their present sufferings, in the knowledge that evil and oppression will finally be overcome, and that suffering and pain will be excluded from the New Jerusalem.

In the present chapter, we have considered aspects of the contents of the New Testament. One theme may be said to dominate the New Testament – Jesus Christ. Martin Luther summarized this point as follows: Jesus Christ is "the mathematical point of Holy Scripture," just as Holy Scripture "is the swaddling clothes and manger in which Christ is laid." Having considered the contents of the New Testament, we must now turn to deal with the New Testament portrayal of the identity and significance of its central figure.

STUDY QUESTIONS

1 You should try to read one of the gospels through from beginning to end, to get a "feel" for its approach. Mark is particularly appropriate, given its brevity and directness.
2 Why were the gospels written down?
3 Why did Luke regard it as important to set out the events of the life of Jesus and the development of the early church?
4 Why are the letters included in the New Testament? What use are they?
5 At some point, you ought to read one of Paul's letters. You will find the letter to the Philippians especially suitable to begin with, as you do not need to know much about the historical background to the letter to make sense of much of what he writes.

The History of Jesus

If Christianity has a center, it is Jesus Christ. It is impossible for the Christian to talk about God, salvation, or worship without bringing Jesus into the discussion, whether explicitly or implicitly. For New Testament writers, Jesus is a window onto the nature, character, and purposes of God. Jesus is the ground of salvation. Since the time of the New Testament onwards, Christians have worshipped Jesus as the risen Lord and Savior of the world.

It is interesting to compare the Christian understanding of the role of Jesus Christ with the Islamic understanding of the role of Muhammed. For Islam, Muhammed himself is not of fundamental importance, except in that he is the bearer of revelation from Allah. Allah is unknown and unknowable. Through Muhammed, Allah's will for humanity is made known. Islam therefore tends to center on principles revealed through Muhammed by Allah. Yet Christianity focuses on the person of Jesus. Islam speaks of a revelation *from* God, where Christianity speaks of a revelation *of* God, seeing that revelation being concentrated and focused on the person of Jesus.

The name "Jesus Christ" needs some explanation. The word "Jesus" (Hebrew *Yeshua*) literally means "God saves." The word "Christ" is actually a title; the name "Jesus Christ" is perhaps better written as "Jesus the Christ." The word "Christ" is the Greek version of the Hebrew term "Messiah," referring to an individual singled out or raised up by God for some special purpose. There seems to have been a general consensus that the Messiah would be like a new king David, opening up a new era in Israel's history. While Israel looked forward to the coming of a messianic age, different groups understood this in different ways. The Jewish desert community at Qumran thought of the messiah in priestly terms, whereas others had more political expectations. Yet despite these differences, the hope of the coming of a "messianic age" seems to have been widespread. It can certainly be detected in the gospel accounts of the ministry of Jesus.

During the first phase of its existence, Christianity existed alongside (or even within) Judaism. Christians insisted that the God who was known and encountered by the great heroes of faith of Israel – such as Abraham, Isaac, Jacob, and Moses – was the same God who was more fully and clearly revealed in Jesus. It was therefore of importance to the early Christians to demonstrate that Jesus of Nazareth, the central figure of the Christian faith, brought the great messianic hopes of Judaism to fulfillment. As the question of the relationship of Christianity to Judaism became of less pressing importance, there is some evidence that the original meaning of the term "Christ" became lost. It seems to have become simply a name, whose implications were not fully understood.

In any case, Jesus was referred to in other ways. In the gospels and Acts of the Apostles (an early compilation of accounts of the expansion of the church in the 40s and 50s), Jesus is often referred to simply as "Jesus of Nazareth." This seems to have been something like a term of contempt. Nazareth was a village about 100 kilometers north of Jerusalem, in the region of Galilee. For historical reasons, Jews from the region of Judea (which includes the city of Jerusalem) tended to look down on Jews from Galilee, seeing them as less Jewish and less cultured than themselves. This sense of religious and cultural superiority underlies one incident reported in the New Testament, in which Jews from Jerusalem refused to take seriously the idea that the Messiah could come from Galilee (John 7:41). From another incident, it is clear that the distinctive accent of Galilean Jews marked them out as strangers in Jerusalem (Matthew 26:73).

Roman Historians on Jesus

There are few references to Jesus in the writings of Roman historians, who had relatively little time for events which took place in the backwaters of their empire. Their histories focused on Rome itself, and the leading figures and events which shaped its destiny. Their interest in Christianity therefore concentrated on its impact at Rome itself. They had little interest in tracing its historical origins, although they were aware that it could be traced back to events in the Roman province of Judea at a time when it was governed by Pontius Pilate. Three Roman historians make reference to Jesus in their writings: Pliny the Younger, writing around AD 111 to Trajan about the rapid spread of Christianity in Asia Minor; Tacitus, who wrote in approximately AD 115 concerning the events of AD 64, in which Nero made Christians the scapegoats for the burning

---

of Rome; and Suetonius, writing around AD 120 concerning certain events in the reign of the emperor Claudius. Suetonius refers to a certain "Chrestus" who was behind rioting at Rome. "Christus" was still an unfamiliar name to Romans at this stage, whereas "Chrestus" was a common name for slaves (meaning "someone who is useful"). Even in the third and fourth centuries, Christian writers were still complaining about people who misspelled "Christus" as "Chrestus." The following points emerge from the brief comments of these historians.

1   Christ had been condemned to death by Pontius Pilate, procurator of Judea, during the reign of the Roman emperor Tiberius (Tacitus). Pilate was procurator of Judea from AD 26–36, while Tiberius reigned from AD 14–37. The traditional date for the crucifixion is some point around AD 30–33.
2   By the time of Nero, Christ had attracted sufficient followers in Rome to make them a suitable scapegoat for the burning of Rome. These followers were named "Christians" after him (Tacitus).
3   "Chrestus" was the founder of a distinctive group within Judaism (Suetonius).
4   In AD 112, Christians worshipped Jesus "as if he were a god," abandoning the worship of the Roman emperor to do so (Pliny).

Our primary sources for the life of Jesus are the four gospels of the New Testament – Matthew, Mark, Luke and John. Roman historians provide relatively little helpful information concerning Jesus, although they are important sources for our understanding of the way in which Jesus was understood within early Christianity. For this reason, we shall focus on the portrayal of the history of Jesus in the gospels. We have already considered their general features, as well as the distinctive characteristics of each of the four gospels (see pp. 55–64). The first three of these are usually referred to as "synoptic gospels." This term derives from the Greek word *synopsis*, meaning "summary" or "list." It points to the way in which each of these gospels presents related, though distinct, accounts of the ministry of Jesus. Matthew's gospel, for example, brings out the importance of Jesus for the Jewish people, and is particularly concerned to explore the way in which Jesus brings the expectations of Israel to their proper fulfillment. Mark's gospel takes the form of a rapidly-paced narrative, often leaving readers breathless, as they are led from one event to another. Luke's gospel has a particular interest in bringing out the importance of Jesus for non-Jewish readers. John's gospel is more reflective in its approach, characterized by a distinctive emphasis on the way in which the coming of Jesus brings eternal life to those who believe in him.

In the previous chapter, we explored the nature of the gospels (pp. 55–60). The reader will recall that we noted that the gospels cannot be thought of as biographies of Jesus, in the modern sense of the term. For example, they do not present us with a full account of the life of Jesus. Mark's gospel, for example, focuses on a few years of Jesus's life, characterized by his intensive public ministry and ending in his crucifixion and resurrection. Matthew and Luke both relate brief accounts of the birth and childhood of Jesus, before resuming their narratives with the public ministry of Jesus. It is clear that the gospels draw on and bring together several sources to build up their overall portrayal of the identity and significance of Jesus. Thus Mark's gospel draws on material which is traditionally attributed to Peter, the leading disciple of Jesus. Furthermore, the gospels are more concerned with bringing out the significance of the life of Jesus than with documenting it in full detail. Nevertheless, the gospels present us with a portrait of Jesus which mingles history and theology to tell us who Jesus is – not simply in terms of his historical identity, but in terms of his continuing importance for the world. In chapter 5, we shall explore something of the New Testament understanding of the significance of Jesus, focusing on the theological aspects of the New Testament witness to Jesus. In the present chapter, we shall consider the gospel accounts of the history of Jesus.

We begin this analysis by considering the background against which the gospels set the coming of Jesus – the history of Israel, as the people of God.

Jesus and Israel

The coming of Jesus did not take place in a vacuum. It is vitally important to appreciate that Jesus was born into Israel, the people of God. Christians stress that the God who was proclaimed and revealed by Jesus is the same God who was known and worshipped by the great saints of Israel, such as Abraham and Moses. From a Christian perspective, the history of Israel is seen as a preparation for the new phase of God's dealings with humanity. The theme of the continuity of God's revelation, initially through Israel, and subsequently through Jesus Christ, is of major importance to Christian writers. This can be seen at point after point in the New Testament, part of the body of writings known as the Bible, and regarded as normative by Christians (see pp. 55–74).

The continuity between Judaism and Christianity is expressed in a number of ways. Judaism placed particular emphasis on the Law, through which the will of God was made known in the form of commands, and the

Prophets, who made known the will of God in certain definite historical situations. Jesus himself stressed that he had "not come to abolish the Law or the Prophets, but to fulfill them" (Matthew 5:17). The same point is made by Paul, who refers to Jesus as "the goal of the Law" (Romans 10:4, using the Greek word *telos*, which means "end" or "objective"). Paul also stresses the continuity between the faith of Abraham and that of Christians (Romans 4:1–25), while the Letter to the Hebrews points out both the continuity of the relationship between Moses and Jesus (Hebrews 3:1–6), and between Christians and the great figures of faith of Israel (Hebrews 11:1–12:2).

Throughout the New Testament, the same theme recurs: Christianity is continuous with Judaism, and brings to completion what Judaism was pointing toward. This has several major consequences, of which the following are the most important. First, both Christians and Jews regard more or less the same collection of books as having authority. The body of writings which Jews refer to as "Law, Prophets and Writings" is referred to by Christians as "the Old Testament." Although there have always been more radical thinkers within Christianity who would like to break the link with Israel, the majority opinion has always been that it is important to affirm and value the historical link with Israel. A body of writings which Jews regard as complete in itself is seen by Christians as pointing forward to something which will bring it to completion. We have already explored the implications of the term "Old Testament" earlier in this book (pp. 9–14).

Second, New Testament writers often stress the manner in which Old Testament prophecies are fulfilled or realized in the life and death of Jesus Christ. By doing this, they draw attention to two important principles – that Christianity is continuous with Judaism, and that Christianity brings Judaism to its true fulfillment. This is particularly important for early Christian writers who have a particular concern to demonstrate the importance of Christianity for Jews, such as Paul and Matthew. Thus at twelve points, Matthew points out how events in the life of Jesus can be seen as fulfilling Old Testament prophecy (Matthew 1:22; 2:15, 23; 3:15; 4:14; 5:17; 8:17; 12:17; 13:14, 35; 21:4; 27:9). In view of the importance of this matter, we shall look at two Old Testament passages, and the way in which New Testament writers saw them as being fulfilled in the life of Christ.

Psalm 22 is of particular significance to Christians. Jesus cited its opening words as he was dying on the cross (Matthew 27:46). The Psalm speaks of the torment of a righteous sufferer, in response to the attacks of enemies who at present are gaining the upper hand. The "righteous sufferer" awaits deliverance from the Lord – yet at present there is no sign of any such deliverance. While the original situation addressed by this Psalm is almost certainly linked with the personal difficulties of David, the Psalm is of especial importance in casting light on the crucifixion of Christ as the righteous suffering servant of God. Even though the Psalm relates well to events of the tenth century before Christ, it seems to Christians to be fulfilled especially in the death of Jesus. The psalm clearly relates to the events of David's lifetime; it is also prophetic, pointing ahead to events which would only be fulfilled in the coming of Jesus Christ.

Thus the Psalm speaks of the "righteous sufferer" being scorned and despised, surrounded by those who mocked him (22:6–7) – a description in anticipation of the scene around the cross (Matthew 27:41). The Psalmist speaks of people taunting him: "he trusted in the Lord; let the Lord rescue him" (22:8). The same words were used by the scoffing crowd who surrounded the dying Christ (Matthew 27:43). The description of the sufferer's anguish (22:12–16) corresponds well to the pain experienced by Christ on the cross. The piercing of Christ's hands and feet at crucifixion are prophesied here (22:16; see John 20:25), as is the casting of lots for his clothes (22:18; see Matthew 27:35; Luke 23:34).

A second Old Testament passage is also of especial importance to Christians. This is one of the "servant songs" found in the prophecy of Isaiah (Isaiah 52:13–53:12), which is generally regarded as one of the most important pieces of Old Testament prophecy concerning Jesus Christ. The passage, which dates from the sixth century before Christ, seems to speak of the suffering of God's servant Israel on behalf of other nations. Yet for Christians, the passage can be seen to have been fulfilled in Jesus Christ. Thus it speaks of the "servant" as being despised and rejected by others, yet at the same time suffering for them and bearing their iniquities. Although the servant was righteous, he was nevertheless "numbered with the transgressors." Jesus was crucified between two criminals (Luke 22:37; 23:32–33). The servant prayed for those who sinned; just as Jesus prayed for those who were crucifying him as he died upon the cross (Luke 22:34). Other New Testament writers pick up this theme of the fulfillment of this prophecy in the suffering of Jesus (most notably at 1 Peter 2:21–25, which explicitly relates this prophecy to Jesus).

In seeing great passages such as these as being fulfilled in the life and death of Jesus, Christians are in no way denying that they had real relevance and application to the situations faced by Jews at the time they were written. They are simply pointing out that their *full* significance was not appreciated at the time. They possessed a deeper – perhaps a more mysterious – meaning, which only became clearer in the fullness of time.

Jesus and Jewish Groups

As has just been stressed, Jesus must be set in the context of Judaism. At the time of Jesus, Judaism was an enormously complex phenomenon. It embraced both Jews who were resident in the region of Judea itself (often referred to as "Palestinian Judaism"), and the various Jewish communities dispersed throughout the civilized world of the time. Jewish communities, of various sizes, were scattered throughout the region of the Mediterranean and beyond. Jews in this category were often referred to as the "Diaspora" (from a Greek word meaning "dispersion" or "scattering"). This raises the question of how Jesus relates to the various groups which existed within Palestinian Judaism of the period. The five most important of such groups are the (1) Samaritans, (2) Pharisees, (3) Sadducees, (4) Zealots and (5) Essenes. In what follows, we shall explore what is known of these groups, and the manner in which Jesus related to them.

The *Samaritans* were a people living in close proximity to Judea, sharing some of the key beliefs of Judaism, yet regarded with intense suspicion and hostility by the Jews. The traditional Jewish account of the origins of the Samaritans lies in the events surrounding the Assyrian overthrow of the northern kingdom of Israel, and the forcible settlement of peoples from elsewhere within the Assyrian empire in the region (described in 2 Kings 17). These peoples mingled their own religious beliefs and practices with those of the Jews who remained in the region, leading to a form of syncretism. However, this view is regarded with some misgivings by historians. Furthermore, there seems to be no Old Testament text which specifically and explicitly refers to "the Samaritans." The Jewish historian Josephus dates the emergence of the Samaritans as a distinctive grouping to the Hellenistic period, rather than the period of the exile. The New Testament represents the Samaritans as a generally conservative religious grouping within Judaism, which recognized Shechem and Mount Gerizim (rather than Jerusalem and Mount Zion) as their place of worship.

Whatever their origins may have been, the Samaritans were regarded as outsiders by Jews. It is this factor which gives the Parable of the Good Samaritan (Luke 10:25–37) and the account of the meeting between Jesus and the Samaritan woman (John 4:4–42) their particular significance within the New Testament.

The origins of the *Pharisees* and *Sadducees* are generally traced back to the Maccabean revolt. This revolt had its origins in 168 BC, in response to the threat posed to Judaism by the political imposition of Greek forms of religion in the region. During the period 333–332 BC, Palestine was conquered by Alexander the Great. This development opened the period in Jewish history often referred to as "the Hellenistic period," in which the Greek language and Greek forms of religion came to play an increasingly prominent role in the region of Palestine. Initially, Judea was controlled by the Ptolemies; later, by the Seleucids. One particularly explosive development took place in 167 BC, and led directly to the Jewish revolt. Antiochus Epiphanes IV, a Seleucid ruler, dismantled the walls of Jerusalem, and massacred those Jews who resisted him. He then forcibly rededicated the

Jewish temple (which, as we have seen, was the political and cultic center of the Jewish religion) to the Greek god Zeus. This act of profanation, linked with various local incidents, sparked off the Maccabean revolt (the word "Maccabee" is a nickname, meaning "hammerer"). By 164 BC, the revolt had achieved its objectives. Jewish worship was formally re-established, and the temple rededicated to the God of Israel (an event which continues to be celebrated at the Jewish festival of Hanukkah). This vigorous reassertion of Jewish national and religious identity caused tensions within Judaism, particularly over the role of the Jewish law or Torah. It is against this background that the emergence of the Pharisees and Sadducees as distinct religious groupings is to be seen.

The Sadducees argued for the priority of the written law, as found in the five books of the law (also known as the Pentateuch: see p. 21). Nothing other than the teachings found in these writings was to be regarded as authoritative. While the Sadducees had their own traditions, these were regarded as subordinate to the law. The Sadducees were particularly hostile to any forms of innovation, such as the adaptation of the law to the new situations which emerged in the late Hellenistic period. Equally, they affirmed that the prophets and other writings of the Old Testament (see pp. 25–38) were not to be regarded as having the same status as the law. For the Sadducees, only the five books of the law were of binding authority. This point underlies the response of Jesus to the Sadducees' question concerning whether there is a resurrection (see Matthew 22:23–33). In responding affirmatively to this question, Jesus cites Exodus 3:6, where a modern reader might have expected a more explicit citation from the book of Isaiah (where the theme of "resurrection" seems to be clearly stated at several points). Yet the Sadducees would not have regarded a citation from Isaiah as having any weight whatsoever. Jesus therefore cites from the Pentateuch, appealing to an authority which he knew would be taken seriously by his questioners.

In contrast to the Sadducees (who, as we have seen, admitted no doctrinal or religious innovations), the Pharisees regarded the law as evolving, rather than static. The issue at stake was therefore to adapt the law to the new situations faced by Judaism. In addition, they permitted doctrinal developments, in that they accepted doctrines which were not explicitly stated in the law, yet seemed consistent with its general thrust – such as the idea of the resurrection of the dead (denied by the Sadducees: see Acts 23:8). The program adopted by the Pharisees could be summed up in the slogan "Torah and tradition," meaning "fidelity to the law as interpreted by the scribes." (The "scribes" were the official teachers of the Torah, many of whom were sympathetic to the Pharisees.) For the Pharisees, the interpretation and application of the law by the scribes was to be given as much weight as the law itself. The written law (the Torah) was thus to be supplemented by the oral law ("the tradition of the elders"), which represented an interpretation and application of the Torah. Both written and oral law were to be regarded as having equal authority. In contrast, the Sadducees refused to acknowledge any concept of a binding tradition or authoritative oral law.

The Pharisees were of considerable importance in early first century Palestinian Judaism, which explains why they are referred to so often in the gospels. The Jewish historian Josephus suggests that there were six thousand Pharisees at the time. It must be stressed that the gospels do not portray the Pharisees as hypocrites, as so many mistakenly assume; indeed, it is clear that the program outlined by Jesus has many points of similarity with that of the Pharisees, most notably their agreement on the summary of the entire law in terms of loving God and their neighbor. Yet there are points of difference between Jesus and the Pharisees. For example, Jesus argued that, at points, the oral law was simply mistaken (a point particularly clear in his teaching on ritual cleanliness: Mark 7:1–23). Of particular importance, however, is the idea of "separation," which needs detailed comment.

The word "Pharisee" is often thought to derive from the Hebrew word *parush* ("separated"). Unlike the Essenes, who chose to separate themselves physically from their contaminated fellow Jews by retreating into the wilderness, the Pharisees remained within Jewish life, while distancing themselves from those of its aspects they regarded as unacceptable. There is no doubt that the Pharisees' emphasis on ritual purity led them to "separate" from other Jews with laxer religious and moral standards. Jesus, however, chose to associate with sinners, particularly those whom the Pharisees regarded as unclean or impure, such as prostitutes (e.g., see Matthew 9:9–13). Jesus clearly regarded his mission as reaching out to the lost, whereas the Pharisees seemed content to shun them, while criticizing them from a safe distance.

Two other groups of importance may be noted. During the period of Jesus' ministry, Palestine was occupied and administered by Rome. The *Zealots* were probably a group of more politically radical Jews, concerned to overthrow the Roman occupation of their native land. Although the term is used primarily to refer to the revolutionaries of 66 AD, in which the Jews revolted against the Roman occupying forces, there are reasons for suspecting that the term was used earlier than this, perhaps dating back to the census of 6 AD. There was fierce nationalist feeling at the time, fuelled by intense resentment at the presence of a foreign occupying power. This is of importance in relation to the overtones of one of the New Testament titles for Jesus – that of "Messiah" or "Christ" (see pp. 108–9). The Roman occupation of Palestine appears to have given a new force to the traditional expectation of the coming of the Messiah. For many, the Messiah would be the deliverer who expelled the Romans from Israel, and restore the line of David. The gospels indicate that Jesus refused to see himself as Messiah in this sense. At no point in his ministry do we find any violence against Rome suggested or condoned, nor even an explicit attack on the Roman administration. Jesus' attacks are directed primarily against his own people. Thus after his triumphal entry into Jerusalem (Matthew 21:8–11), which gives every indication of being a deliberate Messianic demonstration or gesture, Jesus immediately evicts the merchants from the temple (Matthew 21:12–13).

Interestingly, Jesus was not prepared to accept the title "Messiah" in the course of his ministry. Mark's gospel should be read carefully to note this point. When Peter acclaims Jesus as Messiah – "You are the Christ!" – Jesus immediately tells him to keep quiet about it (Mark 8:29–30). It is not clear what the full significance of the "Messianic secret" is. Why should Mark emphasize that Jesus did not make any *explicit* claim to be the Messiah, when he was so clearly regarded as such by so many? Perhaps the answer may be found later in Mark's gospel, when he recounts the only point at which Jesus explicitly acknowledges his identity as the Messiah. When Jesus is led, as a prisoner, before the High Priest, he admits to being the Messiah (Mark 14:61–62). Once violent or political action of any sort is no longer possible, Jesus reveals his identity. He was indeed the deliverer of the people of God – but not, it would seem, in any political sense of the term. The misunderstandings associated with the term, particularly in Zealot circles, appear to have caused Jesus to play down the Messianic side of his mission.

The final group to be considered is the *Essenes.* This group, like the Pharisees, placed considerable emphasis on religious purity. Unlike the Pharisees, however, the Essenes chose to withdraw from everyday Jewish life, forming dedicated communities in the wilderness. The Dead Sea Scrolls (discovered over the period 1947–60) give important insights into the beliefs and practices of the Essenes, although the precise interpretation of these documents is difficult, due to uncertainties over their origins. The scrolls can all be dated to the last two centuries of the Second Temple; it is entirely possible that some date from the lifetime of Jesus. The scrolls are of particular interest in relation to understanding Jewish messianic expectations around the time of Jesus. It has also been suggested that John the Baptist may have been an Essene, or had links with Essene communities. However, there are no grounds for the suggestion, occasionally encountered in sensationalizing media reports, that the Dead Sea Scrolls discredit the gospel narratives, or force a total revision of our understanding of the origins of Christianity.

Having explored this important issue, we may now turn to explore the life of Jesus, as we find it in the gospels.

The Birth of Jesus

Matthew and Luke provide complementary accounts of the birth of Jesus, on which traditional Christmas cards and carols are based. Matthew's ac-

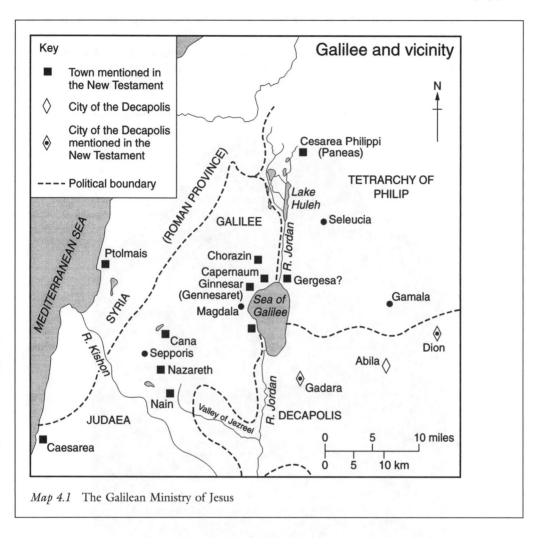

Galilee and vicinity

Key

■ Town mentioned in the New Testament

◇ City of the Decapolis

◈ City of the Decapolis mentioned in the New Testament

---- Political boundary

N

MEDITERRANEAN SEA

(ROMAN PROVINCE)

Cesarea Philippi (Paneas) ■

Lake Huleh

TETRARCHY OF PHILIP

GALILEE

● Seleucia

Ptolmais ■

Chorazin ■

Capernaum ■
Ginnesar ■
(Gennesaret)

R. Jordan

■ Gergesa?

● Gamala

Sea of Galilee

Magdala ●

SYRIA

■ Cana

● Sepporis

◈ Dion

R. Kishon

■ Nazareth

Abila ◇

◇ Gadara

Nain ■

Valley of Jezreel

R. Jordan

JUDAEA

DECAPOLIS

■ Caesarea

| 0 | | 5 | | 10 miles |

| 0 | 5 | | 10 km |

Map 4.1   The Galilean Ministry of Jesus

count is related from the standpoint of Joseph, and Luke's from that of Mary. Neither the day nor the year of Jesus' birth is known for certain. Non-Christians often assume that Christians believe that Jesus was born on 25 December. In fact, Christians have chosen to celebrate the birth of Jesus on Christmas Day; 25 December is the date fixed for the celebration of the birth of Jesus, not the date of his birth itself. Early Christian writers suggested a variety of dates for the celebration of Jesus' birth – for example, Clement of Alexandria (*c*.150–*c*.215) advocated 20 May. By the fourth century, the date of 25 December had been chosen, possibly to take advantage of a traditional Roman holiday associated with this date. For Christians, the precise date of the birth of Jesus is actually something of a non-issue.

What really matters is that he was born as a human being, and entered into human history.

The traditional Christmas story has become somewhat stylized over the years. For example, most traditional versions of the story tell of the "three wise men" and of Jesus "being born in a stable." In fact, the New Testament

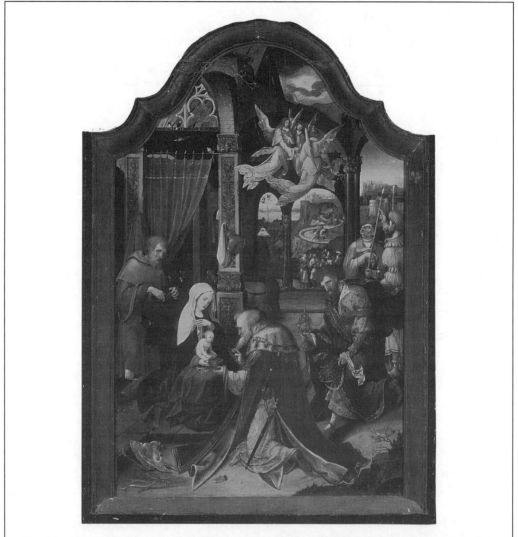

The Adoration of the Magi, by the Flemish painter Jan de Beer. This painting, which dates from the period 1510—25, incorporates many traditional motifs based on the account in Matthew's gospel. The term "Magi" (from the Greek term for "sages") is often used to refer to the "wise men." Sotheby's London.

relates that the wise men brought three gifts to Jesus; many have simply assumed that, as there were three gifts, there must have been three wise men. Similarly, we are told that Jesus was born in a manger; many have assumed that, since mangers are kept in stables, Jesus must have been born in a stable.

A point of particular importance concerns the identity of the birthplace of Jesus. Bethlehem was a minor town in the region of Judea, not far from Jerusalem. Its significance lies in its associations with King David, given particular emphasis in one of the writings of a prophet of Israel. Micah, writing in the eighth century before Christ, made reference to the future emergence of a ruler of Israel from Bethlehem (Micah 5:2). This expectation is noted in Matthew's gospel (Matthew 2:5–6), where it is seen as one of many indications that the birth and ministry of Jesus are in direct fulfillment of Israelite prophecies and hopes.

Luke stresses the humility and lowliness of the circumstances of the birth of Jesus. For example, he notes that Jesus was placed in a manger (normally used for feeding animals), and that the first people to visit him were shepherds. Although the force of the point is easily lost, it needs to be remembered that shepherds were widely regarded as socially and religiously inferior people by Jewish society, on account of their nomadic lifestyle.

Both Matthew and Luke stress the importance of Mary, the mother of Jesus. In later Christian thought, Mary would become a focus for personal devotion, on account of her obedience and humility. She often had a particular appeal to women, who felt marginalized by the strongly masculine ethos of Christianity during, for example, the Middle Ages. The hymn *Stabat Mater* (the Latin title of which means "The mother stood [by the cross]"), which was written during the thirteenth century, describes the deep feeling of sorrow experienced by Mary at the death of her son on the cross. This hymn, which was subsequently set to music by several major composers, had a deep impact on the spirituality of the Middle Ages and beyond. At the time of the Reformation, devotion to Mary was often criticized. It was suggested that this devotion could threaten the central place of Jesus Christ in Christian prayer and worship. Nevertheless, most Christians regard Mary as an excellent example of several central Christian virtues, especially obedience to and trust in God.

The place of Joseph in the gospel accounts of Jesus should also be noted. At no point is Joseph described as the "father of Jesus," despite the numerous references here and elsewhere to Mary as the "mother of Jesus." Matthew shows how Joseph was legally related to David (Matthew 1:1–17), with the result that Jesus possessed the legal status of being descended from David. Yet Joseph is not understood to be the physical father of Jesus. For Matthew and Luke, the conception of Jesus is divine in its origins.

The Virgin and Child, as depicted by an unknown painter of the Bohemian school of the sixteenth century. Sotheby's London.

The Beginning of the Public Ministry of Jesus

The gospels all locate the beginning of the public ministry of Jesus in the countryside of Judea, by the River Jordan. It is specifically linked with the activity of John the Baptist, who attracted widespread attention with his calls to repentance. It is clear that John's ministry takes place at a moment of some significance in the history of Israel. Perhaps there were those who felt that God had abandoned Israel; perhaps there were those who felt that the great acts of divine deliverance and encouragement in the past would never be repeated. Israel was under Roman occupation, and seemed to have lost her identity as the people of God. We shall probably never fully understand the complex web of expectations, fears, and hopes which focused on the appearance of John the Baptist.

The New Testament picks up two themes which may help us understand why John the Baptist attracted such enormous interest at the time. The final work of Jewish prophecy – the book of Malachi, probably dating from the fifth century before Christ – spoke of God sending a messenger, to prepare the way for the coming of God (Malachi 3:1–2). It also hinted at the return of Elijah, one of the great figures of faith in Israel, before this event. When John the Baptist appeared, he wore the same simple clothes of camel's hair as Elijah had before him. Malachi spoke of the need for corporate repentance. The whole people of God needed to repent of their sins, before national restoration to divine favor was possible. John the Baptist spoke of this same need for repentance, and offered baptism as a symbol of an individual's willingness to repent. (The word "baptism" comes from the Greek word meaning "to wash" or "to bathe.")

The implications of these developments would have been clear to anyone steeped in a knowledge of the Jewish prophets, and alert to the signs of the times. The coming of John the Baptist pointed to the coming of God. John himself made this point, declaring that someone who was greater than him would follow him – someone whose sandals he was not worthy to untie (Mark 1:8). And at that moment, Jesus appeared. It is impossible to read Mark's vivid and racy account of this encounter without realizing that Mark clearly wants us to understand that it is Jesus to whom John was referring. John is the forerunner of Jesus, pointing the way to his coming.

After Jesus was baptized by John, he slipped away into a solitary place for forty days and nights. This period of Jesus' ministry – usually referred to as "the temptation of Christ" – involved his being confronted with all the temptations which he would encounter during his ministry. Although Mark only hints at this (Mark 1:12), Matthew and Luke provide fuller details (e.g., Luke 4:1–13), allowing us to see how Jesus was confronted with the temptation to personal power and glory. The New Testament writers subsequently stress the importance of Jesus' obedience to the will of God. The period of Lent, immediately before Easter, marks the time of year when Christians are encouraged to examine themselves in this way, following the example of Christ.

A theme which now develops is that of the rejection of Jesus by his own people. This theme culminates in the crucifixion, in which Jesus is publicly repudiated by a crowd in Jerusalem, and taken off to be crucified by the Roman authorities. The theme also appears at earlier points in the ministry of Jesus, and is particularly linked with the severely hostile criticism of Jesus by the Pharisees and the teachers of the Jewish law. For the New Testament writers, the paradox is that those who were most deeply committed to and familiar with the Jewish law failed to recognize its fulfillment when this took place.

14

STUDY PANEL

Criticism of Jesus by the Pharisees

Mark 2:23–3:6

One Sabbath Jesus was going through the grainfields, and as his disciples walked along, they began to pick some heads of grain. The Pharisees said to him, "Look, why are they doing what is unlawful on the Sabbath?" He answered, "Have you never read what David did when he and his companions were hungry and in need? In the days of Abiathar the high priest, he entered the house of God and ate the consecrated bread, which is lawful only for priests to eat. And he also gave some to his companions." Then he said to them, "The Sabbath was made for man, not man for the Sabbath. So the Son of Man is Lord even of the Sabbath." Another time he went into the synagogue, and a man with a shrivelled hand was there. Some of them were looking for a reason to accuse Jesus, so they watched him closely to see if he would heal him on the Sabbath. Jesus said to the man with the shrivelled hand, "Stand up in front of everyone." Then Jesus asked them, "Which is lawful on the Sabbath: to do good or to do evil, to save life or to kill?" But they remained silent. He looked around at them in anger and, deeply distressed at their stubborn hearts, said to the man, "Stretch out your hand." He stretched it out, and his hand was completely restored. Then the Pharisees went out and began to plot with the Herodians how they might kill Jesus.

Nevertheless, the theme of "rejection" can be seen much earlier than this. One incident in particular illustrates this point: the rejection of Jesus in his home town of Nazareth. Luke's gospel relates how Jesus attended synagogue regularly on the sabbath. On one occasion, he was asked to read a section from the prophecy of Isaiah, which included the following words (Luke 4:18–19):

> The Spirit of the Lord is on me, because he has anointed me to preach good news to the poor. He was sent me to proclaim freedom for the prisoners and recovery of sight for the blind, to release the oppressed, to proclaim the year of the Lord's favor.

Jesus declared that these words were fulfilled in himself, and that his ministry would prove more acceptable to Gentiles than to Israel. The synagogue congregation was outraged, and threw him out of their town, even trying to push him over the edge of a nearby hill. After this, Jesus ministered in the region of Capernaum, on the north-west shore of Lake Galilee.

Jesus then gathered around himself a small group of disciples, who would accompany him as he travelled, and subsequently form the core of the early church. The group of twelve apostles (often referred to simply as "the twelve") were drawn from a variety of backgrounds, mostly from jobs in the rural economy of the region. Two pairs of brothers – Peter and Andrew, and James and John – were called to leave their fishing business behind them, and follow Jesus. At a later stage, possibly a year or so into his ministry, Jesus divided the twelve into two groups of six, sending them out into the countryside to preach the kingdom of God.

Jesus then began his ministry of teaching and healing, initially in the region around Galilee, and subsequently in Judea. On the basis of the accounts provided in the gospels, it may be estimated that this period lasted roughly three years. Important though both the teaching and healing are in their own rights, their true importance lies partly in what they demonstrate about Jesus. This becomes clear from a question posed later by John the Baptist. By this stage, John had been imprisoned by Herod Antipas, ruler (or, more precisely, "tetrarch") of the region of Galilee. Still uncertain as to the true identity of Jesus, John asked him this question: "Are you the one who was to come, or should we expect somone else?" The implications of the question are enormous. Is Jesus the messiah? Has the messianic age arrived?

Jesus (who never directly claimed to be the messiah during his ministry) answers indirectly, by pointing to what has happened in his ministry: "The blind receive sight, the lame walk, those who have leprosy are cured, the deaf hear, the dead are raised, and the good news is preached to the poor" (Matthew 11:6). In other words, the expected signs of the messianic age were evident in his ministry. Jesus does not directly answer the question of whether he is the messiah. The inference, however, is clear. The healing miracles are to be seen as signs, pointing to a right understanding of the identity and significance of Jesus.

John's gospel is also of importance in allowing us to understand the significance of the healings and other works accompanying Jesus' ministry. For example, John notes the constant demand from Jesus' critics to "show a sign" in order to prove his authority to speak on behalf of God (e.g., John 2:18). He also points out the distinct role of these "signs," noting that they both revealed Jesus' glory and allowed his disciples to put their faith in him (John 2:11). The synoptic gospels also allow us to follow the growth of faith in the disciples themselves, as they hear him teach and see the signs which he performed. We shall return to this point presently. Our attention now turns to Jesus' attitude to one social grouping which was marginalized at the time: women.

Jesus and Women.

It is clear from the gospel accounts of the ministry of Jesus that women were an integral part of the group of people who gathered round him. They were affirmed by him, often to the dismay of the Pharisees and other religious traditionalists. Not only were women witnesses to the crucifixion; they were also the first witnesses to the resurrection. The only Easter event to be explicitly related in detail by all four of the gospel writers is the visit of the women to the tomb of Jesus. Yet Judaism dismissed the value of the testimony or witness of women, regarding only men as having significant legal status in this respect. Interestingly, Mark tells us the names of these women witnesses – Mary Magdalene, Mary the mother of James, and Salome – *three times* (Mark 15:40, 47; 16:1), but never mentions the names of any male disciples who were present on this occasion.

It is also of importance to note that the gospels frequently portray women as being much more spiritually perceptive than men. For example, Mark portrays the male disciples as having little faith (Mark 4:40, 6:52), while commending women – a woman is praised for her faith (Mark 5:25–34), a foreign women for responding to Jesus (Mark 7:24–30), and a widow being singled out as an example to follow (Mark 12:41–4). Further, Jesus treated women as human subjects, rather than simply as objects or possessions. Throughout his ministry, Jesus can be seen engaging with and affirming women – often women who were treated as outcasts by contemporary Jewish society on account of their origins (e.g., Syro-Phoenicia or Samaria) or their lifestyle (e.g., prostitutes).

Jesus refused to make women scapegoats in sexual matters – for example, adultery. The patriarchal assumption that men are corrupted by fallen women is conspicuously absent from his teaching and attitudes, most notably toward prostitutes and the woman taken in adultery. The Talmud – an important source of Jewish law and teaching – declared that its readers (who are assumed to be men) should "not converse much with women, as this will eventually lead you to unchastity." This was studiously ignored by Jesus, who made a point of talking to women (the conversation with the Samaritan woman, related in John 4, being an especially celebrated instance). In much the same way, the traditional view that a woman was "unclean" during her period of menstruation was dismissed by Jesus, who made it clear that it is only moral impurity which defiles a person (Mark 7:1–23).

Luke's gospel is of particular interest in relation to understanding Jesus' attitude to women. Luke brings out clearly how women are among the "oppressed" who are liberated by the coming of Jesus. Luke also sets out his material in a parallel manner, to emphasize that both men and women are involved in and benefit from the ministry of Jesus. For example, the following passages demonstrate this parallelism especially clearly:

Luke 1:11–20, 26–38	Zacharias and Mary
Luke 2:25–38	Simeon and Anna
Luke 7:1–17	A centurion and a widow
Luke 13:18–21	A man with mustard seed and a woman with yeast
Luke 15:4–10	A man with sheep and a woman with coins

By this arrangement of material, Luke expresses the fact that men and women stand together side by side before God. They are equal in honor and grace; they are endowed with the same gifts and have the same responsibilities.

Luke also draws our attention to the significant role of women in the spreading of the gospel. For example, Luke 8:2–3 indicates that "many women" were involved in early evangelistic endeavors, referring to the Twelve being accompanied by "some women who had been cured of evil spirits and diseases: Mary (called Magdalene) from whom seven demons had come out; Joanna the wife of Cuza, the manager of Herod's household; Susanna; and many others." The inclusion of women in such a significant role would have seemed incomprehensible to the male-dominated society of contemporary Palestine.

It is probably difficult for western readers, who are used to thinking of women as having equal rights and status as men, to appreciate how novel and radical these attitudes were at the time. Possibly the most radical aspect of Jesus' approach to women is that he associated freely with them and treated them as responsible human beings, indulging in theological conversation with them, encouraging and expecting a response. It is hardly surprising that early Christianity proved to have a deep appeal for women. It is entirely possible that Jesus' teachings attracted women partly on account of the new roles and status they were granted in the Christian community. There were many cults in Greece and Rome that were for men only or which allowed women to participate only in very limited ways. We shall explore later developments in Christian attitudes toward women presently (pp. 238–42).

The Teaching of Jesus: the Kingdom of God

The theme of the "kingdom of God" (or, in the case of Matthew's gospel, "the kingdom of heaven") is widely agreed to be central to the preaching of Jesus. The public ministry of Jesus begins with his declaration that the kingdom of God has "drawn near," and that "the time is fulfilled" (Mark 1:15). The Greek word *basileia*, traditionally translated as "kingdom," does not so much express the idea of a definite political region over which a king rules, but rather the idea of "rule" itself. In other words, the Greek word refers to the idea of "kingship" rather than a "kingdom." The "Sermon on the Mount" (the block of teaching contained in Matthew 5:1–7:29) is widely regarded as setting a remarkably high standard for conduct before other people and God, and is often referred to as setting out the "ethics of the kingdom of God." In other words, the acknowledgment of the rule of God leads to a certain pattern of behavior, which is embodied in the life and ministry of Jesus, and echoed in his teaching. We shall explore this point further when we deal with Jesus as an example for Christians (see pp. 121–3). The basic theme of Jesus' preaching can thus be thought of in terms of the coming of the kingly rule of God. This theme is expressed in the prayer which Jesus instructed his followers to imitate, and which is widely known as "the Lord's Prayer."

STUDY PANEL 15

The Lord's Prayer

The "Lord's Prayer" is widely used in public and private Christian prayer, and is treated by most Christians as a model of the concise form of prayer which Jesus himself favored.

Matthew 6:9–13

> Our Father in heaven
> hallowed be your name
> your kingdom come
> your will be done on earth as it is in heaven.
> Give us today our daily bread.
> Forgive us our debts, as we also have forgiven our debtors.
> And lead us not into temptation, but deliver us from the evil one.

A slightly different version of this prayer may be found at Luke 11:2–4.

Jesus' preaching about the kingdom is best understood in terms of "inauguration." Something has happened which sets in motion a series of events which has yet to reach its fulfillment. A series of parables expresses the idea that the kingdom is something which progresses from a seemingly insignificant starting point to something which is much greater. The Parable of the Mustard Seed (Matthew 13:31–32) is a particularly good example in this respect, as it illustrates the idea of growth and development. The Parable of the Vineyard (Matthew 21:33–41) makes the point that those who are entitled to be tenants of the vineyard are those who produce its fruit, a clear indication of the need for those who claim to be within the kingdom to conform to its ethics. The kingly rule of God carries obligations.

Some Parables of the Kingdom

Mark 4:26–32

"This is what the kingdom of God is like. A man scatters seed on the ground. Night and day, whether he sleeps or gets up, the seed sprouts and grows, though he does not know how. All by itself the soil produces grain – first the stalk, then the head, then the full kernel in the head. As soon as the grain is ripe, he puts the sickle to it, because the harvest has come." Again he said, "What shall we say the kingdom of God is like, or what parable shall we use to describe it? It is like a mustard seed, which is the smallest seed you plant in the ground. Yet when planted, it grows and becomes the largest of all garden plants, with such big branches that the birds of the air can perch in its shade."

So important are the parables in relation to Jesus' teaching about the kingdom that we must consider them in more detail. Parables are often defined as "earthly stories with heavenly meanings." This is a useful way of beginning to understand the importance of parables within the ministry of Jesus. The word "parable" reflects a number of ideas, including that of "illustration" and that of "mystery" or "riddle." A parable illustrates a spiritual truth – but the meaning may not be clear, and may therefore require illustration. Some of the parables are based on shrewd observation of everyday life in rural Palestine. Just as a pearl of great value is worth selling lesser possessions in order to own it, so the kingdom of God is worth giving up everything for (Matthew 13:45–46). Just as a small amount of yeast can raise a large amount of dough, so the kingdom of God can exercise its influence throughout the world (Matthew 13:33). Just as a shepherd will go out and look for a sheep that has got lost, so God will seek out those who have wandered away (Luke 15:4–6).

Sometimes, the parables are more complex. The Parable of the Prodigal Son (Luke 15:11–32) is an example of this kind of parable. It tells of a son who decides to leave his father's home, and seek his fortune in a distant land. Yet life away from his father turns out not to be as rosy as the prodigal son had expected. He falls on hard times. The prodigal son comes to long to return home to his father. However, he is convinced that his father will have disowned him and will no longer wish to acknowledge him as his son. The remarkable feature of the parable is the picture of God which it gives us. The father sees the returning son long before the son notices him, and rushes out to meet him and celebrate the return of the son he had given up for lost.

The parable is clearly intended to be interpreted along the following lines.

The father represents God; the son represents those who have sinned, or turned their backs on God. The message of the parable is therefore simple: just as the father was overjoyed at the return of his son, so God will be overjoyed at the return of sinners.

The teaching of Jesus concerning the kingdom of God is an important element in the Christian faith. However, Christianity is not only about what Jesus taught. It is also about the person of Jesus himself. Who is he? And what is his importance? For the New Testament, the death and resurrection of Jesus are of central importance. We shall turn to consider these in what follows.

The Crucifixion

The theme of the crucifixion of Jesus Christ is deeply embedded in the New Testament. The Latin word "crucifixion" literally means "being placed on a cross." One of the earliest literary witnesses to the central importance of the crucifixion is Paul's first letter to the Christian church at Corinth, which probably dates from the early months of 55. In the first chapter of this letter, Paul lays considerable emphasis upon the fact that Christ was crucified. The subject of his preaching was "Christ crucified" (1:23); the power lying behind the gospel proclamation is "the cross of Christ" (1:17); the entire gospel can even be summarized as "the message of the cross" (1:18). The idea of a crucified savior was immediately seized upon by the opponents of the early church as an absurdity, demonstrating the ridiculous nature of Christian claims. Justin Martyr, attempting to defend Christianity against its more sophisticated critics in the second century, conceded that the Christian proclamation of a crucified Christ appeared to be madness: "[The opponents of Christianity] say that our madness lies in the fact that we put a crucified man in second place to the unchangeable and eternal God, the creator of the world."

The background to this within Judaism is of importance. For a Jew, anyone hanged upon a tree was to be regarded as cursed by God (Deuteronomy 21:23), which would hardly commend the Christian claim that Jesus was indeed the long-awaited Messiah. Indeed, one of the Dead Sea scrolls suggests that crucifixion was regarded as the proper form of execution for a Jew suspected of high treason. Yet the first Christians regarded the preaching of the gospel of Jews as one of their top priorities. Why would they included an idea which would have been so deeply offensive to a Jewish audience? The answer is quite simple: they had to. It was an historical fact, known to all, which had to be acknowledged and preached, even if it could lead to the alienation of many potential Jewish converts.

It is clear from contemporary evidence that crucifixion was a widespread form of execution within the Roman Empire, and that there was an aston-

The city of Jerusalem, seen from the west, showing the Mount of Olives and the garden of Gethsemane. The road leading upwards on the left side of the picture marks the traditional road along which Jesus made his triumphal entry into Jerusalem. Popperfoto.

ishing variety of manners in which this execution might be carried out. The victim was generally flogged or tortured beforehand, and then might be tied or nailed to the cross in practically any position. This form of punishment appears to have been employed ruthlessly to suppress rebellions in the Roman provinces, such as the revolt of the Cantabrians in northern Spain, as well as those of the Jews. Josephus' accounts of the crucifixion of the many Jewish fugitives who attempted to escape from besieged Jerusalem at the time of its final destruction by the Roman armies in 70 make horrifying reading. In the view of most Roman jurists, notorious criminals should be crucified on the exact location of their crime, so that "the sight may deter others from such crimes." Perhaps for this reason, the Roman emperor Quintillian crucified criminals on the busiest thoroughfares, in order that the maximum deterrent effect might be achieved.

It is therefore little wonder that the sophisticated pagan world of the first century reacted with disbelief and disgust to the Christians' suggestion that they should take seriously "an evil man and his cross" (*homo noxius et crux eius*) to the point of worshipping him. Crucifixion was a punishment reserved for the lowest criminals, clearly implying that Jesus belonged to this category of people. Yet the gospels, in common with the remainder of the New Testament, insist that this was the fate which Jesus endured.

The background to the crucifixion is the triumphal entry of Jesus into Jerusalem mounted on a donkey, in fulfillment of a great messianic prophecy of the Old Testament (Zechariah 9:9). Jesus enters Jerusalem as its king, an event especially celebrated by Christians on Palm Sunday. Yet this final week in the life of Jesus is marked by increasing controversy, culminating in his betrayal, arrest, and execution. Luke relates that Jesus and his disciples gather together "in an upper room" to celebrate the passover (Luke 22:14–23). With great solemnity, Jesus tells the gathered disciples that he will never celebrate passover again "until it finds fulfillment in the Kingdom of God." The passover is seen as something which points beyond itself, to something greater which is yet to find its fulfillment. The implications of these words is that the true meaning of the passover is about to find its fulfillment in and through him. In view of the importance of this idea, we may consider it in more detail.

The Jewish feast of Passover celebrates the events leading up to the exodus and the establishment of the people of Israel. The passover lamb, slaughtered shortly before, and eaten at the feast, symbolizes this great act of divine redemption. It is thus very significant that the last supper and the crucifixion of Jesus took place at the feast of Passover. The Synoptic Gospels clearly treat the last supper as a Passover meal, with Jesus initiating a new version of the meal. While Jews celebrated their deliverance by God from Egypt by eating a lamb, Christians would henceforth celebrate their deliverance by God from sin by eating bread and drinking wine. Passover celebrates the great act of God by which the people of Israel came into being; the Lord's Supper celebrates the great saving act of God by which the Christian church came into being, and to which she owes her life and her existence.

John's gospel suggests that Jesus is crucified at exactly the same moment as the slaughter of the passover lambs, indicating even more forcefully that Jesus is the true passover lamb, who died for the sins of the world. The real passover lamb is not being slaughtered in the temple precincts, but on the cross. In the light of this, the full meaning of the words of John the Baptist can be appreciated: "Behold the Lamb of God, who takes away the sin of the world" (John 1:29). The death of Christ takes away our sins, and cleanses us from its guilt and stain.

The coincidence of the last supper and the crucifixion with the Passover feast makes it clear that there is a vitally close connection between the exodus and the death of Christ. Both are to be seen as acts of divine deliverance from oppression. However, while Moses led Israel from a specific captivity in Egypt, Christ is seen as delivering his people from a universal bondage to sin and death. While there are parallels between the exodus and the cross; there are also differences. Perhaps the most important difference relates to the New Testament affirmation of the universality of the redemption accomplished by Christ. For the New Testament, the work of Christ benefits all who put their trust in him, irrespective of their ethnic identity, or historical or geographical location.

The Last Supper

Luke 22:7–23

Then came the day of Unleavened Bread on which the Passover lamb had to be sacrificed. Jesus sent Peter and John, saying, "Go and make preparations for us to eat the Passover." "Where do you want us to prepare for it?" they asked. He replied, "As you enter the city, a man carrying a jar of water will meet you. Follow him to the house that he enters, and say to the owner of the house, 'The Teacher asks: Where is the guest room, where I may eat the Passover with my disciples?' He will show you a large upper room, all furnished. Make preparations there."

They left and found things just as Jesus had told them. So they prepared the Passover. When the hour came, Jesus and his apostles reclined at the table. And he said to them, "I have eagerly desired to eat this Passover with you before I suffer. For I tell you, I will not eat it again until it finds fulfillment in the kingdom of God." After taking the cup, he gave thanks and said, "Take this and divide it among you. For I tell you I will not drink again of the fruit of the vine until the kingdom of God comes." And he took bread, gave thanks and broke it, and gave it to them, saying, "This is my body given for you; do this in remembrance of me." In the same way, after the supper he took the cup, saying, "This cup is the new covenant in my blood, which is poured out for you. But the hand of him who is going to betray me is with mine on the table. The Son of Man will go as it has been decreed, but woe to that man who betrays him." They began to question among themselves which of them it might be who would do this.

STUDY PANEL 17

The "last supper" is of particular importance to Christians, in that it is remembered in Christian worship. Note the explicit command to the disciples to repeat this action in remembrance of Jesus. The use of bread and wine as a remembrance of Jesus – which focuses on the sacrament or ordinance usually referred to as "Holy Communion," "the Lord's Supper," "the eucharist" or "the mass" – has its origins here (see pp. 363–74).

This is followed by an account of the betrayal of Jesus to the Jewish authorities. The betrayal of Jesus by Judas for thirty pieces of silver (Matthew 27:1–10) is seen as the fulfillment of Old Testament prophecy (the prophecy in question seems to bring together both Jeremiah 19:1–13 and Zechariah 11:12–13).

After a theological interrogation, Jesus is handed over to the Roman authorities. The sections of the gospels which relate the betrayal, trial and execution of Jesus are usually known as "the passion narratives," on account of their focusing on the sufferings (Latin: *passiones*) of Jesus. Why should Jesus have been handed over to the Roman authorities? Jesus was accused of blasphemy, specifically in relation to his admission that he was "the Christ, the Son of God." Under Jewish law, the penalty for blasphemy was death. However, with one exception, the Romans had deprived the Sanhedrin (that is, the 71-member supreme Jewish court, consisting of the chief priests, elders, and teachers of the law) of the right to sentence anyone to death. This was now a matter for the Roman authorities.

Jesus is therefore brought before Pontius Pilate, who was the Roman governor of Judea from 26–36. Pilate's inclination would probably have been to order some token punishment, but take things no further. However, the crowd demands that Jesus be crucified. Washing his hands of the whole affair, Pilate sends Jesus off to be flogged and crucified. Jesus is then humiliated by the Roman soldiers, who dress him up in a caricature of royal costume, including a crown of thorns.

The floggings administered by the Romans were vicious; they had been known to cause the death of victims before they were crucified. Under Jewish law, victims were only allowed to be flogged with 40 strokes; this was invariably reduced to 39, as an act of leniency. But under Roman law, there were no limits to the extent of the suffering to be inflicted. The whips used for this purpose generally consisted of several strands of leather with small pieces of metal or broken bones at the end; these tore apart the skin of those being whipped, with the result that many did not survive the ordeal.

Jesus was clearly severely weakened by his beating, and proves unable to carry his own cross. Simon of Cyrene was forced to carry it for him. Finally, they reached Golgotha, the place of execution (Matthew 27:32–43). This place is also often referred to as "Calvary," from the Latin word *Calvaria* meaning "the skull" – the literal meaning of "Golgotha." As Jesus hangs on the cross, he is mocked by those watching him die, while the Roman soldiers cast lots for his clothes. These events can be seen as a fulfillment of the Old Testament prophecy of the fate of the righteous sufferer of Psalm 22 (see

Psalm 22:7–8, 18). The identity of Jesus with this sufferer is confirmed by his cry of despair from the cross – "My God, my God, why have you forsaken me?" (Matthew 27:46) – which draws upon the opening verse of this Psalm (Psalm 22:1). It is here that Jesus experiences a sense of the absence of God. Finally, Jesus dies.

The period of three hours on Good Friday is often commemorated in Christian churches. A common pattern of worship is known as the "three hours of the cross," which typically takes the form of meditations on the passion narratives, prayers, and periods of silence. A particularly common form of meditation is known as "the seven words from the cross," which focus on the words uttered by Jesus during his crucifixion, and which form a framework for the exposition of some of the leading themes of the Christian gospel. Musically, the passion narratives are particularly associated with Johann Sebastian Bach, whose *St Matthew Passion* and *St John Passion* can be regarded as the passion narratives of Matthew and John set to music.

The Seven Words from the Cross

1 Father, forgive them, for they do not know what they are doing (Luke 23:34).
2 I tell you the truth, today you will be with me in paradise (Luke 23:43).
3 Dear woman, here is your son . . . Here is your mother (John 19:26–27).
4 My God, my God, why have you forsaken me? (Matthew 27:46)
5 I am thirsty (John 19:28).
6 It is finished (John 19:30).
7 Father, into your hands I commit my spirit (Luke 23:46).

STUDY PANEL 18

The disciples, we now discover, are nowhere to be found. Matthew carefully identifies some witnesses of the death of Jesus. Not a single disciple is mentioned; it seems that they, like sheep without a shepherd, have scattered – just as Jesus had predicted. The witnesses who are identified are the Roman centurion, who declared that Jesus was the "Son of God" (Matthew 27:54) – a critically important testimony, coming from a Gentile, given that the Jewish high priest, here representing his own people, had refused to accept that Jesus was the Son of God. Yet here we can see the acceptance of this fact among the Gentiles, anticipating both the mission to the Gentiles, and the enormous appeal which the gospel would prove to have to those outside Judaism. The other witnesses are women. Notice how

Matthew names them (Matthew 27:55–56), so that they will not be forgotten. Finally, Jesus is buried in a borrowed tomb (Matthew 27:57–61). That is not, however, the end of the story, according to the New Testament.

The Resurrection

The gospels now turn to narrate a series of events which are of vital importance to the Christian faith. The term "the resurrection" is used to refer to the series of events which took place. In general terms, "the resurrection" refers to a cluster of related happenings, focusing on what happened to Jesus after his death. We may summarize them as follows.

1   The tomb in which the corpse of Jesus was laid late on the Friday afternoon was discovered to be empty on the Sunday morning. Those who discovered the empty tomb were frightened by what they found; their reports were not taken seriously by many of those in Jesus' close circle of friends.

The Removal of Jesus' Body from the Cross, by an unknown sixteenth-century Flemish artist. The central figure of the picture is Mary, who is depicted with tears flowing from her left eye. Note the crown of thorns on Jesus' head, and the wound in his right-hand side. Sotheby's London.

2 The disciples reported personal appearances of Jesus, and experienced him as someone living.
3 The disciples began to preach Jesus as the living Lord, rather than as a past teacher.

The "empty tomb" tradition is of considerable importance here. It is a major element in each of the four gospels (Matthew 28:1–10; Mark 16:1–8; Luke 24:1–11; John 20:1–10) that it must be considered to have a basis in historical fact. The story is told from different aspects in each of the gospels, and includes the divergence on minor points of detail which is so characteristic of eye-witness reports. Interestingly, all four gospels attribute the discovery of the empty tomb to women. The only Easter event to be explicitly related in detail by all four of the gospel writers is the visit of the women to the tomb of Jesus. Yet Judaism dismissed the value of the testimony or witness of women, regarding only men as having significant legal status in this respect. Mark's gospel even names each of them three times: Mary Magdalene, Mary the mother of James, and Salome (Mark 15:40, 47; 16:1), but fails to mention the names of any male disciples who were around at the time.

It is perhaps too easy for modern western readers, accustomed to a firm belief in the equality of men and women, to overlook the significance of this point. At the time, in the intensely patriarchal Jewish culture of that period, the testimony of a woman was virtually worthless. In first-century Palestine, this would have been sufficient to discredit the accounts altogether. If the reports of the empty tomb were invented, as some have suggested, it is difficult to understand why their inventors should have embellished their accounts of the "discovery" with something virtually guaranteed to discredit them in the eyes of their audiences. Why not attribute this discovery to men, if the story was an invention?

A further point of interest here concerns the practice of "tomb veneration" – that is, returning to the tomb of a prophet as a place of worship. This is known to have been common in New Testament times, and is probably hinted at in Matthew 23:29–30. The tomb of David in Jerusalem is still venerated by many Jews to this day. But there is no record whatsoever of any such veneration of the tomb of Jesus by his disciples. This would have been unthinkable, unless there was a very good reason for it. That reason appears to be the simple fact that Jesus' body was quite simply absent from its tomb.

It is quite clear that the resurrection of Jesus came as a surprise to the disciples. It must be pointed out that there was no precedent in Jewish thinking for a resurrection of this kind. Most Jews at this time seem to have believed in the resurrection of the dead. Yet the general belief of the time concerned the future resurrection of the dead, at the end of time itself. Nobody believed in a resurrection before the end of history. The Pharisees may be regarded as typical in this respect: they believed in a future resurrection, and held that men and women would be rewarded or punished after death, according to their actions. The Sadducees, however, insisted that there was no resurrection of any kind. No future existence awaited men and women after death. Paul was able to exploit the differences between the Pharisees and Sadducees on this point during an awkward moment in his career (see Acts 26:6–8). The Christian claim thus did not fit any known Jewish pattern at all. The resurrection of Jesus was not declared to be a future event, but something which had already happened in the world of time and space, in front of witnesses.

Luke records one incident which brings out the unexpected nature of the resurrection of Jesus. This is usually referred to as the "road to Emmaus" (Luke 24:13–35). In this narrative, Luke tells of two disciples, one of whom is named Cleopas, who are discussing the day's bewildering events as they walk along the road from Jerusalem to Emmaus (24:13–17). As they talk, they are joined by a stranger. It is only when he breaks bread with them (an important allusion to the last supper) that they realize who he is.

Jesus appearing to his disciples at the Sea of Galilee, by Pieter Breughel the Younger (1564–1638). This depicts the scene described in John 21:1–14. Sotheby's London.

But what are the implications of the resurrection? We shall discuss these in more detail in chapter 5. In this chapter, we have been documenting the history of Jesus, including the crucifixion and resurrection. But what is the *meaning* of that history? What does the resurrection mean? What does the crucifixion tell us about the identity and the significance of Jesus? To answer such questions, we need to explore the question of the relation between events and meanings.

Events and Meanings

In turning to deal with the question of the significance of Jesus, we need to explore the relation between the events of his life and their meaning. Christianity is not just about the recitation of the history of Jesus; it deals with the meanings of the events in that history, particularly his death on the cross (usually referred to as "the crucifixion"). The Christian faith certainly presupposes that Jesus existed as a real historical figure, and that he was crucified. Christianity is, however, most emphatically not about the mere facts that Jesus existed and was crucified. Let us recall some words of Paul:

> Now, brothers, I want to remind you of the gospel I preached to you, which you received and on which you have taken your stand. By this gospel you are saved . . . For what I received I passed on to you as of first importance: that Christ died for our sins according to the Scriptures, that he was buried, that he was raised on the third day according to the Scriptures, and that he appeared to Peter, and then to the Twelve [Apostles]. (1 Corinthians 15:1–5)

The use of the words "passed on" is of particular interest. These words are taken from the technical Jewish language of tradition, of "handing down" or "handing over," and point to the fact that Paul is passing on to his readers something that had earlier been passed on to him. In other words, Paul was not the first to summarize the Christian faith in terms of the two essential components of Christ's crucifixion and resurrection. He had learned this from others. Paul is not here relying on his own memory at this point, but on the collective memory of a much larger group of people.

It is widely believed that Paul is here reciting a formula, a form of words which was in general use in the early church, and which he had received not just in general terms, but in almost exactly the form which he passes down to the Corinthian Christians. He is not relying on his own memory, but on that of the Christian church in the earliest period of its existence. Earlier in this letter, Paul had made clear that the content of his preaching to the Corinthian Christians, upon which their faith was based, was "Christ crucified" (1 Corinthians 1:17–18; 2:2).

Paul here makes a clear distinction between the *event* of the death of

Christ, and the *significance* of this event. That Christ died is a simple matter of history; that Christ died *for our sins* is an insight which lies right at the heart of the gospel itself. The distinction between an *event* and its *meaning* can be illustrated from an event which took place in 49 BC, when the great Roman commander Julius Caesar crossed a small river with a legion of soldiers. The name of the river was the Rubicon, and it marked an important frontier within the Roman Empire. It was the boundary between Italy and Cisalpine Gaul, a colonized region to the north-west of Italy, in modern-day France.

As an event, it was not especially important. The Rubicon was not a great river, and there was no particular difficulty in crossing it. People have crossed wider and deeper rivers before and since. As a simple event, it was not remarkable. But that is not why the crossing of that river was important. It is the meaning of the event that guarantees its place in the history books, for the political significance of that event was enormous. Crossing this national frontier with an army was a deliberate act of rebellion against Rome. It marked a declaration of war on the part of Caesar against Pompey and the Roman senate. The event was the crossing of a river; the meaning of that event was a declaration of war.

In many ways, the death of Christ may be said to parallel Caesar's crossing of the Rubicon. The event itself appears unexceptional. Similarly, Jesus's death on the cross hardly seems significant at first sight. On the basis of contemporary records, we know that an incalculable number of people died in this way at that time. Jesus would not have been alone in being executed in this way. As an event, the crucifixion hardly seems important or noteworthy.

On the other hand, those aware of the meaning of an event saw behind the mere external event itself, to what it signified, to the reason why it was important. Pompey and the Roman senate were not interested in the mechanics of how Caesar crossed the Rubicon: for them, it meant war. Similarly, Paul was not particularly interested in the mechanics of the crucifixion of Jesus; for him, it meant salvation, forgiveness, and victory over death. Thus the "message of the cross" was not concerned with the simple fact that Jesus was crucified, but with the significance of this event for us. Jesus died, in order that we might live. Jesus was numbered among sinners, so that sinners might be forgiven.

Another example of the link between an event and its meaning can be seen from an incident linked with the death of Jesus on the cross. Matthew's account of the death of Jesus notes one event which happened around this point, which has particular theological significance. The "curtain of the temple" was torn from top to bottom (Matthew 27:51). We are not told how; for Matthew, it is the event that is significant. But what does it mean? The "curtain of the temple" was an especially important feature of the Old

Testament tabernacle (Exodus 26:31–35). It was included in order to provide a means of restricting access to the "most holy place," the region of the tabernacle which was regarded as sacrosanct. Although the curtain served an important practical function in relation to the worship of Israel, it came to have a deeper significance. The fact that the curtain prevented ordinary worshippers from entering the "most holy place" came to be seen as pointing to a much deeper separation between God and sinful humanity. The curtain thus came to be a symbol of the barrier placed between God and humanity by human sinfulness. The tearing of this curtain at the crucifixion can be seen as a symbol of one of the chief benefits brought about by the death of Christ: the barrier between God and humanity caused by sin has been torn down, so that there is now free access for believers to God on account of Christ's death (a theme explored by Paul at Romans 5:1–2).

This line of thinking clearly makes it necessary to move on and consider the significance of Jesus for the writers of the New Testament, which is the subject of chapter 5.

1 In what way does the Old Testament prepare the way for understanding the identity and significance of Jesus?
2 Why was there so much popular interest in John the Baptist?
3 The gospels are critical of the Pharisees. Why?
4 Read one of the "passion narratives" (in other words, the accounts of the trial, suffering, and death of Jesus). Why do the gospels devote so much attention to this aspect of the life of Jesus?
5 What is the difference between the two statements which follow: "Jesus died"; "Jesus died for sinners"?

STUDY QUESTIONS

CHAPTER

The Significance of Jesus: the New Testament

In the previous two chapters, we explored some of the issues concerning the history of Jesus of Nazareth, including the sources we possess concerning him. Our attention now turns to his significance for Christians. What is the Christian understanding of the place of Jesus Christ? What do Christians believe about the identity and significance of Jesus? We have already touched on some aspects of this question in earlier chapters; we shall now try to bring the various strands of these matters together. For the sake of convenience we shall explore the New Testament witness to Jesus under two general headings: the identity of Jesus, and the work of Jesus.

The Identity of Jesus

The New Testament uses a series of major terms to refer to Jesus. These are sometimes known as the "Christological titles" of the New Testament. In what follows, we shall explore several of these titles, and consider their implications for the Christian understanding of the identity of Jesus.

Messiah

It is very easy for a modern western reader to assume that "Christ" was Jesus' surname, and to fail to appreciate that it is actually a title – "Jesus the Christ." The word "Christ" is the Greek form of the Hebrew title "the Messiah," which literally means "the anointed one" – someone who has been anointed with oil. This Old Testament practice indicated that the person anointed in this way was regarded as having been singled out by God as having special powers and functions; thus 1 Samuel 24:6 refers to the king as "the Lord's anointed." The basic sense of the word could be said to be "the divinely appointed King of Israel." As time passed, the term gradually came to refer to a deliverer, himself a descendant of David, who would restore Israel to the golden age she enjoyed under the rule of David.

During the period of Jesus' ministry, Palestine was occupied and administered by Rome. There was fierce nationalist feeling at the time, fuelled by intense resentment at the presence of a foreign occupying power, and this appears to have given a new force to the traditional expectation of the coming of the Messiah. For many, the Messiah would be the deliverer who expelled the Romans from Israel, and restored the line of David. Jesus refused to see himself as Messiah in this sense. At no point in his ministry do we find any violence against Rome suggested or condoned, nor even an explicit attack on the Roman administration. Jesus' attacks are directed primarily against his own people. Thus after his triumphal entry into Jerusalem (Matthew 21:8–11), which gives every indication of being a deliberate Messianic demonstration or gesture, Jesus immediately evicts the merchants from the temple (Matthew 21:12–13).

Interestingly, Jesus was not prepared to accept the title "Messiah" in the course of his ministry. Mark's gospel should be read carefully to note this point. When Peter acclaims Jesus as Messiah – "You are the Christ!" – Jesus immediately tells him to keep quiet about it (Mark 8:29–30). It is not clear what the full significance of the "Messianic secret" is. Why should Mark emphasize that Jesus did not make an explicit claim to be the Messiah, when he was so clearly regarded as such by so many?

Perhaps the answer may be found later in Mark's gospel, when he recounts the only point at which Jesus explicitly acknowledges his identity as the Messiah. When Jesus is led, as a prisoner, before the high priest, he admits to being the Messiah (Mark 14:61–62). Once violent or political action of any sort is no longer possible, Jesus reveals his identity. He was indeed the deliverer of the people of God – but not, it would seem, in any political sense of the term. The misunderstandings associated with the term, particularly in Zealot circles, appear to have caused Jesus to play down the Messianic side of his mission.

Lord

A second significant title is "Lord" (Greek: *kyrios*). The word is used in two main senses in the New Testament. It is used as a polite title of respect, particularly when addressing someone. When Martha addresses Jesus as "Lord" (John 11:21), she is probably, although not necessarily, merely treating Jesus with proper respect. However, the word is also used in another sense. The confession that "Jesus is Lord" (Romans 10:9; 1 Corinthians 12:3) was clearly regarded by Paul as a statement of the essential feature of the gospel. Christians are those who "call upon the name of the

Lord" (Romans 10:13; 1 Corinthians 1:2). But what is implied by this? It is clear that there was a tendency in first-century Palestine to use the word "Lord" (Greek: *kyrios*; Aramaic: *mare*) to designate a divine being, or at the very least a figure who is decidedly more than just human, in addition to its function as a polite or honorific title. But of particular importance is the use of this Greek word *kyrios* to translate the cypher of four letters used to refer to God in the Old Testament (often referred to as the "Tetragrammaton": see p. 43).

When the Old Testament was translated from Hebrew into Greek, the word *kyrios* was generally used to translate the sacred name of God. Of the 6,823 times that this name is used in the Hebrew, the Greek word *kyrios* ("Lord") is used to translate it on 6,156 occasions. This Greek word thus came to be an accepted way of referring directly and specifically to the God who had revealed himself to Israel at Sinai, and who had entered into a covenant with his people on that occasion. Jews would not use this term to refer to anyone or anything else. To do so would be to imply that this person or thing was of divine status. The historian Josephus tells us that the Jews refused to call the Roman Emperor *kyrios*, because they regarded this name as reserved for God alone.

The writers of the New Testament had no hesitation in using this sacred name to refer to Jesus, with all that this implied. A name which was used exclusively to refer to God was regarded as referring equally to Jesus. This was not some error made by ill-informed writers, ignorant of the Jewish background to the name. After all, the first disciples were Jews. Those New Testament writers, such as Paul, who make most use of the term "Lord" to refer to Jesus, were perfectly well aware of its implications. Yet they regarded the evidence concerning Jesus, especially his resurrection from the dead, as compelling them to make this statement concerning his identity. It was a deliberate, considered, informed and justified decision, which is entirely appropriate in the light of the history of Jesus. He has been raised to glory and majesty, and sits at the right hand of God. He therefore shares the same status as God and is to be addressed accordingly.

On occasion, the New Testament takes an Old Testament text which refers to "the Lord" (in other words, "the Lord God"), and deliberately applies or transfers this to "the Lord Jesus." Perhaps the most striking example of this tendency may be seen by comparing Joel 2:32 with Acts 2:21. The passage in Joel refers to a coming period in the history of the people of God, in which the Spirit of God will be poured out upon all people (Joel 2:28). On this "great and dreadful day of the Lord" (that is, God) "everyone who calls upon the name of the Lord will be saved" (Joel 2:31–32) – in other words, all who call upon the name of *God* will be saved.

This prophecy is alluded to in Peter's great sermon on the Day of Pentecost (Acts 2:17–21), which ends with the declaration that "everyone who calls upon the name of the Lord shall be saved" (Acts 2:21). It is then made clear, in what follows, that the "Lord" in question is none other than "Jesus of Nazareth," whom God has made "both Lord and Christ" (Acts 2:36). Peter declares that the resurrection has established that the same Jesus who was crucified has now been publicly declared by God to be the Messiah and Lord, with the right to equal status with God.

A further interesting example may be found in the use made of Isaiah 45:23 in Philippians 2:10–11. Isaiah speaks prophetically of a day in which "the Lord" (that is, "the Lord God") declares that "every knee shall bow" to him, and "every tongue confess him." It is a powerful passage, in which the uniqueness of the God of Israel, and especially his universal claims to authority and sovereignty, are firmly stated (Isaiah 45:22–25).

This practice of transferring from one Lord ("the Lord God") to another ("the Lord Jesus") is known to have infuriated Jews at the time. In the second-century dialogue between Trypho the Jew and Justin Martyr, Trypho complains that Christians have "hijacked" passages referring to God, in order to refer them to Christ. There was, of course, no suggestion that there were two "Lords" (in other words, two Gods), simply that Jesus had to be regarded as having a status at least equal to that of God, which demanded that he be addressed and worshipped as such. The use of the term "Lord" to refer to Jesus may therefore be seen as a recognition of his exalted status, arising from his resurrection.

Son of God

A further title used by the New Testament to refer to Jesus is "Son of God." In the Old Testament, the term is occasionally used to refer to angelic or supernatural persons (see Job 38:7; Daniel 3:25). Messianic texts in the Old Testament refer to the coming Messiah as the "Son of God" (2 Samuel 7:12–14; Psalm 2:7). The New Testament use of the term seems to mark a development of its Old Testament meaning, with an increased emphasis upon its exclusiveness.

Although all people are children of God in some sense of the word, Jesus is *the* Son of God. Paul distinguishes between Jesus as the natural Son of God, and believers as adopted sons. Their relation to God is quite different from Jesus' relationship to him, even though both may be referred to as "sons of God." We shall explore this point further when we consider the idea of "adoption" as a way of thinking about the benefits which Christ obtained for us on the cross. Similarly, in the first letter of John, Jesus is referred to as "the Son," while believers are designated as "children." There is something quite distinct about Jesus' relation to God, as expressed in the title "Son of God."

The New Testament understanding of Jesus' relationship to God, expressed in the Father–Son relationship, takes a number of forms. First, we note that Jesus directly addresses God as "Father," with the very intimate Aramaic word "Abba" being used (Mark 14:36: see also Matthew 6:9; 11:25–26; 26:42; Luke 23:34, 46). Second, it is clear from a number of passages that the evangelists regard Jesus as the Son of God, or that Jesus treats God as his father, even if this is not stated explicitly (Mark 1:11; 9:7; 12:6; 13:32; 14:61–62; 15:39). Third, John's gospel is permeated with the Father–Son relationship (note especially passages such as John 5:16–27; 17:1–26), with a remarkable emphasis upon the identity of will and purpose of the Father and Son, indicating how close the relationship between Jesus and God was understood to be by the first Christians. At every level in the New Testament – in the words of Jesus himself, or in the impression which was created among the first Christians – Jesus is clearly understood to have a unique and intimate relationship to God, which the resurrection demonstrated publicly (Romans 1:3–4).

It must be stressed that the Christian doctrine of Jesus as the "Son of God" is not to be understood that God physically fathered Jesus. Muslims generally regard this way of referring to Jesus as an instance of the heresy of *ittakhadha*, by which Jesus is acknowledged to be the physical Son of God. This is not a correct perception. The point being made by this title for Jesus is fundamentally relational – that is to say, it is an affirmation of the unique status of Jesus in relation to God, and hence the unique role of Jesus within the Christian tradition as a bearer of divine revelation and the agent of divine salvation.

Son of Man

For many Christians, the term "Son of Man" stands as a natural counterpart to "Son of God." It is an affirmation of the humanity of Christ, just as the latter term is an complementary affirmation of his divinity. However, it is not quite as simple as this. The term "Son of Man" (Hebrew: *ben-adam* or Aramaic *bar nasha*) is used in three main contexts in the Old Testament:

1 as a specific form of address to the prophet Ezekiel;
2 to refer to a future eschatological figure (Daniel 7:13–14), whose coming signals the end of history and the coming of divine judgment;
3 to emphasize the contrast between the lowliness and frailty of human nature and the elevated status or permanence of God and the angels (Numbers 23:19; Psalm 8:14).

The third such meaning relates naturally to the humanity of Jesus, and may underlie at least some of its references in the synoptic gospels, especially those stressing the humility of Jesus, and his willingness to suffer alongside others.

However, the sense of the term which has attracted most attention is that of a coming figure of judgment. This is certainly the sense which the term bears in the vision of Daniel in the Old Testament. In one of his visions of a future judgment, Daniel sees someone whom he refers to as "a son of man" coming to judge the world. The term "son of man" is also used in the gospels to refer to a future judge, who will come in glory at the end of time. This way of referring to Jesus would thus stress the continuity between the humble figure of Jesus during the time of his ministry and the future judge, who will come at the end of time. The Nicene Creed refers to Jesus as the one "who will come again in glory to judge the living and the dead"; this affirmation echoes the New Testament understanding of Jesus as one coming judge. It also emphasizes the authority of Jesus as one with the divine right to judge. This is further consolidated by the final New Testament title for Jesus which we shall consider – that of "God".

The Present Humility and Future Glory of Jesus

The theme of the "son of man" brings out the importance of the relationship between the first coming of Jesus in humility and his second coming in power.

The Coming Judge: Daniel 7:13–14
I saw in the night visions, and behold, with the clouds of heaven there came one like a son of man, and he came to the Ancient of Days and was presented before him. And to him was given dominion and glory and kingdom, that all peoples, nations, and languages should serve him; his dominion is an everlasting dominion, which shall not pass away, and his kingdom one that shall not be destroyed.

The Figure of Humility: Matthew 8:20
Jesus said to him, "Foxes have holes, and birds of the air have nests; but the Son of man has nowhere to lay his head."

The Figure of Power and Authority: Matthew 19:28
Jesus said to them, "Truly, I say to you, in the new world, when the Son of man shall sit on his glorious throne, you who have followed me will also sit on twelve thrones, judging the twelve tribes of Israel."

STUDY PANEL 19

Study Panel 19 Continued

This theme of the continuity between the humble Jesus of Palestine and the coming glorious judge is brought out clearly in a Christian prayer used to celebrate the opening of the season of Advent (see p. 376), four weeks before Christmas:

Almighty God, give us grace to cast away the works of darkness, and to put on the armour of light, now in the time of this mortal life, in which your Son Jesus Christ came to us in great humility: so that on the last day, when he shall come again in his glorious majesty to judge the living and the dead, we may rise to life immortal; through him who is alive and reigns with you and the Holy Spirit, one God, now and for ever, Amen.

God

Finally, we must note a group of texts which explicitly refer to Jesus as God. All the other material we have considered in this chapter can be seen as pointing to this conclusion. The affirmation that Jesus is divine is the climax of the New Testament witness to the person of Jesus Christ. At least ten texts in the New Testament seem to speak explicitly of Jesus in this way (John 1:1; 1:18; 20:28; Romans 9:5; Titus 2:13; Hebrews 1:8–9; 2 Peter 1:1 and 1 John 5:20). Others point in this direction, implying the same conclusion (such as Matthew 1:23; John 17:3; Galatians 2:20; Ephesians 5:5; Colossians 2:2; 2 Thessalonians 1:12 and 1 Timothy 3:16). We shall consider some of these verses in what follows.

One of the most remarkable passages in the New Testament describes how the doubts of Thomas concerning the resurrection of Jesus are dispelled (John 20:24–29). Thomas doubted that Jesus really had been raised. However, those doubts give way to faith when the risen Jesus is able to show him the wounds inflicted upon him at the crucifixion. Thomas responds with a declaration of faith in Christ, addressing him with the following words: "My Lord and my God!" (John 20:28). These remarkable words are totally consistent with the witness to the identity of Jesus Christ which is provided by this gospel. We have already noted how the term "Lord" could be used as a way of referring to God. However, Thomas explicitly addresses Jesus, not merely as "Lord" but as "God," making explicit what might otherwise only be implicit.

The second letter of Peter is one of the later writings in the New Testament. The letter is addressed to "those who through the righteousness of our God and Savior Jesus Christ have received a faith as precious as ours" (2 Peter 1:1). A similar phrase is found in Paul's letter to Titus, which refers to Jesus Christ as "God our Savior" (Titus 1:3). The Greek form of both these statements makes it clear that they cannot be translated as if "God" and "Savior" were different persons. Both titles refer to the one and same person, Jesus Christ.

The Significance of Jesus

We can summarize the significance of Jesus for Christians under four broad headings, as follows.

Jesus as the Founder of Christianity

This observation is relatively uncontroversial. Christianity traces its origins back to Jesus, who may be regarded as its founder. However, the interpretation of this observation is complex. Consider, for example, the question of whether Jesus of Nazareth introduced anything *new* into the world. For the writers of the Enlightenment, Jesus of Nazareth did little more than republish a religion of nature, which was promptly corrupted by his followers, including Paul. There was nothing new about his words and deeds. The insights of Jesus, where they were valid, could all be obtained through the use of an omnicompetent human reason. Rationalism thus argued that Jesus had nothing that was both right and new to say; where he was right, he merely agreed with what sound human reason always knew to be the case; if he said anything that was new (that is, hitherto unknown to reason), this would, by definition, be irrational and hence of no value.

A very different approach is associated with German liberal Protestantism (see pp. 326–7), especially as this is developed in the writings of Albrecht Benjamin Ritschl. Ritschl argues that Jesus of Nazareth brings something new to the human situation, something which reason had not known about. "Jesus was conscious of a *new and hitherto unknown relation to God.*" Where rationalists believed in a universal rational religion, of which individual world religions were at best shadows, Ritschl argued that this was little more than a dream of reason, an abstraction without any historical embodiment. Christianity possesses certain definite theological and cultural characteristics as a historical religion, partly due to Jesus of Nazareth.

Important though this historical consideration might be, Christian theology has generally located the significance of Jesus Christ in three specifically *theological* areas, which we shall consider below. Nevertheless, it must be stressed that this historical dimension to the significance of Jesus Christ is of continuing importance. Christianity is not a set of self-contained and free-standing ideas; it represents a sustained response to the questions raised by the life, death, and resurrection of Jesus Christ. Christianity is an historical religion, which came into being in response to a specific set of events, which center upon Jesus Christ, and to which Christian theology is obliged to return in the course of its speculation and reflection.

This point is of importance in understanding the continuing importance of Scripture within the Christian tradition. Christology and scriptural authority are inextricably linked, in that it is Scripture which brings us to a knowledge of Jesus Christ. The New Testament is the only document we possess which the Christian church has recognized as authentically embodying and recollecting its understanding of Jesus, and the impact which he had upon peoples' lives and thought. The reports we have concerning Jesus from extra-canonical sources are of questionable reliability, and strictly limited value. The authority of Scripture thus rests partly upon historical considerations. However, those historical considerations are to be supplemented with theological reflections – for example, that it is through Jesus Christ that the distinctively Christian knowledge of God comes about, and this knowledge of Jesus is given only in Scripture. We shall now move on to consider such explicitly theological considerations.

Jesus Reveals God

The New Testament sets out the idea that god, who is invisible, is in some way made known or made visible through Jesus. One of the dominant themes in the Old Testament is that nobody has ever seen God. A number of factors lie behind this assertion, including the belief that human nature is simply not capable of grasping or coping with the full wonder of God, and the related belief that human sinfulness prevents a clear apprehension of God.

Two passages from the New Testament letters bring this point out with particular clarity. Colossians 1:15 affirms that Jesus "is the image of the invisible God." The Greek word here translated as "image" (*eikon*) has a number of senses, conveying the basic idea of correspondence between the image and the reality which it depicts. It is used elsewhere in the New Testament to refer to the image of the emperor on Roman coinage. The same theme emerges as important at Hebrews 1:3, which refers to Jesus as "the exact representation of [God's] being." The Greek word here translated as "exact representation" (*charakter*) is also used to refer to the imprint on coins, perhaps with the sense of the exact reproduction of a likeness. The word occasionally seems to have the sense of "a copy." Both these passages express the idea that Jesus in some way makes God known in a way which would otherwise not be possible.

"Anyone who has seen me has seen the Father" (John 14:9). These remarkable words, so characteristic of John's gospel, emphasize that God the Father speaks and acts in the Son. God is revealed through, in, and by Jesus. The Christian claim that God is most fully and authentically revealed in the face of Jesus Christ is simply a summary statement of the kaleidoscope of New Testament descriptions of the intimate relation between the Father and the Son, between God and Jesus. To have seen Jesus is to have seen the Father. Martin Luther makes this point as follows. For Luther, Islam has the Qur'an and Judaism the Torah; yet for Christians:

> God does not want to be known except through Christ; nor can he be known in any other way. Christ is the offspring promised to Abraham; on him God has grounded all his promises. Therefore Christ alone is the means, the life, and the mirror through which we see God and know his will. Through Christ God declares his favor and mercy to us. In Christ we see that God is not an angry master and judge but a gracious and kind father, who blesses us, that is, who delivers us from the law, sin, death, and every evil, and gives us righteousness and eternal life through Christ. This is a certain and true knowledge of God and divine persuasion, which does not fail, but depicts God himself in a specific form, apart from which there is no God.

Jesus is understood, once more, to function as God, in that God chooses to be revealed definitively in this form and in this way. This point is stated clearly by the Swiss theologian Karl Barth (1886–1968), widely regarded as one of the greatest theological writers of the twentieth century. For Barth, Jesus is the key to an understanding of the nature of God:

> When Holy Scripture speaks of God, it does not permit us to let our attention or thoughts wander at random . . . When Holy Scripture speaks of God, it concentrates our attention and thoughts upon one single point and what is to be known at that point . . . If we ask further concerning the one point upon which, according to Scripture, our attention and thoughts should and must be concentrated, then from first to last the Bible directs us to the name of Jesus Christ.

This point is developed further in the doctrine of the incarnation (see pp. 123–34) – the characteristically Christian idea that God entered into the world of time and space in the person of Jesus Christ. The doctrine of the incarnation provides a basis for the distinctively Christian belief that Jesus provides a "window into God." It also underlies the practice, especially associated with the Orthodox church, of using icons in worship and personal devotion.

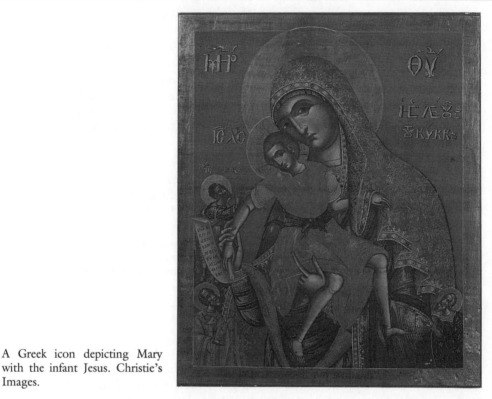

A Greek icon depicting Mary with the infant Jesus. Christie's Images.

John of Damascus on the Incarnation and Icons

In one of his works, originally written in Greek in the first half of the eighth century, John of Damascus argues that the theological fact of the incarnation of Christ provides a solid foundation for the use of icons in devotion. An "icon" (*eikōn*) is a religious painting or picture, which is understood to act as a window through which the worshipper may catch a closer glimpse of the divine than would otherwise be possible.

> Previously there was absolutely no way in which God, who has neither a body nor a face, could be represented by any image. But now that he has made himself visible in the flesh and has lived with people, I can make an image of what I have seen of God . . . and contemplate the glory of the Lord, his face having been unveiled.

Jesus as the Ground of Salvation

One of the more significant titles used in the New Testament to refer to Jesus is "Savior." Jesus is the "Savior, who is Christ the Lord" (Luke 2:11). One of the earliest symbols of faith used by Christians was a fish. The use of this symbol may partly reflect the fact that the first disciples were fishermen. But the real reason is that the five Greek letters (see p. 395) spelling out "fish" in Greek (I-CH-TH-U-S) are an acronym of the Christian slogan "Jesus Christ, Son of God, Savior." According to the New Testament, Jesus saves his people from their sins (Matthew 1:21); in his name alone is there salvation (Acts 4:12); he is the "author of their salvation" (Hebrews 2:10). And in these affirmations, and many others like them, Jesus is understood to function as God, doing something which, properly speaking, only God can do.

So what does this "salvation" mean? And how does the New Testament understand this to relate to the death of Jesus? To explore this matter, we may spend some time looking at three of the images used by the New Testament to refer to the nature of the salvation which results from the work of Jesus. Many more could be considered; our intention here is simply to illustrate the kinds of ideas and approaches found within the New Testament.

Ransom

Jesus himself declared that he came "to give his life as a ransom for many" (Mark 10:45). This understanding of the meaning of the death of Jesus is of particular interest, as it comes from Jesus himself. The idea is also found elsewhere. 1 Timothy 2:5–6 speaks of Jesus Christ being a "mediator between God and humanity . . . who gave his life as a ransom for all." A ransom is a price which is paid to achieve someone's freedom. As used in the Old Testament, however, the emphasis falls primarily upon the idea of being freed, of liberation, rather than speculation about the nature of the price paid, or the identity of the person to whom it is paid. Thus Isaiah 35:10 and 51:11 refer to the liberated Israelites as the "ransomed of the Lord." The basic idea is that God intervenes to deliver people from captivity, whether from the political power of Babylon (Isaiah 51:10–11) or from the physical and spiritual threat of death (Hosea 13:14).

To speak of Jesus' death as a "ransom" immediately suggests three ideas.

1 *Liberation.* A ransom is something which achieves freedom for a person who is held in captivity. When someone is kidnapped, and a ransom demanded, the payment of that ransom leads to liberation.
2 *Payment.* A ransom is a sum of money which is paid in order to achieve an individual's liberation.

3 *Someone to whom the ransom is paid.* A ransom is usually paid to an individual's captor, or an intermediate.

These three ideas thus seem to be implied by speaking of Jesus' death as a "ransom" for sinners.

But are all three present in the New Testament? There is no doubt whatsoever that the New Testament proclaims that we have been liberated from captivity through the death and resurrection of Jesus. We have been set free from captivity to sin and the fear of death (Romans 8:21; Hebrews 2:15). It is also clear that the New Testament understands the death of Jesus as the price which had to be paid to achieve our liberation (1 Corinthians 6:20; 7:23). Our liberation is a costly and a precious matter. In these two respects, the scriptural use of "redemption" corresponds to the everyday associations of the term. But what of the third aspect?

There is not a hint in the New Testament that Jesus' death was the price paid to someone (such as the devil) to achieve our liberation. Some of the writers of the first four centuries, however, assumed that they could press this analogy to its limits, and declared that God had delivered us from the power of the devil by offering Jesus as the price of our liberation. This idea surfaces repeatedly in patristic discussions of the meaning of the death of Christ. Yet it needs to be asked whether it rests upon pressing an analogy beyond its acceptable limits!

Redemption

The basic idea expressed in the idea of "redemption" is that of "buying back." The practice of redeeming slaves, a familiar event in New Testament times, seems to lie behind this important New Testament image for salvation. Slavery resulted from a number of factors; for example, occasionally individuals who were unable to meet their financial obligations would sell themselves into slavery, until such time as they had accumulated enough money to but back their freedom. Slaves could thus redeem themselves by purchasing their freedom. The word used to describe this event could literally be translated as "being taken out of the forum [the slave market]." As with the idea of ransom, we are dealing with the notion of restoring someone to a state of liberty, with the emphasis laid upon liberation, rather than upon the means used to achieve it.

The New Testament can use the term "redeemed" in the sense of being liberated from bondage – for example, bondage to the Old Testament law (Galatians 3:13; 4:5). More often, however, the word is used in a more general sense – simply being set free (Revelation 5:9; 14:3 4). Here, as with the image of ransom, we are dealing with the idea of Christ's death and resurrection setting man free from his bondage to sin and death. Paul's repeated emphasis that Christians are slaves who have been "bought at a price" (1 Corinthians 6:20; 7:23) represents an important statement of the principle that Christian liberty is directly related to the death of Christ, which is somehow seen as purchasing that freedom.

Reconciliation

"God was reconciling the world to himself in Christ" (2 Corinthians 5:19). This famous statement picks up the theme of "reconciliation." Paul uses the same word in another context to refer to the reconciliation of an estranged husband and wife (1 Corinthians 7:11). The idea of reconciliation is fundamental to human experience, especially in the area of personal relationships. The parable of the prodigal son (Luke 15:11 32) is perhaps the supreme illustration of the importance of reconciliation in the New Testament. It illustrates vividly the reconciliation of father and son, and the restoration of their broken relationship.

How, then, is Jesus understood by New Testament writers to be involved in the reconciliation between God and sinners? There are two ways of looking at this question. First, the phrase "God was in Christ" can be taken as a reference to the incarnation – that is, to God entering into human history in the human person of Jesus. The word "incarnation" literally means "in the flesh". As God incarnate, Jesus takes the initiative in proclaiming the overwhelming love of God for us and God's desire that we should be reconciled. In proclaiming the need and possibility of reconciliation to God, Christ addresses us as God and on behalf of God.

The phrase "in Christ" can also be understood in a second way. It may reflect a Hebrew grammatical construction with which Paul would have been familiar, which could be translated as "through Christ." In other words, "God was reconciling the world to himself in Christ" is to be understood as meaning that Christ is the agent of divine reconciliation, the one through whom God reconciles us – a mediator or go-between. This idea can clearly be seen at other points in the New Testament: "You were alienated from God . . . But now he has reconciled you by Christ's physical body through death to present you holy in his sight" (Colossians 1:21–22). The ideas of "estrangement" (or "alienation," as it could also be translated) and "hostility" are used to refer to the alienated human relationship with God, which is transformed through the death of Christ into reconciliation.

Jesus as an Example

For the New Testament, Jesus Christ is not only the basis of salvation; he embodies the features of the Christian life. Christians are meant to become like Christ. This should not be understood to mean that it is by imitating Jesus that one becomes a Christian. Rather, the New Testament clearly assumes that it is by coming to faith that some kind of process of transformation is initiated by God, which ends up by making the believer become more like Jesus. Thus when Paul urges his readers to be "imitators of Christ," as he is (1 Corinthians 11:1), his words seem to suggest that being a Christian is to enter into so close and deep a relationship with Christ that believers in some way begin to imitate him in consequence of that relationship. Imitation of Jesus is thus the result of faith, not its precondition.

An understanding of Jesus Christ which sees him as nothing more than a religious or moral example is thus inadequate. The New Testament affirms that Jesus is indeed such an example – but that he is more than this. Jesus establishes both the basis of the Christian life (through his saving death on the cross) and the shape of that life (through the example of his life). The view that Jesus is only an example is linked with a very weak view of human nature, which sees it as requiring nothing more than education before it can be transformed. As the noted nineteenth-century English theologian Charles Gore pointed out:

> Inadequate conceptions of Christ's person go hand in hand with inadequate conceptions of what human nature wants. The Nestorian conception of Christ . . . qualifies Christ for being an example of what man can do, and into what wonderful union with God he can be assumed if he is holy enough; but Christ remains one man among many, shut in within the limits of a single human personality, and influencing man only from outside. He can be a Redeemer of man if man can be saved from outside by bright example, but not otherwise . . . The Nestorian Christ is the fitting Saviour of the Pelagian man.

For the New Testament writers – particularly Paul – the life, death, and resurrection of Jesus Christ make possible a new form of existence, which is received through faith. In the previous section we noted how the New Testament understands Jesus to be the basis of the salvation of humanity. Once that salvation has been appropriated, believers can begin to become like Jesus.

It will be clear from this brief survey of the New Testament material that Jesus is of central importance to Christians. Our attention now turns to the development of these New Testament themes concerning the identity and significance of Jesus in the Christian tradition after the New Testament.

1   Why is it important to the gospel writers (especially Matthew) to establish that Jesus is "the Messiah"?
2   What are the implications of referring to Jesus as "Lord"?
3   Why is it inadequate to summarize the Christian understanding of Jesus as a "good religious teacher"?
4   Why is the cross so important for Christians?
5   Why does Karl Barth see Jesus as being of such central significance?

CHAPTER 6

The Significance of Jesus: the Christian Tradition

In the previous chapter we explored the significance of Jesus, as set out within the New Testament. Christians have seen it as an issue of major importance to ensure that the significance of Jesus for humanity is articulated as accurately and adequately as possible. As a result, the Christian tradition has developed a number of ways of explaining and defending the identity and relevance of Jesus, several of which have become classic. In what follows we shall be exploring some classic approaches to the identity of Jesus – a general area of Christian thought dealing with the identity of Jesus is often referred to as "Christology." In the course of this analysis the reader will encounter a number of important technical terms, all of which will be explained as they are introduced.

The Use of Philosophical Ideas in Christology

As we have seen from our analysis of the view of Jesus found in the New Testament, the first Christians were confronted with something so exciting and novel in the life, death, and resurrection of Jesus that they were obliged to employ a whole range of images, terms, and ideas to describe it. There was simply no single term available which could capture the richness and profundity of their impressions and experience of Jesus. They were forced to use a whole variety of terms to illuminate the different aspects of their understanding of him. Taken together, these combine to build up an overall picture of Christ.

At times they may even have drawn upon ideas or concepts ultimately deriving from paganism to try and build up this picture. For example, it is often thought that the opening section of John's gospel (John 1:1–18), with its distinctive emphasis on the "Word" (Greek: *Logos*), is trying to show that Jesus occupies the same place in the Christian understanding of the world as the idea of the *Logos* in secular Greek philosophy. But this does not mean that Christians invented their understanding of Jesus' significance because they happened to read a few textbooks of Stoic philosophy. Rather, they noticed an analogy or parallel, and saw the obvious advantages to be gained by exploiting it to express something which they already knew about. It also went some way to make Christianity more understandable to an educated Greek audience. Even at this early stage in the Christian tradition, we can see a principled determination to make the gospel both intelligible and accessible to those outside the church. The gospel was thus expressed using ideas and concepts which helped to bring out its central themes, and make them understandable to non-believers. Christian writers of the patristic period thus used analogies and ideas which would express their understanding of the identity and significance of Jesus in terms that their Greek readers could understand.

An excellent example of this process within the New Testament is provided by Paul's "Areopagus Sermon" (Acts 17:16–34). This sermon, preached to philosophers at the Areopagus (or "Mars Hill") in Athens, seems to have aimed to gain a hearing for the gospel by engaging with ideas and terms which were already familiar to Paul's audience. Luke's gospel is another case in point. Luke is clearly writing for an audience which includes non-Jews (usually referred to as "Gentiles"). The word "Messiah" would have meant little to such a readership, who would not have been fully aware of its implications and nuances. However, many of the Greek religions were already used to terms such as "Savior" or "Redeemer." By using such terms, and always interpreting them in a rigorously Christian manner, Luke could express the significance of Jesus Christ in terms which would have made sense to his readers. In doing this, Luke was in no way inventing the significance of Jesus, nor was he forcing Jesus into a pagan religious context. He was simply bringing out the full significance of Jesus, using words and ideas to which his readers could respond. In this way, Luke opened the way for a pagan readership to discover that the true fulfillment of their religious hopes lay only in Jesus Christ.

All that such Christian writers were doing was expressing something they already knew, something that was already there and already true, in new and different ways, in order to get their message across. The fact that Christianity found it so easy to cross cultural barriers at the time is a remarkable testimony to the effectiveness of the first Christians' attempts to express their beliefs in ways that made sense outside a Jewish context.

In the case of patristic writers, this often involved making use of ideas drawn from the Greek philosophy of the period. Thus the idea of the "Logos" (noted above) was seen as especially important as a means of enabling a philosophically literate secular audience to gain insights into the identity of Jesus. Aristotelian insights were used in the same way in thirteenth-century Paris, just as Hegelian insights were used in nineteenth-century Germany, or existentialist approaches in North America during the 1960s. The principle was the same: attempt to explain the Christian understanding of Jesus in terms which made sense to the prevailing culture.

Some works dealing with Christian theology draw a sharp distinction between "the person of Christ" (or "Christology") on the one hand, and "the work of Christ" (or "soteriology," from the Greek work *soteria*, "salvation") on the other. While this distinction has some value in some respects, it is increasingly regarded as unhelpful, partly on account of the growing realization of the affinities between what are generally referred to as *functional* and *ontological* Christologies – that is, between Christologies which make affirmations about the function or work of Jesus, and those which make affirmations concerning his identity or being. Christology and soteriology are here seen as two sides of the same coin, rather than two independent areas of thought.

The Person of Jesus

As we noted earlier (pp. 108–23), the person of Jesus Christ is of central importance to Christianity. This is especially the case in the New Testament. Whereas "theology" could be defined as "talk about God" in general, "Christian theology" accords a central role to Jesus Christ. The nature of that role is perhaps best understood by considering the three aspects of the central role of Jesus in Christian thought, noted earlier (see pp. 116–23). In what follows, we shall explore the major debates of the patristic period over the identity of Jesus, which acted as a catalyst to the definite Christian statements concerning the identity of Jesus at the Council of Chalcedon (451).

The patristic period saw considerable attention being paid to the doctrine of the person of Christ. The task confronting the writers of this period was basically the development of a unified Christological scheme, which would bring together and integrate the various Christological hints and statements, images and models, found within the New Testament – some of which have been considered briefly earlier (pp. 108–23). That task proved complex. In view of its importance for Christian theology, we shall consider its main stages of development in what follows.

Early Christological Heresies

The first period of the development of Christology centered on the question of the divinity of Jesus. That Jesus was human appeared to be something of a truism to most early patristic writers. What required explanation about Jesus concerned the manner in which he differed from, rather than the ways in which he was similar to, other human beings.

Two early viewpoints were quickly rejected as heretical. *Ebionitism*, promoted by a Jewish sect which flourished in the early first centuries of the Christian era, regarded Jesus as an ordinary human being, the human son of Mary and Joseph. This reduced Christology was regarded as totally inadequate by its opponents, and soon passed into oblivion. More significant was the diametrically opposed view, which came to be known as *Docetism*, from the Greek verb "*dokein*" (to seem or appear). This approach – which is probably best regarded as a tendency within theology rather than a definite theological position – argued that Christ was totally divine, and that his humanity was merely an appearance. The sufferings of Christ are thus treated as apparent rather than real. Docetism held a particular attraction for the Gnostic writers of the second century, during which period it reached its zenith. By this time, however, other viewpoints were in the process of emerging, which would eventually eclipse this tendency. Justin Martyr represents one such viewpoint, generally known as a "Logos-Christology."

The Logos Christologies

Justin Martyr, amongst the most important of the second-century Apologists, was especially concerned to demonstrate that the Christian faith brought to fruition both the insights of classical Greek philosophy and Judaism. Of particular interest is the Logos-Christology which Justin develops, in which he exploits the apologetic potential of the idea of the "Logos," current in both Stoicism and the Middle Platonism of the period. The Logos (a Greek term which is usually translated as "word" – e.g., as it occurs at John 1:14) is to be thought of as the ultimate source of all human knowledge. The one and the same Logos is known by both Christian believers and pagan philosophers; the latter, however, only have partial access to it, whereas Christians have full access to it, on account of its manifestation in Christ. Justin allows that pre-Christian secular philosophers, such as Heraclitus or Socrates, thus had partial access to the truth, on account of the manner in which the Logos is present in the world. It is in the writings of Origen that the Logos-Christology appears to find its fullest development. It must be made clear that Origen's Christology is complex, and that its interpretation at points is highly problematical. What follows is a simplification of his approach. In the incarnation, the human soul of Christ is united with the Logos. On account of the closeness of this union, Christ's human soul comes to share in the properties of the Logos. Origen illustrates this idea with an often quoted analogy:

> If a lump of iron is constantly kept in a fire, it will absorb its heat through all
> its pores and veins. If the fire is continuous, and the iron is not removed, it
> becomes totally converted to the other . . . In the same way, the soul which
> has been constantly placed in the Logos and Wisdom and God, is God in all
> that it does, feels and understands.

Nevertheless, Origen insists that the Logos must be regarded as subordinate
to the Father. Although both the Logos and Father are co-eternal, the
Logos is subordinate to the Father.

We noted above that Justin Martyr argued that the Logos was accessible
to all, even if only in a fragmentary manner. Its full disclosure only came in
Christ. Similar ideas can be found in the writings of other theologians of this
period, including Origen. Origen adopts an illuminationist approach to
revelation, in which God's act of revelation is compared to being enlightened by the "rays of God," which are caused by "the light which is the
divine Logos." For Origen, both truth and salvation can be found outside
the Christian faith.

The Arian Controversy

One controversy of especial importance to the formation of the definitive
Christian statement of the identity of Jesus broke out in the fourth century,
and is known as the "Arian controversy." This controversy, which focused
on the teaching of the writer Arius, remains a landmark in the development
of classical Christology, and therefore needs to be considered in a little
detail. Arius emphasizes the self-subsistence of God. God is the one and only
source of all created things; nothing exists which does not ultimately derive
from God. This view of God, which many commentators have suggested is
due more to Hellenistic philosophy than to Christian theology, clearly raises
the question of the relation of the Father to the Son. Arius' critic Athanasius
represents him as making the following statements on this point.

> God was not always a father. There was a time when God was all alone, and
> was not yet a father; only later did he become a father. The Son did not always
> exist. Everything created is out of nothing . . . so the Logos of God came into
> existence out of nothing. There was a time when he was not. Before he was
> brought into being, he did not exist. He also had a beginning to his created
> existence.

These statements are of considerable importance, and bring us to the heart
of Arianism. The following points are of especial significance.

The Father is regarded as existing before the Son. "There was when he
was not," to quote one of Arius' fighting slogans. This decisive affirmation
places Father and Son on different levels, and is consistent with Arius'

rigorous insistence that the Son is a creature. Only the Father is "unbegotten"; the Son, like all other creatures, derives from this one source of being. However, Arius is careful to emphasize that the Son is like every other creature. There is a distinction of rank between the Son and other creatures, including human beings. Arius has some difficulty in identifying the precise nature of this distinction. The Son, he argued, is "a perfect creature, yet not as one among other creatures; a begotten being, yet not as one among other begotten beings." The implication seems to be that the Son outranks other creatures, while sharing their essentially created and begotten nature.

An important aspect of Arius' distinction between Father and Son concerns the unknowability of God. Arius emphasizes the utter transcendence and inaccessibility of God. God cannot be known by any other creature. Yet, as we noted above, the Son is to be regarded as a creature, however elevated above all other creatures. Arius presses home his logic, arguing that the Son cannot know the Father. "The one who has a beginning is in no position to comprehend or lay hold of the one who has no beginning." This important affirmation rests upon the radical distinction between Father and Son. Such is the gulf fixed between them, that the latter cannot know the former unaided. In common with all other creatures, the Son is dependent upon the grace of God if the Son is to perform whatever function has been ascribed to him. It is considerations such as these which have led Arius' critics to argue that, at the levels of revelation and salvation, the Son is in precisely the same position as other creatures.

But what about the many biblical passages which seem to suggest that the Son is far more than a mere creature? Arius' opponents were easily able to bring forward a series of biblical passages, pointing to the fundamental unity between Father and Son. On the basis of the controversial literature of the period, it is clear that the Fourth Gospel was of major importance to this controversy, with John 3:35, 10:30, 12:27, 14:10, 17:3 and 17:11 being discussed frequently. Arius's reponse to such texts is significant: the language of "sonship" is variegated in character, and metaphorical in nature. To refer to the "Son" is an honorific, rather than theologically precise, way of speaking. Although Jesus Christ is referred to as "Son" in Scripture, this metaphorical way of speaking is subject to the controlling principle of a God who is totally different in essence from all created beings – including the Son.

The basic elements of Arius' position can be summarized in the following manner. The Son is a creature, who, like all other creatures, derives from the will of God. The term "Son" is thus a metaphor, an honorific term intended to underscore the rank of the Son among other creatures. It does not imply that Father and Son share the same being or status.

Athanasius had little time for Arius' subtle distinctions. If the Son is a creature, then the Son is a creature like any other creature, including human beings. After all, what other kind of creaturehood is there? For Athanasius, the affirmation of the creaturehood of the Son had two decisive consequences, each of which had uniformly negative implications for Arianism.

First, Athanasius makes the point that it is only God who can save. God, and God alone, can break the power of sin, and bring us to eternal life. An essential feature of being a creature is that one requires to be redeemed. No creature can save another creature. Only the creator can redeem the creation. Having emphasized that it is God alone who can save, Athanasius then makes the logical move which the Arians found difficult to counter. The New Testament and the Christian liturgical tradition alike regard Jesus Christ as Savior. Yet, as Athanasius emphasized, only God can save. So how are we to make sense of this?

The only possible solution, Athanasius argues, is to accept that Jesus is God incarnate. The logic of his argument at times goes something like this:

1   No creature can redeem another creature.
2   According to Arius, Jesus Christ is a creature.
3   Therefore, according to Arius, Jesus Christ cannot redeem humanity.

At times, a slightly different style of argument can be discerned, resting upon the statements of Scripture and the Christian liturgical tradition. The way in which Christians worship is of major importance to the way in which they think.

1   Only God can save.
2   Jesus Christ saves.
3   Therefore Jesus Christ is God.

Salvation, for Athanasius, involves divine intervention. Athanasius thus draws out the meaning of John 1:14 by arguing that the "word became flesh": in other words, God entered into our human situation, in order to change it.

The second point that Athanasius makes is that Christians worship and pray to Jesus Christ. This represents an excellent case study of the importance of Christian practices of worship and prayer for Christian theology. By the fourth century, prayer to and adoration of Christ were standard features of the way in which public worship took place. Athanasius argues that if Jesus Christ is a creature, then Christians are guilty of worshipping a creature instead of God – in other words, they had lapsed into idolatry. Christians, Athanasius stresses, are totally forbidden to worship anyone or anything except God himself. Athanasius thus argued that Arius seemed to be guilty of making nonsense of the way in which Christians prayed and worshipped. Athanasius argued that Christians were right to worship and adore Jesus Christ, because by doing so they were recognizing him for what he was – God incarnate.

The Arian controversy had to be settled somehow, if peace was to be established within the church. Debate came to center upon two terms as possible descriptions of the relation of the Father to the Son. The term *homoiousios*, "of like substance" or "of like being," was seen by many as representing a judicious compromise, allowing the proximity between Father and Son to be asserted without requiring any further speculation on the precise nature of their relation. However, the rival term *homoousios*, "of the same substance" or "of the same being," eventually gained the upper hand. Though differing by only one letter from the alternative term, it embodied a very different understanding of the relationship between Father and Son.

The Chalcedonian Definition

The Nicene Creed – or, more accurately, the Niceno-Constantinopolitan Creed – of 381 ended the Arian controversy by declaring that Christ was "of the same substance" with the Father. This affirmation has since widely become regarded as a benchmark of Christological orthodoxy within all the mainstream Christian churches, whether Protestant, Catholic or Orthodox.

The Chalcedonian Definition of the Identity of Jesus (451)

The Council of Chalcedon (451) laid down an understanding of the relation of the humanity and divinity of Jesus Christ which became normative for the Christian churches, both east and west. Notice how the Council is adamant that Christ must be accepted to be truly divine and truly human, without specifying precisely how this is to be understood. In other words, a number of Christological models are legitimated, providing they uphold this essential Christological affirmation.

> We all with one voice confess our Lord Jesus Christ to be one and the same Son, perfect in divinity and humanity, truly God and truly human, consisting of a rational soul and a body, being of one substance with the Father in relation to his divinity, and being of one substance with us in relation to his humanity, and is like us in all things apart from sin (Hebrews 4:15). He was begotten of the Father before time in relation to his divinity, and in these recent days was born from the Virgin Mary, the *Theotokos*, for us and for our salvation. In relation to the

STUDY PANEL 21

> ### Study Panel 21 Continued
>
> humanity he is one and the same Christ, the Son, the Lord, the Only-begotten, who is to be acknowledged in two natures, without confusion, without change, without division, and without separation. This distinction of natures is in no way abolished on account of this union, but rather the characteristic property of each nature is preserved, and concurring into one Person and one subsistence, not as if Christ were parted or divided into two persons, but remains one and the same Son and only-begotten God, Word, Lord, Jesus Christ; even as the Prophets from the beginning spoke concerning him, and our Lord Jesus Christ instructed us, and the Creed of the Fathers was handed down to us.

The classic Christian position is therefore summarized in the "doctrine of the two natures" – that is to say, that Jesus is perfectly divine and perfectly human. This view was definitively stated by the Council of Chalcedon (451). This laid down a controlling principle for classical Christology, which has been accepted as definitive within orthodox Christian theology ever since. The principle in question could be summarized as follows: provided that it is recognized that Jesus Christ is both truly divine and truly human, the precise manner in which this is articulated or explored is not of fundamental importance. Oxford patristic scholar Maurice Wiles (*The Making of Christian Doctrine*, Cambridge: Cambridge University Press, 1967, p. 106) summarized Chalcedon's aims as follows:

> On the one hand was the conviction that a saviour must be fully divine; on the other was the conviction that what is not assumed is not healed. Or, to put the matter in other words, the source of salvation must be God; the locus of salvation must be humanity. It is quite clear that these two principles often pulled in opposite directions. The Council of Chalcedon was the church's attempt to resolve, or perhaps rather to agree to live with, that tension. Indeed, to accept both principles as strongly as did the early church is already to accept the Chalcedonian faith.

Chalcedon simply states definitively what the first five centuries of Christian reflection on the New Testament had already established. It defines the point from which we start the recognition that, in the face of Christ, we see none other than God himself. That is a starting point, not an end. But we must be sure of our starting point, the place at which we begin, if the result is to be reliable. Chalcedon claims to have established that starting point, and whatever difficulties we may find with its turgid language and outdated expressions, the basic ideas which it lays down are clear and crucial, and are obviously a legitimate interpretation of the New Testament witness to Jesus Christ.

Chalcedon was content to reaffirm the "two natures" of Christ, without imposing a binding interpretation and it was wise to do so. Interpretations vary from one age to another, depending upon the time and place. Thus Platonism might be used to interpret the doctrine of the incarnation in third-century Alexandria, Aristotelianism in thirteenth-century Paris, and Hegelianism in nineteenth-century Berlin. In every case, a prevailing philosophical system is drawn upon to illuminate aspects of the doctrine. But philosophies go out of date, whereas the doctrine of the incarnation does not. The truth expressed by the doctrine – that God has entered into and made possible a transformation of our human existence – thus remains constant, whatever additional ideas or concepts may be used in explaining it. Christianity has thus avoided becoming enslaved to any one philosophy.

Chalcedon did not commit itself to any one philosophical system or outlook which would probably have been abandoned as outdated within centuries, and been an embarrassment to the church ever afterwards. Rather, it attempted to safeguard an essential fact, which could be interpreted in terms of philosophical ideas or concepts which might make sense at any particular point in history, provided these explanations do not deny or explain away any part of the fact. As a result, Christian theologians and apologists have enjoyed a considerable degree of liberty in defending and explaining this central Christian doctrine to different audiences throughout Christian history.

Every explanation of the person and work of Jesus Christ must, in the final analysis, be recognized to be inadequate, and Chalcedon merely stated with great clarity what the essential fact was which required explanation and interpretation: Jesus really is both God and a human being. To make this point absolutely clear, the Council used the Greek term *homoousios,* which is usually translated into English as "of one substance," or "of one being." Although this term was not itself biblical (a fact which caused some concern at the time), it was widely regarded as expressing some central biblical insights.

In part, it should be noted that Chalcedon's decision to insist upon the two natures of Christ, while accepting a plurality of interpretations regarding their relation, reflects the political situation of the period. At a time in which there was considerable disagreement within the church over the most reliable way of stating the "two natures of Christ," the Council was obliged to adopt a realistic approach, and give its weight to whatever consensus it could find. That consensus concerned the recognition that Christ was both divine and human, but not how the divine and human natures related to each other.

An important minority viewpoint must, however, be noted. Chalcedon did not succeed in establishing a consensus throughout the entire Christian world. A minority viewpoint became established during the sixth century, and is now generally known as *Monophysitism* – literally, the view that there is "only one nature" (Greek: *monos*, "only one," and *physis*, "nature") in Christ. The nature in question is understood to be divine, rather than human. The intricacies of this viewpoint lie beyond the scope of this volume; the reader should note that it remains normative within most Christian churches of the eastern Mediterranean world, including the Coptic, Armenian, Syrian, and Abyssinian churches.

The Work of Jesus

The Apostles' Creed is emphatic that Jesus was a real historical person, who lived and died. Jesus was a first-century Jew who lived in Palestine in the reign of Tiberius Caesar, and who was executed by crucifixion under Pontius Pilate. The Roman historian Tacitus refers to Christians deriving their name from "Christ, who was executed at the hands of the procurator Pontius Pilate in the reign of Tiberius." The Christian faith certainly presupposes that Jesus existed as a real historical figure, and that he was crucified. Christianity is, however, most emphatically not about the *mere facts* that Jesus existed and was crucified. As we have seen, the *interpretation* of his life and death is of critical importance. In the section which follows we shall look in particular at the interpretations of the death of Christ, which are sometimes referred to as "theories of the atonement."

Before exploring these, we may look at the phrase used by the creed in referring to the death of Jesus. According to the Creed, Jesus "descended to hell." This is the traditional translation of the Greek original; however, the Greek version of this statement is better translated as "descended to the place of the dead." What does this mean? For the New Testament writers, Christ was not raised "from death" (an abstract idea), but "from the dead" (Acts 2:24; Romans 1:4, Colossians 2:12). The Greek term literally means "out of those who are dead." In other words, Jesus shared the fate of all those who have died. Again, we find the same point being stressed: Jesus really was human, like us. His divinity does not compromise his humanity in this respect. Being God incarnate did not mean he was spared from tasting death. He did not merely seem to die; he really did die, and joined those who had died before him. This is a particularly important statement, as there are known to have been those in the early church who interpreted the suffering and death of Jesus as apparent rather than real.

Ignatius of Antioch on Docetism

Ignatius' letter to the Christians at Trallia, written several years before his martyrdom around 107, is an important witness to an early form of the Docetist heresy, which declared that Christ did not suffer in reality, but suffered only in appearance, and was thus not truly human. In this letter, Ignatius affirms that Christ really was a true human being, in nature as well as in appearance. Note that Ignatius in no way regards the affirmation of the full humanity of Jesus as in any way compromising his full divinity.

> So do not pay attention when anyone speaks to you apart from Jesus Christ, who was of the family of David, the child of Mary, who was truly born, who ate and drank, who was truly persecuted under Pontius Pilate, was truly crucified and truly died, in full view of heaven, earth and hell, and who was truly raised from the dead. It was his Father who raised him again, and it is him [i.e., the Father] who will likewise raise us in Jesus Christ, we who believe in him, apart from whom we have no true life. But if, as some godless people, that is, unbelievers, say, he suffered in mere appearance – being themselves mere appearances – why am I in bonds?

STUDY PANEL 22

We may now move on to consider the second major aspect of the Christian understanding of the importance of Jesus. The doctrine of the "work of Jesus" focuses on the issue of salvation. The Christian faith affirms that the death of Jesus on the cross is of central importance to the salvation of the world. It is therefore of importance to consider the Christian under-standing of the grounds and nature of salvation. For Christians, salvation is grounded in the death and resurrection of Jesus Christ. The New Testament affirmation of the necessity and uniqueness of the saving death of Christ has been taken up by Christian writers. Discussions of the meaning of the cross and resurrection of Christ are best grouped around four central controlling themes or images. It must be stressed that these are not mutually exclusive, and that it is normal to find Christian writers adopting approaches which incorporate elements drawn from more than one such category. Indeed, it can be argued that the views of most writers on this subject cannot be reduced to or confined within a single category, without doing serious violence to their ideas.

The Cross as a Sacrifice

The New Testament, drawing on Old Testament imagery and expectations, presents Christ's death upon the cross as a sacrifice. This approach, which is especially associated with the Letter to the Hebrews, presents Christ's sacrificial offering as an effective and perfect sacrifice, which was able to accomplish that which the sacrifices of the Old Testament were only able to intimate, rather than achieve. In particular, Paul's use of the Greek term *hilasterion* (Romans 3:25) points to a sacrificial interpretation of Christ's death.

This idea is developed subsequently within the Christian tradition. For example, in taking over the imagery of sacrifice, Augustine states that Christ "was made a sacrifice for sin, offering himself as a whole burnt offering on the cross of his passion." In order for humanity to be restored to God, the mediator must sacrifice himself; without this sacrifice, such restoration is an impossibility.

The sacrificial offering of Christ on the cross came to be linked especially with one aspect of the "threefold office of Christ." According to this typology, which dates from the middle of the sixteenth century, the work of Christ could be summarized under three "offices": prophet (by which Christ declares the will of God), priest (by which he makes sacrifice for sin), and king (by which he rules with authority over his people). The general acceptance of this taxonomy within Protestantism in the late sixteenth and seventeenth centuries led to a sacrificial understanding of Christ's death becoming of central importance within Protestant soteriologies.

Since the Enlightenment, however, there has been a subtle shift in the meaning of the term "sacrifice." A metaphorical extension of meaning of the term has come to be given priority over the original. Whereas the term originally referred to the ritual offering of slaughtered animals as a specifically religious action, the term increasingly came to mean heroic or costly action on the parts of individuals, especially the giving up of one's life, with no transcendent reference or expectation.

The use of sacrificial imagery has become noticeably less widespread since 1945, especially in German-language theology. It is highly likely that this relates directly to the rhetorical debasement of the term in secular contexts, especially in situations of national emergency. The secular use of the imagery of sacrifice, often degenerating to little more than slogan-mongering, is widely regarded as having tainted and compromised both the word and the concept. The frequent use of such phrases as "he sacrificed his life for King and country" in British circles during the First World War, and Adolf Hitler's extensive use of sacrificial imagery in justifying economic hardship and the loss of civil liberties as the price of German national revival in the late 1930s, served to render the term virtually unusable for many in Christian teaching and preaching, on account of its negative associations. Nevertheless, the idea continues to be of importance in modern Roman Catholic sacramental theology, which continues to regard the eucharist as a sacrifice, and to find in this image a rich source of theological imagery.

The Cross as Victory

The New Testament and early church laid considerable emphasis upon the victory gained by Christ over sin, death, and Satan through his cross and resurrection (see pp. 96–105). This theme of victory, often linked liturgically with the Easter celebrations, was of major importance within the western Christian theological tradition until the Enlightenment. The theme of "Christ the victor" brought together a series of themes, centering on the idea of a decisive victory over forces of evil and oppression.

The imagery of Jesus' victory over the devil proved to have enormous popular appeal. The medieval idea of "the harrowing of hell" bears witness to its power. According to this, after dying upon the cross, Christ descended to hell, and broke down its gates in order that the imprisoned souls might go free. The idea rested (rather tenuously, it has to be said) upon 1 Peter 3:18–22, which makes reference to Christ "preaching to the spirits in prison." The hymn "Ye choirs of New Jeruslem," written by Fulbert of Chartres, expresses this theme in two of its verses, picking up the theme of Christ as the "lion of Judah" (Revelation 5:5) defeating Satan, the serpent (Genesis 3:15):

> For Judah's lion bursts his chains
> Crushing the serpent's head;
> And cries aloud through death's domain
> To wake the imprisoned dead.
>
> Devouring depths of hell their prey
> At his command restore;
> His ransomed hosts pursue their way
> Where Jesus goes before.

A similar idea can be found in a fourteenth-century English mystery play, which describes the "harrowing of hell" in the following manner. "And when Christ was dead, his spirit went in haste to hell. And soon he broke down the strong gates that were wrongfully barred against him . . . He bound Satan fast with eternal bonds, and so shall Satan ever remain bound until the day of doom. He took with him Adam and Eve and others that were dear to him . . . all these he led out of hell and set in paradise."

Perhaps the most well-known portrayal of this powerful image familiar to modern readers is found in that most remarkable of religious allegories C. S. Lewis' *The Lion, The Witch and the Wardrobe.* The book tells the story of

Narnia, a land which is discovered by accident by four children rummaging around in an old wardrobe. In this work we encounter the White Witch, who keeps the land of Narnia covered in wintry snow. As we read on we realize that she rules Narnia not as a matter of right, but by stealth. The true ruler of the land is absent; in his absence the witch subjects the land to oppression. In the midst of this land of winter stands the witch's castle, within which many of the inhabitants of Narnia have been imprisoned as stone statues.

As the narrative moves on we discover that the rightful ruler of the land is Aslan, a lion. As Aslan advances into Narnia, winter gives way to spring, and the snow begins to melt. The witch realizes that her power is beginning to fade. In the fourteenth chapter of the book, Lewis describes the killing of Aslan, perhaps the most demonic episode ever to have found its way into a children's story. The forces of darkness and oppression seem to have won a terrible victory and yet, in that victory lies their defeat. Aslan surrenders himself to the forces of evil, and allows them to do their worst with him and by so doing, disarms them.

In the sixteenth chapter of this modern version of the "harrowing of hell," Lewis graphically describes how Aslan the lion of Judah, who has burst his chains breaks into the castle, breathes upon the statues, and restores them to life, before leading the liberated army through the shattered gates of the once great fortress to freedom. Hell has been harrowed. It has been despoiled, and its inhabitants liberated from its imprisonment.

The Cross and Forgiveness

A third approach centers on the idea of the death of Christ providing the basis by which God is enabled to forgive sin. This notion is traditionally associated with the eleventh-century writer Anselm of Canterbury. Anselm's emphasis falls upon the righteousness of God. God redeems humanity in a manner that is totally consistent with the divine quality of righteousness. In the course of his analysis he argues for both the necessity of the incarnation of the Son of God, and the saving potential of his death and resurrection. The complex argument can be summarized as follows:

1 God created humanity in a state of original righteousness, with the objective of bringing humanity to a state of eternal blessedness.
2 That state of eternal blessedness is contingent upon human obedience to God. However, through sin, humanity is unable to achieve this necessary obedience, which appears to frustrate God's purpose in creating humanity in the first place.
3 In that it is impossible for God's purposes to be frustrated, there must be some means by which the situation can be remedied. However, the

situation can only be remedied if a *satisfaction* is made for sin. In other words, something has to be done, by which the offense caused by human sin can be purged.

4　However, there is no way in which humanity can provide this necessary satisfaction. It lacks the resources which are needed. On the other hand, God possesses the resources needed to provide the required satisfaction.

5　Therefore a "God-man" would possess both the *ability* (as God) and the *obligation* (as a human being) to pay the required satisfaction. Therefore the incarnation takes place, in order that the required satisfaction may be made, and humanity redeemed.

In taking up Anselm's approach, later writers were able to place it on a more secure foundation by grounding it in the general principles of law. The sixteenth century was particularly appreciative of the importance of human law, and saw it as an appropriate model for God's forgiveness of human sin. Three main models came to be used at this time to understand the manner in which the forgiveness of human sins is related to the death of Christ.

1　*Representation*. Christ is here understood to be the covenant representative of humanity. Through faith, believers come to stand within the covenant between God and humanity. All that Christ has achieved through the cross is available on account of the covenant. Just as God entered into a covenant with his people Israel, so he has entered into a covenant with his church. Christ, by his obedience upon the cross, represents his covenant people, winning benefits for them as their representative. By coming to faith, individuals come to stand within the covenant, and thus share in all its benefits, won by Christ through his cross and resurrection – including the full and free forgiveness of our sins.

2　*Participation*. Through faith, believers participate in the risen Christ. They are "in Christ," to use Paul's famous phrase. They are caught up in him, and share in his risen life. As a result of this, they share in all the benefits won by Christ, through his obedience upon the cross. One of those benefits is the forgiveness of sins, in which they share through our faith. Participating in Christ thus entails the forgiveness of sins, and sharing in his righteousness. This idea is central to both Luther and Calvin's soteriology, as Luther's image of the marriage between Christ and the believer makes clear.

3　*Substitution*. Christ is here understood to be a substitute, the one who goes to the cross in our place. Sinners ought to have been crucified, on account of their sins. Christ is crucified in their place. God allows Christ to stand in our place, taking our guilt upon himself, so that his righteousness – won by obedience upon the cross – might become ours.

23

STUDY PANEL

George Herbert on the Death of Christ and Redemption

In the poem "Redemption," which forms part of the collection known as "The Temple," composed around 1633, the noted English poet George Herbert explores the associations of the term "redemption." Alluding to the Old Testament notion of "redeeming land," Herbert develops the idea of the death of Christ as the price by which God takes legitimate possession of a precious piece of land. While also exploring the idea of the shame and humility of the cross, Herbert is able to bring out the legal and financial dimensions of redemption.

> Having been tenant long to a rich Lord,
>   Not thriving, I resolved to be bold,
>   And make a suit unto him, to afford
> A new small-rented lease, and cancell th'old,
> In heaven at his manour I him sought:
>   They told me there, that he was lately gone
>   About some land, which he had dearly bought,
> Long since on earth, to take possession.
> I straight return'd, and knowing his great birth,
>   Sought him accordingly in great resorts;
>   In cities, theatres, gardens, parks, and courts:
> At length I heard a ragged noise and mirth
>   Of theeves and murderers: there I him espied,
>   Who straight, *Your suit is granted*, said, & died.

These themes are developed by the modern Swiss Protestant theologian Karl Barth. In writing of "The Judge Judged in Our Place," Barth argues that we can see God exercising his rightful judgment of sinful humanity. The cross exposes human delusions to self-sufficiency and autonomy of judgment, which Barth sees encapsulated in the story of Genesis 3: "the human being wants to be his own judge."

Yet alteration of the situation demands that its inherent wrongness be acknowledged. For Barth, the cross of Christ represents the locus, in which the righteous judge makes known his judgment of sinful humanity, and simultaneously takes that judgment upon himself.

> What took place is that the Son of God fulfilled the righteous judgement on us human beings by himself taking our place as a human being, and in our place undergoing the judgement under which we had passed . . . Because God willed to execute his judgement on us in his Son, it all took place in his person,

as *his* accusation and condemnation and destruction. He judged, and it was the judge who was judged, who allowed himself to be judged . . . Why did God become a human being? So that God as a human being might do and accomplish and achieve and complete all this for us wrongdoers, in order that in this way there might be brought about by him our reconciliation with him, and our conversion to him.

The Cross and Love

A central aspect of the New Testament understanding of the meaning of the cross relates to the demonstration of the love of God for humanity.

New Testament Affirmations of the Love of God in Jesus

"For God so loved the world that he gave his one and only Son, that whoever believes in him shall not perish but have eternal life" (John 3:16).

"God demonstrates his own love for us in this: While we were still sinners, Christ died for us" (Romans 5:8).

"I have been crucified with Christ and I no longer live, but Christ lives in me. The life I live in the body, I live by faith in the Son of God, who loved me and gave himself for me" (Galatians 2:20).

STUDY PANEL 24

Augustine of Hippo was but one of many patristic writers to stress that one of the motivations underlying the mission of Christ was the "demonstration of the love of God towards us." Perhaps the most important medieval statement of this emphasis can be found in the writings of Peter Abelard. It must be stressed that Abelard does not, as some of his interpreters suggest, reduce the meaning of the cross to a demonstration of the love of God. This is one among many components of Abelard's soteriology, which includes traditional ideas concerning Christ's death as a sacrifice for human sin. It is Abelard's emphasis upon the subjective impact of the cross that is distinctive.

For Abelard, "the purpose and cause of the incarnation was that Christ might illuminate the world by his wisdom, and excite it to love of himself." In this, Abelard restates the Augustinian idea of Christ's incarnation as a public demonstration of the extent of the love of God, with the intent of evoking a response of love from humanity. "The Son of God took our nature, and in it took upon himself to teach us by both word and example even to the point of death, thus binding us to himself through love."

This theme continues to be of central importance to Christian thinking about the meaning of the cross. The cross demonstrates and affirms the love of God for us. For Christians, the full wonder of the love of God for us can only be appreciated in the light of the cross of Jesus. According to the Christian tradition, God – though angered and grieved by our sin – comes to meet us where we are. Christians believe that Jesus was the embodiment of God, God incarnate, God willingly accepting the suffering, pain, and agony of the world in order to forgive and renew it. Jesus did not come to explain away, or to take away, suffering. He came to take it upon himself, to assume human suffering, and lend it dignity and meaning through his presence and sympathy. It is this which is the full-blooded meaning of the love of God, in the Christian understanding of the idea.

In contemplating the spectacle of Jesus dying on the cross, Christian tradition affirms that we see none other than God taking up the agony of the world which God created and loves. It is this which is the "love of God" in the full-blooded sense of the word. In its deepest sense, the love of God is that of someone who stoops down from heaven to enter into our fallen world, with all its agony and pain, culminating in the grim cross of Calvary.

STUDY PANEL 25

John Donne on the Love of God

The English poet John Donne (1571–1631) was noted for his "divine sonnets," in which he gave expression to some of the most fundamental Christian ideas and values. His reflections on the love of God are of especial interest. The poem stresses the extent of the love of God by focusing on the way in which this love was expressed in the coming and death of Jesus. Note especially the emphasis placed on the voluntary humiliation of Jesus.

> Wilt thou love God, as he thee? then digest
> My soul, this wholesome meditation,
> How God the Spirit, by angels waited on
> In heaven, doth make his temple in thy breast.
> The Father having begot a Son most blessed,
> And still begetting (for he ne'er begun)
> Hath deigned to choose thee by adoption,
> Coheir to his glory, and Sabbath's endless rest;
> And as a robbed man, which by search doth find

Study Panel 25 Continued

> His stol'n stuff sold, must lose or buy it again:
> The Son of glory came down, and was slain,
> Us whom he had made, and Satan stol'n, to unbind.
> T'was much, that man was made like God before,
> But, that God should be made like man, much more.

Christianity thus makes the astonishing assertion, which it bases upon the life, death and resurrection of Jesus Christ, that God is profoundly interested in us and concerned for us, despite our apparent indifference to God. We are special in the sight of God. In the midst of an immense and frightening universe, we are given meaning and significance by the realization that the God who called the world into being, who created us, also loves us and cares for us, coming down from heaven and going to the cross to prove the full extent of that love to a disbelieving and wondering world.

Charles Wesley on the Love of God in Christ

On 21 May 1738, Charles Wesley underwent a profound conversion experience through the ministry of the Moravian Peter Böhler. In this hymn, written a year after this experience, Wesley put into verse his understanding of the significance of the death of Christ for Christian believers. The first two verses, which are reproduced here, stress the way in which the love of God is shown in and through the death of Jesus.

> And can it be that I should gain
>   An int'rest in the Saviour's blood!
> Dy'd he for me? – who caus'd his pain?
>   For me? – who Him to Death pursued?
> Amazing love! How can it be
> That Thou, my God, shouldst die for me?
>
> 'Tis mystery all! th'Immortal dies!
>   Who can explore his strange Design?
> In vain the first-born Seraph tries
>   To sound the Depths of Love divine.
> 'Tis mercy all! Let earth adore;
> Let Angel Minds inquire no more.

STUDY PANEL 26

A final issue which must be addressed at this early stage concerns the chronology of salvation. Is salvation to be understood as something which has happened to the believer? Or is it something currently happening? Or is there an eschatological dimension to it – in other words, is there something which has yet to happen? The only answer to such questions which can be given on the basis of the New Testament is that salvation includes past, present, and future reference. Salvation is an exceptionally complex idea, embracing not simply a future event, but something which has happened in the past (Romans 8:24; 1 Corinthians 15:2), or which is taking place now (1 Corinthians 1:18). The Christian understanding of salvation thus presupposes that something *has* happened, that something *is now happening*, and that something further *will still happen* to believers. We shall return to this point when we consider the teachings of the Christian creeds about eternal life and the hope of heaven.

With this, we bring our analysis of the founder of Christianity to an end. It will be clear that it totally fails to do justice to the Christian understanding of Jesus to refer to him simply as a "teacher." The World Council of Churches, founded in 1948, adopted as its basis the following affirmation: "The World Council of Churches is a fellowship of Churches which accept our Lord Jesus Christ as God and Savior." This basic assertion identifies the critically important affirmations to be the recognition of Jesus as "God" and as "Savior." This can be seen as an excellent summary of the basic Christian understanding of the identity of Jesus.

Yet although Christianity is strongly Jesus-centered and Jesus-focused, it affirms other ideas as well. In what follows, we shall explore some more of the basic ideas of the Christian faith.

STUDY QUESTIONS

1 John's gospel refers to Jesus as "the word (Greek: *logos*)." What does this suggest?
2 What issues were at stake in the Arian debate?
3 What did Chalcedon intend us to understand by affirming that Jesus is both divine and human?
4 In what way is the death of Jesus a sacrifice?
5 How can the death and resurrection of Jesus be described as a "victory"?

The Teachings of Christianity

In Part I of this work we explored the basic Christian understandings of the identity and significance of the Jesus Christ, and the nature and importance of the Bible as a source of our knowledge of Jesus, and of the basic teachings of the Christian faith. Some of those teachings center on Jesus himself, and have already been explored. However, there remains a significant body of Christian teachings which need to be examined. In this second part, we shall consider some further teachings of the Christian faith. However, it is appropriate to begin by considering the nature of the "creeds" in Christian thought.

7

The Creeds of Christianity

The second part of this volume is devoted to an explanation of the basic teachings of Christianity. It must be appreciated from the outset that limitations on space make it impossible to give any more than a sketch of the basic themes of Christian doctrine. To do justice to the richness, complexity, and occasional diversity of the teachings of Christianity would require a major volume in its own right. All that I can hope to achieve in this volume is a sketch map of a complex terrain. Readers who wish to explore this fascinating landscape in more detail are referred to the major works dealing with Christian theology noted at the end of this book. We shall use the Apostles' Creed as the basic structure for our exploration of Christian doctrine.

The Apostles' Creed

The document known as the "Apostles' Creed" is widely used in the western church as a succinct summary of the leading themes of the Christian faith. Its historical evolution is complex, with its origins lying in declarations of faith which were required of those who wanted to be baptized. The twelve individual statements of this Creed, which seems to have assumed its final form in the eighth century, are traditionally ascribed to individual apostles, although there is no historical justification for this belief. During the twentieth century, the Apostle's Creed has become widely accepted by most churches, eastern and western, as a binding statement of Christian faith despite the fact that

Study Panel 27 Continued

its statements concerning the "descent into hell" and the "communion of saints" (here printed within brackets) are not found in eastern versions of the work.

1   I believe in God, the Father almighty, creator of the heavens and earth;
2   and in Jesus Christ, his only Son, our Lord;
3   who was conceived by the Holy Spirit and born of the Virgin Mary;
4   suffered under Pontius Pilate, was crucified, dead and buried; [he descended to hell;]
5   on the third day he was raised from the dead;
6   he ascended into the heavens, and sits at the right hand of God the Father almighty;
7   from where he will come to judge the living and the dead.
8   I believe in the Holy Spirit;
9   in the holy catholic church; [the communion of saints;]
10   the forgiveness of sins;
11   the resurrection of the body;
12   and eternal life.

The Nature of Creeds

Many words in the English language owe their origins to Latin. This is especially true of words relating to Christianity. For more than a thousand years, Latin was the language of educated Christians. For centuries, Christians in western Europe knew the Creed only in Latin. The opening words of the creed in Latin are *credo in Deum*, "I believe in God." Many will be familiar with these Latin words, or some very similar to them, from the choral works of composers such as Bach, Haydn, Mozart, or Beethoven. The English word "creed" derives from that word *credo*. As the word suggests, it is a statement of faith. It is an attempt to summarize the main points of what Christians believe. It is not exhaustive; nor is it meant to be. Cyril of Jerusalem is one of many early Christian writers to stress that creeds are simply convenient summaries of faith, based on the Bible.

Cyril of Jerusalem on the Role of Creeds

In a series of 24 lectures given in Jerusalem around the year 350 to those who were about to be baptized, Cyril explains the various aspects of the Christian faith and its practices. In the section which follows he explains the origins and role of creeds, noting their importance as summaries of Scripture. The creed, he argues, is basically a summary of the leading ideas and themes of the Old and New Testaments.

> This synthesis of faith was not made to be agreeable to human opinions, but to present the one teaching of the faith in its totality, in which what is of greatest importance is gathered together from all the Scriptures. And just as a mustard seed contains a great number of branches in its tiny grain, so also this summary of faith brings together in a few words the entire knowledge of the true religion which is contained in the Old and New Testaments.

STUDY PANEL 28

The origins of the creed may be found within the New Testament itself. There are frequent calls to be baptized "in the name of Jesus Christ" (Acts 2:28; 8:12; 10:48), or "in the name of the Lord Jesus" (Acts 8:16, 19:5). In its simplest form, the earliest Christian creed seems to have been simply "Jesus is Lord!" (Romans 10:9; 1 Corinthians 12:3; 2 Corinthians 4:5; Philippians 2:11). Anyone who made this declaration was regarded as being a Christian. The Christian is one who "receives Jesus Christ as Lord" (Colossians 2:16). This involves two related claims. In the first place, it declares the believers loyalty and commitment to Jesus Christ. As we shall see, for someone to confess that "Jesus Christ is Lord" is to declare that Jesus is the Lord of his or her life. To recognize that Jesus is Lord is to seek to do his will. The refusal of the first Christians to worship the Roman emperor reflects this belief: you can only serve one master, and for the Christian that is, and must be, none other than Jesus himself. In the second place, "Jesus is Lord" declares certain things about Jesus, especially his relation to God.

As time went on, however, it became necessary to explain what Christians believed in more detail. The full implications of declaring that "Jesus is Lord" needed to be explained and explored in more detail. What did Christians believe about God? about Jesus? about the Holy Spirit? By the fourth century the Apostles' Creed as we now know it had assumed a more or less fixed form; what variations did exist were slight, and were finally eliminated in the seventh century. The Apostles' Creed is an excellent summary of the apostolic teaching concerning the gospel, even though it was not actually written by the apostles.

When someone became a Christian and wished to join the early church, great emphasis was placed on the importance of his or her baptism. During the period of Lent (the period from Ash Wednesday to Easter), those who had recently come to faith were given instruction in Christian beliefs. They were obliged to undergo an extended period of instruction in the Christian faith, under the guidance of a skilled teacher, usually the local bishop. During this period they were known as "catechumens" (from the Greek word for "instruction"). Finally, when they had mastered the basics of faith they would recite the creed together, as a corporate witness to the faith in which they believed – and which they now understood. Faith had been reinforced with understanding. They would then be baptized with great ceremony and joy on Easter Day itself, as the church celebrated the resurrection of its Lord and Savior. In this way the significance of the baptism of the believer could be fully appreciated: he or she had passed from death to life (Romans 6:3–10). Baptism was a public demonstration of the believer's death to the world, and being born to new life in Jesus Christ.

A central part of the baptism celebration was the public declaration of faith by each candidate. Anyone who wished to be baptized had to declare publicly his faith in Jesus Christ. At many times in the history of the Christian church, this was exceptionally dangerous: to admit to being a Christian could mean imprisonment, victimization, suffering, or even death. (The English word "martyr," incidentally, derives from the Greek word meaning "witness." To be a martyr was seen as the finest witness possible to Jesus Christ and his gospel.) New believers did not, however, merely recite the creed; they were also asked, as individuals, whether they personally believed in the gospel, before they could be baptized. Here is part of a sermon preached in the fourth century to those who had just been baptized, in which this practice is described. (Incidentally, note the important references to Romans 6:3–4; those who have died to their past have risen to new life in Christ.)

> You were asked, "Do you believe in God the father almighty?" You replied, "I believe," and were immersed, that is, were buried. Again, you were asked, "Do you believe in our Lord Jesus Christ and his cross?" You replied, "I believe," and were immersed. Thus you were buried with Christ, for he who is buried with Christ rises again with him. A third time you were asked, "Do you believe in the Holy Spirit?" You replied, "I believe," and were immersed for a third time. Your three-fold confession thus wiped out the many sins of your previous existence.

Historically, then, the creed was the profession of faith made by converts at their baptism, and formed the basis of their instruction.

The Apostles' Creed, however, was not the only creed to come into existence in the period of the early church. Two major controversies in the early church made it necessary to be more precise about certain matters of doctrine. The first controversy (the Arian controversy of the fourth century) centered on the relationship of Jesus and God. In order to avoid inadequate understandings of the relation of the Father and Son, the Council of Chalcedon (451 AD) endorsed a creed now generally known as the "Nicene Creed." This creed, roughly twice as long as the Apostles' Creed, begins with the words "We believe in one God." In its efforts to insist upon the reality of the divinity of Jesus Christ, this creed speaks of Jesus as "being of one substance with the Father." A second major controversy centered on the doctrine of the Trinity. In order to avoid inadequate understandings of the relation of the Father, Son and Spirit, the "Athanasian Creed" was drawn up. This creed, which opens with the words "Whoever wishes to be saved . . .", is by far the longest of the three creeds, and is nowadays rarely used in any form of public worship.

Our attention in this chapter, however, concerns the Apostles' Creed, which is the oldest and simplest creed of the church. All Christian churches, both eastern and western, catholic and evangelical, recognize its authority and its importance as a standard of doctrine. It is a central element of the common Christian heritage, and an affirmation of the basic beliefs which unite Christians throughout the world and across the centuries. For this reason, it will serve as the basis for an exposition of the basic features of Christian teaching in this work.

The Nature of Faith

The opening words of the Apostles' Creed are: "I believe." Clearly, it is of importance to establish what this opening affirmation means. What are the implications of "believing in God"? What are we to understand by "faith"?

Since the time of the Enlightenment, the word "faith" has come to mean something like "a lower form of knowledge." Faith is here understood to mean "partial knowledge," characterized by a degree of uncertainty, and based upon either a lack of evidence, or evidence which is inadequate to convince fully. Thus the eighteenth-century German philosopher Immanuel Kant argued that faith is basically a belief which is held on grounds that are subjectively adequate, but objectively inadequate. Faith is thus seen as a firm commitment to a belief which is not adequately justified on the basis of the evidence available.

Although this understanding of faith may be adequate for many purposes, it is seriously inadequate for the purposes of Christian theology. Faith, as understood within the Christian tradition, has both epistemological and soteriological aspects; that is, it concerns how things (especially things about

God) may be known, and also how salvation may be grasped. For example, Luther's fundamental doctrine of justification by faith alone (see p. 153) simply cannot be understood if faith is understood to mean "a belief which goes beyond the evidence available."

To explore this point further, we may consider these two aspects of faith in more detail. The cognitive or epistemological aspects of faith are best discussed with reference to the works of Thomas Aquinas, while the soteriological aspects of faith are best brought out in the early writings of Martin Luther.

Faith and Knowledge

Aquinas adopts a strongly intellectualist approach to faith, treating it as something which is midway between knowledge (*scientia*) and opinion. For Aquinas, *scientia* has the sense of "something which is self-evidently true," or "something which can be demonstrated to be derived from something which is self-evidently true." In the case of *scientia*, truth compels assent on the part of the human intellect either because it is self-evidently correct, or because it is supported by such powerfully persuasive logical arguments that no rational mind could fail to be convinced. In the case of faith, however, the evidence is not sufficient to compel the human intellect to accept it.

Faith accepts as true the articles of the Christian faith, as they are summarized, for example, in the creeds. The object of faith is propositions about God, or about the Christian faith in general. To "have faith" is to accept these articles of faith as true, even though they cannot be demonstrated to be so beyond doubt, on the basis of the evidence available. Aquinas insists upon the rationality of the Christian faith. In other words, he stresses that the contents of the Christian faith can be shown to be consistent with human reason. His arguments for the existence of God (the "Five Ways": see pp. 181–2) are basically an attempt to show that the Christian belief in God is consistent with rational reflection on the world of human experience. Nevertheless, Aquinas is also concerned to insist that Christian faith and theology are ultimately a response to something which lies beyond human reason – divine revelation.

The commonsense understanding of faith, as a lower form of knowledge, thus seems to be well grounded in the writings of Thomas Aquinas. It has had a profound impact upon the philosophy of religion, as well as upon popular understandings of the nature of Christian faith. For example, the popular understanding of the first statement of the creed, "I believe in God," is little more than "I believe that there is a god." Yet with the sixteenth-century Reformation, there came a sustained attempt to rediscover aspects of the biblical understanding of the nature of faith, which had become obscured by the scholastic concern for right knowledge of God. We can explore this by considering Luther's emphasis upon the soteriological aspects of faith.

Faith and Salvation

The most significant contribution to the classic evangelical understanding of faith was unquestionably made by Martin Luther. Luther's doctrine of justification by faith alone made faith, rightly understood, the cornerstone of his spirituality and theology. Luther's fundamental point is that "the Fall" (Genesis 1–3) is first and foremost a fall from faith. Faith is the right relationship with God (cf. Genesis 15:6). To have faith is to live as God intends us to live. Luther's notion of faith has three basic elements, which we shall explore in what follows.

1   *Faith is not simply historical knowledge.* Luther argues that a faith which is content to believe in the historical reliability of the gospels is not a saving faith. Sinners are perfectly capable of trusting in the historical details of the gospels; but these facts of themselves are not adequate for true Christian faith. Saving faith concerns believing and trusting that Christ was born for us personally, and has accomplished for us the work of salvation.

2   *Faith includes an element of trust.* The notion of trust is prominent in the Reformation conception of faith, as a nautical analogy used by Luther indicates. "Everything depends upon faith. The person who does not have faith is like someone who has to cross the sea, but is so frightened that he does not trust the ship. And so he stays where he is, and is never saved, because he will not get on board and cross over." Faith is not merely believing that something is true; it is being prepared to act upon that belief, and relying upon it. To use Luther's analogy: faith is not simply about believing that a ship exists – it is about stepping into it, and entrusting ourselves to it.

But what are we being asked to trust? Are we being asked simply to have faith in faith? The question could perhaps be phrased more accurately: *who* are we being asked to trust? For Luther, the answer was unequivocal: faith is about being prepared to put one's trust in the promises of God, and the integrity and faithfulness of the God who made those promises. Faith is only as strong as the one in whom we believe and trust. The efficacy of faith does not rest upon the intensity with which we believe, but in the reliability of the one in whom we believe. Trust is not, however, an occasional attitude. For Luther, it is an undeviating trusting outlook upon life, a constant stance of conviction of the trustworthiness of the promises of God.

3 *Faith unites the believer to Christ.* Luther states this principle clearly in his 1520 writing, *The Liberty of a Christian*, in which he sets out the nature of the relationship between Jesus and the believer as follows:

> Faith unites the soul with Christ as a bride is united with her bridegroom. As Paul teaches us, Christ and the soul become one flesh by this mystery (Ephesians 5:31–2). And if they are one flesh, and if the marriage is for real – indeed, it is the most perfect of all marriages, and human marriages are poor examples of this one true marriage – then it follows that everything that they have is held in common, whether good or evil. So the believer can boast of and glory of whatever Christ possesses, as though it were his or her own; and whatever the believer has, Christ claims as his own. Let us see how this works out, and see how it benefits us. Christ is full of grace, life and salvation. The human soul is full of sin, death and damnation. Now let faith come between them. Sin, death and damnation will be Christ's. And grace, life and salvation will be the believer's.

Faith, then, is not assent to an abstract set of doctrines. Rather, it is a "wedding ring" (Luther), pointing to mutual commitment and union between Christ and the believer. It is the response of the whole person of the believer to God, which leads in turn to the real and personal presence of Christ in the believer. Faith makes both Christ and his benefits – such as forgiveness, justification, and hope – available to the believer.

Christianity and Other Religions

A final question which needs to be considerered here is the Christian understanding of the relationship between Christianity and other religions. This question has become of particular importance within the modern western world, which is acutely aware of a plurality of cultures within its midst. As the British theologian Lesslie Newbigin remarks:

> It has become a commonplace to say that we live in a pluralist society – not merely a society which is in fact plural in the variety of cultures, religions and lifestyles which is embraces, but pluralist in the sense that this plurality is celebrated as things to be approved and cherished.

Newbigin, who spent a significant part of his career working in the Church of South India, here makes an important distinction between pluralism as a fact of life, and pluralism as an ideology – that is, the belief that pluralism is to be encouraged and desired, and that normative claims to truth are to be censured as imperialist and divisive (an important aspect of the postmodern worldview). Our concern here is with the former.

So how does Christianity relate to other religious traditions? The question is not modern; it has been asked throughout Christian history. Initially the question focused on Christianity's relationship with Judaism, from whose matrix it emerged in the period 30–60 AD (see pp. 235–8). And as Christianity expanded, it encountered other religious beliefs and practices, such as classical paganism. The Acts of the Apostles often relates incidents illustrating the tensions between Christianity and classic pagan culture. As Christianity became established in India in the fifth century it encountered the diverse native Indian cultural movements which western scholars of religion have misleadingly grouped together, and termed "Hinduism." Arab Christianity has long learned to co-exist with Islam in the eastern Mediterranean.

In the modern period the question of the relation of Christianity has assumed a new importance in western academic theology, partly on account of the rise of multiculturalism in western society. As will become clear, three main approaches have gained currency. However, it will be helpful to begin by considering the idea of "religion" itself.

A naïve view of religion might be that it is an outlook on life which believes in, or worships, a Supreme Being. This outlook, characteristic of Deism and Enlightenment rationalism, is easily shown to be inadequate. Buddhism is classified as a religion by most people; yet here a belief in some supreme being is conspicuously absent. The same problem persists, no matter what definition of "religion" is offered. No unambiguously common features can be found among the religions, in matters of faith or practice. Thus Edward Conze, the great scholar of Buddhism, recalled that he "once read through a collection of the lives of Roman Catholic saints, and there was not one of whom a Buddhist could fully approve . . . They were bad Buddhists though good Christians."

There is a growing consensus that it is seriously misleading to regard the various religious traditions of the world as variations on a single theme. "There is no single essence, no one content of enlightenment or revelation, no one way of emancipation or liberation, to be found in all that plurality" (David Tracy). John B. Cobb Jr. also notes the enormous difficulties confronting anyone wishing to argue that there is an "essence of religion": "Arguments about what religion truly is are pointless. There is no such thing as religion. There are only traditions, movements, communities, peoples, beliefs, and practices that have features that are associated by many people with what they mean by religion."

Cobb also stresses that the assumption that religion has an essence has bedevilled and seriously misled recent discussion of the relation of the religious traditions of the world. For example, he points out that both Buddhism and Confucianism have "religious" elements – but that does not necessarily mean that they can be categorized as "religions." Many "religions" are, he argues, better understood as cultural movements with religious components.

The idea of some universal notion of religion, of which individual religions are subsets, appears to have emerged at the time of the Enlightenment. To use a biological analogy, the assumption that there is a genus of religion, of which individual religions are species, is a very western idea, without any real parallel outside western culture – except on the part of those who have been educated in the west, and uncritically absorbed its presuppositions.

What, then, of Christian approaches to understanding the relation between Christianity and other religious traditions? In what way can such traditions be understood, within the context of the Christian belief in the universal saving will of God, made known through Jesus Christ? It must be stressed that Christian theology is concerned with evaluating other religious traditions from the perspective of Christianity itself. Such reflection is not addressed to, or intended to gain approval from, members of other religious traditions, or their secular observers.

Two main approaches can be identified: particularism, which holds that only those who hear and respond to the Christian gospel may be saved; and inclusivism, which argues that, although Christianity represents the normative revelation of God, salvation is nonetheless possible for those who belong to other religious traditions. A third approach, usually referred to as "pluralism," holds that all the religious traditions of humanity are equally valid paths to the same core of religious reality. This position is not typical of historical Christianity, and is often regarded as a culturally-accommodated response to western pluralist culture.

The most significant exponent of a pluralist approach to religious traditions is John Hick (b. 1922). In his *God and the Universe of Faiths* (1973), Hick argued for a need to move away from a Christ-centered to a God-centered approach. Describing this change as a "Copernican Revolution," Hick declared that it was necessary to move away from "the dogma that Christianity is at the centre to the realization that it is *God* who is at the centre, and that all religions . . . including our own, serve and revolve around him." Developing this approach, Hick suggests that the aspect of God's nature of central importance to the question of other faiths was his universal saving will. If God wishes everyone to be saved, it is inconceivable that God should be revealed in such a way that only a small portion of humanity could be saved. In fact, as we shall see, this is not a necessary feature of either particularist or inclusivist approaches. However, Hick draws the conclusion that it is necessary to recognize that all religions lead to the same God. Christians have no special access to God, who is universally available through all religious traditions.

Hick's suggestion is not without its problems. For example, it is fairly clear that the religious traditions of the world are radically different in their beliefs and practices. Hick deals with this point by suggesting that such differences must be interpreted in terms of a "both–and" rather than an "either–or." They should be understood as complementary, rather than contradictory, insights into the one divine reality. This reality lies at the heart of all the religions; yet "their differing experiences of that reality, interacting over the centuries with the different thought-forms of different cultures, have led to increasing differentiation and contrasting elaboration." (This idea is very similar to the "universal rational religion of nature," propounded by Deist writers, which became corrupted through time.) Equally, Hick has difficulties with those non-theistic religious traditions, such as Advaitin Hinduism or Theravada Buddhism, which have no place for a god.

These difficulties relate to observed features of religious traditions. In other words, the beliefs of non-Christian religions make it difficult to accept that they are all speaking of the same God. But a more fundamental theological worry remains: is Hick actually talking about the Christian God at all? A central Christian conviction – that God is revealed definitively in Jesus Christ – has to be set to one side to allow Hick to proceed. Hick argues that he is merely adopting a theocentric, rather than a Christocentric approach. Yet the Christian insistence that God is known normatively through Christ (see pp. 116–19) implies that authentically Christian knowledge of God is derived through Christ. For a number of critics, Hick's desertion of Christ as a reference-point means abandoning any claim to speak from a Christian perspective.

Traditional Christianity is strongly resistant to the homogenizing agenda of religious pluralists, not least on account of its high Christology. The suggestion that all religions are more or less talking about vaguely the same "God" finds itself in difficulty in relation to certain essentially Christian ideas – most notably, the doctrines of the incarnation and the Trinity (see pp. 197–200). For example, if God is Christ-like, as the doctrine of the divinity of Christ affirms in uncompromising terms, then the historical figure of Jesus, along with the witness to him in Scripture, becomes of foundational importance to Christianity. Many pluralists thus find themselves rejecting a series of central Christian teachings – such as that of the divinity and the resurrection of Jesus, and the doctrine of the Trinity. This strongly reductionist approach to Christianity is regarded with distaste by many Christians, who feel that serious liberties are being taken with their faith to serve the notion that all religions are saying the same thing.

In what follows, then, we shall explore the two main lines of approach found within the Christian tradition in relation to other religions.

The Particularist Approach

Perhaps the most influential statement of this position may be found in the writings of Hendrik Kraemer (1888–1965), especially his *Christian Message in a Non-Christian World* (1938). Kraemer emphasized that "God has revealed *the* Way and *the* Truth and *the* Life in Jesus Christ, and wills this to be known throughout the world." This revelation is absolutely distinctive, and exists in a category of its own, and cannot be set alongside the ideas of revelation found in other religious traditions.

At this point, a certain breadth of opinion can be discerned within this approach. Kraemer himself seems to suggest that there is real knowledge of God outside Christ when he speaks of God shining through "in a broken, troubled way, in reason, in nature and in history." The question is whether such knowledge is only available through Christ, or whether Christ provides the only framework by which such knowledge may be discerned and interpreted elsewhere.

Some particularists (such as Karl Barth) adopt the position that there is no knowledge of God to be had apart from Christ; others (such as Kraemer) allow that God reveals himself in many ways and places – but insist that this revelation can only be interpreted correctly, and known for what it really is, in the light of the definitive revelation of God in Christ. (There are important parallels here with the debate over natural and revealed knowledge of God: see pp. 165–8.)

What, then, of those who have not heard the gospel of Christ? What happens to them? Are not particularists denying salvation to those who have not heard of Christ – or, who having heard of him, choose to reject him? This criticism is frequently leveled against particularism by its critics, especially from a pluralist perspective. Thus John Hick, arguing from a pluralist perspective, suggests that the doctrine that salvation is only possible through Christ is inconsistent with belief in the universal saving will of God. That this is not, in fact, the case is easily demonstrated by considering the view of Karl Barth, easily the most sophisticated of twentieth-century defenders of this position.

Barth declares that salvation is only possible through Christ. He nevertheless insists on the ultimate eschatological victory of grace over unbelief – that is, at the end of history. Eventually, God's grace will triumph completely, and all will come to faith in Christ. This is the only way to salvation — but it is a way that, through the grace of God, is effective for all. For Barth, the particularity of God's revelation through Christ is not contradicted by the universality of salvation.

In closing this brief discussion of particularism it should be noted that a number of works published in the 1980s termed this type of approach as "exclusivism." This term has now been generally abandoned, mainly because it is considered to be polemical. The approach is now generally described as "particularism," on account of its affirmation of the particular and distinctive features of the Christian faith.

The Inclusivist Approach

The most significant advocate of this model is the leading Jesuit writer Karl Rahner (1904–84). In the fifth volume of his *Theological Investigations*, Rahner develops four theses, setting out the view, not merely that individual non-Christians may be saved, but that the non-Christian religious traditions in general may have access to the saving grace of God in Christ.

1 Christianity is the absolute religion, founded on the unique event of the self-revelation of God in Christ. But this revelation took place at a specific point in history. Those who lived before this point, or who have yet to hear about this event, would thus seem to be excluded from salvation – which is contrary to the saving will of God.
2 For this reason, despite their errors and shortcomings, non-Christian religious traditions are valid and capable of mediating the saving grace of God, until the gospel is made known to their members. After the gospel has been proclaimed to the adherents of such non-Christian religious traditions, they are no longer legitimate, from the standpoint of Christian theology.
3 The faithful adherent of a non-Christian religious tradition is thus to be regarded as an "anonymous Christian."
4 Other religious traditions will not be displaced by Christianity. Religious pluralism will continue to be a feature of human existence.

We may explore the first three theses in more detail. It will be clear that Rahner strongly affirms the principle that salvation may only be had through Jesus, as he is interpreted by the Christian tradition. "Christianity understands itself as the absolute religion, intended for all people, which cannot recognize any other religion beside itself as of equal right." Yet Rahner supplements this with an emphasis upon the universal saving will of God: God wishes that all shall be saved, even though not all know Christ. "Somehow all people must be able to be members of the church."

For this reason, Rahner argues that saving grace must be available outside the bounds of the church – and hence in other religious traditions. He vigorously opposes those who adopt too-neat solutions, insisting that either a religious tradition comes from God or that it is an inauthentic and purely human invention. Where Kraemer argues that non-Christian religious traditions were little more than self-justifying human constructions, Rahner argues that such traditions may well include elements of truth.

Rahner justifies this suggestion by considering the relation between the Old and New Testaments. Although the Old Testament, strictly speaking, represents the outlook of a non-Christian religion (Judaism), Christians are able to read it and discern within it elements which continue to be valid. The Old Testament is evaluated in the light of the New, and as a result, certain practices (such as food laws) are discarded as unacceptable, while others are retained (such as the moral law). The same approach can and should, Rahner argues, be adopted in the case of other religions.

The saving grace of God is thus available through non-Christian religious traditions, despite their shortcomings. Many of their adherents, Rahner argues, have thus accepted that grace, without being fully aware of what it is. It is for this reason that Rahner introduces the term "anonymous Christians," to refer to those who have experienced divine grace without necessarily knowing it. This term has been heavily criticized. For example, John Hick has suggested that it is paternalist, offering "honorary status granted unilaterally to people who have not expressed any desire for it." Nevertheless, Rahner's intention is to allow for the real effects of divine grace in the lives of those who belong to non-Christian traditions. Full access to truth about God (as it is understood within the Christian tradition) is not a necessary precondition for access to the saving grace of God.

Rahner does not allow that Christianity and other religious traditions may be treated as equal, or that they are particular instances of a common encounter with God. For Rahner, Christianity and Christ have an exclusive status, denied to other religious traditions. The question is: can other religious traditions give access to the same saving grace as that offered by Christianity? Rahner's approach allows him to suggest that the beliefs of non-Christian religious traditions are not necessarily true, while allowing that they may, nevertheless, mediate the grace of God by the lifestyles which they evoke – such as a selfless love of one's neighbor.

A somewhat different approach is associated with the Second Vatican Council. In its decree on other faiths (*Nostra Aetate*, 28 October 1965), the Council followed Rahner in affirming that rays of divine truth were indeed to be found in other religions. However, where Rahner allowed other faiths to have soteriological potential, the Council maintained the distinctiveness of the Christian faith at this point.

> The Catholic Church rejects nothing of what is true and holy in these religions. She has a high regard for the manner of life and conduct, the precepts and doctrines which, although differing in many ways from her own teaching, nevertheless often reflect a ray of that truth which enlightens all men. Yet she proclaims and is in duty bound to proclaim without fail, Christ

who is the way, the truth and the life (John 14:6). In him, in whom God reconciled all things to himself (2 Corinthians 5:18–19), men find the fullness of their religious life.

The distinction between Rahner and Vatican II can be summarized as follows, using some theological jargon. Rahner is both revelationally and soteriologically inclusive; Vatican II tends to be revelationally inclusive, yet soteriologically particularist.

Having considered some of the basic questions which relate to the nature of Christian faith, we may now turn to consider some Christian teachings. We have already explored the Christian understanding of the identity and significance of Jesus in some detail. The discussion which follows will introduce some new themes of importance, focusing on the question of how Christians understand their beliefs to be grounded. Where do the teachings of Christianity come from? On what are they based? Are they just human ideas? Or do they rest on and derive from something more fundamental? We shall explore such questions in what follows.

1 Why did the Christian church start developing and using Creeds?
2 You will find it helpful to learn the Apostles' Creed. It provides you with a neat summary of some of the central themes of Christianity.
3 What do Christians understand by "faith"?
4 What is the difference between the two following statements: "I believe that there is a god"; "I believe in God"?
5 Outline the two main Christian approaches to other religions.

STUDY QUESTIONS

8

CHAPTER

The Sources of Christian Teaching

On what are the distinctive ideas of Christianity based? It must be stressed that Christians are offended by attempts on the part of some individuals, heavily influenced by the social sciences, to argue that Christianity is a purely sociological phenomenon. For Christians, their faith represents a response to something which has its origins outside them. This is the basic idea of "revelation," which designates the central Christian belief that unaided human reason cannot fully grasp the identity and character of God. We shall explore the importance of this idea in Christian theology presently.

However, a word has been used which needs explanation. What is "theology"? It is appropriate at this point to introduce the technical term "theology," which is often used to refer to the systematic study of the ideas of the Christian faith.

Introducing "Theology"

The word "theology" derives from the Greek word for "God" (*theos*), and can be understood as "the study of God" in much the same way as biology is the study of life (Greek: *bios*) and pharmacology is the study of drugs (Greek: *pharmakon*). The word is potentially a little misleading, in that theology is about more than just the Christian understanding of *God* – it embraces every aspect of Christian teaching, including but extending beyond the Christian doctrine of God. To talk about "Christian theology" is to talk about the teachings of the Christian faith, and the sources on which they are based. In chapter 9 we shall consider some of those teachings; our attention in the present chapter focuses on the sources on which they are based.

Christian theology, like most disciplines, draws upon a number of sources. There has been considerable discussion within the Christian tradition concerning the identity of these sources, and their relative importance for theological analysis. The present chapter aims to explore the identity of these sources, and provide an assessment of their potential for constructive theology. Broadly speaking, three main sources have been acknowledged within the Christian tradition:

1 The Bible
2 Reason
3 Tradition

Each of these sources has a distinct contribution to make within the discipline of theology, and will be considered in detail at the appropriate point in our discussion. We begin, however, by considering an idea which is of fundamental importance to Christian theology – that of revelation.

The Concept of Revelation

A central theme of Christian theology down the ages has been that human attempts to discern fully the nature and purposes of God are ultimately unsuccessful. Although a natural knowledge of God is generally held to be possible (the early writings of Karl Barth being a notable exception to this consensus), this is limited both in scope and depth. The idea of "revelation" expresses the basic Christian belief that we need to be "told what God is like" (Eberhard Jüngel).

The 1960s saw a major upheaval in Christian theology, with many traditional ideas being challenged and redefined. One such challenge was to the notion of revelation. Two issues emerged, each of which seemed to call into doubt the traditional Christian understanding of revelation. In the first place, some radical writers suggested that the modern interest in revelation was not due to the biblical material itself, but to the prominence of epistemological issues in modern philosophy. The prominence of questions concerning "right knowledge" in, for example, the philosophy of science had been improperly transferred to theology. The Bible, it was argued, was concerned with salvation, not knowledge. The dominant question in the New Testament was "What must I do to be saved?", not "What must I know?" In response to this it was pointed out that the biblical conception of salvation is often expressed in terms of "knowledge," and that human salvation was understood to rest upon the knowledge of the possibility of salvation in Christ, and the proper response which was necessary for salvation to take place. "Knowledge of God," understood biblically, does not mean simply "information about God," but a life-giving and salvation-bringing self-disclosure of God in Christ.

In the second place, some biblical scholars argued that the issue of revelation appeared to be of marginal importance to both the Old and New Testaments. They suggested that revelational language was neither fundamental to, nor uniform within, the biblical writings. However, it soon became clear that their analyses rested upon the uncritical acceptance of systematically-developed ideas of "revelation," rather than a careful consideration of the revelational vocabulary of Scripture itself. It is certainly true that medieval or modern notions of revelation are not found explicitly stated in either the Old or New Testaments. However, this by no means indicates that revelational language is absent from, or marginalized within, Scripture.

It is certainly correct to say that the New Testament does not regard "revelation" as meaning "disclosure of a hitherto unknown God." In its everyday use, the term "revelation" might be taken to imply "making something known in all its fullness," or "the total disclosure of what had hitherto been obscure or unclear." Yet to speak of a "revelation of God" in a theological context is not to imply that God is revealed totally. As the much respected Catholic theologian Gerald O'Collins put it:

> Revelation can occur between persons without there being an utterly complete disclosure of personalities. Take the following statement: "He revealed to me his wishes in the matter." No full, continuing personal communion is asserted. But something has been disclosed and that too in a context which affords some insight into the other's personality. To see something of his personality is not equivalent to seeing nothing at all. May we not use "reveal" in some such qualified sense of God, and speak of a genuine experience of God which communicates something, and yet falls short of being full disclosure?

O'Collins here expresses a general consensus within Christian theology. For example, many writers within the Greek Orthodox tradition stress that the revelation of God does not abolish the mystery of God. John Henry Newman's doctrine of "reserve" emphasizes the same point. There is always more to God than what he chooses to make known. Again, Luther suggests that God can only be known in part – yet that partial revelation is reliable and adequate. He develops the idea of a "hidden revelation of God" – one of the most important aspects of his "theology of the cross" – to make this point.

There is a consensus within Christian theology to the effect that nature (or creation) bears a witness to God its creator. Yet this natural knowledge of God is to be supplemented by revelation, which gives access to information that is not otherwise available. Yet the idea of revelation implies more than imparting knowledge of God; it carries with it the idea of the self-disclosure of God. In speaking about other persons, we might draw a distinction between "knowing about someone" and "knowing someone." The former implies cerebral knowledge, or an accumulation of data about an individual (such as her height, weight, and so on). The latter implies a personal relationship.

In its developed sense, "revelation" does not mean merely the transmission of a body of knowledge, but the personal self-disclosure of God within history. God has taken the initiative through a process of self-disclosure, which reaches its climax and fulfillment in the history of Jesus of Nazareth. This point has been stressed in the twentieth century by writers influenced by various types of personalist philosophies – such as Friedrich Gogarten, Dietrich Bonhoeffer and Emanuel Hirsch. Emil Brunner, who also belongs to this group of thinkers, emphasized the importance of the doctrine of the incarnation to revelation: in Christ may be seen the personal self-disclosure of God. Believers are "God's dialogue partners in history." Revelation takes a personal form. We shall explore this question further in dealing with the idea of a personal God (pp. 190–1).

At this point, we need to consider a related question of interest. What can be known of God from nature? This question opens up the area of Christian thought which is generally known as "natural theology," to which we now turn.

Natural Theology: its Scope and Limits

It is impossible to read the Bible without becoming aware that the biblical writers are aware of the majesty and wonder of God being revealed in some way through nature. "The heavens declare the glory of God; the skies proclaim the work of his hands" (Psalm 19:1). The doctrine of creation gives theological foundation to the notion of a natural knowledge of God. If God created the world, it is to be expected that his creation should bear the mark of God's special handiwork. Just as an artist's distinctive style might be evident in her sculpting, or a painter might sign his name on his work, so the presence of God, it is argued, can be discerned within the creation. But what part of creation? Three answers may be picked out from the considerable variety offered by Christian theology down the centuries.

1 *Human reason.* Augustine of Hippo addresses this question at some length in *De Trinitate* ("On the Trinity"). His line of argument can be summed up as follows. If God is indeed to be discerned within his creation,

we ought to expect to find him at the height of that creation. Now the height of God's creation, Augustine argues (basing himself on Genesis 1 and 2), is human nature. And, on the basis of the neo-Platonic presuppositions which he inherited from his cultural milieu, Augustine further argued that the height of human nature is the human capacity to reason. Therefore, he concluded, one should expect to find traces of God (or, more accurately, "vestiges of the Trinity") in human processes of reasoning.

2 *The ordering of the world.* We shall presently explore how Thomas Aquinas' important arguments for the existence of God base themselves on the perception that there is an ordering within nature, which requires to be explained. Equally, the fact that the human mind can discern and investigate this ordering of nature is of considerable significance. There seems to be something about human nature which prompts it to ask questions about the world. And there seems to be something about the world which allows answers to those questions to be given. The noted theoretical physicist and Christian apologist John Polkinghorne comments on this point as follows:

> We are so familiar with the fact that we can understand the world that most of the time we take it for granted. It is what makes science possible. Yet it could have been otherwise. The universe might have been a disorderly choas rather than an orderly cosmos. Or it might have had a rationality which was inaccessible to us ... There is a congruence between our minds and the universe, between the rationality experienced within and the rationality observed without.

There is a deep-seated congruence between the rationality present in our minds, and the rationality – the orderedness – which we observe as present in the world. Thus the abstract structures of pure mathematics – a free creation of the human mind – provide important clues to understanding the world. All of this, Polkinghorne argues, is a form of natural theology, preparing the way for the full knowledge of the Christian revelation.

3 *The beauty of the world.* A number of theologians have developed natural theologies, based on the sense of beauty which arises from contemplating the world. Hans Urs von Balthasar is an example of a twentieth-century writer who stresses the theological importance of beauty. But perhaps the most powerful exploration of this theme is due to the celebrated American theologian, Jonathan Edwards. In his *Personal Narrative*, Edwards wrote thus of his "sheer beholding of God's beauty":

> As I was walking there and looking up into the sky and clouds, there came into my mind so sweet a sense of the glorious majesty and grace of God, that I know not how to express. I seemed to see them both in a sweet

conjunction . . . it was a sweet and gentle, and holy majesty; and also a majestic meekness.

This sense of aesthetic ecstasy pervades Edwards' autobiographical writings, especially his *Miscellanies*. The perception of beauty that we experience "when we are delighted with flowery meadows and gentle breezes" is, for Edwards, an intimation of the holiness of God, which Scripture clarifies and confirms, placing it upon a reliable theological foundation.

These, then, are merely some of the ways in which Christian theologians have attempted to describe the manner in which God can be known, however fleetingly, through nature.

Nevertheless, the issue of the extent to which God can be known through nature has led to some serious disagreements between Christian writers. One of the most interesting of these dates from 1934, and will be explored in what follows.

The Barth–Brunner Debate

In 1934, The Swiss theologian Emil Brunner published a work entitled *Nature and Grace*. In this work he argued that "the task of our theological generation is to find a way back to a legitimate natural theology." Brunner located this approach in the doctrine of creation, specifically the idea that human beings are created in the "the image of God." Human nature is constituted in such a way that there is an analogy with the being of God. Despite the sinfulness of human nature, the ability to discern God in nature remains. Sinful human beings remain able to recognize God in nature and the events of history, and to be aware of their guilt before God. There is thus a "point of contact" for divine revelation within human nature.

In effect, Brunner is arguing that human nature is constituted in such a way that there is a ready-made point of contact for divine revelation. Revelation addresses a human nature which already has some idea of what that revelation is about. For example, take the gospel demand to "repent of sin." Brunner argues that this makes little sense, unless human beings already have some idea of what "sin" is. The gospel demand to repent is thus addressed to an audience which already has at least something of an idea of what "sin" and "repentance" might mean. Revelation brings with it a fuller understanding of what sin means – but in doing so, it builds upon an existing human awareness of sin.

Brunner's fellow-countryman Karl Barth reacted with anger to this suggestion. His published reply to Brunner – which brought their long-standing friendship to an abrupt end – has one of the shortest titles in the history of religious publishing. Its title was the German word for "no": Nein! Barth was determined to say "no!" to Brunner's positive evaluation of natural theology. It seemed to imply that God needed help to become known, or that human beings somehow cooperated with God in the act of revelation. "The Holy Spirit . . . needs no point of contact other than that which that same Spirit establishes," was his angry retort. For Barth, there was no "point of contact" inherent within human nature. Any such "point of contact" was itself the result of divine revelation. It is something that is evoked by the Word of God, rather than something which is a permanent feature of human nature.

Underlying this debate is another matter, which is too easily overlooked. The Barth–Brunner debate took place in 1934, the year in which Hitler gained power in Germany. Underlying Brunner's appeal to nature is an idea, which can be traced back to Luther, known as "the orders of creation." According to Luther, God providentially established certain "orders" within creation, in order to prevent it collapsing into chaos. Those orders included the family, the church and the state. (The close alliance between church and state in German Lutheran thought reflects this idea.) Nineteenth-century German Liberal Protestantism had absorbed this idea, and developed a theology which allowed German culture, including a positive assessment of the state, to become of major importance theologically. Part of Barth's concern is that Brunner, perhaps unwittingly, laid a theological foundation for allowing the state to become a model for God. And who wanted to model God on Adolf Hitler?

Having explored the concept of revelation in a little detail, we may now move on to look at the Christian understanding of the sources of revelation. The most important of these is the Bible, to which we now turn.

The Bible

The terms "Bible" and "Scripture," along with the derived adjectives "biblical" and "scriptural," are virtually interchangeable. Both designate a body of texts which are recognized as authoritative for Christian thinking (although the nature and extent of that authority is a matter of debate). It must be stressed that the Bible is not merely the object of formal academic study within Christianity; it is also read and expounded within the context of public worship, and is the subject of meditation and devotion on the part of individual Christians.

We have already explored many aspects of the Christian understanding of the Bible (see pp. 5–74). In what follows, we shall consider some aspects of that understanding in more detail.

The Catechism of the Catholic Church (1994) on the Authority of Scripture

This major document, widely regarded as an authoritative statement of Catholic teaching, here sets out a traditional understanding of the basis of biblical authority.

In order to reveal himself to men, in the condescension of his goodness God speaks to them in human words: indeed, the words of God, expressed in the words of men, are in every way like human language, just as the Word of the eternal Father, when he took on himself the flesh of human weakness, became like men. Through all the words of Sacred Scripture, God speaks only one single Word, his one Utterance in whom he expresses himself completely . . . In Sacred Scripture, the Church constantly finds her nourishment and her strength, for she welcomes it not as a human word, but as what it really is, the word of God. In the sacred books, the Father who is in heaven comes lovingly to meet his children, and talks with them.

God is the author of Sacred Scripture. The divine revealed realities, which are contained and presented in the text of Sacred Scripture, have been written down under the inspiration of the Holy Spirit. For Holy Mother Church, relying on the faith of the apostolic age, accepts as sacred and canonical the books of the Old and the New Testaments, whole and entire, with all their parts, on the grounds that, written under the inspiration of the Holy Spirit, they have God as their author and have been handed on as such to the Church herself. God inspired the human authors of the sacred books. To compose the sacred books, God chose certain men who, all the while he employed them in this task, made full use of their own faculties and powers so that, though he acted in them and by them, it was as true authors they consigned to writing whatever he wanted written, and no more.

The Authority of the Bible

As has been stressed, the Bible is of major importance to Christians. It is regarded as possessing authority in matters of teaching and ethics. The idea of "inspiration" is often used to explain the specific authority of the Bible for Christians. The notion that the special status of Scripture within Christian theology rests upon its divine origins, however vaguely this may be stated, can be discerned both in the New Testament itself, and in subsequent reflection on its contents. 2 Timothy 3:16–17, which speaks of Scripture as "God-breathed (*theopneustos*)," is an important element in any discussion of the manner in which Scripture is inspired, and the significance which is to be attached to this. This idea was common in early Christian thought, and was not regarded as controversial. The Greek-speaking Jewish philosopher Philo of Alexandria (*c*.30 BC–*c*.45 AD) regarded Scripture as fully inspired, and argued that God used the authors of scriptural books as passive instruments for communicating God's will.

The issue began to surface as potentially controversial at the time of the Reformation, especially through the writings of John Calvin. Calvin was concerned to defend the authority of Scripture against two groups of people. On the one hand were those on the more catholic wing of the church (who argued that the authority of Scripture rested in it being recognized as authoritative by the Church). On the other were the more radical evangelical writers (such as the Anabaptists, who argued that every individual had the right to ignore Scripture altogether in favor of some direct personal divine revelation). Calvin declared that the Spirit worked through Scripture (not bypassing it, as the radicals held), and that the Spirit lent direct authority to Scripture by inspiring it, thus doing away with the need for any external support to its authority (such as that of the Church).

This point is important, in that it indicates that the reformers did not see the issue of inspiration as linked with the absolute historical reliability or factual inerrancy. Calvin's doctrine of accommodation implied that God revealed himself in forms tailored to the abilities of the communities which were to receive this revelation; thus in the case of Genesis 1, Calvin suggests that a whole series of ideas – such as the "days of creation" – are simply accommodated ways of speaking, a kind of divine "baby-talk." The development of ideas of "biblical infallibility" or "inerrancy" within Protestantism can be traced to the United States in the middle of the nineteenth century.

With the coming of the Enlightenment, the idea of the Bible having special status was called into question, largely on account of the presuppositions of the rationalism of the period, and increased interest in the critical study of Scripture. A number of approaches to the issue of inspiration which developed around this period are of interest.

1   J. G. Herder, strongly influenced by the outlook of Romanticism, argued that the idea of inspiration was to be interpreted in an artistic or aesthetic sense. In his Spirit of Hebrew Poetry (1782–3), Herder suggested that the most appropriate model for biblical inspiration was provided by works of art. Just as one might speak of a great novel, poem or painting as "inspired," so the same idea can be applied to Scripture. Inspiration is thus seen as a human achievement, rather than a gift of God.

2   The Old Princeton School, represented by Charles Hodge (1797–1878) and Benjamin B. Warfield (1851–1921), developed strongly super-

natural theories of inspiration, in conscious opposition to the naturalist approach favoured by Herder. "Inspiration is that extraordinary, supernatural influence . . . exerted by the Holy Ghost on the writers of our Sacred Books, by which their words were rendered also the words of God, and, therefore, perfectly infallible." Although Warfield is careful to stress that the humanity and individuality of biblical writers is not abolished by inspiration, he nonetheless insists that their humanity "was so dominated that their words became at the same time the words of God, and thus, in every case and all alike, absolutely infallible."

3 Others held that inspiration was also to be regarded as God's guidance of the reader of Scripture, which enabled that reader to recognize the word of God in the biblical text. As we have just seen, Warfield located the inspiration of scripture in the biblical text itself, thus implying that scripture was objectively, in itself, the word of God for all who read it. Others argued for a subjective understanding of inspiration, by which the reader's perception of Scripture – rather than Scripture itself – was to be regarded as "inspired." Augustus H. Strong (1836–1921) stressed that the authority of Scripture could not be located simply in the words of Scripture, as if these could have authoritative status apart from their reception by individual believers, or the community of faith. Inspiration thus had to be recognized to have objective and subjective aspects.

The "Word of God"

The phrases "the Word of God" or "the Word of the Lord" are at least as deeply rooted in Christian worship as they are in Christian theology. "Word" implies action and communication. Just as a person's character and will is expressed through the words they use, so Scripture (especially the Old Testament) understands God to address people, and thus to make known God's intentions and will for them.

The term "word of God" is complex and highly nuanced, bringing together a cluster of ideas. Three broad, and clearly related, senses of the term may be discerned both within the Christian tradition, and Scripture itself.

1 To refer to Jesus Christ as the word of God made flesh (John 1:14). This is the most highly developed use of the term in the New Testament. In speaking of Christ as the "word of God incarnate," Christian theology has attempted to express the idea that the will, purposes and nature of God are made known in history through the person of Jesus Christ. It is the deeds, character and theological identity of Jesus Christ, and not

merely the words that he uttered, which make known the nature and purpose of God.

2   The term is also used to refer to "the gospel of Christ," or "the message or proclamation about Jesus." In this sense, the term refers to what God achieved and made known through the life, death and resurrection of Christ.

3   The term is used in a general sense to refer to the whole Bible, which can be regarded as setting the scene for the advent of Christ, telling the story of his coming, and exploring the implications of his life, death, and resurrection for believers.

Considerations of this kind lie behind Karl Barth's use of the phrase "word of God." Barth's doctrine of "the threefold form of the word of God" distinguishes a threefold movement, from the word of God in Christ, to the witness to this word in Scripture, and finally to the proclamation of this word in the preaching of the community of faith. There is thus a direct and organic connection between the preaching of the church and the person of Jesus Christ.

Interpreting the Bible

Every text demands to be interpreted; Scripture is no exception. There is a sense in which the history of Christian theology can be regarded as the history of biblical interpretation. In what follows we shall explore some of the approaches to biblical interpretation likely to be of interest to students of theology. It will, however, be clear that the vastness of the subject makes it impossible to do more than give a representative selection of approaches to the matter.

We open our discussion by dealing with the patristic period. The Alexandrian school of biblical interpretation drew on the methods devised by the Jewish writer Philo of Alexandria (*c.*30 BC–*c.*45 AD). Philo here draws on earlier Jewish traditions, which allowed the literal interpretation of scripture to be supplemented by an appeal to allegory. But what is an allegory? The Greek philosopher Heraclitus had defined it as "saying one thing, and meaning something other than what is said." Philo argued that it was necessary to look beneath the surface meaning of scripture, to discern a deeper meaning which lay beneath the surface of the text. These ideas were taken up by a group of theologians based in Alexandria, of which the most important are generally agreed to be Clement, Origen, and Didymus the Blind. Indeed, Jerome playfully referred to the last-mentioned as "Didymus the Sighted," on account of the spiritual insights which resulted from his application of the allegorical method of biblical interpretation.

The scope of the allegorical method can be seen from Origen's interpretation of key Old Testament images. Joshua's conquest of the promised land, interpreted allegorically, referred to Christ's conquest of sin upon the cross, just as the sacrificial legislation in Leviticus pointed ahead to the spiritual sacrifices of Christians. It might at first sight seem that this means that the interpreter simply reads any meaning he or she likes into the text of Scripture. However, as the writings of Didymus (which were rediscovered in an ammunition dump in Egypt during the Second World War) make clear, this need not be the case. It seems that a consensus developed about the images and texts of the Old Testament which were to be interpreted allegorically. For example, Jerusalem regularly came to be seen as an allegory of the church.

In contrast, the Antiochene school placed an emphasis upon the interpretation of Scripture in the light of its historical context. This school, especially associated with writers such as Diodore of Tarsus, John Chrysostom and Theodore of Mospsuestia, gave an emphasis to the historical location of Old Testament prophecies, which is quite absent from the writings of Origen and other representatives of the Alexandrian tradition. Thus Theodore, in dealing with Old Testament prophecy, stresses that the prophetic message was relevant to those to whom it was directly addressed, as well as having a developed meaning for a Christian readership. Every prophetic oracle is to be interpreted as having a single consistent historical or literal meaning. In consequence, Theodore tended to interpret relatively few Old Testament passages as referring directly to Christ, whereas the Alexandrian school regarded Christ as the hidden content of many Old Testament passages, both prophetic and historical.

In the western church a slightly distinct approach can be seen to develop. In many of his writings, Ambrose of Milan developed a threefold understanding of the senses of Scripture: in addition to the "natural" sense, the interpreter may discern a "moral" and "rational" or "theological" sense. Augustine chose to follow this approach, and instead argued for a twofold sense – a "literal–fleshly–historical" approach and an "allegorical–mystical–spiritual" sense, although Augustine allows that some passages can possess both senses. "The sayings of the prophets are found to have a threefold meaning, in that some have in mind the earthly Jerusalem, others the heavenly city, and others refer to both." To understand the Old Testament at a purely historical level is unacceptable; the key to its understanding lies in its correct interpretation. Among the major lines of "spiritual" interpretation, the following should be noted: Adam represents Christ; Eve represents the church; Noah's ark represents the cross; the door of Noah's ark represents Christ's pierced side; the city of Jerusalem represents the heavenly Jerusalem.

These hidden meanings of inspired Scripture we can track down to the best of our ability, with varying degrees of success. Yet we all hold firmly to the principle that all these historical events and their narrative always have some foreshadowing of things to come, and that they are always to be interpreted with reference to Christ and his church.

By the use of such lines of analysis, Augustine is able to stress the unity of both Old and New Testaments. They bear witness to the same faith, even if its modes of expression may be different (an idea developed by John Calvin). Augustine expresses this idea in a text which has become of major importance to biblical interpretion, especially as it bears on the relation between Old and New Testaments: "The New Testament is hidden in the Old; the Old is made accessible by the New (*in Vetere Novum latet et in Novo Vetus patet*)."

This distinction between the "literal" or "historical" sense of Scripture on the one hand, and a deeper "spiritual" or "allegorical" meaning on the other, came to be generally accepted within the church during the early Middle Ages. The standard method of biblical interpretation used during the Middle Ages is usually known as the Quadriga, or the "fourfold sense of Scripture." The origins of this method lie specifically in the distinction between the literal and spiritual senses. Scripture possesses four different senses. In addition to the literal sense, three non-literal senses could be distinguished: the allegorical, defining what Christians are to believe; the tropological or moral, defining what Christians are to do; and the anagogical, defining what Christians were to hope for. The four senses of Scripture were thus the following:

1 The literal sense of Scripture, in which the text could be taken at face value.
2 The allegorical sense, which interpreted certain passages of Scripture to produce statements of doctrine. Those passages tended to be either obscure, or to have a literal meaning which was unacceptable, for theological reasons, to their readers.
3 The tropological or moral sense, which interpreted such passages to produce ethical guidance for Christian conduct.
4 The anagogical sense, which interprets passages to indicate the grounds of Christian hope, pointing toward the future fulfillment of the divine promises in the New Jerusalem.

A potential weakness was avoided by insisting that nothing should be believed on the basis of a non-literal sense of Scripture, unless it could first be established on the basis of the literal sense. This insistence on the priority of the literal sense of Scripture may be seen as an implied criticism of the allegorical approach adopted by Origen, which virtually allowed interpreters of Scripture to read into any passage whatever "spiritual" interpretations they liked. As Luther states this principle in 1515: "in the Scriptures no allegory, tropology or anagogy is valid, unless that same truth is explicitly stated literally somewhere else. Otherwise, Scripture would become a laughing matter."

Having considered some questions relating to Scripture as a source of Christian theology, we may now turn to a consideration of the role of reason.

Reason

The second major resource to be considered is human reason. Although the importance of reason for Christian theology has always been recognized within Christian theology, it assumed an especial importance at the time of the Enlightenment (see pp. 312–14). We open our discussion by considering the changing emphasis which has come to be placed upon reason within the Christian tradition.

Reason and Revelation: Three Models

In that human beings are rational, it is to be expected that reason should have a major role to play in theology. There has, however, been considerable debate within Christian theology concerning what that role might be. Three broad categories of positions can be discerned.

1   *Theology is a rational discipline.* This position, associated with writers such as Thomas Aquinas, works on the assumption that the Christian faith is fundamentally rational, and can thus be both supported and explored by reason. Aquinas' Five Ways, considered earlier, illustrate his belief that reason is capable of lending support to the ideas of faith.

But Aquinas, and the Christian tradition which he represented, did not believe that Christianity was limited to what could be ascertained by reason. Faith goes beyond reason, having access to truths and insights of revelation, which reason could not hope to fathom or discover unaided. Reason has the role of building upon what is known by revelation, exploring what its implications might be. In this sense, theology is a rational discipline, using rational methods to build upon and extend what is known by revelation.

The noted historian of medieval Christian thought, Etienne Gilson, made a delightful comparison between the great theological systems of the Middle Ages and the cathedrals which sprang up throughout Christian Europe at this time: they were, he remarked, "cathedrals of the mind." Christianity is like a cathedral which rests upon the bedrock of human reason, but whose superstructure rises beyond the realms accessible to pure reason. It rests upon rational foundations; but the building erected on that foundation went far beyond what reason could uncover.

2 *Theology is the republication of the insights of reason.* By the middle of the seventeenth century, especially in England and Germany, a new attitude began to develop. Christianity, it was argued, was reasonable. But where Thomas Aquinas understood this to mean that faith rested securely upon rational foundations, the new school of thought had different ideas. If faith is rational, they argued, it must be capable of being deduced in its entirety by reason. Every aspect of faith, every item of Christian belief, must be shown to derive from human reason.

An excellent example of this approach is to be found in the writings of Lord Herbert of Cherbury, who argued for a rational Christianity based upon the innate sense of God and human moral obligation. This had two major consequences. First, Christianity was in effect reduced to those ideas which could be proven by reason. If Christianity was rational, then any parts of its system which could not be proved by reason could not be counted as "rational." They would have to be discarded. And second, reason was understood to take priority over revelation. Reason comes first, revelation comes second.

Reason thus came to be regarded as being capable of establishing what is right without needing any assistance from revelation; Christianity has to follow, being accepted where it endorses what reason has to say, and being disregarded where it went its own way. So why bother with the idea of revelation, when reason could tell us all we could possibly wish to know about God, the world, and ourselves? This absolutely settled conviction in the total competence of human reason underlies the rationalist depreciation of the Christian doctrine of revelation in Jesus Christ and through Scripture.

3 *Theology is redundant; reason reigns supreme.* Finally, this potentially rationalist position was pushed to its logical outcome. As a matter of fact, it was argued, Christianity does include a series of major beliefs which are inconsistent with reason. Reason has the right to judge religion, in that it stands above it. This approach is usually termed "Enlightenment rationalism," and is of such importance that it will be considered in more detail. We begin by looking at an English movement which laid the foundations of this form of rationalism in religion – Deism.

The term "deism" (from the Latin *deus*, "god") is often used in a general sense to refer to that view of God which maintains God's creatorship, but denies a continuing divine involvement with, or special presence within, that creation. It is often contrasted with "theism" (from the Greek *theos*, "god"), which allows for continuing divine involvement within the world.

In its more specific sense, Deism is used to refer to the views of a group of English thinkers during the "Age of Reason," in the late seventeenth century and early eighteenth centuries. In his *Principal Deistic Writers* (1757), Leland grouped together a number of writers – including Lord Herbert of Cherbury, Thomas Hobbes, and David Hume – under the broad term "deist." Close examination of their religious views shows that they have relatively little in common, apart from a general scepticism of specifically Christian ideas.

John Locke's *Essay Concerning Human Understanding* (1690) developed an idea of God which became characteristic of much later Deism. Indeed, Locke's Essay can be said to lay much of the intellectual foundation of Deism. Locke argued that "reason leads us to the knowledge of this certain and evident truth, that there is an eternal, most powerful and most knowing Being." The attributes of this being are those which human reason recognizes as appropriate for God. Having considered which moral and rational qualities are suited to the deity, Locke argues that "we enlarge every one of these with our idea of infinity, and so, putting them together, make our complex idea of God." In other words, the idea of God is made up of human rational and moral qualities, projected to infinity.

Matthew Tindal's *Christianity as Old as Creation* (1730) argued that Christianity was nothing other than the "republication of the religion of nature." God is understood as the extension of accepted human ideas of justice, rationality and wisdom. This universal religion is available at all times and in every place, whereas traditional Christianity rested upon the idea of a divine revelation which was not accessible to those who lived before Christ. Tindal's views were propagated before the modern discipline of the sociology of knowledge created scepticism of the idea of "universal reason," and are an excellent model of the rationalism characteristic of the movement, and which later became influential within the Enlightenment.

The ideas of English Deism percolated through to the continent of Europe through translations (especially in Germany), and through the writings of individuals familiar with and sympathetic to them, such as Voltaire's *Philosophical Letters*. Enlightenment rationalism, to which we may now turn, is often considered to be the final flowering of the bud of English Deism.

Enlightenment Rationalism

The basic presupposition of Enlightenment rationalism is that human reason is perfectly capable of telling us everything we need to know about the world, ourselves and God (if there is one). At this point, we need to stress the difference between "reason" and "rationalism," which may appear identical to some readers. Reason is the basic human faculty of thinking, based on argument and evidence. It is theologically neutral, and poses no threat to faith – unless it is regarded as the only source of knowledge about God. It then becomes rationalism, which is an exclusive reliance upon human reason alone, and a refusal to allow any weight to be given to divine revelation.

Enlightenment rationalism may be said to rest upon the belief that unaided human reason can deliver everything that humanity needs to know. There is no need to listen to other voices, except first having consulted reason. By definition, the Christian cannot have anything to say that is at one and the same time distinctive and right. If it is distinctive, it departs from the path of reason – and thus must be untrue. To be different is, quite simply, to be wrong.

An excellent example of this rational critique of Christianity can be seen in relation to the doctrine of Christ (how could Jesus be both God and man at one and the same time?), and the doctrine of the Trinity (how can one God be three persons simultaneously, without lapsing into crude logical contradiction?) One of the early American presidents, Thomas Jefferson, who was deeply influenced by eighteenth-century French rationalism, poured reasoned scorn upon the doctrine of the Trinity:

> When we shall have done away with the incomprehensible jargon of the Trinitarian arithmetic, that three are one and one is three; when we shall have knocked down the artificial scaffolding, reared to mask from view the very simple structure of Jesus; when, in short, we shall have unlearned everything which has been taught since his day, and got back to the pure and simple doctrines he inculcated, we shall then be truly and worthily his disciples.

Jesus was really a very simple rational teacher, who taught a very simple and reasonable gospel about a very simple rational idea of God. And at every point, Christianity chose to make things more complicated than they need be.

A direct consequence of this was the movement in New Testament studies known as the "Quest of the Historical Jesus." This quest, which dates from the late eighteenth century, was based upon the belief that the New Testament seriously misrepresents Jesus. The real Jesus – the "Jesus of history" – was a simple Galilean teacher, who taught entirely sensible ideas based upon reason. The New Testament got him quite wrong, and presented him as the risen savior of sinful humanity.

Reason was thus held to be able to judge Christ. In his celebrated work *Religion Within the Limits of Reason Alone*, Immanuel Kant argued powerfully for the priority of reason and conscience over the authority of Jesus

Christ. Where Jesus endorses what reason has to say, he is to be respected; where he goes against or goes beyond reason, he is to be rejected. Enlightenment rationalism, then, upheld the sovereignty of reason, arguing that human reason was capable of establishing all that it was necessary to know about religion without recourse to the idea of "revelation." Furthermore, reason possessed an ability to judge the truths of religions, such as Christianity, and eliminate vast tracts of its ideas as "irrational." Influential though such ideas were in the late eighteenth and nineteenth centuries, they are now regarded with suspicion. A series of developments, of which we may here note a few, have destroyed the credibility of this approach.

We may begin by exploring reason itself. Surely human reason is capable of basing itself upon self-evident first principles, and, by following these through logically, deducing a complete system? Just about everyone who favors this approach makes some sort of appeal to Euclid's five principles of geometry. On the basis of his five principles, he was able to construct his entire geometrical system. Philosophers, such as Spinoza, were deeply attracted to this: maybe they could use the same method in philosophy. From a set of certain assumptions, a great secure edifice of philosophy and ethics could be erected. But the dream turned sour. The discovery of non-Euclidian geometry during the nineteenth century destroyed the appeal of this analogy. It turned out that there were other ways of doing geometry, each just as internally consistent as Euclid's. But which is right? The question cannot be answered. They are all different, each with their own special merits and problems.

Much the same observation is now made concerning rationalism itself. Where once it was argued that there was one single rational principle, it is now conceded that there are – and always have been – many different "rationalities." Enlightenment thinkers appear to have been shielded from this disconcerting fact by the limitations of their historical scholarship, which remained firmly wedded to the classical western tradition. But this illusion has now been shattered. At the end of his exhaustive analysis of rationalist approaches to reason, the philosopher Alasdair MacIntyre concludes:

> Both the thinkers of the Enlightenment and their successors proved unable to agree as to precisely what those principles were which would be found undeniable by all rational pesons. One kind of answer was given by the authors of the Encyclopédie, a second by Rousseau, a third by Bentham, a fourth by Kant, a fifth by the Scottish philsophers of common sense and their French and American disciples. Nor has subsequent history diminished the extent of such disagreement. Consequently, the legacy of the Enlightenment has been the provision of an ideal of rational justification which it has proved impossible to attain.

According to MacIntyre, reason promises much, yet fails to deliver what it promises. It is for such reasons that the German writer Hans-Georg Gadamer wrote of the "Robinson Crusoe dream of the historical Enlightenment, as artificial as Crusoe himself." The notion of "universal rationality" is today viewed by many as little more than a fiction. Postmodernism has argued that there exists a variety of "rationalities," each of which has to be respected in its own right; there is no privileged vantage point, no universal concept of "reason," which can pass judgment upon them.

Can God's Existence be Proved by Reason?

The relation of faith and reason is often discussed in terms of whether God's existence can be proved, and whether such proof would be adequate to bring a non-believer to faith. Although some writers have suggested that this is the case, the general consensus within Christian theology seems to be that, although reason does not bring individuals to faith in God, believers are nonetheless able to give rational reasons for their faith in God.

The classic statement of such questions, to which all modern discussion makes reference, is to be found in the writings of the medieval Christian authors and thinkers Anselm of Canterbury and Thomas Aquinas. The former developed what has come to be known as "the ontological argument" for the existence of God. The second developed the "Five Ways," arguing from the effects of nature to their cause in God its creator. We shall consider these two categories of arguments individually.

The "ontological argment" is first set out by Anselm in a work which dates from 1079. (The term "ontological" refers to the branch of philosophy which deals with the notion of "being" or "existence.") In the course of this work, Anselm reflects on how self-evident the idea of God has become to him, and what the implications of this might be.

Anselm begins by offering a crucially important definition of God. God is "that than which nothing greater can be conceived." This definition, which seems self-evidently true to Anselm (given his Christian understanding of what God is like), has important implications. Anselm expresses his point in a rather contorted manner, which requires a little explanation:

> It is possible to conceive of a being which cannot be conceived not to exist. Now this is greater than one which can be conceived not to exist. So if that than which nothing greater can be conceived, can be conceived not to exist, it is not that than which nothing greater can be conceived. But this is an irreconcilable contradiction. So there really is a being than which nothing greater can be conceived to exist, that it cannot be conceived not to exist; and you are that being, O Lord our God . . . For if a mind could conceive of a being better than you, the creature would rise above the creator, and this would be absurd.

This is not the easiest of arguments to follow, and it might be helpful if we simplify the argument, to bring out the central point at issue.

God is defined as "that than which nothing greater can be conceived." Now the idea of such a being is one thing; the reality is another. Thinking of a hundred dollar bill is quite different from having a hundred dollar bill in your hands – and much less satisfying, as well. Anselm's point is this: the idea of something is inferior to the reality. So the idea of God as "that than which nothing greater can be conceived" contains a potential contradiction – because the reality of God would be superior to this idea. In other words, if this definition of God is correct, and exists in the human mind, then the corresponding reality must also exist.

There is an obvious logical weakness in this "argument" (although it must be stressed that Anselm does not really regard it as an argument in the first place). It is brought out clearly by Anselm's early critic Gaunilo, who made a response known as "A Reply on Behalf of the Fool" (the reference being to Psalm 14:1, cited by Anselm, "The fool says in his heart that there is no God"). Imagine, Gaunilo suggests, an island, so lovely that a more perfect island cannot be conceived. By the same argument, Gaunilo suggests, that island must exist, in that the reality of the island is necessarily more perfect that the mere idea. In much the same way, we might argue that the idea of a hundred dollar bill seems, according to Anselm, to imply that we have such a bill in our hands.

Anselm, however, is not so easily dismissed. Part of his argument is that it is an essential part of the definition of God that God is "that than which nothing greater can be conceived." God belongs in a totally different category to islands or hundred dollar bills. It is part of the nature of God to transcend everything else. Once the believer has come to understand what the word "God" means, then God really does exist for him or her. This is the intention of Anselm's meditation: to reflect on how the Christian understanding of the nature of God reinforces belief in his reality. The "argument" does not really have force outside this context of faith, and Anselm never intended it to be used in this general philosophical manner.

Thomas Aquinas' "Five Ways" adopt a somewhat different approach. Aquinas believed that it was entirely proper to identify pointers toward the existence of God, drawn from general human experience of the world. So what kind of pointers does Aquinas identify? The basic line of thought guiding Aquinas is that the world mirrors God, as its creator. Just as an artist might sign a painting to identify it as his handiwork, so God has stamped a divine "signature" upon the creation. What we observe in the world – for example, its signs of ordering – can be explained on the basis of the existence of God as its creator. God is both its first cause and its designer. God both brought the world into existence, and impressed the divine image and likeness upon it.

So where might we look in creation to find evidence for the existence of God? Aquinas argues that the ordering of the world is the most convincing evidence of God's existence and wisdom. This basic assumption underlies each of the "Five Ways," although it is of particular importance in the case of the argument often referred to as the "argument from design" or the "teleological argument." We shall consider each of these individually.

The first way begins from the observation that things in the world are in motion or change. The world is not static, but is dynamic. Examples of this are easy to list. Rain falls from the sky. Stones roll down valleys. The earth revolves around the sun (a fact, incidentally, unknown to Aquinas). But how did nature come to be in motion? Why is it not static?

Aquinas argues that everything which moves is moved by something else. For every motion, there is a cause. Things don't just move by themselves – they are moved by something else. Now each cause of motion must itself have a cause. And that cause must have a cause as well. And so Aquinas argues that there is a whole series of causes of motion lying behind the world as we know it. Now unless there is an infinite number of these causes, Aquinas argues, there must be a single cause right at the origin of the series. From this original cause of motion, all other motion is ultimately derived. This is the origin of the great chain of causality which we see reflected in the way the world behaves. From the fact that things are in motion, Aquinas argues for the existence of a single original cause of all this motion – and this, he concludes, is none other than God.

The second way begins from the idea of causation. In other words, Aquinas notes the existence of causes and effects in the world. One event (the effect) is explained by the influence of another (the cause). The idea of motion, which we looked at briefly above, is a good example of this cause-and-effect sequence. Using a line of reasoning similar to that used above, Aquinas thus argues that all effects may be traced back to a single original cause – which is God.

The third way concerns the existence of contingent beings. In other words, the world contains beings (such as human beings) which are not there as a matter of necessity. Aquinas contrasts this type of being with a necessary being (one who is there as a matter of necessity). Whilst God is a necessary being, Aquinas argues that humans are contingent beings. The fact that we are here itself needs explanation. Why are we here? What happened to bring us into existence?

Aquinas argues that a being comes into existence because something which already exists brought it into being. In other words, our existence is caused by another being. We are the effects of a series of causation. Tracing this series back to its origin, Aquinas declares that this original cause of being can only be someone whose existence is necessary – in other words, God.

The fourth way begins from human values, such as truth, goodness and nobility. Where do there values come from? What causes them? Aquinas argues that there must be something which is in itself true, good and noble, and that this brings into being our ideas of truth, goodness, and nobility. The origin of these ideas, Aquinas suggests, is God, who is their original cause.

The fifth and final way is the teleological argument itself. Aquinas notes that the world shows obvious traces of intelligent design. Natural processes and objects seem to be adapted with certain definite objectives in mind. They seem to have a purpose. They seem to have been designed. But things don't design themselves: they are caused and designed by someone or something else. Arguing from this observation, Aquinas concludes that the source of this natural ordering must be conceded to be God.

It will be obvious that most of Aquinas' arguments are rather similar. Each depends on tracing a causal sequence back to its single origin, and identifying this with God. A number of criticisms of these arguments were developed by the leading thinkers of the later Middle Ages, such as Duns Scotus and William of Ockham. The following are especially important.

1   Why is the idea of an infinite regression of causes impossible? For example, the argument from motion only really works if it can be shown that the sequence of cause and effect stops somewhere. There has to be, according to Aquinas, a Prime Unmoved Mover. But he fails to demonstrate this point.
2   Why do these arguments lead to belief in only one God? The argument from motion, for example, could lead to belief in a number of Prime Unmoved-Movers. There seems to be no reason for insisting that there can only be one such cause.
3   These arguments do not demonstrate that God continues to exist. Having caused things to happen, God might cease to exist. The continuing existence of events does not necessarily imply the continuing existence of their originator. Aquinas' arguments, Ockham suggests, might lead to a belief that God existed once upon a time – but not necessarily now. Ockham developed a somewhat complex argument, based on the idea of God continuing to sustain the universe, which attempts to get round this difficulty.

In the end, Aquinas' arguments only go some way toward suggesting that it is reasonable to believe in a creator of the world, or an intelligent being who is able to cause effects in the world. Nevertheless, a leap of faith is still required. It still remains to be shown that this creator or intelligent being is the God whom Christians know, worship, and adore. Aquinas' arguments could lead to faith in the existence of a god rather like that favored by the Greek philosopher Aristotle – an Unmoved Mover, who is distant from and uninvolved in the affairs of the world. However, if interpreted from a specifically Christian perspective, a very different understanding of God will result!

Having considered Scripture and reason as theological resources, we may now turn to consider the idea of tradition.

Tradition

The word "tradition" implies not merely something that is handed down, but an active process of reflection by which theological or spiritual insights are valued, assessed, and transmitted from one generation to another. Three broad approaches to tradition may be detected within Christian theology.

A Single-Source Approach to Tradition

In response to various controversies within the early church, especially the threat from Gnosticism, a "traditional" method of understanding certain passages of Scripture began to develop. Second-century patristic theologians such as Irenaeus of Lyons began to develop the idea of an authorized way of interpreting certain texts of Scripture, which he argued went back to the time of the apostles themselves. Scripture could not be allowed to be interpreted in any arbitrary or random way: it had to be interpreted within the context of the historical continuity of the Christian church. The parameters of its interpretation were historically fixed and "given." "Tradition" here means simply "a traditional way of interpreting Scripture within the community of faith." This is a single-source theory of theology: theology is based upon Scripture, and "tradition" refers to a "traditional way of interpreting Scripture."

The mainstream Reformation adopted this approach, insisting that traditional interpretations of Scripture – such as the doctrine of the Trinity or the practice of infant baptism – could be retained, provided they could be shown to be consistent with Scripture. On the basis of this observation, it will be clear that it is incorrect to suggest that the magisterial reformers elevated private judgment above the corporate judgment of the church, or that they descended into some form of individualism. This judgment is unquestionably true of the radical Reformation (see below).

This approach remains the "majority report" within modern Christian thought. Nevertheless, two significant alternative positions should be noted.

A Dual-Source Approach to Tradition

In the fourteenth and fifteenth centuries a somewhat different understanding of tradition than that noted above developed. "Tradition" was understood to be a separate and distinct source of revelation in addition to Scripture. Scripture, it was argued, was silent on a number of points – but God had providentially arranged for a second source of revelation to supplement this deficiency: a stream of unwritten tradition, going back to the apostles themselves. This tradition was passed down from one generation to another within the church. This is a dual-source theory of theology: theology is based upon two quite distinct sources, Scripture and unwritten tradition.

A belief which is not to be found in Scripture may thus, on the basis of this dual-source theory, be justified by an appeal to an unwritten tradition. This position was defended strongly at the Council of Trent, which was charged with stating and defending the Roman Catholic position against the threat posed by the Reformation. Trent ruled that Scripture could not be regarded as the only source of revelation; tradition was a vital supplement, which Protestants irresponsibly denied. "All saving truths and rules of conduct . . . are contained in the written books and in the unwritten traditions, received from the mouth of Christ himself or from the apostles themselves." Interestingly, however, Vatican II seems to move away from this approach, in favor of the "traditional interpretation of Scripture" approach, noted above.

These two approaches just discussed affirm the value of tradition. A third approach, which in effect rejected tradition, came to be influential within the radical wing of the Reformation, often known as "Anabaptism," and subsequently was developed by writers sympathetic to the Enlightenment.

The Rejection of Tradition

For radical theologians of the sixteenth century, such as Thomas Müntzer and Caspar Schwenkfeld, every individual had the right to interpret Scripture as he or she pleased, subject to the guidance of the Holy Spirit. For the radical Sebastian Franck, the Bible "is a book sealed with seven seals which none can open unless he has the key of David, which is the illumination of the Spirit." The way was thus opened for individualism, with the private judgment of the individual raised above the corporate judgment of the church. Thus the radicals rejected the practice of infant baptism (to which the magisterial Reformation remained committed) as non-scriptural. (There is no explicit reference to the practice in the New Testament.) Similarly, doctrines such as the Trinity and the divinity of Christ were rejected as resting upon inadequate scriptural foundations. The radicals had no place whatsoever for tradition. As Sebastian Frank wrote in 1530: "Foolish Ambrose, Augustine, Jerome, Gregory – of whom not one even knew the Lord, so help me God, nor was sent by God to teach. Rather, they were all apostles of Antichrist."

This approach was developed further during the Enlightenment, which was anxious to liberate itself from the shackles of tradition. Political emancipation from the oppression of the past (a key theme of the French Revolution) meant a total abandoning of the political, social, and religious ideas of the past. One of the reasons why Enlightenment thinkers placed such a high value upon human reason was that it relieved them of the need to appeal to tradition for ideas – any ideas worth knowing about were accessible to reason alone.

A respect for tradition was thus seen as capitulation to the authority of the past, a self-imposed bondage to outdated social, political, and religious structure. The Enlightenment thus represented a radical rejection of tradition. Reason required no supplementation by voices from the past.

Theology and Worship: the Role of Liturgical Tradition

One of the most important elements of the Christian tradition is fixed forms of worship, usually known as "liturgy." In recent years there has been a rediscovery of the fact that Christian theologians pray and worship, and that this doxological context shapes their theological reflections. This point has been appreciated since the first centuries of the Christian church. The Latin maxim *lex orandi, lex credendi*, which could roughly be translated as "the way you pray determines what you believe," expresses the fact that theology and worship interact with each other. What Christians believe affects the manner in which they pray and worship; the manner in which Christians pray and worship affects what they believe.

Two controversies within the early church, centering on Gnosticism and Arianism, illustrate the importance of this point particularly well. On the basis of their radical dualism between the "physical" and the "spiritual," the Gnostics argued that matter was inherently evil. In refuting this position, Irenaeus pointed to the fact that bread, wine, and water were used in the Christian sacraments. How could they be evil, if they were given so prominent a position in Christian worship?

Arius argued that Christ was supreme among God's creatures. His opponents, such as Athanasius, retorted that this Christology was totally inconsistent with the way in which Christians worshipped. Athanasius stressed the theological importance of the practice of praying to Christ and worshipping him. If Arius was right, Christians were guilty of idolatry, through worshipping a creature, rather than God. Where Arius believed that theology should criticize liturgy, Athanasius believed that worship patterns and practices had to be taken into account by theologians.

This chapter has provided a brief exploration of the resources available to Christian theology, and some of the debates concerning their potential and their limitations. We may now return to the ideas of Christianity, and consider some further aspects of Christian teaching. We have already noted the central importance of Jesus Christ to Christians, and some of the key ideas of Christianity concerning his identity and significance. But what else do Christians believe? We shall explore this question in chapter 9.

1   What do Christians mean by "revelation"?
2   What can be known about God by looking at the world around us?
3   Why is the Bible so important to Christians?
4   Can God's existence be proved?
5   Try to summarize the argument set out by Anselm of Canterbury. Does it make sense?

STUDY QUESTIONS

9

CHAPTER

The Teachings of Christianity

As has already been stressed, Christianity is not just a set of ideas. The central figure of Christianity is Jesus. It is possible to gain the impression that Christianity is simply a set of ideas or moral values. For this reason, this book has devoted a major section to setting out the importance of Jesus for Christianity. The relevant parts of this section (pp. 108–44) should be studied in depth.

Christianity is thus about a way of living, focusing on Jesus Christ. Part of that way of living is a way of understanding the world, including ways of understanding the nature of God, the origin and destiny of human beings, and what lies beyond death. Underlying and sustaining that Christian way of living is a set of controlling beliefs. To gain a proper understanding of Christianity, it is therefore vitally important to understand what Christians believe. The present chapter aims to provide an overview of the classic themes of the Christian faith.

It must be understood that it is impossible to give a full account of the leading themes of the Christian faith in the brief space possible in the present volume. The reader should consider what follows as being nothing more than an introduction. Christians have been exploring and debating matters of theology for some two thousand years, with the result that there is an enormously rich theological heritage awaiting exploration. The present chapter can only hope to introduce the main themes of Christian teaching; readers wishing to proceed further with their explorations and reflections should consult more detailed works, such as those noted at the end of this book.

In what follows we shall use the western form of the Apostles' Creed (see p. 147) as a basis for our analysis of the leading themes of the Christian faith. This creed has long been used as a convenient summary of the main points of Christian belief, particularly for new converts who wish to be baptized.

Notice how the creed is dominated by statements directly relating to Jesus. Of the twelve statements in the creed, six (2–7) relate directly to Jesus. Three (10–12) can be argued to state the Christian understanding of the significance of Jesus, in that forgiveness of sins and the hope of resurrection and eternal life are understood by Christians to be based directly on the cross and resurrection of Jesus.

The Apostles' Creed (Western Form)

The Creed is restated here for ease of reference.

1 I believe in God, the Father almighty, creator of the heavens and earth;
2 and in Jesus Christ, his only Son, our Lord;
3 who was conceived by the Holy Spirit and born of the Virgin Mary;
4 suffered under Pontius Pilate, was crucified, dead and buried; he descended to hell;
5 on the third day he was raised from the dead;
6 he ascended into the heavens, and sits at the right hand of God the Father almighty;
7 from where he will come to judge the living and the dead.
8 I believe in the Holy Spirit;
9 in the holy catholic church; the communion of saints;
10 the forgiveness of sins;
11 the resurrection of the body;
12 and eternal life.

STUDY PANEL 30

We have already considered the Christian understanding of the identity and significance of Jesus in some detail. As a result, the present chapter will pick up on those aspects of the creed which set out additional Christian teachings. Readers who wish to engage with Christian views about Jesus are referred to the substantial discussions of these issues earlier in this work (pp. 108–44).

The Christian Doctrine of God

Christianity affirms the existence of God. But which God? And what is this God like? The creeds of Christianity do more than simply state the belief that God exists; they begin to give shape and substance to a series of specifically Christian understandings about the nature and character of this

God. Of particular importance is the Christian affirmation that God is known through Jesus. As we have seen, one of the most fundamental Christian insights is that God is revealed in the person and work of Jesus (see pp. 116–19).

God as Father

The creed opens with an affirmation of belief in "God the Father." This statement is intended to affirm that Christians believe in a personal God, rather than in an abstract impersonal idea. This can be seen clearly from the language both the Old and New Testaments use about God. For example, both use strongly personal language in describing the nature and character of God. God can be spoken of as "faithful" and "loving" (words which immediately imply a personal relationship). Many Christian writers have pointed out that prayer seems to be modeled on the relationship between a child and a parent. Prayer expresses a gracious relationship which "is simply trust in a person whose whole dealing with us proves him worthy of trust" (John Oman). Furthermore, one of Paul's leading ideas concerning the effects of Christ's death on the cross is that it gives rise to "reconciliation." This profound theological idea is clearly modeled on human personal relationships. It implies that the transformation through faith of the relationship between God and sinful human beings is like the reconciliation of two persons – perhaps an alienated husband and wife.

To refer to God as "Father" is thus to affirm belief in a personal dynamic God, rather than an impersonal static divine force. But it also implies more than this. For example, it implies that we derive our origin from God, and that God cares for us in that way that human fathers are meant to care for their children.

The major medieval Christian theologian Thomas Aquinas argues that the image of "God as Father" should be understood to mean that God is *like* a human father. In other words, God is *analogous* to a father. In some ways God is like a human father, and in others not. There are genuine points of similarity. God cares for us, as human fathers care for their children (note Matthew 7:9–11). God is the ultimate source of our existence, just as our fathers brought us into being. He exercises authority over us, as do human fathers. Equally, there are genuine points of dissimilarity. God is not a human being, for example.

The point that Aquinas is trying to make is clear. God reveals himself in images and ideas which tie in with our world of everyday existence – yet which do not reduce God to that everyday world. To say that "God is our father" is not to say that God is just yet another human father. Rather, it is to say that thinking about human fathers helps us think about God. They are analogies. Like all analogies, they break down at points. However, they are still extremely useful and vivid ways of thinking about God, which allow us to use the vocabulary and images of our own world, to describe something which ultimately lies beyond that world.

Biblical models of God are firmly located in real life. Just as Jesus used real-life parables to make theological points, so the writers of Scripture use models drawn from the experiential world of ancient Palestine to allow us insights into the nature and purposes of God. In that this society was male-dominated, many of these models are male. For example, the idea of the authority of God can only be represented using male imagery – for example, that of a father, a judge, or a king. Nevertheless, other models are used. God is often compared to a (genderless) rock, for example, conveying the idea of strength, stability and permanence. Feminine imagery abounds to describe God's care and compassion for his people, which is often likened to the love of a mother for her children. Yet it is not the imagery, but what is being said about God, that is of fundamental importance.

Scripture affirms that kings, shepherds, and fathers in ancient Israelite society are appropriate models for God. But this use of male models does not mean that God is male, any more than the use of genderless models (such as a rock) means that God is impersonal, or the use of female models (such as mother) imply that God is female. To speak of God as father is to say that the role of the father in ancient Israel allows us insights into the nature of God. It is not to say that God *is* a male human being! Neither male nor female sexuality is to be attributed to God. Sexuality is an attribute of the created order, which cannot be assumed to correspond directly to any such polarity within the Godhead.

The Old Testament avoids attributing sexual functions to God, on account of the strongly pagan overtones of such associations. The Canaanite fertility cults emphasized the sexual functions of both gods and goddesses; the Old Testament refuses to endorse the idea that the gender or the sexuality of God is a significant matter. There is no need to revert to pagan ideas of gods and goddesses to recover the idea that God is neither masculine or feminine; those ideas are already firmly embedded in the Old and New Testaments.

We shall return to consider the idea of God as creator, already hinted at in the present discussion, in a later section of this chapter. Our attention now turns to one of the more challenging aspects of the Christian understanding of God – the doctrine of the Trinity.

God as Trinity

The doctrine of the Trinity is one of the most distinctive Christian teachings. It also one of the most difficult doctrines to understand. In what follows we shall attempt to present an outline sketch of the main features of this teaching. The doctrine is not explicitly taught in the New Testament, although there are two passages which are certainly open to an explicitly Trinitarian interpretation: Matthew 28:19 and 2 Corinthians 13:14.

Trinitarian Hints in the New Testament?

STUDY PANEL 31

Matthew 28:18–20
Then Jesus came to [the disciples] and said, "All authority in heaven and on earth has been given to me. Therefore go and make disciples of all nations, baptizing them in the name of the Father and of the Son and of the Holy Spirit, and teaching them to obey everything I have commanded you. And surely I am with you always, to the very end of the age."

2 Corinthians 13:14
May the grace of the Lord Jesus Christ, and the love of God, and the fellowship of the Holy Spirit be with you all.

Both of the verses cited in Study Panel 31 have become deeply rooted in the Christian consciousness, the former on account of its baptismal associations, and the latter through the common use of the formula in Christian prayer and devotion. Yet these two verses, taken together or in isolation, can hardly be thought of as constituting a doctrine of the Trinity.

The biblical foundations of this doctrine are not, however, to be found in these two verses, but in the pervasive pattern of divine activity to which the New Testament bears witness. The Father is revealed in Christ through the Spirit. There is the closest of connections between the Father, Son, and Spirit in the New Testament writings. Time after time, New Testament passages link together these three elements as part of a greater whole. The totality of God's saving presence and power can only, it would seem, be expressed by involving all three elements (for example, see 1 Corinthians 12:4–6; 2 Corinthians 1:21–2; Galatians 4:6; Ephesians 2:20–22; 2 Thessalonians 2:13–14; Titus 3:4–6; 1 Peter 1:2).

The same Trinitarian structure can be seen in the Old Testament. Three major "personifications" of God can be discerned within its pages, which naturally lead on to the Christian doctrine of the Trinity. These are:

1   *Wisdom*. This personification of God is especially evident in the Wisdom literature, such as Proverbs, Job, and Ecclesiasticus. The attribute of divine wisdom is here treated as if it were a person (hence the idea of

"personification"), with an existence apart from, yet dependent upon, God. Wisdom (who is always treated as female, incidentally) is portrayed as active in creation, fashioning the world in her imprint (see Proverbs 1:20–3; 9:1–6; Job 28; Ecclesiasticus 24).

2   *The Word of God.* Here, the idea of God's speech or discourse is treated as an entity with an existence independent of God, yet originating with him. The Word of God is portrayed as going forth into the world to confront men and women with the will and purpose of God, bringing guidance, judgment and salvation (see Psalm 119:89; Psalm 147:15–20; Isaiah 55:10–11).

3   *The Spirit of God.* The Old Testament uses the phrase "the spirit of God" to refer to God's presence and power within his creation. The spirit is portrayed as being present in the expected Messiah (Isaiah 42:1–3), and as being the agent of a new creation which will arise when the old order has finally passed away (Ezekiel 36:26; 37:1–14).

These three "hypostatizations" of God (to use a Greek word in place of the English "personification") do not amount to a doctrine of the Trinity in the strict sense of the term. Rather, they point to a pattern of divine activity and presence in and through creation, in which God is both immanent and transcendent. A purely unitarian conception of God proved inadequate to contain this dynamic understanding of God. And it is this pattern of divine activity which is expressed in the doctrine of the Trinity.

The doctrine of the Trinity can be regarded as the outcome of a process of sustained and critical reflection on the pattern of divine activity revealed in Scripture, and continued in Christian experience. This is not to say that Scripture contains a doctrine of the Trinity; rather, Scripture bears witness to a God who demands to be understood in a Trinitarian manner.

The development of the doctrine of the Trinity is best seen as organically related to the evolution of the Christian understanding of the identity and significance of Jesus (see pp. 115–23; 126–34). It became increasingly clear that there was a consensus to the effect that Jesus was "of the same substance" (Greek: *homoousios*) as God, rather than just "of similar substance" (Greek: *homoiousios*). But if Jesus was God, in any meaningful sense of the word, what did this imply about God? If Jesus was God, were there now two Gods? Or was a radical reconsideration of the nature of God appropriate? Historically, it is possible to argue that the doctrine of the Trinity is closely linked with the development of the doctrine of the divinity of Christ. The more emphatic the church became that Christ was God, the more it came under pressure to clarify how Christ related to God.

The starting point for Christian reflections on the Trinity is, as we have seen, the New Testament witness to the presence and activity of God in Christ and through the Spirit. For Irenaeus, the whole process of salvation, from its beginning to its end, bore witness to the action of Father, Son, and Holy Spirit. Irenaeus made use of a term which features prominently in future discussion of the Trinity: "the economy of salvation." That word "economy" needs clarification. The Greek word *oikonomia* basically means "the way in which one's affairs are ordered" (the relation to the modern sense of the word will thus be clear). For Irenaeus, the "economy of salvation" means "the way in which God has ordered the salvation of humanity in history."

At the time, Irenaeus was under considerable pressure from Gnostic critics, who argued that the creator god was quite distinct from (and inferior to!) the redeemer god (see pp. 11–12). In the form favored by Marcion, this idea took the following form: the Old Testament god is a creator god, and totally different from the redeemer god of the New Testament. As a result, the Old Testament should be shunned by Christians, who should concentrate their attention upon the New Testament. Irenaeus vigorously rejected this idea. He insisted that the entire process of salvation, from the first moment of creation to the last moment of history, was the work of the one and the same God. There was a single economy of salvation, in which the one God – who was both creator and redeemer – was at work to redeem his creation.

In his *Demonstration of the Preaching of the Apostles,* Irenaeus insisted upon the distinct yet related roles of Father, Son, and Spirit within the economy of salvation. He affirmed his faith in:

> God the Father uncreated, who is uncontained, invisible one God, creator of the universe . . . and the Word of God, the Son of God, our Lord Jesus Christ, who . . . in the fulness of time, to gather all things to himself, became a human among humans, to . . . destroy death, bring life, and achieve fellowship between God and humanity . . . And the Holy Spirit . . . was poured out in a new way on our humanity to make us new throughout the world in the sight of God.

This passage brings out clearly the idea of an economic Trinity – that is to say, an understanding of the nature of the Godhead in which each person is responsible for an aspect of the economy of salvation. Far from being a rather pointless piece of theological speculation, the doctrine of the Trinity is grounded directly in the complex human experience of redemption in Christ, and is concerned with the explanation of this experience.

By the second half of the fourth century, the debate concerning the relation of the Father and Son gave every indication of having been settled.

The recognition that Father and Son were "of one being" settled the Arian controversy, and established a consensus within the church over the divinity of the Son. But further theological construction was necessary. What was the relation of the Spirit to the Father? and to the Son? There was a growing consensus that the Spirit could not be omitted from the Godhead. The Cappadocian fathers, especially Basil of Caesarea, defended the divinity of the Spirit in such persuasive terms that the foundation was laid for the final element of Trinitarian theology to be put in its place. The divinity and co-equality of Father, Son, and Spirit had been agreed; it now remained to develop Trinitarian models to allow this understanding of the Godhead to be visualized.

In general, eastern theology tended to emphasize the distinct individuality of the three persons, and safeguard their unity by stressing the fact that both the Son and the Spirit derived from the Father. The relation between the persons is grounded in what those persons *are*. Thus the relation of the Son to the Father is defined in terms of "being begotten" and "sonship." Augustine moves away from this approach, preferring to treat the persons in *relational* terms. The western approach was thus more marked by its tendency to begin from the unity of God, especially in the work of revelation and redemption, and to interpret the relation of the three persons in terms of their mutual fellowship.

The eastern approach might seem to suggest that the Trinity consists of three independent agents, doing quite different things. This possibility was excluded by two later developments, which are usually referred to by the terms "mutual interpenetration (*perichoresis*)" and "appropriation." Although these ideas find their full development at a later stage in the development of the doctrine, they are unquestionably hinted at in both Irenaeus and Tertullian, and find more substantial expression in the writings of Gregory of Nyssa. We may usefully consider both these ideas at this stage.

1   *Perichoresis.* This Greek term, which is often found in either its Latin (*circumincessio*) or English ("mutual interpenetration") forms, came into general use in the sixth century. It refers to the manner in which the three persons of the Trinity relate to one another. The concept of *perichoresis* allows the individuality of the persons to be maintained, while insisting that each person shares in the life of the other two. An image often used to express this idea is that of "a community of being," in which each person, while maintaining its distinctive identity, penetrates the others and is penetrated by them.

2   *Appropriation.* The modalist heresy argued that God could be considered as existing in different "modes of being" at different points in the economy of salvation, so that, at one point, God existed as Father and

created the world; at another God existed as Son and redeemed it. The doctrine of appropriation insists that the works of the Trinity are a unity; every person of the Trinity is involved in every outward action of the Godhead. Thus Father, Son, and Spirit are all involved in the work of creation, which is not to be viewed as the work of the Father alone. For example, Augustine of Hippo pointed out that the Genesis creation account speaks of God, the Word and the Spirit (Genesis 1:1–3), thus indicating that all three persons of the Trinity were present and active at this decisive moment in salvation history.

A representation of the Trinity found in a collection of Latin antiphons, produced in Siena around 1480. The three persons of the Trinity are here depicted as three "faces" of the one God. The divine unity is emphasized by the single figure sitting upon the throne. Note also the orb and scepter, which have been placed in the hands of God as symbols of divine authority. Christie's Images.

Yet it is appropriate to think of creation as the work of the Father. Despite the fact that all three persons of the Trinity are implicated in creation, it is properly seen as the distinctive action of the Father. Similarly, the entire Trinity is involved in the work of redemption. It is, however, appropriate to speak of redemption as being the distinctive work of the Son.

Taken together, the doctrines of *perichoresis* and appropriation allow us to think of the Godhead as a "community of being," in which all is shared, united, and mutually exchanged. Father, Son, and Spirit are not three isolated and diverging compartments of a Godhead, like three subsidiary components of an international corporation. Rather, they are differentiations within the Godhead, which become evident within the economy of salvation and the human experience of redemption and grace. The doctrine of the Trinity affirms that, beneath the surface of the complexities of the history of salvation and our experience of God lies one God, and one God only.

One of the most significant events in the early history of the church was agreement throughout the Roman Empire, both east and west, on the Nicene Creed. This document was intended to bring doctrinal stability to the church in a period of considerable importance in its history. Part of that agreed text referred to the Holy Spirit "proceeding from the Father." By the ninth century, however, the western church routinely altered this phrase, speaking of the Holy Spirit "proceeding from the Father *and from the Son*" (my emphasis). The Latin term *filioque* ("and from the Son") has since come to refer to this addition, now widely accepted within the western church, and the theology which it expresses. This idea of a "double procession" of the Holy Spirit was a source of intensive irritation to Greek Christians. Not only did it raise serious theological difficulties for them; it also involved tampering with the supposedly inviolable text of the creeds. Many scholars see this bad feeling as contributing to the split between the eastern and western churches, which took place around 1054 (see p. 261).

The *filioque* debate is of importance, both as a theological issue in itself, and also as a matter of some importance in the contemporary relations between the eastern and western churches. We therefore propose to explore the issues in some detail. The basic issue at stake is whether the Spirit may be said to proceed *from the Father alone*, or *from the Father and the Son*. The former is associated with the eastern church, and is given its most weighty exposition in the writings of the Cappadocian fathers; the latter is associated with the western church, and particularly with Augustine.

The Greek patristic writers insisted that there was only one source of being within the Trinity. The Father alone was the sole and supreme cause of all things, including the Son and the Spirit within the Trinity. The Son and the Spirit derive from the Father, but in different manners. In searching for suitable terms to express this relationship, theologians eventually fixed on two quite distinct images: the Son is *begotten* of the Father, while the Spirit *proceeds* from the Father. These two terms are intended to express the idea that both Son and Spirit derive from the Father, but are derived in different ways. The vocabulary is clumsy, reflecting the fact that the Greek words involved (*gennesis* and *ekporeusis*) are difficult to translate into modern English.

To assist in understanding this complex process, the Greek fathers used two images. The Father pronounces his word; at the same time as he utters this word, he breathes out in order to make this word capable of being heard and received. The imagery used here, which is strongly grounded in the biblical tradition, is that of the Son as the Word of God, and the Spirit as the breath of God. An obvious question arises here: why should the Cappadocian fathers, and other Greek writers, spend so much time and effort on distinguishing Son and Spirit in this way? The answer is important. A failure to distinguish the ways in which Son and Spirit derive from the one and the same Father would lead to God having two sons, which would have raised insurmountable problems.

Within this context, it is unthinkable that the Holy Spirit should proceed from the Father and the Son. Why? Because it would totally compromise the principle of the Father as the sole origin and source of all divinity. It would amount to affirming that there were two sources of divinity within the one Godhead, with all the internal contradictions and tensions that this would generate. If the Son were to share in the exclusive ability of the Father to be the source of all divinity, this ability would no longer be exclusive. For this reason, the Greek church regarded the western idea of a "double procession" of the Spirit with something approaching total disbelief.

Augustine, however, argued that the Spirit had to be thought of as proceeding from the Son. One of his main proof texts was John 20:22, in which the risen Christ is reported as having breathed upon his disciples, and said: "Receive the Holy Spirit." In particular, Augustine developed the idea of relation within the Godhead, arguing that the persons of the Trinity are defined by their relations to one another. The Spirit is thus to be seen as the relation of love and fellowship between the Father and Son, a relation which Augustine believed to be foundational to the Fourth Gospel's presentation of the unity of will and purpose of Father and Son.

We can summarize the basic differences between these two approaches to the Trinity as follows. The Greek intention was to safeguard the unique position of the Father as the sole source of divinity. In that both the Son

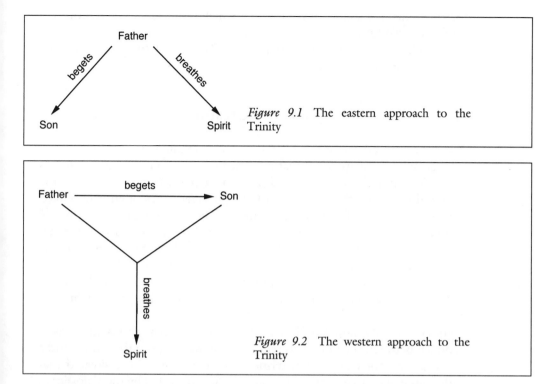

Figure 9.1 The eastern approach to the Trinity

Figure 9.2 The western approach to the Trinity

and Spirit derive from him, although in different but equally valid manners, their divinity is in turn safeguarded. To the Greeks, the Latin approach seemed to introduce two separate sources of divinity into the Godhead, and to weaken the vital distinction between Son and Spirit. The Son and Spirit are understood to have distinct, yet complementary roles; whereas the western tradition sees the Spirit as the Spirit of Christ. Indeed, a number of modern writers from this tradition, such as the Russian writer Vladimir Lossky, have criticized the western approach. In his essay "The Procession of the Holy Spirit," Lossky argues that the western approach inevitably depersonalizes the Spirit, leads to a misplaced emphasis upon the person and work of Christ, and reduces the Godhead to an impersonal principle.

The Latin intention was to ensure that the Son and Spirit were adequately distinguished from one another, yet shown to be mutually related to one another. The strongly relational approach adopted to the idea of "person" made it inevitable that the Spirit would be treated in this way. Sensitive to the Greek position, later Latin writers stressed that they did not regard their approach as presupposing two sources of divinity in the Godhead. The Council of Lyons stated that "the Holy Spirit proceeds from the Father and the Son, yet not as from two origins but as from one origin." However, the doctrine remains a source of contention, which is unlikely to be removed in the foreseeable future.

The differences between these two conceptions of the Trinity can be illustrated diagrammatically (see p. 199):

God the Creator

One important aspect of the Christian understanding of God focuses on God's activity in the work of creation. The doctrine of God as creator has its foundations firmly laid in the Old Testament (e.g., Genesis 1, 2). In the history of theology, the doctrine of God the creator has often been linked with the authority of the Old Testament. The continuing importance of the Old Testament for Christianity is often held to be grounded in the fact that the god of which it speaks is the same god to be revealed in the New Testament. The creator and redeemer god are one and the same. In the case of Gnosticism, a vigorous attack was mounted on both the authority of the Old Testament, and the idea that God was creator of the world.

For Gnosticism, in most of its significant forms, a sharp distinction was to be drawn between the God who redeemed humanity from the world, and a somewhat inferior deity (often termed "the demiurge") who created that world in the first place. The Old Testament was regarded by the Gnostics as dealing with this lesser deity, whereas the New Testament was concerned with the redeemer God. As such, belief in God as creator and in the authority of the Old Testament came to be interlinked at an early stage. Of the early writers to deal with this theme, Irenaeus of Lyons is of particular importance.

Irenaeus argued that the Christian doctrine of creation affirmed the basic goodness of the created order. Whereas Gnostic writers argued that the material world was evil, Irenaeus insisted that it remained the good creation of God. The development of this insight within early Christianity is especially associated with Celtic Christianity (see pp. 257–60), which was noted for its emphasis on the goodness of creation. The strongholds of Celtic Christianity tended to be on the tiny islands off the Scottish mainland, or in isolated regions of Ireland. These contexts brought the Celtic Christians into close contact with nature, and led to a deep appreciation of the wonder of nature. Celtic manuscripts, including biblical and liturgical texts, often incorporated ornamental designs based on animals, plants, foliage, and fruit. However, perhaps the most familiar affirmation of the goodness of the creation is found in the famous "Canticle of the Sun" of Francis of Assisi (1181–1226), which uses the language of "brother" and "sister" to refer to elements of the creation.

Francis of Assisi on the Creation

Francis's *Canticle of the Sun*, probably written in 1225, represents an important affirmation of a positive attitude towards the creation, typical of Franciscan spirituality. Note especially the underlying theology of providence, in which the benefit of each aspect of creation for humanity is identified. The most famous feature of the canticle is its use of the terms "brother" and "sister" to refer to various aspects of the created order. Traditional English translations of this familiar poem have been heavily influenced by the need to ensure rhyming. My prose translation of the original Italian ignores such considerations in order to convey the sense of the poem. The lines of the original have been retained.

The Praises of the Creatures

Most high, all-powerful and good Lord!
To you are due the praises, the glory, the honor and every blessing,
To you only, O highest one, are they due
and no human being is worthy to speak of you.

Be praised, my Lord, with all your creatures
especially by brother sun
by whom we are lightened every day
for he is fair and radiant with great splendor
and bears your likeness, O highest one.

Be praised, my Lord, for sister moon and the stars
you have set them in heaven, precious, fair and bright.

Be praised, my Lord, by brother wind
and by air and cloud and sky and every weather
through whom you give life to all your creatures.

Be praised, my Lord, by sister water
for she is useful and humble and precious and chaste.

By praised, my Lord, by brother fire
by him we are lightened at night
and he is fair and cheerful and sturdy and strong.

Be praised, my Lord, by our sister, mother earth
she sustains and governs us
and brings forth many fruits and coloured flowers and plants.

Another debate of importance within early Christianity centered on the question of whether creation was *ex nihilo* ("out of nothing"). In one of his dialogues, the classical Greek philosopher Plato developed the idea that the world was made out of pre-existent matter, which was fashioned into the present form of the world. This idea was taken up by most Gnostic writers, who were here followed by a few Christian theologians such as Theophilus and Justin Martyr. According to these writers, God created the world out of pre-existent matter (that is, material which was already to hand), which was then shaped into the specific shape of the world as we know it in the act of creation. In other words, creation was not *ex nihilo*; rather, it was an act of construction, on the basis of material which was already to hand, in much the same way as one might speak of someone "creating" a house from brick or stone.

On the basis of this approach, the presence of evil in the world was thus to be explained on the basis of the intractability of this pre-existent matter. God's options in creating the world were limited by the poor quality of the material available. The presence of evil or defects within the world are thus not to be ascribed to God, but to deficiencies in the material from which the world was constructed. This view gained widespread acceptance within Gnostic circles.

However, the growing conflict between early Christian writers and Gnosticism forced reconsideration of this specific issue. In part, the idea of creation from pre-existent matter was seen as discredited by its Gnostic associations; in part, it was called into question by an increasingly sophisticated reading of the Old Testament creation narratives. Writers such as Theophilus of Antioch insisted upon the doctrine of creation *ex nihilo*, which may be regarded as gaining the ascendency from the end of the second century onwards. From that point onwards, it became the received doctrine within the church.

Implications of the Doctrine of Creation

The doctrine of God as creator has several major implications, of which some may be noted here.

1   A distinction must be drawn between God and the creation. A major theme of Christian theology from the earliest of times has been to resist the temptation to merge the creator and the creation. The theme is clearly stated in Paul's letter to the Romans, the opening chapter of which criticizes the tendency to reduce God to the level of the world. According to Paul, there is a natural human tendency, as a result of sin, to serve "created things rather than the creator" (Romans 1:25). A central task of a Christian theology of creation is to distinguish God from the creation, while at the same time to affirm that it is God's creation.

This process may be seen at work in the writings of Augustine; it is of considerable importance in the writings of reformers such as Calvin, who were concerned to forge a world-affirming spirituality in response to the general monastic tendency to renounce the world, evident in writings such as Thomas à Kempis' *Imitation of Christ*, with its characteristic emphasis upon the "contempt of the world." There is a dialectic in Calvin's thought between the world, as the creation of God himself, and the world as the fallen creation. In that it is God's creation, it is to be honored, respected, and affirmed; in that it is a fallen creation, it is to be criticized with the object of redeeming it. The doctrine of creation thus leads to a critical world-affirming spirituality, in which the world is affirmed, without falling into the snare of treating it as if it were God.

The importance of this point has been stressed by more recent writers, including Lesslie Newbigin. Elements of creation can easily become demonic, by being invested with the authority and power which properly belong to God alone.

> They can come to usurp the place to which they have no right, the place which belongs to Christ and to him alone. They can, as we say, become absolutized, and then they become demonic. [The state] power ordained by God in Romans 13 becomes the Beast of Revelation. The Torah, that loving instruction which God gives his people and the beauty of which is celebrated in Psalm 119, becomes a tyrant from which Christ has to deliver us.

A proper doctrine of creation prevents this process of demonization from taking place, by insisting that creational elements may be good, but are never divine. It thus provides a framework by which we are protected against the usurpation of divine authority by any aspect of the creation – whether it is a person, a set of values, or an institution.

2   Creation implies God's authority over and possession of the world. As the Dutch Reformed theologian Abraham Kuyper once famously affirmed, "there is not one square inch of creation about which Jesus Christ does not say: that is *mine.*" A characteristic biblical emphasis is that the creator has authority over the creation. Humans are thus regarded as part of that creation, with special functions within it. The doctrine of creation leads to the idea of *human stewardship of the creation*, which is to be contrasted with a secular notion of *human ownership of the world*. The creation is not ours; we hold it in trust for God. We are meant to be the stewards of God's creation, and are responsible for the manner in which we exercise that stewardship. This insight is of major importance in relation to ecological and environmental concerns, in that it provides a theoretical foundation for the exercise of human responsibility towards the planet.

Recognition that the world belongs to God thus has important consequences for understanding our own responsibilities within that world. We have been placed within God's creation to tend it and take care of it (Genesis 2:15). We may be superior to the remainder of that creation, and exercise authority over it (Psalm 8:4–8) – but we remain under the authority of God, and responsible to him for the way in which we treat his creation. We are the stewards, not the owners, of creation. We hold it in trust. There is a growing realization today that past generations have seriously abused that trust. They have exploited the creation and its resources. There is a real danger that we shall spoil what God so wonderfully created.

Fortunately, there has been a growing awareness recently of the need to take a more responsible attitude towards creation. Reflecting on our responsibilities as stewards of God's creation is the first step in undoing the harm done by past generations. It matters to God that vast areas of our world are made uninhabitable through nuclear or toxic chemical waste. It matters that the delicate balance of natural forces is disturbed by human carelessness. Sin affects the way we treat the environment as much as it does our attitude towards God, other people, and society as a whole. This article of the creed is the basis of a new – and overdue – attitude towards creation.

3   The doctrine of God as creator implies the goodness of creation. Throughout the first biblical account of creation, we encounter the affirmation "And God saw that it was good" (Genesis 1:10; 18; 21; 25; 31). (The only thing that is "not good" is that Adam is alone. Humanity is created as a social being, and is meant to exist in relation with others.) There is no place in Christian theology for the Gnostic or dualist idea of the world as an inherently evil place. As we shall explore elsewhere, even though the world

is fallen through sin, it remains God's good creation, and capable of being redeemed.

This is not to say that the creation is presently perfect. An essential component of the Christian doctrine of sin is the recognition that the world has departed from the trajectory upon which God placed it in the work of creation. It has become deflected from its intended course. It has fallen from the glory in which it was created. The world as we see it is not the world as it was intended to be. The existence of human sin, evil, and death are themselves tokens of the extent of the departure of the created order from its intended pattern. For this reason, most Christian reflections on redemption include the idea of some kind of restoration of creation to its original integrity, in order that God's intentions for his creation might find fulfillment. Affirming the goodness of creation also avoids the suggestion, unacceptable to most theologians, that God is responsible for evil. The constant biblical emphasis upon the goodness of creation is a reminder that the destructive force of sin is not present in the world by God's design or permission.

4   The doctrine of creation has important implications for our understanding of ourselves, and particularly our place within creation. Human beings are created in the image of God. This insight, central to any Christian doctrine of human nature, is of major importance as an aspect of the doctrine of creation itself. The divine intention in creating humanity is that they should exist in a relationship with him. Until and unless that relationship exists, humanity will not fulfill its true intention, and will remain unfulfilled. "You made us for yourself, and our hearts are restless until they find their rest in you" (Augustine of Hippo).

At a more existential level, the doctrine has important implications for our attitude toward existing in the world. The doctrine of creation allows us to feel at home in the world. It reminds us that we, like the rest of creation, were fashioned by God. We are here because God wants us to be here. We are not alone, but are in the very presence of the God who made and owns everything. We are in the presence of a friend, who knows us and cares for us. Behind the apparently faceless universe lies a person.

Yet this attitude of "being at home in the world" needs to be qualified. We are to see ourselves as passing through the world, not belonging there permanently. We are, so to put it, tourists rather than residents. In his *Geneva Catechism*, Calvin suggests that we should "earn to pass through this world as though it is a foreign country, treating all earthly things lightly and declining to set our hearts upon them."

Perhaps one of the finest statements of this attitude may be found in the sermon of the eighteenth-century American writer Jonathan Edwards entitled "The Christian Pilgrim", in which he affirms that "It was never designed by God that this world should be our home." Speaking with the eighteenth-century situation in New England in mind, Edwards declared:

> Though surrounded with outward enjoyments, and settled in families with desirable friends and relations; though we have companions whose society is delightful, and children in whom we see many promising qualifications; though we live by good neighbors and are generally beloved where known; yet we ought not to take our rest in these things as our portion . . . We ought to possess, enjoy and use them, with no other view but readily to quit them, whenever we are called to it, and to change them willingly for heaven.

5   The doctrine of creation also calls into question the western distinction between "sacred" and "secular." To describe one area of our lives (such as leading a Sunday School) as "sacred" and another (such as working in an office) as "secular" implies that only part of our lives is dedicated to God, and that only part of God's creation can be said to be his. This attitude is particularly associated with the Protestant reformers, who supplemented the doctrine of the "priesthood of all believers" with the idea of "being called to serve God in the world." All Christians were called to be priests – and that calling extended to the everyday world. Christians were called to be priests to the world, purifying and sanctifying its everyday life from within. Luther stated this point succinctly, when commenting on Genesis 13:13: "what seem to be secular works are actually the praise of God and represent an obedience which is well pleasing to him." Luther even extolled the religious value of housework, declaring that although "it had no obvious appearance of holiness, yet these very household chores are more to be valued than all the works of monks and nuns."

Underlying this new attitude is the notion of the "calling." God calls his people not just to faith, but to express that faith in quite definite areas of life in the world. One is called, in the first place, to be a Christian, and in the second, to live out that faith in a quite definite sphere of activity within the world. Whereas medieval monastic spirituality generally regarded the idea of "vocation" as a calling *out* of the world into the seclusion and isolation of the monastery, Luther and Calvin understood it as a calling *into* the everyday world. The doctrine of creation thus leads to a strong work ethic, in the sense that work in the world can be seen as work for God.

Jesus

The area of Christian theology traditionally known as "Christology" deals with the person of Jesus Christ. This has already been dealt with in some detail in our analysis of the significance of Jesus in the New Testament (pp. 108–23), and the elaboration of these views in the Christian tradition (pp. 124–44). You are referred to these major sections for further discussion.

The Holy Spirit

The Christian interest in the doctrine of the Holy Spirit has perceptibly grown in the last hundred years, on account of the rise of the charismatic movement (see pp. 334–6). It is important that we begin our discussion of this area of Christian teaching by noting the difficulties of translating the biblical words for "spirit." The English language uses at least three words – "wind," "breath," and "spirit" – to translate the one Hebrew word *ruach*. This important Hebrew word has a depth of meanings which it is virtually impossible to reproduce in English. *Ruach*, traditionally translated simply as "spirit," is associated with a range of meanings, each of which casts some light on the complex associations of the Christian notion of the Holy Spirit.

1 *Spirit as wind.* The Old Testament writers are careful not to identify God with the wind, and thus reduce God to the level of a natural force. Nevertheless, a parallel is drawn between the power of the wind, and that of God. To speak of God as spirit is to remind Israel of the power and dynamism of the God who had called Israel out of Egypt. This image of the spirit as redemptive power is perhaps stated in its most significant form in the account of the Exodus from Egypt, in which a powerful wind divides the Red Sea (Exodus 14:21). Here, the idea of *ruach* conveys both the power and the redemptive purpose of God.

The image of the wind also allowed the pluriformity of human experience of God to be accounted for, and visualized in a genuinely helpful manner. The Old Testament writers were conscious of experiencing the presence and activity of God in two quite distinct manners. Sometimes God was experienced as a judge, one who condemned Israel for its waywardness; yet at other times, God is experienced as one who refreshes Israel, like water in a dry land. The image of the wind conveyed both these ideas in a powerful manner. It must be remembered that Israel bordered the Mediterranean Sea on the west, and the great deserts on the east. When the wind blew from the east, it was experienced as a mist of fine sand which scorched vegetation and parched the land. Travellers' accounts of these winds speak of their remarkable force and power. Even the light of the sun is obliterated by the sand-storm thrown up by the wind. This wind was seen by the biblical writers as a model for the way in which God demonstrated the finitude and transitoriness of the creation. "The grass withers and the flowers fall, because the breath of the Lord blows on them" (Isaiah 40:7).

The western winds, however, were totally different. In the winter, the west and south-west winds brought rain to the dry land as they blew in from the sea. In the summer, the western winds did not bring rain, but coolness. The intensity of the desert heat was mitigated through these gentle cooling breezes. And just as this wind brought refreshment, by moistening the dry ground in winter and cooling the heat of the day in summer, so God was understood to refresh human spiritual needs. In a series of powerful images, God is compared by the Old Testament writers to the rain brought by the western wind (Hosea 6:3), refreshing the land.

2 *Spirit as breath.* The idea of spirit is associated with life. When God created Adam, God breathed into him the breath of life, as a result of which he became a living being (Genesis 2:7). The basic difference between a living and a dead human being is that the former breathes, and the latter does not. This led to the idea that life was dependent upon breath. God is the one who breathes the breath of life into empty shells, and brings them to life. God brought Adam to life by breathing into him. The famous vision of the valley of the dry bones (Ezekiel 37:1–14) also illustrates this point: can these dry bones live? The bones only come to life when breath enters into them (Ezekiel 37:9–10). The model of God as spirit thus conveys the fundamental insight that God is the one who gives life, even the one who is able to bring the dead back to life. It is thus important to note that *ruach* is often linked in the Old Testament with God's work of creation (e.g., Genesis 1:2; Job 26:12–13; 33:4; Psalm 104:27–31), even if the precise role of the Spirit is left unspecified. There is clearly an association between "Spirit" and the giving of life through creation.

3 *Spirit as charism.* The technical term "charism" refers to the "filling of an individual with the spirit of God," by which the person in question is enabled to perform tasks which would otherwise be impossible. In the Old Testament, the gift of wisdom is often portrayed as a consequence of the endowment of the Spirit (Genesis 41:38–9; Exodus 28:3; 35:31; Deuteronomy 34:9). At times, the Old Testament attributes gifts of leadership or military prowess to the influence of the Spirit (Judges 14:6, 19; 15:14, 15). However, the most pervasive aspect of this feature of the Spirit relates to the question of prophecy. The Old Testament does not offer much in the way of clarification concerning the manner in which the prophets were inspired, guided or motivated by the Holy Spirit. In the pre-exilic era, prophecy is often associated with ecstatic experiences of God, linked with wild behavior (1 Samuel 10:6; 19:24). Nevertheless, the activity of prophecy gradually became associated with the message rather than the behavior of the prophet. The prophet's credentials rest upon an endowment with the Spirit (Isaiah 61:1; Ezekiel 2:1–2; Micah 3:8; Zechariah 7:12), which authenticates the

prophet's message – a message which is usually described as "the word of the Lord."

The Debate over the Divinity of the Holy Spirit

The early church, with occasional exceptions, does not appear to have devoted much attention to clarifying its teaching on the Holy Spirit. The relative absence of extensive discussion of the role of the Holy Spirit in the first three centuries reflects the fact that theological debate centered elsewhere. The Greek patristic writers had, in their view, more important things to do than worry about the Spirit, when vital political and Christological debates were raging all around them. This point was made by the fourth-century writer Amphilochius of Iconium, who pointed out that the Arian controversy had first to be resolved before any serious discussion over the status of the Holy Spirit could get under way. The theological development of the early church was generally a response to public debates; once a serious debate got under way, doctrinal clarification was the inevitable outcome.

The debate in question initially centered upon a group of writers known as the *pneumatomachoi* or "opponents of the spirit," who argued that neither the person nor the works of the Spirit were to be regarded as having the status or nature of a divine person. In response to this writers such as Athanasius and Basil of Caesarea made an appeal to the formula which had by then become universally accepted for baptism. Since the time of the New Testament (see Matthew 28:18–20) Christians were baptized in the name of "the Father, Son, and Holy Spirit." Athanasius argued that this had momentous implications for an understanding of the status of the person of the Holy Spirit. In his *Letter to Serapion*, Athanasius declared that the baptismal formula clearly pointed to the Spirit sharing the same divinity as the Father and the Son. This argument eventually prevailed.

However, patristic writers were hesitant to speak openly of the Spirit as "God," in that this practice was not sanctioned by Scripture – a point discussed at some length by Basil of Caesarea in his treatise on the Holy Spirit (374–5). Even as late as 380, Gregory of Nazianzen conceded that many orthodox Christian theologians were uncertain as to whether to treat the Holy Spirit "as an activity, as a creator, or as God." This caution can be seen in the final statement of the doctrine of the Holy Spirit, formulated by a Council meeting at Constantinople in 381. The Spirit was here described, not as God, but as "the Lord and giver of life, who proceeds from the Father, and is worshipped and glorified with the Father and Son." The language is unequivocal; the Spirit is to be treated as having the same dignity and rank as the Father and Son, even if the term "God" is not to be used explicitly. The precise relation of the Spirit to Father and Son would subsequently become an item of debate in its own right, as the *filioque* controversy indicates (see pp. 197–200).

The following considerations seem to have been of decisive importance in establishing the divinity of the Holy Spirit during the later fourth century. First, as Gregory of Nazianzen stressed, Scripture applied all the titles of God to the Spirit, with the exception of "unbegotten." Gregory drew particular attention to the use of the word "holy" to refer to the Spirit, arguing that this holiness did not result from any external source, but was the direct consequence of the nature of the Spirit. The Spirit was to be considered as the one who sanctifies, rather than the one who requires to be sanctified.

Second, the functions which are specific to the Holy Spirit establish the divinity of the Spirit. Didymus the Blind (died 398) was one of many writers to point out that the Spirit was responsible for the creating, renewing and sanctification of God's creatures. Yet how could one creature renew or sanctify another creature? Only if the Spirit was divine could sense be made of these functions. If the Holy Spirit performed functions which were specific to God, it must follow that the Holy Spirit shares in the divine nature. For Basil, the Spirit makes creatures to be like God and to be god – and only one who is divine can bring this about.

Third, the reference to the Spirit in the baptismal formula of the church was interpreted as supporting the divinity of the Spirit. Baptism took place in the name of the "Father, Son and Holy Spirit" (Matthew 28:17–20). Athanasius and others argued that this formula established the closest of connections between the three members of the Trinity, making it impossible to suggest that the Father and Son shared in the substance of the Godhead, while the Spirit was nothing other than a creature. In a similar way, Basil of Caesarea argued that the baptismal formula clearly implied the inseparability of Father, Son, and Spirit. This verbal association, according to Basil, clearly had considerable theological implications.

The admission of the full divinity of the Spirit thus took place at a relatively late stage in the development of patristic theology. In terms of the logical advance of doctrines, the following historical sequence can be discerned.

Stage 1: the recognition of the full divinity of Jesus Christ.
Stage 2: the recognition of the full divinity of the Spirit.
Stage 3: the definitive formulation of the doctrine of the Trinity, embedding and clarifying these central insights, and determining their mutual relationship.

This sequential development is acknowledged by Gregory of Nazianzen, who pointed to a gradual progress in clarification and understanding of the mystery of God's revelation in the course of time. It was, he argued, impossible to deal with the question of the divinity of the Spirit, until the issue of the divinity of Christ had been settled.

> The Old Testament preached the Father openly and the Son more obscurely. The New Testament revealed the Son, and hinted at the divinity of the Holy Spirit. Now the Spirit dwells in us, and is revealed more clearly to us. It was not proper to preach the Son openly, while the divinity of the Father had not yet been admitted. Nor was it proper to accept the Holy Spirit before [the divinity of] the Son had been acknowledged . . . Instead, by gradual advances and . . . partial ascents, we should move forward and increase in clarity, so that the light of the Trinity should shine.

The Functions of the Spirit

What does the Holy Spirit do? The Christian tradition has generally understood the work of the Holy Spirit to focus on three broad areas: revelation, salvation, and the Christian life. In what follows we shall provide a brief indication of the richness of the Christian understanding of the role of the Spirit in each of these three areas.

1   *Revelation.* There has been a widespread recognition of the pivotal role of the Spirit in relation to the making of God known to humanity. Irenaeus wrote of the "Holy Spirit, through whom the prophets prophesied, and our forebears learned of God and the righteous were led in the paths of justice." Similarly, in his 1536 commentary on the gospels, Martin Bucer argues that revelation cannot occur without the assistance of God's Spirit:

> Before we believe in God and are inspired by the Holy Spirit, we are unspiritual and for that reason we are completely unable to apprehend anything relating to God. So all the wisdom and righteousness which we possess in the absence of the Holy Spirit are the darkness and shadow of death.

The task of the Holy Spirit is to lead us into God's truth; without that Spirit, truth remains elusive.

The role of the Spirit in relation to the most important theological source of the Christian tradition is of particular importance. The doctrine of the "inspiration of Scripture" affirms that the Bible has a God-given authority by virtue of its origins. This doctrine, in various forms, is the common tradition of Christianity, and has its origins in the Bible itself, most notably the affirmation that "every Scripture is God-breathed (*theopneustos*)" (1 Timothy 3:16). In Protestant theology, however, the doctrine of the inspiration of Scripture serves an additional purpose – that of insisting on the primacy of Scripture over the church. Whereas more catholic writers point to the formation of the canon of Scripture as indicating the authority of the church over that of Scripture, Protestant writers argue that the church merely recognized an authority which was already present within Scripture itself.

Yet it is not simply God's revelation which is linked with the work of the Spirit; the Spirit is also widely regarded as being involved in the human response to that revelation. Most Christian theologians have regarded faith itself as the result of the work of the Holy Spirit. John Calvin is one writer who draws attention to the pivotal role of the Spirit in revealing God's truth and applying or "sealing" this truth to humanity.

> Now we shall have a right definition of faith if we say that it is a steady and certain knowledge of the divine benevolence towards us, which is founded upon the truth of the gracious promise of God in Christ, and is both revealed to our minds and sealed in our hearts by the Holy Spirit.

2   *Salvation.* We have already noted how patristic writers justified the divinity of the Spirit with reference to the functions of the Spirit. Many of those functions relate directly to the doctrine of salvation – for example, the role of the Spirit in sanctification, making humanity like God, and divinization. This point is particularly important within the eastern Christian tradition, with its traditional emphasis on deification; western concepts of salvation, which tend to be relational rather than ontological, nevertheless find room for a role for the Spirit. Thus in Calvin's doctrine of the application of salvation, the Holy Spirit plays a major role in relation to the establishment of a living relationship between Christ and the believer.

3   *The Christian life.* For many writers, the Holy Spirit plays an especially important role in relation to the Christian life, both at the individual and corporate level. The fifth-century writer Cyril of Alexandria is one of many to stress the role of the Spirit in bringing unity within the church.

> All of us who have received the one and the same Spirit, that is, the Holy Spirit, are in a sense merged together with one another and with God . . . Just as the power of the holy flesh of Christ united those in whom it dwells into one body, I think that, in much the same way, the one and undivided Spirit of God, who dwells in us all, leads us all into spiritual unity.

A further development of this aspect of the work of the Holy Spirit is due to Augustine. Augustine regards the Spirit as the bond of unity between Father and Son on the one hand, and between God and believers on the other. The Spirit is a gift, given by God, which unites believers both to God and to other believers. The Holy Spirit forges bonds of unity between believers, upon which the unity of the church ultimately depends. The church is the "temple of the Holy Spirit," within which the Holy Spirit dwells. The same Spirit which binds together the Father and Son in the unity of the godhead also binds together believers in the unity of the church.

However, any properly Christian understanding of the role of the Spirit will go far beyond this, and will include reference to at least two other areas. First, the "making real" of God in personal and corporate worship and devotion. The importance of the role of the Spirit in relation to Christian prayer, spirituality, and worship has been stressed by many writers, classic and modern. Second, the enabling of believers to lead a Christian life, particularly in relation to morality. In his 1536 gospels commentary, Martin Bucer draws attention to the necessity of the Spirit, if believers are to keep the law.

> So those who believe are not under the law, because they have the Spirit within them, teaching them everything more perfectly than the law ever could, and motivating them much more powerfully to obey it. In other words, the Holy Spirit moves the heart, so that believers wish to live by those things which the law commands, but which the law could not achieve by itself.

This aspect of the role of the Holy Spirit has become increasingly prominent in modern Christian discussions, on account of the rise of the charismatic movement, which places an emphasis on the energizing role of the Spirit within the Christian life.

The Church

The Greek word *ekklesia*, used in the New Testament to refer to the church, does not denote a building, but a group of people. It literally means "those who are called out." The church consists of those who have been called out of the world into a community of faith – those who God has "called out of darkness into his wonderful light" (1 Peter 2:9). Ecclesiology was not a major issue in the early church. The eastern church showed no awareness of the potential importance of the issue. Most Greek patristic writers of the first five centuries contented themselves with describing the church using recognizably scriptural images, without choosing to probe further. The following elements can be discerned as having achieved a wide consensus at the time:

1   The church is a spiritual society, which replaces Israel as the people of God in the world.

2 All Christians are made one in Christ, despite their different origins and backgrounds.

3 The church is the repository of true Christian teaching.

4 The church gathers the faithful throughout the world together, in order to enable them to grow in faith and holiness.

In part, this lack of interest in the doctrine of the church reflected the political situation of the time. The church was at best a barely tolerated, and at worst a vigorously persecuted, organization within the sphere of authority of a hostile pagan state – namely, the Roman Empire. With the conversion of Constantine, however, the situation changed radically. In what follows, we shall concentrate on the key elements of Christian understandings of the nature of the church. It is traditional to speak of the "four marks of the church" – in other words, four characteristic identifying features. The Apostles' Creed notes two, implies one more, and omits reference to a fourth. For the sake of fulness, we shall consider all four "notes." These are: "one," "holy," "catholic," and "apostolic."

One

The unity of the church has been of central importance to Christian thinking on the subject. The World Council of Churches, one of the more important agencies in the modern period to be concerned with Christian unity, defines itself as "a fellowship of churches, which confess our Lord Jesus Christ as God and Savior." Yet that very definition concedes the existence of a plurality of churches – Anglican, Baptist, Lutheran, Methodist, Orthodox, Presbyterian, Roman Catholic, and so on. How can one speak of "one church" when there are so many churches? Or "the unity of the church," when it is so clearly disunited at the institutional level?

Two episodes in church history may be noted as being of especial importance in relation to this question. The first relates to North Africa in the third century, when division within the church became a potentially destructive issue. The Decian persecution (250–1) led to many Christians lapsing or abandoning their faith in the face of persecution. Division arose immediately over how these individuals should be treated: did such a lapse mark the end of their faith, or could they be reconciled to the church by penance? Opinions differed sharply, and serious disagreement and tension resulted. (The Donatist controversy, noted earlier, may be regarded as a development of this unresolved problem, in response to the later Diocletian persecution.)

In his treatise *On the Unity of the Catholic Church* (251), written in direct response to the crisis arising from the Decian persecution, Cyprian of Carthage insisted upon the absolute unity of the church, comparing it to the "seamless robe of Christ," which could not be divided because it had been woven from the top throughout. Destroy its unity, and its identity was simultaneously devastated.

> Whoever is separated from the church is joined with an adultress, and separated from the promises of the church. None who leaves the church of Christ can attain the rewards of Christ. None can have God for a father unless they have the church as their mother. If any had been able to escape outside Noah's Ark, there might be a way of escape for those who are outside the church.

There is only one church, and outside its bounds salvation is impossible.

The sixteenth-century Reformation also witnessed controversy over this issue. How, it was asked, could the reformers justify forming breakaway churches, and thus compromising the unity of the church? (It must be remembered that the Reformation took place in a western European context, where the only significant ecclesiastical body was the hitherto more or less undivided Roman Catholic church.) The reformers responded by arguing that the medieval church had become corrupted to a point at which it could no longer be regarded as a church, in the strict sense of the word. The scene was thus set for an explosive increase in denominations.

Once the principle of breaking away from a parent ecclesiastical body for doctrinal reasons was established, little could be done to check it. Thus the Church of England broke away from the medieval Catholic church in the sixteenth century; in the eighteenth century, Methodism broke away from the Church of England; in the nineteenth century, Methodism subdivided into Welseyan and Calvinist churches, divided over the issue of predestination. From the sixteenth century onwards, it became clear that the idea of "one church" could not longer be understood sociologically or institutionally.

Faced with this apparent contradiction between a theoretical belief in "one church" and the brute reality of a plurality of churches, some Christian writers have developed approaches to allow the latter to be understood within the framework of the former. Four approaches may be noted, each with distinctive strengths and weaknesses.

1 An imperialist approach, which declares that there is only one empirical church which deserves to be treated as the true church, with all others being fraudulent, or at best approximations to the real thing. The position was characteristic of Roman Catholicism prior to the Second Vatican Council. The Second Vatican Council took the momentous step of recognizing other churches as separated Christian brothers and sisters.

2 A Platonic approach, which draws a fundamental distinction between the empirical church (that is, the church as a visible historical reality) and the ideal church. This has found relatively little support in mainstream Christian theology, although some scholars have argued that this idea may be detected in the Reformation distinction between the "visible" and "invisible" church. However, this distinction is better interpreted along eschatological lines, as we shall see shortly.

3 An eschatological approach, which suggests that the present disunity of the church will be abolished on the last day. The present situation is temporary, and will be resolved at the time of eschatological fulfillment. This understanding lies behind Calvin's distinction between the "visible" and "invisible" church.

4 A biological approach, which likens the historical evolution of the church to the development of the branches of a tree. This image, developed by the eighteenth-century German Pietist writer Nicolas von Zinzendorf, and taken up with enthusiasm by Anglican writers of the following century, allows the different empirical churches – e.g., the Roman Catholic, Orthodox, and Anglican churches – to be seen as possessing an organic unity, despite their differences.

However, in recent years, many theologians concerned with ecumenism (deriving from the Greek word *oecumene*, "the whole world," and now generally understood to mean "the movement concerned with the fostering of Christian unity") argued that the true basis of the "unity of the church" required to be recovered, after centuries of distortion. Throughout the New Testament, they argued, the diversity of local churches is not regarded as compromising the unity of the church. The church already possesses a unity through its common calling from God, which expresses itself in different communities in different cultures and situations. Hans Küng stresses this point as follows:

> The unity of the church is a spiritual entity . . . It is one and the same God who gathers the scattered from all places and all ages and makes them into one people of God. It is one and the same Christ who through his word and Spirit unites all together in the same bond of fellowship of the same body of Christ . . . The Church *is* one, and therefore *should be* one.

The unity of the church is grounded in the saving work of God in Christ. This is in no way inconsistent with that one church adapting itself to local cultural conditions, leading to the formations of local churches.

> The unity of the Church presupposes a multiplicity of Churches; the various churches do not need to deny their origins or their specific situations; their language, their history, their customs and traditions, their way of life and

thought, their personal structure will differ fundamentally, and no one has the right to take this from them. The same thing is not suitable for everyone, at every time, and in every place.

The rapid growth of evangelicalism in the modern church is of considerable importance in relation to the doctrine of the church. Evangelicalism is a world-wide transdenominational movement, which is able to co-exist within every major denomination in the western church, including the Roman Catholic church. Evangelicalism is not inextricably locked into any specific denominational constituency. An evangelical commitment to a corporate conception of the Christian life does not entail the explicit definition of a theology of the church (see pp. 331–4). Precisely because evangelicalism has no defining or limiting ecclesiology, it can accommodate itself to virtually any form of church order – including that of Roman Catholicism.

This is well illustrated by the history of the movement. Evangelical attitudes are now known to have been deeply embedded within the Italian church during the 1520s and 1530s, with prominent Italian church leaders (including several cardinals) meeting regularly in a number of cities to study Scripture and the writings of the Protestant reformers. No tension was seen between an evangelical spirituality and a Catholic ecclesiology; it was only when the situation was radically politicized in the 1540s through the intrusion of imperial politics into theological debate that evangelicalism came to be seen as a destabilizing influence within the Italian church.

Similar developments are now known to be taking place within the Roman Catholic church in the United States, as an increasing number of members find evangelicalism conducive to their spiritual needs – yet do not feel (and are not made to feel) that their espousal of an evangelical spirituality entails abandoning their loyalty to Catholic church structures. The unity of the church is here grounded, not in any specific ecclesiastical organizational system, but in a common commitment to the good news of Jesus Christ.

Holy

Earlier, we noted that the idea of the unity of the church appeared to be fatally compromised by rampant denominationalism. The theoretical unity of the church appeared to be contradicted by the empirical reality, in which the church appeared as divided and fragmented. Precisely the same tension between theory and experience arises through the assertion that the church is "holy," when both the past history and present experience of that institution point to such sinfulness on the part of both the church and its members.

So how is the theoretical holiness of the church to be reconciled with the sinfulness of Christian believers? The most significant attempt to bring experience into line with theory can be seen in sectarian movements, such as Donatism and Anabaptism. Both these movements laid considerable emphasis upon the empirical holiness of church members, leading to the exclusion from the church of members who were deemed to have lapsed from these public standards of sanctity. This rigorist approach seemed to contradict substantial parts of the New Testament, which affirmed the fallibility and forgivability – if the neologism may be excused – of believers. Others have asserted that a distinction may be made between the holiness of the church, and the sinfulness of its members. This raises the theoretical difficulty of whether a church can exist without members, and seems to suggest a disembodied church without any real connection with human beings.

A second approach adopts an eschatological perspective. The church is at present as sinful as its members; nevertheless, it will finally be purified in the last day. "Whenever I have described the church as being without spot or wrinkle, I have not intended to imply that it was like this already, but that it should prepare itself to be like this, at the time when it too will appear in glory" (Augustine). "That the church will be . . . without spot or wrinkle . . . will only be true in our eternal home, not on the way there. We would deceive ourselves if we were to say that we have no sin, as 1 John 1:8 reminds us" (Thomas Aquinas).

Catholic

In modern English, the term "catholic" is often confused, especially in non-religious circles, with "Roman Catholic." Although this confusion is understandable, the distinction must be maintained. It is not only Roman Catholics who are catholic, just as it is by no means Eastern Orthodox writers who are orthodox in their theology. Indeed, many Protestant churches, embarrassed by the use of the term "catholic" in the creeds, have replaced it with "universal." The word "catholic," however, comes from the Greek phrase *kath' holou* ("referring to the whole"). The Greek words subsequently found their way into the Latin word *catholicus*, which came to have the meaning "universal or general." This sense of the word is retained in the English phrase "catholic taste," meaning "a wide-ranging taste" rather than "a taste for things that are Roman Catholic." Older versions of the English Bible often refer to some of the New Testament letters (such as those of James and John) as "catholic epistles," meaning that they are directed to all Christians (rather than those of Paul, which are directed to the needs and situations of individually identified churches, such as those at Rome or Corinth).

At no point does the New Testament use the term "catholic" to refer to the church as a whole. The New Testament uses the term *ekklesia* to refer to local churches or worshipping communities, which it nevertheless understands to represent or embody something which transcends that local body. While an individual church is not the church in its totality, it nevertheless shares in that totality. It is this notion of "totality" which is subsequently encapsulated in the term "catholic." The term is introduced in later centuries, in an attempt to bring together central New Testament insights, and attach them to a single term. The first known use of the phrase "the catholic church" occurs in the writings of Ignatius of Antioch, who was martyred at Rome around 110: "Where Jesus Christ is, there is the catholic church." Other writings of the second century use the term to refer to the existence of a universal church alongside local congregations.

The meaning of the term changed fundamentally with the conversion of Constantine. By the end of the fourth century, the term "the catholic church" came to mean "the imperial church" – that is, the only legal religion within the Roman empire. Any other form of belief, including Christian beliefs which diverged from the mainline, were declared to be illegal. Further expansion of the church in this period contributed to a developing understanding of the term. By the beginning of the fifth century, Christianity was firmly established throughout the entire Mediterranean world. In response to this development, the term "catholic" came to be interpreted as "embracing the entire world."

A fundamental re-examination of the notion of "catholicity" took place at the time of the Reformation. It seemed to many that the catholicity and unity of the church were destroyed simultaneously with the fragmentation of the western European church in the sixteenth century. Protestant writers argued that the essence of catholicity lay, not in church institutions, but in matters of doctrine. The fifth-century writer Vincent of Lérins had defined catholicity in terms of "that which is believed everywhere, at all times, and by all people." The reformers argued that they remained catholic, despite having broken away from the medieval church, in that they retained the central and universally-recognized elements of Christian doctrine. Historical or institutional continuity was secondary to doctrinal fidelity. For this reason, the mainline Protestant churches insisted they were simultaneously catholic and reformed – that is, maintaining continuity with the apostolic church at the level of teaching, having eliminated spurious non-biblical practices and beliefs.

The notion of "catholicity" which has come to the fore in recent years, especially in ecumenical discussions subsequent to the Second Vatican Council, is the oldest sense of the term — namely, that of totality. Local churches and particular denominations are to be seen as the manifestation, representation, or embodiment of the one universal church. As Hans Küng states this position:

> The catholicity of the church therefore consists in a notion of entirety, based on identity, and resulting in universality. From this it is clear that unity and catholicity go together; if the church is one, it must be universal; if it is universal, it must be one. Unity and catholicity are two interwoven dimensions of one and the same church.

STUDY PANEL 33

Philip Melanchthon on the Nature of Catholicity

In his treatise on the use of the word "catholic," Melanchthon emphasizes the importance of doctrinal correctness as its defining element. Although the church may be dispersed throughout the world, it nevertheless remains universally faithful to the same teaching. This is a typically Protestant approach to the meaning of the word, which avoids an institutional understanding of the concept of "catholicity" and focuses instead on the importance of "universal Christian teaching."

What does "catholic" mean? It means the same as universal. *Kath'holou* means "universally" and "in general" . . . Why is this term added in the article of the creed, so that the church is called catholic? Because it is an assembly dispersed throughout the whole world and because its members, wherever they are, and however separated in place, accept and externally profess one and the same utterance or true doctrine throughout all ages from the beginning until the very end . . . It is one thing to be called catholic, something else to be catholic in reality. Those are truly called catholic who accept the doctrine of the truly catholic church, i.e., that which is supported by the witness of all time, of all ages, which believes what the prophets and apostles taught, and which does not tolerate factions, heresies, and heretical assemblies. We must all be catholic, i.e., accept this word which the rightly-thinking church holds, separate from, and unentangled with, those sects which oppose that word.

Apostolic

The term "apostolic," like "catholic," is not used to refer to the church in the New Testament. The fundamental sense of the term is "originating with the apostles" or "having a direct link with the apostles." It is a reminder that the church is founded on the apostolic witness and testimony. The term "apostle" requires explanation. The use of the term in the New Testament suggests that it bears two related meanings:

1   an apostle as one who has been commissioned by Christ, and charged
    with the task of preaching the good news of the kingdom;
2   an apostle as one who was a witness to the risen Christ, or to whom
    Christ revealed himself as risen.

In declaring the church to be "apostolic," the creeds thus appear to emphasize the historical roots of the gospel, the continuity between the church and
Christ through the apostles whom he appointed, and the continuing evangelistic and missionary tasks of the church.

The Resurrection of the Body and Eternal Life

The creed links together two ideas at this point, as it gives expression to the
Christian hope. Earlier, it proclaimed the reality of the resurrection of
Jesus Christ. We have already explored the importance of this point for
the Christian understanding of the identity of Jesus (see pp. 102–5). The
Creed now affirms the common Christian hope that all believers will one day
share in that resurrection.

   This raises the question of the connection between the resurrection of
Jesus and the resurrection of believers. Earlier, we noted that one aspect of
the Christian understanding of faith is that it concerns being "united to
Christ," sharing in a relationship with him and all his benefits. It is helpful
to consider the New Testament image of adoption in exploring this point
(Romans 8:15; 8:23; 9:4; Galatians 4:5; Ephesians 1:5). The image expresses the important idea that the adopted children have the same inheritance rights as the natural son. The adopted children are entitled to receive
the same inheritance as the natural son. Paul points out that the inheritance
which Jesus received from God is suffering and glory. Christians may expect
to receive the same, in that they are the children of God and co-heirs with
Christ. "Now if we are children, then we are heirs – heirs of God and co-
heirs with Christ, if indeed we share in his sufferings in order that we may
also share in his glory" (Romans 8:17). In other words, resurrection and
eternal life are the inheritance of Christians (1 Peter 1:3–4). What Jesus
obtained by his obedience will one day be ours. He is the "first-fruits" of the
dead (1 Corinthians 15:20–23): that is, the first of a rich harvest (for the
idea of "first-fruits," see Exodus 23:16). Christ *has* been raised; we *shall* be
raised, as those who share in him.

   So what form does the resurrected body take? The New Testament
affirms the reality of the resurrection hope, but sees little point in speculat-
ing about it. Paul compares the relation of our present bodies and our
resurrection bodies as being like the relation of a seed and the plant which
results when the seed is planted in the ground. There is both continuity and

development in the relationship. Christian theologians have often specu-
lated, however, about this relationship, going far beyond the modest statements found in the New Testament. One particularly interesting approach
is found in the writings of Methodius of Olympus.

In his dialogue with Aglaophon, dating from around 300, Methodius
offers another approach, which retains an emphasis on the physical reality of
the future resurrection of the body, based on the analogy of the melting
down and recasting of a metal statue.

> So it seems that it is as if some skilled artificer had made a noble image, cast
> in gold or other material, which was beautifully proportioned in all its features.
> Then the artificer suddenly notices that the image had been defaced by some
> envious person, who could not endure its beauty, and so decided to ruin it for
> the sake of the pointless pleasure of satisfying his jealousy. So the craftsman
> decides to recast this noble image. Now notice, most wise Aglaophon, that if
> he wants to ensure that this image, on which he has expended so much effort,
> care and work, will be totally free from any defect, he will be obliged to melt
> it down, and restore it to its former condition . . . Now it seems to me that
> God's plan was much the same as this human example . . . God dissolved
> humanity once more into its original materials, so that it could be remodelled
> in such a way that all its defects could be eliminated and disappear. Now in the
> melting down of a statue corresponds to the death and dissolution of
> the human body, and the remoulding of the material to the resurrection after
> death.

The basic theme to emerge from this analogy is that of continuity
and difference, as with Paul's analogy of a seed; however, the point is
made in a different way. In the end, Christians have never attached great
importance to this kind of speculation, being content to affirm the reality of
the hope of resurrection, without feeling the need to be too specific over the
fine details.

But what of the related idea of eternal life? Having affirmed that we will
one day share Christ's resurrection, the creed now hints at what form our
existence will take. The idea of "eternal life" might initially seem to suggest
little more than life that goes on and on and on – a perennially extended
version of our present existence. This is not what is intended. The Greek
language, in which the New Testament was written, has two words for life.
One (*bios*) could be understood to mean something like "biological existence;" the other (*zoe*) to mean something like "life in all its fullness." The
Christian gospel concerns the gift of fullness of life (John 10:10), a totally
fulfilled life which not even death itself can destroy. We are not being offered
an endless extension of our biological existence, but rather a transformation
of that existence. Eternal life means that our present relationship with God
is not destroyed or thwarted by death, but is continued and deepened by it.

The fundamental Christian theme of coming to a fulfilled relationship with God through Christ is thus understood to mean that this relationship is begun now, and fulfilled later.

It will therefore be clear that eternal life is not to be seen as something which lies totally in the future. It is something that we can begin to experience now. It is certainly true that eternal life, in all its fullness, is something we can only hope to gain in the age to come (Luke 18:30). Nevertheless, we are able to gain a foretaste of that eternal life now. To come to faith in Jesus Christ is to begin a new relationship with God which is not abolished by death, but which is actually deepened, in that death sweeps away the remaining obstacles to our experiencing the presence of God. This is not to say that our resurrection has already taken place (a view which is rejected by New Testament writers, as at 2 Timothy 2:18); it is to say that we may catch a glimpse of what eternal life is like here and now. Eternal life is inaugurated, but not fulfilled, in our present life as believers. To enter fully into eternal life is not to experience something totally strange and unknown. Rather, it is to extend and deepen our experience of the presence and love of God.

The Resurrection and Christian Funerals

The Christian faith places a particular emphasis on the hope of resurrection and eternal life. This has considerable implications for Christian attitudes toward death. The impact of these beliefs can probably be seen most clearly at Christian funeral services, in which the theme of sorrow at a believer's death is set alongside the theme of rejoicing at the hope of resurrection. This can be seen clearly in the old English order of service for "the burial of the dead" (1662), in which the theme of hope is clearly set out.

The service opens with the priest meeting the funeral party at the churchyard gate, and speaking some words from John's gospel (John 15:25–26), in which the theme of the Christian hope is clearly set out:

> I am the resurrection and the life, saith the Lord: he that believeth in me, though he were dead, yet shall he live; and whosoever liveth and believeth in me shall never die.

The service then proceeds with the reading of 1 Corinthians 15, a chapter in which Paul stresses the importance of the resurrection, and the difference it makes to Christians. This reading includes the following words:

STUDY PANEL 34

Study Panel 34 Continued

> Death is swallowed up in victory. O death, where is thy sting? O grave, where is thy victory? The sting of death is sin, and the strength of sin is the law. But thanks be to God, which giveth us the victory through our Lord Jesus Christ. Therefore, my beloved brethren, be ye steadfast, unmoveable, always abounding in the work of the Lord, forasmuch as ye know that your labor is not in vain in the Lord.

Finally, as the corpse is lowered into the grave, the priest speaks these words. Again, note the theme of hope.

> Forasmuch as it has pleased Almighty God of his great mercy to take unto himself the soul of our dear *brother* here departed, we therefore commit *his* body to the ground; earth to earth, ashes to ashes, dust to dust; in sure and certain hope of the resurrection to eternal life, through our Lord Jesus Christ.

The traditional form of Christian funerals is that of burial. Christianity was initially hostile to the use of cremation, on account of the pagan associations of the practice. However, this hostility has waned considerably, particularly during the twentieth century. Most Christian denominations now permit their dead to be cremated, believing that this practice is in no way inconsistent with the hope of final resurrection.

Christianity is thus a religion of hope, which focuses on the resurrection of Jesus as the grounds for believing and trusting in a God who is able to triumph over death, and give hope to all those who suffer and die. The word "eschatology" is used to refer to Christian teachings about the "last things" (Greek: *ta eschata*). Just as "Christology" refers to the Christian understanding of the nature and identity of Jesus Christ, so "eschatology" refers to the Christian understanding of such things as heaven and eternal life. In view of the importance of the New Testament material to the shaping of Christian thinking on eschatology, we shall consider some of its leading themes. The two sources of leading importance are generally agreed to be the preaching of Jesus himself, and the writings of Paul. We shall consider each of these in more detail in what follows.

As we have already noted (pp. 93–6), the dominant theme in the preaching of Jesus is the coming of the Kingdom of God. It is clear that this term has both present and future associations. The kingdom is something which is "drawing near" (Mark 1:15), yet which still belongs in its fullness to the future. The Lord's Prayer, which remains of central importance to individual and corporate Christian prayer and worship, includes reference to the future coming of the kingdom (Matthew 6:10). At the Last Supper, Jesus spoke to his disciples of a future occasion when they would drink wine in the kingdom of God (Mark 14:25). The general consensus among New Testament scholars is that there is a tension between the "now" and the "not yet" in relation to the Kingdom of God, similar to that envisaged by the parable of the growing mustard seed (Mark 4:30–32). The term "inaugurated eschatology" has become widely used to refer to the relation of the present inauguration and future fulfillment of the Kingdom.

Paul's eschatology also shows a tension between the "now" and the "not yet." This is articulated in terms of a number of key images, which may be summarized as follows.

1 The presence of a "new age." At several points, Paul emphasizes that the coming of Christ inaugurates a new era or "age" (Greek: *aionos*). Although this new age – which Paul designates a "new creation" (2 Corinthians 5:17) – has yet to be fulfilled, its presence can already be experienced. For this reason, Paul can refer to the "end of the ages" in Christ (1 Corinthians 10:11). The position which Paul opposes in the early chapter of 1 Corinthians clearly corresponds to a realized eschatology, in which each and every aspect of the age to come has been fulfilled in the present. For Paul, there is an element of postponement: the ultimate transformation of the world is yet to come, but may be confidently awaited.

2 The resurrection of Jesus is seen by Paul as an eschatological event, which affirms that the "new age" really has been inaugurated. Although this does not exhaust the meaning of Christ's resurrection (which has significant soteriological implications: see p. 137), Paul clearly sees Christ's resurrection as an event which enables believers to live in the knowledge that death – a dominant feature of the "present age" – has been overcome.

3 Paul looks forward to the future coming of Jesus Christ in judgment at the end of time, confirming the new life of believers and their triumph over sin and death. A number of images are used to refer to this, including "the day of the Lord." At one point (1 Corinthians 16:22), Paul uses an Aramaic term, *maranatha* (literally, "Come, our Lord!") as an expression of the Christian hope. The Greek term *parousia* is often used to refer to the future coming of Christ (e.g., 1 Corinthians 15:23; 2 Thessalonians 2:1, 8–9). For Paul, there is an intimate connection between the final coming of Christ and the execution of final judgment.

4 A major theme of Paul's eschatology is the coming of the Holy Spirit. This theme, which builds on a longstanding aspect of Jewish expectations, sees the gift of the Spirit as a confirmation that the new age has dawned in Christ. One of the most significant aspects of Paul's thought at this point is his interpretation of the gift of the Spirit to believers as an *arrabon* (2 Corinthians 1:22; 5:5). This unusual word has the basic sense of a "guarantee" or "pledge," affirming that the believer may rest assured of ultimate salvation on account of the present possession of the Spirit. Although salvation remains something which will be consummated in the future, the believer may have present assurance of this future event through the indwelling of the Spirit.

It will therefore be clear that the eschatology of the New Testament is complex. However, a leading theme is that something which happened in the past inaugurates something new, which will reach its final consummation in the future. The Christian believer is thus caught up in this tension between the "now" and the "not yet." We have already noted the importance of this point in relation to Christian teaching on the nature of salvation, which includes past, present, and future elements.

The term "heaven" is used frequently in the Pauline writings of the New Testament to refer to the Christian hope. Although it is natural to think of heaven as a future entity, Paul's thinking appears to embrace both a future reality and a spiritual sphere or realm which co-exists with the material world of space and time. Thus "heaven" is referred to both as the future home of the believer (2 Corinthians 5:1–2; Philippians 3:20) and as the present dwelling-place of Jesus Christ, from which he will come in final judgment (Romans 10:6; 1 Thessalonians 1:10; 4:16). One of Paul's most significant statements concerning heaven focuses on the notion of believers being "citizens of heaven" (Philippians 3:20), and in some way sharing in the life of heaven in the present. The tension between the "now" and the "not yet" (see pp. 93–5) is evident in Paul's statements concerning heaven, making it very difficult to sustain the simple idea of heaven as something which will not come into being until the future, or which cannot be experienced in the present.

Probably the most helpful way of conceiving heaven is to regard it as a consummation of the Christian doctrine of salvation, in which the presence, penalty, and power of sin have all been finally eliminated, and the total presence of God in individuals and the community of faith has finally been achieved. It should be noted that the New Testament parables of heaven are strongly communal in nature – for example, heaven is portrayed as a banquet, a wedding feast, or as a city – the new Jerusalem. Individualist interpretations of heaven or eternal life are also excluded on account of the Christian understanding of God as Trinity. Eternal life is thus not a projection of an individual human existence, but is rather to be seen as sharing, with the redeemed community as a whole, in the community of a loving God.

A major point of difference between Christians should be noted at this point. The Catholic church teaches the existence of "purgatory," while the Protestant and Eastern Orthodox Christians do not. In view of the importance of this difference, we shall consider it in a little more detail.

Purgatory is perhaps best understood as an intermediate state, in which those who have died in a state of grace are given an opportunity to purge themselves of the guilt of their sins before finally entering heaven. The idea does not have explicit scriptural warrant, although a passage in 2 Maccabees 12:39–45 (regarded as apocryphal, and hence as lacking in authority, by Protestant writers) speaks of Judas Maccabeus making "propitiation for those who had died, in order that they might be released from their sin."

The idea was developed during the patristic period. Clement of Alexandria and Origen both taught that those who had died without time to perform works of penance would be "purified through fire" in the next life. The practice of praying for the dead – which became widespread in the eastern church in the first four centuries – exercised a major impact upon theological development, and provides an excellent case study of the manner in which liturgy influences theology. What was the point of praying for the dead, it was asked, if those prayers could not alter the state in which they existed? Similar views are found in Augustine, who taught the need for purification from the sins of the present life, before entering the joys of the next.

While the practice of praying for the dead appears to have become well established by the fourth century, the explicit formulation of a notion of "purgatory" seems to date from two centuries later, in the writings of Gregory the Great. In his exposition of Matthew 12:31, dating from 593 or 594, Gregory picks up the idea of sins which can be forgiven "in the age to come." He interprets this in terms of a future age in which sins which have not been forgiven on earth may be forgiven subsequently.

> As for certain lesser faults, we must believe that, before the final judgment, there is a purifying fire, for he who is the truth declares that "whoever utters blasphemy against the Holy Spirit will not be pardoned either in this age, or in the age which is to come" (Matthew 12:31). From this statement, it is to be understood that certain offenses can be forgiven in this age, whereas certain others will be forgiven in the age which is to come.

Note especially the reference to the "purifying fire (*purgatorius ignis*)," which became incorporated into most medieval accounts of purgatory, and from which the term "purgatory" derives.

The theme of a fire which purifies – as opposed to a fire which punishes – is developed with particular enthusiasm in Catherine of Genoa's *Treatise on Purgatory*, which probably dates from around the year 1490:

> Because the souls in purgatory are without the guilt of sin, there is no obstacle between them and God except their pain, which holds them back so that they cannot reach perfection through this instinct. They can also see that this instinct is held back by a need for righteousness. For this reason, a fierce fire comes into being, which is like that of Hell, with the exception of guilt. This is what makes evil the wills of those who are condemned to Hell, on whom God does not bestow his goodness; they therefore remain in their evil wills, and opposed to the will of God.

The idea of purgatory was rejected by the reformers during the sixteenth century. Two major lines of criticism were directed against it. First, it was held to lack any substantial scriptural foundations. Second, it was inconsistent with the doctrine of justification by faith, which declared that an individual could be put "right with God" (or "justified") through faith, thus establishing a relationship which obviated the need for purgatory. Having dispensed with the idea of purgatory, the reformers saw no pressing reason to retain the practice of prayer for the dead, which was henceforth omitted from Protestant liturgies. Both the concept of purgatory and the practice of praying for the dead continue to find acceptance within Catholicism.

Mention should also be made of the idea of "Hell." The New Testament draws a clear distinction between "Hades" (which is understood in neutral terms as the place of the dead) and "hell" (which is understood as a place of permanent separation from God). The two ideas were often confused; for example, early versions of the creed sometimes speak about Christ "descending to Hades" (that is, descending to the place of the dead, which is a biblical idea), and sometimes of "descending to Hell" (which is not a biblical idea).

The traditional imagery of hell owes virtually nothing to the New Testament. Interest in hell reached a climax during the Middle Ages, with artists of the period taking, one assumes, a certain delight in portraying the righteous watching sinners being tormented by burning and other means of torture. Satan is often portrayed as a gentlemen dressed in red, with a forked tail. The source of this imagery? Wherever it comes from, it is not the Bible! The most graphic portrayal of the medieval view of hell is due to Dante, in the first of the three books of his *Divine Comedy*. Dante portrays hell as nine circles at the center of the earth, within which Satan dwells. On the gate, Dante notices the inscription: "Abandon hope, all who enter here!"

The first circle of hell consists of "limbo," and is populated by those who have died without being baptized and virtuous pagans. Dante declares that it is this circle which was visited by Christ during his "descent into hell," between the time of the crucifixion and resurrection. There is no torment of any kind in this circle. As Dante advances further into hell, he discovers those who are guilty of increasingly serious sins. The second circle is populated by the lustful, the third by the gluttonous, the fourth by the miserly, and the fifth by the wrathful. These circles, taken together, constitute "upper hell." At no point does Dante refer to fire in this part of hell. Dante then draws upon Greco-Roman mythology, and suggests that the River Styx divides "upper hell" from "lower hell." Now we encounter fire for the first time. The sixth circle is populated by heretics, the seventh by the violent, the eighth by fraudsters (including several popes), and the ninth by traitors.

This static medieval view of hell was unquestionably of major influence at the time, and continues to be of importance into the modern period. It may be found clearly stated in Jonathan Edwards' famous sermon "Sinners in the Hands of An Angry God," preached on 8 July 1741:

> It would be dreadful to suffer this fierceness and wrath of Almighty God for one moment; but you must suffer it for all eternity. There will be no end to this exquisite horrible misery . . . You will know that you must wear out long ages, millions of millions of ages, in wrestling and conflicting with this almighty merciless vengeance.

However, the very idea of hell has been subjected to increasing criticism, of which the following should be noted.

1   Its existence is seen as a contradiction of the Christian assertion of the final victory of God over evil. This criticism is especially associated with the patristic writer Origen, whose doctrine of universal restoration ultimately rests upon an affirmation of the final and total triumph of God over evil. In the modern period, the philosopher Leibnitz identified this consideration as a major difficulty with the doctrine of hell:

    > It seems strange that, even in the great future of eternity, evil must triumph over good, under the supreme authority of the one who is the sovereign good. After all, there will be many who are called, and yet few who are chosen or saved.

2   The notion of vindictive justice seemed unChristian to many writers, especially in the light of many New Testament passages speaking of the compassion of God. A number of writers, especially during the nine-

teenth century, found it difficult to reconcile the idea of a loving God with the notion of the continuing vindictive or retributive punishment of sinners. The main difficulty was that there seemed to be no point to the suffering of the condemned.

While answers may be given to these objections, there has been a perceptible loss of interest in the idea of hell in both popular and more academic Christian circles. One of the more noticeable features of western culture since about 1960 onward is that any form of lingering popular belief in hell seems to have evaporated. Evangelistic preaching now seems to concentrate upon the positive affirmation of the love of God, rather than on the negative implications of the rejection of that love. Nevertheless, the idea of a permanent separation from God as a result of a decision to reject God remains an integral part of the Christian tradition, however this may be stated.

One aspect of the Christian expectation of heaven merits especial attention — the idea of the beatific vision. The Christian is finally granted a full vision of the God who has up to this point been known only in part. This vision of God in the full splendor of the divine majesty has been a constant theme of much Christian theology, especially during the Middle Ages. Perhaps the most famous statement of this hope can be found in Dante's *Divine Comedy*, a major literary work written in or about the first decade of the fourteenth century, which sets out some central themes of Christian teaching in poetical form. The work has three major sections, entitled "Hell," "Purgatory," and "Paradise."

Dante (1265–1321), based in the city of Florence, wrote the *Divine Comedy* in order both to give poetic expression to the Christian hope, and to make comments on the life of both the church and city of Florence of his own day. The poem is set in the year 1300, and describes how Dante is led into the depths of the earth by the pagan Roman poet Virgil, who will act as his guide through hell and purgatory. The work is an important representation of the medieval worldview, in which the souls of the departed were understood to pass through a series of purifying and cleansing processes (see the discussion of purgatory, pp. 227–9), before being enabled to catch a glimpse of the vision of God – the ultimate goal of the Christian life. The third and final section thus concludes with the poet finally capturing a glimpse of God, who is described as

the love which moves the sun and the other stars.

The anticipation of the wonder and glory of this vision was seen as a powerful incentive to keep going in the Christian life. Christian theology can never fully capture the wonder of that vision of God. But it can at least challenge us to think more deeply about God, and whet our appetites for what is yet to come – a fitting note on which to end this very brief introduction to some of its themes.

1 What does it mean to speak of God as "father"?
2 What are the implications of the Christian doctrine of creation?
3 The Christian church celebrates the gift of the Holy Spirit at Pentecost. What difference does that coming of the Spirit make?
4 What does it mean to say that the church is "holy"?
5 What does it mean to be a "citizen of heaven"?

The History of Christianity

This third part of this introduction to Christianity focuses on the historical development of Christianity down the ages. It traces they way in which Christianity established itself as a global religion, and the issues which it confronted in doing so. During the course of this analysis we shall examine some of the landmarks of the history of Christianity – the conversion of the Roman emperor Constantine, the rise of scholasticism, the dawn of the Reformation, the American and French Revolutions of the eighteenth century, and the Russian and Chinese Revolutions of the twentieth. We shall explore the way in which a religion which came to birth in Palestine gradually established a presence in Europe, and thence in the Americas, sub-Saharan Africa, and parts of Asia. It will be clear that this vast and complex story can only be told in part; the reader must expect to come away with a longing for more information about various aspects of the matters discussed so briefly here. However, it is hoped that what is presented in these sections will whet the reader's appetite to follow up issues through the further reading list provided on pp. 436–9.

10

The Early Church to c.700

The first two major periods of Christian history are usually understood to be the period of the New Testament itself (often referred to as "the apostolic era"), and the period between the closing of the New Testament (*c*.100) and the Council of Chalcedon in 451. During this period the distinctive shape of the Christian faith emerged. In the present section we shall explore some of the events and issues which emerged as significant during this first phase in the global expansion of Christianity. We begin by exploring an issue which is of major importance within the New Testament, and continues to be important today – the relation between Christianity and Judaism.

Christianity and Judaism

In one sense, Christianity can be said to begin with the coming of Jesus Christ. Yet Christians themselves have always been clear that Christianity is continuous with Judaism. The "God of Abraham, Isaac and Jacob" is the same as the "God of Jesus Christ." Early Christianity emerged within Judaism, and most of the first converts to the movement were Jews. The New Testament frequently mentions Christians preaching in local synagogues. So similar were the two movements that outside observers, such as the Roman authorities, tended to treat Christianity as a sect within Judaism, rather than as a new movement with a distinct identity.

As we have seen (p. 10), this relationship was expressed in terms of two "covenants." This terminology is used in the New Testament, especially the Letter to the Hebrews, and became normative within Christian thought over the following centuries. The "Old Covenant" refers to God's dealings with Israel, expressed in Judaism; the "New Covenant" refers to God's dealings with humanity as a whole, revealed in Jesus Christ. The Christian belief that the coming of Christ inaugurates something new expresses itself in a distinctive attitude toward the Old Testament, which could basically be summarized thus: *religious principles and ideas* (such as the notion of a sovereign God who is active in human history) are appropriated; religious *practices* (such as dietary laws and sacrificial routines) are not.

One option which has generally been rejected completely is to treat the Old Testament as the writings of a religion which had nothing to do with Christianity. This approach is especially associated with the second-century writer Marcion, who was excommunicated in the year 144. According to Marcion, Christianity was a religion of love, which had no place whatsoever for law. The Old Testament relates to a different god than the New; the Old Testament god, who merely created the world, was obsessed with the idea of law. The New Testament god, however, redeemed the world, and was concerned with love. According to Marcion, the purpose of Christ was to depose the Old Testament God (who bears a considerable resemblance to the Gnostic "demiurge," a semi-divine figure responsible for fashioning the world), and usher in the worship of the true God of grace.

The emphasis on the continuity between Christianity and Judaism raised a number of serious difficulties for the early Christians. First, there was the question of the role of the Jewish Law in the Christian life. Did the traditional rites and customs of Judaism have any continuing place in the Christian church? There is evidence that this issue was of particular importance during the 40s and 50s, when non-Jewish converts to Christianity came under pressure from Jewish Christians to maintain such rites and customs. The issue of circumcision was particularly sensitive, with Gentile converts to Christianity often being pressed to become circumcised, in accord with the Law. This controversy is recorded in the Acts of the Apostles, which notes how, in the late 40s, a section of the church argued that it was essential that male Christians should be circumcised. In effect, they seemed to regard Christianity as an affirmation of every aspect of contemporary Judaism, with the addition of one extra belief – that Jesus was the Messiah. Unless males were circumcised, they could not be saved (Acts 15:1).

In order to resolve this issue, Paul and Barnabas set out to Jerusalem from Antioch. Luke provides us with an account of the first General Council of the Christian church – the Council of Jerusalem in 49 (Acts 15:2–29). The debate is initially dominated by converted Pharisees, who insist upon the need to uphold the law of Moses, including the circumcision requirements. Yet Paul's account of the growing impact of the Christian gospel among the Gentiles causes the wisdom of this approach to be questioned. If so many Gentiles are becoming Christians, why should anything unnecessary be put in their way? Paul conceded the need to avoid food which had been sacrificed to idols – an issue which features elsewhere in his letters (1

Corinthians 8:7–13). But there is no need for circumcision. This position won widespread support, and was summarized in a letter which was circulated at Antioch (Acts 15:30–35).

Yet although the issue was resolved at the theoretical level, it would remain a live issue for many churches in the future. Having sorted out this issue in Palestine, Paul determined to return to the region of Galatia (in the center of modern-day Turkey) to make sure that the churches which he had planted would know of this decision. Paul's letter to the Galatians, probably written around 53, deals explicitly with this question, which had clearly become a contentious issue in the region. Paul notes the emergence of a Judaizing party in the region – that is, a group within the church which insisted that Gentile believers should obey every aspect of the law of Moses, including the need to be circumcised. According to Paul, the leading force behind this party was James – not the apostle James, who died in 44 AD, but the brother of Jesus Christ who was influential in calling the Council of Jerusalem, and wrote the New Testament letter known by his name.

For Paul, this trend was highly dangerous. If Christians could only gain salvation by the rigorous observance of the law, what purpose did the death of Christ serve? It is faith in Christ, not the scrupulous and religious keeping of the law of Moses, which is the basis of salvation. Nobody can be justified (that is, put in a right relationship with God) through keeping the law. The righteousness on which our salvation depends is not available through the law, but only through faith in Christ. Aware of the importance and sensitivity of this issue, Paul then explores this question in some detail (see Galatians 3:1–23). The Galatians have fallen into the trap of believing that salvation came by doing works of the law, or by human achievement. So what has happened to faith? Did the gift of the Holy Spirit ever come through keeping the law? Paul then makes an appeal to the example of Abraham to make his point. Paul argues that Abraham was "justified" (that is, put in a right relationship with God) through his faith (Galatians 3:6–18). The great patriarch was not put in a right relationship with God through circumcision; that came later. That relationship with God was established through Abraham's faith in God's promise to him (Genesis 15:6). Circumcision was simply the external sign of that faith. It did not establish that faith, but confirmed something that was already there. Nor does the law, or any aspect of it, abolish the promises which God had already made. The promise to Abraham and his descendants – which includes Christians, as well as Jews – remains valid, even after the introduction of the law.

So the basic point is that the promise of God to Abraham was made before either circumcision or the law of Moses were delivered. Thus all who share in the faith of Abraham are the children of Abraham. It is possible for the Gentiles to share Abraham's faith in the promises of God – and all the benefits that result from this faith – without the need to be circumcised, or be bound to the fine details of the law of Moses. It is Christ's death and resurrection, not external observance of the law, which constitute the ultimate grounds of our relationship with God.

This controversy is important for several reasons. It casts light on tensions within the early church; it also raises the question of whether Jewish Christians enjoyed special privileges or status in relation to Gentile Christians. The final outcome of the debate was that Jews and Gentiles were to be given equal status and acceptance within the church. While the theological and ethical teaching of the Old Testament was to be honored and accepted by Christians, they were under no obligation to obey the ceremonial or cultic aspects of the Law, including circumcision or sacrifice. Those were both fulfilled and superseded by the coming of Jesus Christ. For many early Christians, the fact that Jesus was circumcised removed any need for them to undergo the same painful process.

Yet the relationship of Jew and Gentile within the church was not the only subject of discussion. What about the relationship between men and women?

Early Christianity and Women

Our most important source for the history of early Christianity is the Acts of the Apostles, written by the same Luke who compiled the third of the four gospels. Acts emphasizes the vitally important role of women in providing hospitality for missionaries, which was of major importance in establishing the church in Europe, with women converts such as Lydia making their homes available as house churches and staging-posts for missionaries. Luke appears to be concerned to bring out clearly the important historical point that the early church attracted significant numbers of prominent women in cultures which gave them a much greater social role than in Judaism, and offered them a significant role in the overall evangelistic and pastoral ministry of the early church.

In particular, Luke singles out Priscilla and Aquila as a husband-and-wife team who were engaged in an evangelistic and teaching ministry (Acts 18:1–3, 24–26), not least in relation to Apollos. Interestingly, the name of the woman precedes that of her husband. As many scholars of antiquity point out, it is unusual for a woman's name to precede that of her husband. Perhaps Priscilla had a higher social rank than her husband, or was more significant in Christian circles. The priority given to Priscilla clearly suggests that Luke regards her as taking priority over Aquila in terms of the teaching ministry exercised by the couple. Many other examples could be given. Paul commends to the Roman church "our sister Phoebe, a servant of the church at Cenchrea" (Romans 16:1), commenting on how helpful she had been to him. 1 Timothy 3:11 and 5:9–10 also clearly point to women having a ministerial role, exercising a recognized and authorized ministry of some form within the church.

"There is neither Jew nor Greek, slave nor free, male nor female, for you are all one in Christ Jesus" (Galatians 3:28). This verse stands as the foundation of Paul's approach to differences of gender, class, or race. Paul affirms that being "in Christ" transcends all social, ethnic, and sexual barriers. Perhaps this vigorous and unambiguous statement was provoked by the local situation in Galatia, in which Judaizers (that is to say, people who wished Christians to retain the traditions of Judaism) were attempting to retain customs or beliefs which encouraged or justified such distinctions. Paul does not mean that people stop being Jews or Greeks, or male and female, as a result of their conversions. It does mean that these distinctions, while remaining, cease to have any saving significance. They may have importance in the eyes of the world; yet in the sight of God, and within the Christian community, they are transcended by the union between Christ and the believer. Paul's affirmation has two major consequences. First, it declares that there are no barriers of gender, race, or social status to the gospel. The gospel is universal in its scope. Secondly, it clearly implies that, while Christian faith does not abolish the particularities of one's existence, they are to be used to glorify God in whatever situation we find ourselves.

Christianity thus laid the foundations for the radical undermining of traditional attitudes toward both women and slaves at two levels:

1 It asserted that all were one in Christ – whether Jew or Gentile, whether male or female, whether master or slave. Differences of race, gender or social position were declared to place no obstacles between all believers sharing the same common relationship with the risen Christ.
2 It insisted that all – whether Jew or Gentile, whether male or female, whether master or slave – could share in the same Christian fellowship, and worship together. Society might force each of these groups to behave in different manners; but within the Christian community, all were to be regarded as brothers and sisters in Christ.

These developments did not lead to an immediate alteration in existing attitudes towards either women or slaves. Theory always appears to have preceded practice, with the practice being affected by a variety of factors, including the cultural acceptability of the development in question. Nevertheless, it was equivalent to placing a theoretical time bomb under them. It was only a matter of time before the foundations of these traditional distinctions would be eroded to the point at which they could no longer be maintained. As the Roman historian Harold Mattingley once pointed out, "Christianity made no attempt to abolish slavery at one blow, but it undermined its basis by admitting slaves into the same religious fellowship as their masters."

The general principle which thus emerges can be stated as follows. The New Testament makes it clear that there is a theoretical equality amongst Christians. Differences of racial origin, gender, or class are relativized and abolished by the new relationship with the risen Christ which arises through faith in him. Yet the practical outworking of these developments is seen as a long-term issue. Cultural attitudes modify these radical theoretical beliefs. The theoretical equality of all believers may not be culturally acceptable in certain contexts. As a result, theory may not be able to pass into practice in one cultural context, while it may in another.

It is clear that Paul's approach is profoundly liberating, implying new freedoms for women. Spiritual gifts, Paul insists, are not bestowed on the basis of gender, race, or class. Whatever gifts God has bestowed must be recognized and put to use. But Paul is clearly aware that this universalization will raise problems in terms of its practical application in matters of church life and within Christian families. His letters therefore include discussion of a number of sensitive areas, which I propose to deal with. Both the passages in question are drawn from Paul's letters to Corinth.

It must be stressed that the Corinthian situation appears to have been especially difficult, with the issue of personal freedom emerging as being of major importance. Paul is obliged to lay down limits to Christian freedom, particularly in relation to spiritual gifts, in order to prevent the church from degenerating into chaos, or hindering the spread of the gospel by scandalizing people for cultural, not theological, reasons.

A passage which is often singled out for discussion in relation to this question is 1 Corinthians 11:2–16, which raises the issue of whether women should cover their heads in public worship. The passage in question is notoriously difficult to interpret, largely because we do not know enough about the Corinthian church, or local Corinthian culture, to be sure that we have understood Paul's point. There seems to be no explanation forthcoming from modern scholars as to why Paul regards it as obvious that men should have their heads uncovered, and women their heads covered, at worship. One suggestion has been that a woman with an uncovered head might have been mistaken for a prostitute. In that Corinth was noted as a center of prostitution, partly on account of the fact that it was a port, it is possible that this explanation would make sense of Paul's recommendation. However, there is not enough evidence to support this contention. Nor is it clear quite why he regards it as obvious that men should cut their hair shorter than women.

The issue of length of hair is generally thought to relate to pagan religious beliefs and practices, which Paul would have wished to forbid in his congregation. For example, a number of scholars have pointed out that, within contemporary Corinthian culture, hair style or length was a sign of sexual or religious practices. Long hair for a man could indicate homosexuality, as could short hair on a women. Equally, dishevelled hair on the part of a woman was often linked with the ecstatic mystery cults, such as the frenzied rituals associated with the Isis cult. If this is the case, we are dealing with recommendations from Paul which are grounded in the particularities of the Corinthian situation of the time, and which need not be regarded as binding upon Christians for all time. Paul's recommendations would seem to relate to local Corinthian circumstances, which no longer apply.

On the basis of what has been said, it is clear that the Christian gospel gave a new status to women, as it did to others (such as Gentiles and slaves) who had hitherto been regarded as marginalized within Judaism. However, there was, as we have seen, a genuine tension between these new attitudes and values and the generally patriarchal structure of family and society in the first century. The New Testament is not revolutionary, in the sense that it does not make demands for a radical and violent overthrow of the existing order of things. Rather, it lays the foundations for a new set of attitudes which, if generally accepted, would have transformed society.

But how could the church get those values accepted in a society which was clearly not ready to receive them? To get society to accept Christian values and attitudes, society had first to be made Christian. This meant that evangelism was seen as a priority. Yet evangelism, then as now, had to proceed by ensuring that people outside the church were not unnecessarily scandalized. The acceptance of the gospel itself was prior to the acceptance of the new values which it embodied. As a result, there is a tension between the theological affirmation of the equality of all, and the apologetic recognition of divergence and diversity.

Many scholars have noted how Christianity was treated with contempt by educated Romans and Greeks in its first two centuries. In order to gain any kind of hearing for the good news of the gospel, at least some degree of cultural accommodation was necessary. The early Christians chose not to dilute the gospel message, but attempted to demonstrate the social acceptability of Christianity. Inevitably, this meant bringing Christian attitudes toward women more into line with those which prevailed in the wider community. By the end of the fourth century such social presures seem to have led to the neglect, or perhaps even suppression, of the ministerial roles of women within the church. But this is to be regarded as a response to a set of specific historical circumstances encountered during this early period in the development of the church, rather than something which is permanently binding on all Christians.

The Expansion of the Gospel: Paul

The gospel had its origins in Palestine. However, it spread rapidly through-out the Roman empire. One of the most important agents of this develop-ment was Paul.

We possess two significant sources for Paul's life: the letters written by Paul himself, and the Acts of the Apostles, compiled by Luke. These two sources are significantly different. Paul's primary concern in his letters is to establish his credentials as an apostle. In affirming that God has called both Jews and Gentiles to be equal partners in the Christian faith, Paul often finds it appropriate to emphasize his Jewish pedigree and in particular his high standing within Judaism as a Pharisee. For example, in defending the view that Christians are under no obligation to be circumcised, Paul appeals to his earlier period as a zealous defender of Jewish traditions. He knew their value and importance; he was now, however, convinced that they had been superseded by the new revelation through Christ.

Paul particularly draws attention to the radical changes in values and outlook which he experienced as a result of his conversion, but gives little historical detail concerning the manner in which this conversion took place. Luke's account, however, is told from the standpoint of the overall develop-ment of Christianity in the first two or three decades after the crucifixion and resurrection of Jesus of Nazareth. Luke brings out the way in which there is a close connection between the conversion or calling of Paul and the origins of the mission to the Gentiles, while providing historical details concerning the conversion itself.

There are five explicit references to this "conversion" or "calling" of Paul in the New Testament (Acts 9:1–19; 22:1–21; 26:2–23; Galatians 1:11–17; Philippians 3:3–17). Of the three accounts in Acts, two take the form of statements by Paul in defense of his activities, in which he relates his personal narrative to his critics (in one case, a Jewish audience; in the other, King Agrippa). Both statements highlight Paul's Jewish background, and show a clear concern to address Jewish sensitivities. The first account takes the form of an historical narrative, relating the events which took place on the road to Damascus. It is this account (Acts 9:1–19) which has had the greatest impact on Christian thinking.

This narrative tells of how Paul originally bore the name of "Saul." He had established a reputation as a zealous persecutor of the church in Pales-tine during its initial period of growth. (Paul elsewhere mentions that he was a Pharisee, an established teacher of the Jewish law.) As he travels to the city of Damascus, in order to extend his persecutions of Christians in the region, he experiences a vision of Jesus of Nazareth. This is then interpreted by Ananias, a Christian at Damascus, in terms of a divine commissioning to be an apostle to the Gentiles. It must be noted that this account places its emphasis more on the theme of "calling" than of "conversion." The impact of the experience relates to its significance for Paul's mission, rather than to his personal experience, although a link between the two is clearly assumed.

The narrative now shifts to the realization of this calling to be an apostle to the Gentiles. Acts subsequently records three major missionary journeys undertaken by Paul, and hints at a fourth. Paul's first missionary journey (decribed in Acts 13:4–15:35) would probably have taken place at some time around 46–48 AD. Paul was now about 44 years old. Some fourteen years had passed since his conversion, during which time he had been occupied primarily with missionary work in the region of Syria. Paul and Barnabas are joined by John Mark, more usually known as Mark, and generally thought to have been the author of the gospel now known by his name. In 46 these three companions set out on their way to the south coast of Asia Minor, a region of the north-eastern Mediterranean coast which constitutes modern-day Turkey. Their journey initially takes them to the

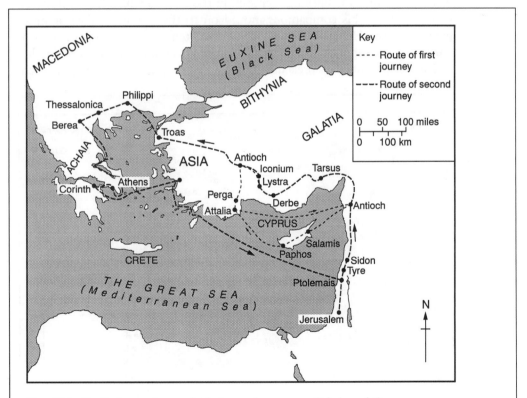

Map 10.1 Paul's first and second missionary journeys to Galatia and Greece

The History of Christianity

island of Cyprus, and subsequently to Iconium, Lystra and Derbe in the region of Galatia. Paul established small Christian communities in the area, before returning to Antioch.

Paul's second missionary journey (described in Acts 15:36–18:22) was undertaken in the aftermath of the Council Of Jerusalem, which had given equal status to Jews and Gentiles within the church. The first stage of the journey took them overland once more to Galatia, where they are joined by Timothy, who will become one of Paul's most trusted colleagues. They then proceeded to Troas, at the north-western tip of Asia Minor, close to the site of the ancient city of Troy. There they are joined by Luke himself, who is generally regarded as a primary source for many of the accounts relating to this part of the journey (notice the use of "we" in many of the reports from this section). Crossing the Aegean Sea, they landed in the area of Macedonia, where they spent some time in the city of Philippi, a major Roman colony.

The visit to Philippi was of especial importance on account of its symbolic role. For the first time, the Christian gospel was preached on the continent of Europe. After establishing a church in the city, to which he would later write, Paul and his companions moved on to the region of Thessalonica, further south. Here, Paul may have taken temporary employment as a tentmaker to support himself while undertaking missionary work in the region. As a result of his preaching in the local synagogue (17:1–9), a church

Map 10.2 Paul's third missionary journey in the Aegean Sea

The theatre of the city of Ephesus, with the Arcadian Way in the background. Paul's speech in this theatre (which was capable of holding some 24,000 people) is described in the Acts of the Apostles. Sonia Halliday Photographs.

was established (to which he would later write his two earliest letters, 1 Thessalonians and 2 Thessalonians).

From there, they moved on to Athens, still widely regarded as the intellectual center of the ancient world (Acts 17:15–34). The city had a reputation for its short-lived interest in the latest ideas and intellectual fashion, and appears to have seen in Paul the course of some exciting new ideas. It was here that Paul delivered his famous address on the Areopagus, or "Mars Hill," in which Paul argued that Christianity put a name to the god whose existence ancient philosophy had recognized. There is no letter from Paul to the Athenians; it seems that no church was founded in this city. But in the port city of Corinth, further south, Paul gained a much more sympathetic hearing (Acts 18:1–28). Corinth was a huge seaport, with many openings for evangelism within the local Jewish community, as well as within the vastly larger Gentile population. Paul stayed there for eighteen months. It was clearly an important time in his ministry. Encouraged by the reports of church growth in the region of Macedonia, Paul wrote both his letters to the Thessalonian Christians.

At some point in 53 AD, Paul set off from Corinth on his third missionary journey, described in Acts 18:23–21:17. His visit to the city of Ephesus was of particular importance. At the time of his visit, the city was a stronghold of pagan superstition, centering on the goddess Diana. As a result of Paul's visit to the city, a church is established, which seems to have acted as a major resource for the evangelization of the region in later years.

The Expansion of the Gospel: Rome

Rome was the administrative center of the empire which embraced the whole Mediterranean region. Indeed, the Romans tended to refer to the Mediterranean as "Mare Nostrum" – "our sea." Judea was part of this vast empire – and a rather insignificant part at that. Although the languages spoken in this region of the empire were Aramaic (a language closely related to Hebrew) and Greek, Latin was used for administrative purposes. John's gospel makes reference to the charge against Jesus to the effect that he claimed to be "King of the Jews" being written in all three languages (John 19:19–20). In many paintings and representations of the crucifixion, this inscription is represented by four letters: INRI – the initial letters of the Latin phrase *Iesus Nazarenus Rex Iudaeorum*, meaning "Jesus of Nazareth, King of the Jews."

It is clear that Greek was the first language of the early Christians. It is no accident that the entire New Testament was written in an everyday form of Greek (usually referred to as *koine*). Yet Christianity is soon a presence at Rome. There is evidence that Mark's gospel may have been written in Rome at some point around 64, on the eve of Nero's persecution of Christians in the city. (Mark 12:42 notes that two copper coins make one *quadrans*, a coin not in circulation in the eastern part of the empire. Similarly, Mark 15:16 explains that a Greek word corresponds to the Latin *praetorium*.) Paul's letter to the Romans, dating from around 57, refers to a number of individuals with Latin names, such as Urbanus, Aquila, Rufus and Julia. Yet the letter is written in Greek! So how could a Greek-speaking movement gain such acceptance in a Latin-speaking city?

The answer is quite simple. Many Romans knew Greek. Huge numbers of Greek-speaking immigrants from the eastern regions of the empire had made their home in Rome, to the irritation of many indigenous Romans. Seneca is one of many Roman writers to complain about the vast numbers of immigrants in his city, and the cultural disruption which they caused. To speak Greek was, in the eyes of many Romans, a sign of being an immigrant, and hence of lower social status.

However, the situation was more complex than this. Many educated Romans cultivated the study of Greek as a result of their interest in Greek

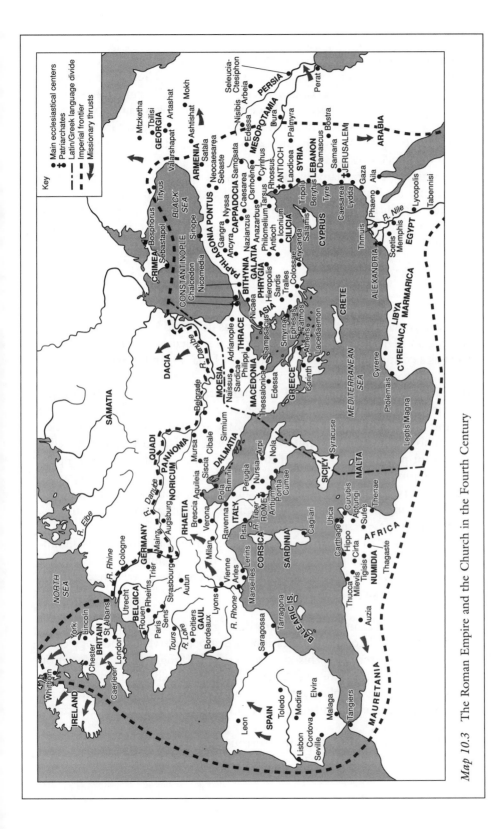

Map 10.3 The Roman Empire and the Church in the Fourth Century

philosophy and poetry. To be able to speak the refined Greek of the philosophers and poets (as opposed to the common Greek of the masses) was a sign of cultural accomplishment. Claudius, the emperor who was responsible for the expulsion of large numbers of Jews (along with some Jewish Christians) from Rome in 49, spoke both Latin and Greek; indeed, he even attempted to modify the Latin alphabet, adding three new letters based on Greek originals.

It was therefore relatively easy for Greek-speaking Christians to gain a hearing at Rome. The evidence indicates that the movement had gained a significant following by the end of the century, although a significant Christian literature in Latin only begins to emerge in the following century.

The Consolidation of Christianity

As we have seen, Christianity had its origins in Palestine – more specifically, the region of Judea, especially the city of Jerusalem. Christianity regarded itself as a continuation and development of Judaism, and initially flourished in regions with which Judaism was traditionally associated, supremely Palestine. However, it rapidly spread to neighboring regions, partially through the efforts of early Christian evangelists such as Paul of Tarsus. By the end of the first century, Christianity appears to have become established throughout the eastern Mediterranean world, and even to have gained a significant presence in the city of Rome, the capital of the Roman Empire. As the church at Rome became increasingly powerful, tensions began to develop between the Christian leadership at Rome and at Constantinople, foreshadowing the later schism between the western and eastern churches, centered on these respective centers of power.

In the course of this expansion, a number of regions emerged as significant centers of theological debate. Three may be singled out as having especial importance, the first two of which were Greek-speaking, and the third Latin-speaking.

1   The city of Alexandria, in modern-day Egypt, which emerged as a center of Christian theological education. A distinctive style of theology came to be associated with this city, reflecting its long-standing association with the Platonic tradition. "Alexandrian" approaches to matters such as Christology and biblical interpretation soon developed, reflecting both the importance and distinctiveness of the style of Christianity associated with the area.
2   The city of Antioch and the surrounding region of Cappadocia, in

modern-day Turkey. A strong Christian presence came to be established in this northern region of the eastern Mediterranean at an early stage. As we have already seen, Paul's missionary journeys often involved church-planting in this region, and Antioch features significantly at several points in the history of the very early church, as recorded in the Acts of the Apostles. Antioch itself soon became a leading center of Christian thought. Like Alexandria, it became associated with particular approaches to Christology and biblical interpretation. The term "Antiochene" is often used to designate this distinct theological style. The "Cappadocian fathers" were also an important theological presence in this region in the fourth century, notable especially for their contribution to the doctrine of the Trinity.

3 Western north Africa, especially the area of modern-day Algeria. In the late classical period this was the site of Carthage, a major Mediterranean city and at one time a political rival to Rome for dominance in the region. During the period when Christianity expanded in this region it was a Roman colony. Major writers of the region include Tertullian, Cyprian of Carthage, and Augustine of Hippo.

This is not to say that other cities in the Mediterranean were devoid of significance. Rome, Constantinople, Milan and Jerusalem were also centers of Christian theological reflection, even if none was destined to achieve quite the significance of its rivals.

The period during which Christianity established itself as a dominant religious force in the Mediterranean region is usually referred to as "the patristic period." The term "patristic" comes from the Latin word *pater*, "father," and designates both the period of the church fathers, and the distinctive ideas which came to develop within this period. The term "patristic period" is rather vaguely defined, but is usually taken to refer to the period from the closing of the New Testament writings (*c.*100) to the definitive Council of Chalcedon (451). However, many scholars argue that the term ought to be used in a broader sense, and include developments up to about 750. A third term which is often encountered in the literature is "patristics," which is usually understood to mean the branch of theological study which deals with the study of "the fathers."

The patristic period is one of the most exciting and creative periods in the history of Christian life and thought. This feature alone is enough to ensure that it will continue to be the subject of study for many years to come. The period is also of importance for theological reasons. Every mainstream Christian body – including the Anglican, Eastern Orthodox, Lutheran, Reformed and Roman Catholic churches – regards the patristic period as a definitive landmark in the development of Christian doctrine.

Each of these churches regards themselves as continuing, extending and, where necessary, criticizing the views of the early church writers. For example, the leading seventeenth-century Anglican writer Lancelot Andrewes (1555–1626) declared that orthodox Christianity was based upon two testaments, three creeds, four gospels, and the first five centuries of Christian history.

The period was of major importance in clarifying a number of issues. A task of initial importance was sorting out the relationship between Christianity and Judaism. The letters of Paul in the New Testament bear witness to the importance of this issue in the first century of Christian history, as a series of doctrinal and practical issues came to the fore. Should Gentile (that is, non-Jewish) Christians be obliged to be circumcised? And how was the Old Testament to be correctly interpreted?

However, other issues soon came to the fore. One which was of especial importance in the second century is that of *apologetics* – the reasoned defense and justification of the Christian faith against its critics. During the first period of Christian history, the church was often persecuted by the state. Its agenda was that of survival; there was limited place for theological disputes when the very existence of the Christian church could not be taken for granted. This observation helps us understand why apologetics came to be of such importance to the early church, through writers such as Justin Martyr (*c*.100–*c*.165), concerned to explain and defend the beliefs and practices of Christianity to a hostile pagan public. Although this early period produced some outstanding theologians – such as Irenaeus of Lyons (*c*.130–*c*.200) in the west, and Origen (*c*.185–*c*.254) in the east – theological debate could only begin in earnest once the church had ceased to be persecuted.

Pliny the Younger on the Persecution of Christians

STUDY PANEL 35

In his letter to Trajan, dating from about 112, Pliny the Younger asked advice as to how to deal with the growing number of Christians who refused to worship the image of the Roman emperor, and reports on what he has been told about the customs of these Christians. Note in particular the reference to an "oath." The Latin term used here is *sacramentum*. Pliny understands this to refer to a military oath, and thus suspects some kind of secret political or military society. In fact, the word passed into use as a reference to the communion service (which involves bread and wine: see pp. 363–74), which is almost certainly the "food" referred to by Pliny. Note also the early Christian

Study Panel 35 Continued

practice of praising Christ "as a god," and the reference to "deaconesses" (an order of Christian ministry).

> I ask them if they are Christians. If they admit this, I ask them the question again and second and third time, threatening them with the death sentence if they persist . . . But they declared that their only crime or error was that they used to meet regularly before daybreak on an appointed day, and to sing a hymn to Christ as to a god, and to bind themselves by an oath (not to commit any crime, but to abstain from theft, robbery, adultery or breach of trust, and not to deny a deposit when this was required). After the end of this ceremony, they would leave, and then meet again to take food. But it is ordinary and harmless food . . . I found out what truth there was in this by torturing two maidservants (who were called "deaconesses"), but found nothing but a depraved and extravagant superstition.

These conditions became possible during the fourth century, with the conversion of the emperor Constantine. So important is this development that it needs further discussion. Since it has established a presence at Rome in the 40s, Christianity had an ambiguous legal status. On the one hand, it was not legally recognized, and so did not enjoy any special rights; on the other, it was not forbidden. However, its growing numerical strength led to periodic attempts to suppress it by force. Sometimes these persecutions were local, restricted to regions such as North Africa; sometimes, they were sanctioned throughout the Roman empire as a whole.

A particularly significant period of persecution dates from the accession of the emperor Decius in 249. His first major act of hostility toward Christianity was the execution of Fabian, Bishop of Rome, in January 250. The Decian persecution resulted from the Edict of Decius, issued in June 250, which commanded provincial governors and magistrates to ensure that there was universal observance of the requirement to offer sacrifices to the Roman gods, and to the emperor. A certificate (*libellus pacis*) was issued to those who offered such sacrifices. The Edict seems to have been widely ignored, but was nevertheless enforced in some regions. Thousands of Christians were martyred during this difficult period. Some offered sacrifices to the gods in order to get hold of the required certificates; some were able to obtain the certificates without actually offering sacrifices.

A Certificate of Sacrifice from the Decian Persecution

This certificate, which is dated 26 June 250, was discovered in Egypt in 1893. It affirms that an unknown individual, distinguished only by a scar, has completed all the sacrificial formalities, and includes his personal statement of his regular practice of offering sacrifices. A local magistrate is recorded as witnessing the sacrifice taking place.

To: The Commissioners for Sacrifices in the village of Alexander's Island.
From: Aurelius Diogenes, son of Sabatus
Re: A 72 year old man, from the village of Alexander's island, with a scar on his right eyebrow.

I have always sacrificed to the gods. Now, in your presence, in accordance with the terms of the Edict, I have offered a sacrifice, poured libations, and tasted the sacrifices. I request you to certify to this effect. Farewell.

Presented by me, Aurelius Diogenes
I certify that I witnessed his sacrifice. Aurelius Syrus.

The Decian persecution ended in June 251, when Decius was killed on a military expedition. The persecution led to many Christians lapsing or abandoning their faith in the face of persecution. Division arose immediately within the church over how these individuals should be treated: did such a lapse mark the end of their faith, or could they be reconciled to the church by penance? Opinions differed sharply, and serious disagreement and tension resulted. Very different views were promoted by Cyprian of Carthage and Novatian. Both of these writers were martyred during the persecution instigated by the emperor Valerian in 257–258.

One of the most severe outbursts of persecution came about in February 303, under the emperor Diocletian. An edict was issued ordering the destruction of all Christian places of worship, the surrender and destruction of all their books, and the cessation of all acts of Christian worship. Christian civil servants were to to lose all privileges of rank or status and be reduced to the status of slaves. Prominent Christians were forced to offer sacrifice according to traditional Roman practices. It is an indication of how influential Christianity had become that Diocletian forced both his wife and daughter, who were known to be Christians, to comply with this order. The persecution continued under successive emperors, including Galerius, who ruled the eastern region of the empire.

In 311, Galerius ordered the cessation of the persecution. It had been a failure, and had merely hardened Christians in their resolve to resist the reimposition of classical Roman pagan religion. Galerius issued an edict which permitted Christians to live normally again and "hold their religious assemblies, provided that they do nothing which would disturb public order." The edict explicitly identified Christianity as a religion, and offered it the full protection of the law. The legal status of Christianity, which had been ambiguous up to this point, was now resolved. The church no longer existed under a siege mentalilty.

Galerius' Edict of Toleration, 313

We have tried to restore universal observance of the ancient institutions and public order of Rome. In particular, we have aimed to bring Christians, who had abandoned the religion of their forebears, back to a right observance . . . We are now pleased to grant indulgence to these people, allowing Christians the right to exist once more, and to establish their places of worship, providing that they do not offend against public order. We will explain to the magistrates how they should conduct themselves in this matter in a later communication. In return for our toleration, it will be the duty of Christians to pray to God for our recovery, for the common good as well as for their own, and that the state may be preserved from all dangers, and that they themselves may live safely in their homes.

STUDY PANEL 37

Christianity was now a legal religion; it was, however, merely one among many such religions. The conversion of the emperor Constantine changed this irreversibly, and brought about a complete change in the situation of Christianity throughout the Roman empire. Constantine was born to pagan parents in 285. (His mother would eventually become a Christian, apparently through her son's influence.) Although he showed no particular attraction to Christianity in his early period, Constantine certainly seems to have regarded toleration as an essential virtue. Following Maxentius' seizure of power in Italy and North Africa, Constantine led a body of troops from western Europe in an attempt to gain authority in the region. The decisive battle took place on 28 October 312 at the Milvian Bridge, to the north or Rome. Constantine defeated Maxentius, and was proclaimed emperor. At some point shortly afterwards, he declared himself to be a Christian.

This point is affirmed by both Christian and pagan writers. What is not clear is precisely why or when this conversion took place. Some Christian writers (such as Lactantius and Eusebius) suggest that the conversion may have taken place before the decisive battle, with Constantine seeing a heavenly vision ordering him to place the sign of the cross on his soldiers' shields. Whatever the reasons for the conversion, and whether it dates from before or after the battle of Milvian Bridge, the reality and consequences of this conversion are not in doubt. Gradually, Rome became Christianized. On his own instructions, the statue of the emperor erected in the Forum depicts Constantine bearing a cross – "the sign of suffering that brought salvation," according to the inscription provided by Constantine. In 321, Constantine decreed that Sundays should become public holidays. Christian symbols began to appear on Roman coins. Christianity was now more than just legitimate; it was on its way to becoming the established religion of the empire.

As a result, constructive theological debate became a public affair. Apart from a brief period of uncertainty during the reign of Julian the Apostate (361–3), the church could now count upon the support of the state. Theology thus emerged from the hidden world of secret church meetings, to become a matter of public interest and concern throughout the Roman Empire. Increasingly, doctrinal debates became a matter of both political and theological importance. Constantine wished to have a united church throughout his empire, and was thus concerned that doctrinal differences should be debated and settled as a matter of priority.

As a result, the later patristic period (from about 310 to 451) may be regarded as a high watermark in the history of Christian theology. Theologians now enjoyed the freedom to work without the threat of persecution, and were able to address a series of issues of major importance to the consolidation of the emerging theological consensus within the churches. That consensus involved extensive debate, and a painful learning process in which the church discovered that it had to come to terms with disagreements and continuing tensions. Nonetheless, a significant degree of consensus, eventually to be enshrined in the ecumenical creeds, can be discerned as emerging within this formative period.

Theological Divisions of the Period

The patristic period saw a number of major disputes developing within the church. Three can be singled out as being of particular importance to the development of Christian theology.

1 *The Donatist controversy.* This debate centered on Roman north Africa, particularly the region around Carthage. Christians in this region suffered particularly during the Diocletian persecution. Such was the ferocity of the persecution that many Christians, including some senior

church figures, collaborated with the Roman authorities, in the hope that the storm would pass and they could get back to a normal way of life. Others fiercely resisted the persecution. As a result, controversy developed within the church over the treatment of those who had compromised their principles during the persecution. One group, which centered on the figure of Donatus took a hard line. No compromise could be permitted. Clergy who had collaborated in any way during the persecution could not be readmitted within the church. This controversy, which became particularly important during the fourth century, forced the western church to give careful thought to two areas of Christian doctrine – the doctrine of the church, and the doctrine of the sacraments (see pp. 363–74).

2 *The Arian controversy.* This controversy broke out in the eastern section of the church during the fourth century. It focused on Arius, based in the Egyptian city of Alexandria. Arius argued that Jesus Christ could not be described as being fully divine. Rather, Jesus was to be thought of as supreme among God's creatures (see pp. 128–31). Arius met stiff resistance from various opponents, especially Athanasius. The resulting dispute became so serious that the unity of the Roman empire was threatened. As a result, the emperor Constantine convened a council of 220 bishops at the city of Nicea in Asia Minor. He demanded that they settle the issue. The Council of Nicea decided against Arius, and affirmed that Jesus Christ was "of one substance" with God – in other words, that Jesus was both human and divine. This doctrine, which is generally referred to as "the doctrine of the two natures" (see pp. 131–4) is of particular importance to Christian thought, and will be explored in depth later.

3 *The Pelagian controversy.* This debate broke out in the final years of the fourth century, and continues into the first two decades of the fifth century. The basic question under debate was the respective roles played by God and humanity in salvation. Does God have the upper hand? Or do we? Is salvation something which is given to us by God? Or is it something which we earn or merit by our good works? Such questions caused significant divisions within the church at the time, and would become controversial once more during the sixteenth century (see pp. 280–6; 288–91).

The Origins of Monasticism

One of the most important developments to take place during the patristic period was the development of monasticism. The origins of the movement are generally thought to lie in remote hilly areas of Egypt and parts of eastern Syria. Significant numbers of Christians began to make their homes in these regions, in order to get away from the population centers, with all the distractions that these offered. One such person was Anthony of Egypt, who left his parents' home in 273 to seek out a life of discipline and solitude in the desert.

The theme of withdrawal from a sinful and distracting world became of central importance to these communities. While some lone figures insisted on the need for individual isolation, the concept of a communal life in isolation from the world gained the ascendancy. One important early monastery was founded by Pachomius during the years 320–325. This monastery developed an ethos which would become normative in later monasticism. Members of the community agreed to submit themselves to a common life which was regulated by a Rule, under the direction of a superior. The physical structure of the monastery was significant: the complex was surrounded by a wall, highlighting the idea of separation and withdrawal from the world. The Greek word *koinōnia* (often translated as "fellowship"), frequently used in the New Testament, now came to refer to the idea of a common corporate life, characterized by common clothing, meals, furnishing of cells (as the monks' rooms were known) and manual labor for the good of the community.

The monastic ideal proved to have a deep attraction for many. By the fourth century monasteries had been established in many locations in the Christian east, especially in the regions of Syria and Asia Minor. It was not long before the movement was taken up in the western church. By the fifth century, monastic communities had come into existence in Italy (especially along the western coastline), Spain and Gaul. Augustine of Hippo, one of the leading figures of the western church at this time, established two monasteries in North Africa at some point during the period 400–425. For Augustine, the common life (now designated by the Latin phrase *vita communis*) was essential to the realization of the Christian ideal of love. He supplemented this emphasis on community life with an appreciation of the importance of intellectual activity and spiritual study.

During the sixth century, the number of monasteries in the region grew considerably. It was during this period that one of the most comprehensive of monastic "Rules" – the "Rule of Benedict" – made its appearance. Benedict of Nursia (*c*.480–*c*.550) established his monastery at Monte Cassino at some point around 525. The Benedictine community followed a rule which was dominated by the notion of the unconditional following of Christ, sustained by regular corporate and private prayer, and the reading of Scripture.

The Rise of Celtic Christianity

The rise of Christianity in the Celtic regions of Europe – more specifically, Ireland, Scotland, Cornwall, Brittany and Wales – is of considerable interest, not least in that this form of Christianity found itself in opposition to the more Romanized forms which rapidly gained the ascendancy in England. Although the origins of Celtic Christianity seem to lie in Wales, it is Ireland which established itself as a missionary center of distinction in the fifth and sixth centuries. Other centers of missionary activity in the Celtic sphere of influence are known from this period, most notably Candida Casa (modern-day Whithorn, in the Galloway region of Scotland), which was established by bishop Ninian in the fifth century. The significance of this missionary station was that it lay outside the borders of Roman Britain, and was thus able to operate without the restrictions then associated with Roman forms of Christianity.

The person who is traditionally held to be responsible for the evangelization of Ireland was a Romanized Briton by the name of Magonus Sucatus Patricius, more usually known by his Celtic name "Patrick" (*c*.390–*c*.460). Born into a wealthy family, Patrick was taken captive by a raiding party at the age of sixteen, and sold into slavery in Ireland, probably in the region of Connaught. Here, he appears to have discovered the basics of the Christian faith, before escaping and making his way back to his family. He had been in captivity for six years. It is not clear precisely what happened between Patrick's escape from captivity and his subsequent return to Ireland as a missionary. A tradition, dating back to the seventh or eighth century, refers to Patrick spending time in Gaul before his return to Ireland. It is possible that some of Patrick's views on church organization and structures may reflect first-hand acquaintance with the monasticism of certain regions of southern France. There is excellent historical evidence for trading links between Ireland and the Loire Valley around this time.

At any rate, Patrick returned to Ireland and established Christianity in the region. It is clear that some form of Christianity already existed; not only does Patrick's conversion account presuppose that others in the region knew about the gospel, contemporary records dating from as early as 429 speak of one Palladius as the bishop of Ireland, indicating that at least some form of rudimentary ecclesiastical structures existed in the region. Irish representatives are also known to have been present at the Synod of Arles (314). Patrick's achievement is perhaps best understood in terms of the consolidation and advancement of Christianity, rather than its establishment in the first place.

The monastic idea took hold very quickly in Ireland. Historical sources indicate that Ireland was largely a nomadic and tribal society at this time, without any permanent settlements of any importance. The monastic quest for solitude and isolation was ideally suited to the Irish way of life. Whereas in western Europe as a whole, monasticism was marginalized within the life of the church, in Ireland it rapidly became its dominant form. It is no exaggeration to say that the Irish church was monastic, with the abbot rather than the bishop being seen as pre-eminent.

The authority structures which emerged within Celtic Christianity were thus rather different to those which came to dominate the Roman–British church at this time. The Irish monastic model came to be seen as a threat to the Roman model of the episcopate, in which the government of the church resided firmly in the hands of the bishops. None of the abbots of Iona ever allowed bishops to ordain formally then, rejecting the need for any such "official" recognition. In Ireland, some of the older bishoprics (including Armagh) were reorganized on a monastic basis, with others being absorbed by monasteries. Abbeys were responsible for the pastoral care of the churches which grew up in their vicinity. The Roman episcopal system was thus marginalized. The Celtic church leaders were openly critical of worldly wealth and status, including the use of horses as a mode of transport, and any form of luxury. Theologically, Celtic Christianity also stressed the importance of the world of nature as a means of knowing God. This is especially clear from the ancient Irish hymn traditionally ascribed to Patrick, and known as "St Patrick's Breastplate." The theme of a "breastplate" was common in Celtic Christian spirituality. It is based upon Paul's references to the "armor of God" (Ephesians 6:10–18), and develops the theme of the believer being protected by the presence of God and a whole range of associated powers. Although strongly trinitarian in its structure, it shows a fascination with the natural world as a means of knowing God. The God who made the world is the same God who will protect Christians from all dangers.

STUDY PANEL 38

St Patrick on the Wonder of Creation

This section from "St Patrick's Breastplate" makes an appeal to the creation itself as a witness to the power and the reliability of God.

> I bind unto myself today
> The virtues of the star-lit heaven,
> The glorious sun's life-giving ray,
> The whiteness of the moon at even,
> The flashing of the lightning free,

Study Panel 38 Continued

> The whirling wind's tempestuous shocks,
> The stable earth, the deep salt sea,
> Around the old eternal rocks.

The Irish monasteries acted as centers for missionary activity, often using sea lanes as channels for the transmission of Christianity. Brendan (died *c.*580) and Columba (died *c.*597) are excellent examples of this type of missionary. In a poem entitled "The Navigation of St Brendan" (*c.*1050), Brendan is praised for his journeys to the "northern and western isles" (usually assumed to be the Orkneys and Hebrides, off the coast of Scotland). Columba brought Christianity from the north of Ireland to the western Isles of Scotland, and established the abbey of Iona as a missionary outpost. From there, Christianity spread southwards and eastwards. Aidan (died 651) is an excellent example of a monk from Iona who acted as a missionary in this way. At the invitation of the king of the region of Northumbria, he established a missionary monastery on the island of Lindisfarne, off the east coast of northern England. Celtic Christianity began to penetrate into France, and become increasingly influential in the region.

The tensions between Celtic Christianity and its Roman rivals could not be ignored. Celtic Christianity threatened to undermine the episcopate, reduce the power of Rome, make it more difficult for Christianity to become culturally acceptable, and to make monasticism the norm for Christian living. By 597, the year of Columba's death, the ascendancy of the Celtic vision seemed inevitable. However, the following century saw a series of developments which led to its gradual eclipse outside its heartland of Ireland. By a coincidence of history, the event which led to its eclipse took place in the very year of Columba's death. In 597, Augustine was sent to England by Pope Gregory to evangelize the English. As Roman forms of Christianity became established in England, tensions arose between northern and southern English Christians, the former remaining faithful to Celtic traditions, and the latter to Roman. The Synod of Whitby (664) is widely seen as establishing the dominance of Roman Christianity in England. Although the Synod focused on the question of when Easter should be celebrated (Celtic and Roman traditions differing on the issue), the real issue concerned the growing influence of the see of Canterbury. The Saxon invasions of England in the previous century had resulted in major cultural changes in the region, making inevitable the gradual erosion of Celtic culture, including its distinctive approach to Christianity.

The year 700 may be seen as marking the end of the growth of Celtic Christianity, and also a convenient point at which to interrupt this narrative. A period of cultural and intellectual consolidation lay ahead, as what is now known as "the Middle Ages" began to dawn. We shall resume our account of the growth of Christianity by exploring this development.

STUDY QUESTIONS

1 The expansion of Christianity during the patristic period is thought to be linked to its potential appeal to marginalized groups, such as slaves or women. Are there any hints of this in the New Testament?
2 Why were so few churches built during the first three centuries of the Christian era?
3 What difference did the conversion of Constantine make to the fortunes of the church?
4 Why did monasticism become such an important force in the early church?
5 How is the growing power of Roman Christianity illustrated by the decline of Celtic Christianity?

11

The Middle Ages, c.700 to c.1500

By the fifth century, Christianity had begun to establish itself securely in the Mediterranean region. Five major centers emerged within the region, each of which served as the nucleus of groups of churches: Alexandria, Antioch, Constantinople, Jerusalem, and Rome. These five centers, generally referred to as "patriarchates," were intended to be seen as equal partners within the church as a whole. In fact, however, there was a considerable degree of rivalry between them, with frequent jostling for position as the pre-eminent center of the Christian faith. The growing power of the Roman church was a cause of particular concern to the four eastern patriarchates.

An event of fundamental importance to the history of the church took place during this period. For a variety of reasons, relations between the eastern church, based at Constantinople, and the western, based at Rome, became increasingly strained during the ninth and tenth centuries. Growing disagreement over the wording of the Nicene creed (see pp. 197–8) was of no small importance to this increasingly sour atmosphere. However, other factors contributed, including the political rivalry between Latin-speaking Rome and Greek-speaking Constantinople, and the increasing claims to authority of the Roman pope. The final break between the Catholic west and Orthodox east is usually dated to 1054; however, this date is slightly arbitrary.

The patristic period centered on the Mediterranean world, and centers of power such as Rome and Constantinople. Instability was widespread throughout the region during this period. The following developments were of particular importance in relation to this unstable situation.

1   *The fall of Rome.* The northern frontier of the Roman empire was more or less defined by the River Rhine. In 404, this frontier collapsed in the face of assault by "barbarians." Huge areas of the Roman empire were

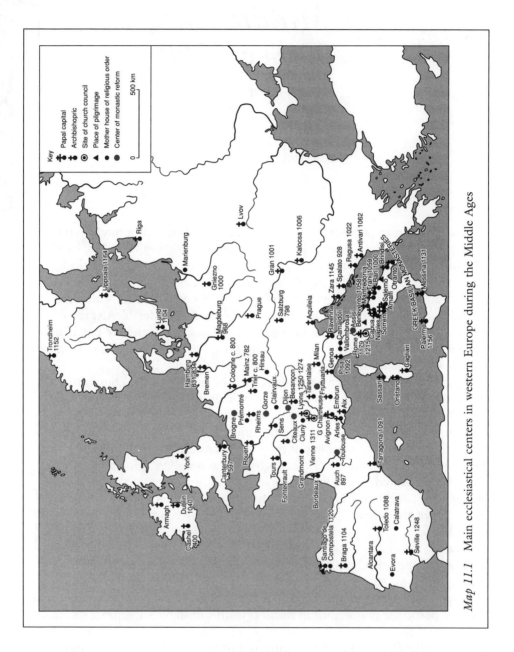

Map 11.1 Main ecclesiastical centers in western Europe during the Middle Ages

now under the control of the Franks, Goths, and Vandals. Rome itself was sacked twice, most notably by the forces of Alaric the Goth in 410. By 476, the western regions of the Roman empire were in ruins. The political stability of the region was eroded, with the result that Christianity found itself facing a period of considerable uncertainty.

2 *The Arab invasions.* Islam became a significant religious movement amongst the Arab people in the seventh century. A program of conquest was initiated, which eventually led to Arab forces taking control of the entire coastal region of north Africa by about 750. Islamic forces also moved north, posing a serious threat to Constantinople itself. Arab forces laid siege to the city during the period 711–78, eventually being forced to withdraw. The enforcement of Islam in the conquered regions of the Holy Land led to intense concern in the western church, and was one of the factors which led to the crusades during the period 1095–1204.

By the eleventh century, a degree of stability had settled upon the region, with three major power groupings having emerged to take the place of the former Roman empire.

1 Byzantium, centered on the city of Constantinople (now Istanbul, in modern-day Turkey). The form of Christianity which predominated in this region was based on the Greek language, and was deeply rooted in the writings of patristic writers of the eastern Mediterranean region, such as Athanasius, the Cappadocians, and John of Damascus.

2 Western Europe, encompassing regions such as France, Germany, the Lowlands and northern Italy. The form of Christianity which came to dominate this region was based particularly in the city of Rome, and its bishop, known as "the pope." (However, in the period known as the "Great Schism," some confusion developed: there were two rival claimants for the papacy, one based at Rome, the other at the southern French city of Avignon.) Here, theology came to center on the great cathedral and university schools of Paris and elsewhere, based largely on the Latin writings of Augustine, Ambrose and Hilary of Poitiers.

3 The Caliphate, an Islamic region embracing much of the extreme eastern and southern parts of the Mediterranean. The expansion of Islam continued, with the fall of Constantinople (1453) sending shock waves throughout much of Europe. By the end of the fifteenth century, Islam had established a significant presence in several regions of the continent of Europe, including Spain, parts of southern Italy, and the Balkans. This advance was eventually halted by the defeat of the Moors in Spain in the final decade of the fifteenth century, and the defeat of Islamic armies outside Vienna in 1523.

Christianity in the East to 1453

The particular style of Christianity which flourished in the eastern region of the Roman empire is generally referred to as "Byzantine," taking its name from the Greek city of Byzantium, which Constantine chose as the site of his new capital city in 330. At this point, it was renamed "Constantinople" ("city of Constantine"). However, the name of the older town remained, and gave its name to the distinctive type of Christianity which flourished in this region until the fall of Constantinople to invading Islamic armies in 1453. Constantinople was not the only center of Christian thought in the eastern Mediterranean. Egypt and Syria had been centers of theological reflection for some time. However, as political power increasingly came to be concentrated on the imperial city, so its status as a theological center advanced correspondingly.

Constantinople soon became a center of missionary activity. At some point around the year 860, the Moravian ruler Rastislav asked the Byzantine emperor to send missionaries to his people in central Europe. Two Greek brothers, Cyril and Methodius, were sent in response to this request. This development was of particular importance to the formation of eastern European culture. Not only did it eventually lead to the dominance of Orthodoxy in the region of eastern Europe; it also had a major impact on the alphabets used in the region. Cyril devised an alphabet, suitable for writing down the Slavic languages, which became the basis for the modern Cyrillic alphabet, named after the younger of the two "apostles of the Slavs." The conversion of Moravia was followed by that of Bulgaria and Serbia later that century. This was followed by the conversion of the Russians, at some point around the year 988.

As the eastern and western churches became increasingly alienated from each other (a process which had begun long before the final schism of 1054), so Byzantine thinkers often emphasized their divergence from western theology (for example, in relation to the *filioque* clause: see p. 197), thus reinforcing the distinctiveness of their approach through polemical writings. For example, Byzantine writers tended to understand salvation in terms of *deification*, rather than western legal or relational categories. Any attempt to achieve a degree of reunion between east and west during the Middle Ages was thus complicated by a complex network of political, historical, and theological factors. By the time of the fall of Constantinople, the differences between east and west remained as wide as ever. With the fall of Byzantium, intellectual and political leadership within Orthodoxy tended to pass to Russia. The Russians, who had been converted through Byzantine missions in the tenth century, took the side of the Greeks in the schism of 1054. By the end of the fifteenth century, Moscow and Kiev were firmly established as patriarchates, each with its own distinctive style of Orthodox Christianity, which remains of major importance today. Other regions which converted to Orthodoxy during this period include Serbia and Bulgaria.

It is clear that the flourishing of the eastern Orthodox church in Russia during the Middle Ages was of major importance to the shaping of Moscovite Russia. It is estimated that during the fourteenth, fifteenth and sixteenth centuries, more than 250 monasteries and convents were established in the region. The monastic revival, under the guidance of leaders such as St Sergius of Radonezh (died 1392), gave further impetus to the missionary efforts of the Russian church. During the thirteenth century, for example, the Finnish-speaking peoples of the Karelia region were converted to Orthodoxy.

The fall of Constantinople in 1453 caused a major development within Russian Orthodoxy. Traditionally, each new metropolitan of the Russian church was installed by the patriarch of Constantinople, and looked to the Byzantine emperor (based in Constantinople) for its political leadership. The Russian church was very much a daughter of the Byzantine church. But with the fall of Constantinople, this traditional approach became a thing of the past. What could replace it? In the event, the eastern Orthodox church in Moscow became autocephalous – that is, self-governing. As a result, the political and cultural links between the Russian church and state became deeper. By 1523, the relation between church and state was so close that some writers began to refer to Moscow as the "Third Rome," to be treated with respect equal to Rome and Constantinople. Philotheus of Pskov proclaimed that, now that Rome and Byzantium had become corrupt, the leadership of the Christian world had passed to Moscow: "two Romes have fallen; the third stands; there will be no fourth."

Two controversies are of particular importance within eastern Christianity during this period. The first of these, which broke out during the period 725–842, is usually referred to as the iconoclastic ("breaking of images") controversy. It erupted over the decision of emperor Leo III (717–742) to destroy icons, on the grounds that they were barriers to the conversion of Jews and Muslims. The controversy was mainly political, although there were some serious theological issues at stake, most notably the extent to which the doctrine of the incarnation justified the depiction of God in the form of images (see pp. 117–18). The second, which broke out in the fourteenth century, focused on the issue of hesychasm (Greek: *hesychia* = silence), a style of meditation through physical exercises which enabled believers to see the "divine light" with their own eyes. Hesychasm placed considerable emphasis upon the idea of "inner quietness" as a means of achieving a direct inner vision of God. It was particularly associated with writers such as Simeon the New Theologian and Gregory Palamas (*c.*1296–1359), who was elected as archbishop of Thessalonica in 1347. Its oppo-

St Basil's Cathedral, in Red Square, Moscow. The distinctive architecture of the building has made it one of the best-known buildings in the world. Hutchison Library.

nents argued that its methods tended to minimize the difference between God and creatures, and were particularly alarmed by the suggestion that God could be "seen."

The Development of Western Christianity to 1050

After the collapse of the western section of the Roman empire in the later fifth century, Christianity was forced to go through a period of reconstruction. Since the conversion of Constantine, the church could more or less rely on the support of the emperor. With the destruction of the western Roman empire, the church was suddenly exposed to uncertainty and instability. Christianity had become quite Roman in its culture and outlook; it now found itself having to adapt to a new environment in which Roman ideas and values carried little weight. Furthermore, Christianity had never really taken hold in the extreme regions of the empire. Its future in the regions seemed highly uncertain.

However, a program of consolidation and expansion began to get under way. Pope Gregory the Great encouraged missionary work in the outlying regions of the empire. As we noted in the previous chapter (see pp. 257–60), Ireland had been converted to Christianity in the fifth century by Patrick and Palladius; it soon became a center for missionary activity in Wales and

England. This was supplemented by missionary work undertaken by Augustine, with the support of the pope. As a result, two rather different styles of Christianity were established in England by the seventh century, one Celtic, the other Roman. This led to tensions – for example, over the date of Easter. These were largely resolved by the Synod of Whitby (664), which settled this particular debate. With the conversion of England, a base was established for the evangelization of other northern European nations. Missionaries from England became active in Germany. Under the rule of Charlemagne (*c.742–814*), Christianity was given new institutional and social stability. The importance of Charlemagne in the consolidation of Christianity in western Europe was given formal recognition by the pope, who crowned him as the first "Holy Roman Emperor" on Christmas Day, 800. Although this coronation further strained relations between the eastern and western churches, it nevertheless gave Christianity a new authority in the western regions of Europe. By the end of the first millennium, Christianity was more or less established as the dominant religion of much of the region. The scene was set for further consolidation and renewal.

The Renewal of Christianity in Western Europe

An important aspect of the Christian Renaissance of the period was a new flowering of interest in Christian theology. The period 1050–1350 saw a remarkable consolidation of Christian thought at the intellectual level. When the Dark Ages finally lifted from over western Europe, giving birth to the Middle Ages, the scene was set for revival in every field of academic work. The restoration of some degree of political stability in France in the late eleventh century encouraged the re-emergence of the University of Paris, which rapidly became recognized as the intellectual center of Europe. A number of theological "schools" were established on the Left Bank of the Seine, and on the Île de la Cité, in the shadow of the newly-built cathedral of Notre-Dame de Paris.

One such school was the Collège de la Sorbonne, which eventually achieved such fame that "the Sorbonne" eventually came to be a shorthand way of referring to the University of Paris. Even in the sixteenth century, Paris was widely recognized as a leading center for theological and philosophical study, including among its students such names as Erasmus of Rotterdam and John Calvin. Other such centers of study were soon established elsewhere in Europe. A new program of theological development began, concerned with consolidating the intellectual, legal, and spiritual aspects of the life of the Christian church.

The early part of the medieval period is dominated by developments in France. Several monasteries produced outstanding Christian writers and thinkers. For example, the monastery at Bec, in Normandy, produced such outstanding writers as Lanfranc (*c.*1010–89) and Anselm (*c.*1033–1109). The University of Paris soon established itself as an outstanding center of theological speculation, producing such leading writers as Peter Abelard (1079–1142), Albert the Great (*c.*1200–80), Thomas Aquinas (*c.*1225–74), and Bonaventure (*c.*1217–74). The fourteenth and fifteenth centuries witnesses an expansion of the university sector in western Europe, with major new universities being founded in Germany and elsewhere.

A central resource to the new medieval interest in theology is also linked with Paris. At some point shortly before 1140, Peter Lombard arrived at the university to teach. One of his central concerns was to get his students to wrestle with the thorny issues of theology. His contribution was a textbook – perhaps one of the most boring books that has ever been written. The *Four Books of the Sentences* bring together quotations from Scripture and the patristic writers, arranged topically. The task Peter set his students was simple: make sense of the quotes. The book proved to be of major importance in developing the Augustinian heritage, in that students were obliged to wrestle with the ideas of Augustine, and reconcile apparently contradictory texts by devising suitable theological explanations of the inconsistencies. By 1215 the work was firmly established as the most important textbook of the age. It became obligatory for theologians to comment on the work. The resulting works, known as *Commentaries on the Sentences,* became one of the most familiar theological genres of the Middle Ages. Outstanding examples include those of Thomas Aquinas, Bonaventure, and Duns Scotus.

Perhaps the most important intellectual development associated with this period was the rise of scholasticism. Scholasticism is best regarded as the medieval movement, flourishing in the period 1200–1500, which placed emphasis upon the rational justification of religious belief, and the systematic presentation of those beliefs. "Scholasticism" thus does not refer to a *specific system of beliefs,* but to a *particular way of organizing theology* – a highly-developed method of presenting material, making fine distinctions, and attempting to achieve a comprehensive view of theology. It is perhaps understandable why, to its humanist critics, scholasticism seemed to degenerate into little more than logical nitpicking. However, scholasticism may be argued to have made vitally important contributions to a number of key areas of Christian theology, especially in relation to the role of reason and logic in theology. The writings of Thomas Aquinas, Duns Scotus, and William of Ockham – often singled out as the three most influential of all scholastic writers – make massive contributions to this area of theology, which have served as landmarks ever since.

Yet it was not only the life of the mind which underwent renewal during this period. The western church was subjected to a sustained program of reform under Gregory VII (*c*.1021–95), who was elected pope in 1073. Although the "Gregorian Reform" was intensely controversial at the time, modern scholars are generally agreed that it led to the renewal of the church at this critical period in its history. In particular, Gregory managed to achieve an inversion of the existing understanding of the relation of church and state. Whereas it had been assumed that the church was subservient to the state, Gregory managed to establish the principle that, at least in some areas, the church has authority over the state.

The scene was set for further consolidation of papal authority during the later Middle Ages. One major development was the weakness of the empire following the death of emperor Henry IV in 1197. Henry's predecessor as emperor, Frederick I (also known as "Barbarossa") ruled during the period 1152–90. He established his authority over much of northern Italy. Henry consolidated these gains. Yet in 1197 Henry died, leaving his empire to his three-year-old son. Chaos resulted, leaving the empire weak and divided. As it happened, a strong pope was elected the following year, who seized the opportunity to re-establish the authority of the papacy. Under Innocent III (pope from 1198 to 1216), the medieval papacy reached an unprecedented level of power throughout western Europe. Innocent adopted the title of "Vicar of Christ" (the term "vicar" here means "representative" or "substitute"). For Innocent, "no king can reign correctly unless he serves the Vicar of Christ."

Innocent III on the Church and State

In his decree *Sicut universitatis conditor*, issued in October 1198, Innocent set out the principle of the subordination of the state to the church in the following way.

> Just as the creator of the universe established two great lights in the firmament of heaven (the greater one to rule the day, and the lesser one to rule the night), so he also appointed two dignitaries for the firmament of the universal church (which is referred to as "heaven"). The greater of these rules souls (the "days"), and the lesser of them rules bodies (the "nights"). These dignitaries are the authority of the pope and the power of the king. And just as the moon derives her light from the sun, and is inferior to the sun in terms of its size and its quality, so the power of the king derives from the authority of the pope.

STUDY PANEL 39

Nevertheless, other developments undermined this process of consolidation. Of particular importance was the emergence of the Avignon papacy during the period 1378–1417. This development resulted from the temporary withdrawal of the papacy from Rome to Avignon for political reasons during the period 1309–77. On the return of the papacy to Rome in 1378, two pro-French anti-popes ruled in Avignon. The resulting schism was finally settled through the Council of Pisa (1409) and the Council of Constance (1417).

The period was of enormous importance in other respects. Several major new religious orders were founded in the region. In 1097, the Cistercian order was founded at Cîteaux, in the middle of the wild countryside around the River Saône. This order placed an emphasis on the importance of manual labor, rather than of scholarship, and on private rather than corporate prayer. The Cistercian order was noted for its severe rule of life, which denied virtually all of the comforts of life. For example, fires were only permitted once a year, on Christmas Day. One of the most noted Cistercian leaders was the great spiritual writer and preacher Bernard of Clairvaux (1090–1153). By the dawn of the fourteenth century it is estimated that some 600 Cistercian monasteries or convents had come into being.

Two other major orders were founded more than a century later – the Franciscans and Dominicans. The Franciscans were founded by Francis of Assisi (*c*.1181–1226), who renounced a life of wealth to life a life of prayer and poverty. The order was often referred to as "the grey friars," on account of the dark grey habits they wore. The order was distinguished by its emphasis on individual and corporate poverty. The order was often viewed as anti-intellectual; nevertheless, some of the greatest theologians of the period, such as Bonaventure, were members of the order.

The Dominicans (sometimes referred to as "Black Friars" on account of their black mantle worn over a white habit) were founded by the Spanish priest Dominic de Guzman (1170–1221), with a particular emphasis on education. By the end of the Middle Ages the Dominicans had established houses in most major European cities, and made a significant contribution to the intellectual life of the church. Thus Thomas Aquinas, perhaps the greatest medieval theologian, was a Dominican.

The Renaissance

The French term "Renaissance" is now universally used to designate the literary and artistic revival in fourteenth- and fifteenth-century Italy. In 1546 Paolo Giovio referred to the fourteenth century as "that happy century in which Latin letters are conceived to have been reborn," anticipating this development. Certain historians, most notably Jacob Burckhardt, argued that the Renaissance gave birth to the modern era. It was in this era, Burckhardt argued, that human beings first began to think of themselves as *individuals.* In many ways, Burckhardt's definition of the Renaissance in purely individualist terms is highly questionable. But in one sense, Burckhardt is unquestionably correct: *something* novel and exciting developed in Renaissance Italy, which proved capable of exercising a fascination over generations of thinkers.

It is not entirely clear why Italy became the cradle of this brilliant new movement in the history of ideas. A number of factors have been identified as having some bearing on the question.

1   Scholastic theology – the major intellectual force of the medieval period – was never particularly influential in Italy. Although many Italians achieved fame as theologians (such as Thomas Aquinas and Gregory of Rimini), they generally operated in northern Europe. There was thus an intellectual vacuum in Italy during the fourteenth century. Vacuums tend to be filled – and Renaissance humanism filled this particular gap.
2   Italy was saturated with visible and tangible reminders of the greatness of antiquity. The ruins of ancient Roman building and monuments were scattered throughout the land, and appear to have aroused interest in the civilization of ancient Rome at the time of the Renaissance, acting as a stimulus to its thinkers to recover the vitality of classical Roman culture at a time which was culturally arid and barren.
3   As Byzantium began to crumble – Constantinople finally fell to Islamic invaders in 1454 – there was an exodus of Greek-speaking intellectuals westward. Italy happened to be conveniently close to Constantinople, with the result that many such emigrès settled in her cities. A revival of the Greek language was thus inevitable, and with it a revival of interest in the Greek classics.

It will be clear that a central component of the worldview of the Italian Renaissance is a return to the cultural glories of antiquity, and a marginalization of the intellectual achievements of the Middle Ages. Renaissance writers had scant regard for these, regarding them as outweighed by the greater achievements of antiquity. What was true of culture in general was also true of theology: they regarded the late classical period as totally overshadowing the theological writings of the Middle Ages, both in substance and in style. Indeed, the Renaissance may partly be regarded as a reaction against the type of approach increasingly associated with the faculties of arts and theology of northern European universities. Irritated by the technical nature of the language and discussions of the scholastics, the writers of the Renaissance bypassed them altogether. In the case of Christian theology, the key to the future lay in a direct engagement with the text of Scripture and the writings of the patristic period.

The intellectual force within the Renaissance is generally referred to as "humanism." Humanism is a cultural and educational movement, primarily concerned with the promotion of eloquence in its various forms. Its interest in morals, philosophy, and politics are of secondary importance. To be a humanist is to be concerned with eloquence first and foremost, and with other matters incidentally. Humanism was essentially a cultural program, which appealed to classical antiquity as a model of eloquence. In art and architecture, as in the written and spoken word, antiquity was seen as a cultural resource, which could be appropriated by the Renaissance. Humanism was thus concerned with *how ideas were obtained and expressed*, rather than with *the actual substance of those ideas*. A humanist might be a Platonist or an Aristotelian – but in both cases, the ideas involved derived from antiquity. A humanist might be a skeptic or a believer – but both attitudes could be defended from antiquity.

The form of "humanism" which proved to be of especial importance to Christianity is primarily northern European humanism. We must therefore consider what form this northern European movement took. It is becoming increasingly clear that northern European humanism was decisively influenced by Italian humanism at every stage of its development. Three main channels for the diffusion of the methods and ideals of the Italian Renaissance into northern Europe have been identified.

1   Through northern European scholars moving south to Italy, perhaps to study at an Italian university or as part of a diplomatic mission. On returning to their homeland, they brought the spirit of the Renaissance back with them.
2   Through the foreign correspondence of the Italian humanists. Humanism was concerned with the promotion of written eloquence, and the writing of letters was seen as a means of embodying and spreading the ideals of the Renaissance. The foreign correspondence of Italian humanists was considerable, extending to most parts of northern Europe.
3   Through printed books, originating from sources such as the Aldine Press in Venice. These works were often reprinted by northern European presses, particularly those at Basel in Switzerland. Italian humanists often dedicated their works to northern European patrons, thus ensuring that they were taken notice of in potentially influential quarters.

Although there are major variations within northern European humanism, two ideals seem to have achieved widespread acceptance throughout the movement. First, we find the same concern for written and spoken eloquence, after the fashion of the classical period, as in the Italian Reformation. Second, we find a religious program directed towards the corporate revival of the Christian church. The Latin slogan *Christianismus renascens*, "Christianity being born again," summarizes the aims of this program, and indicates its relation to the "rebirth" of letters associated with the Renaissance.

A central element of the humanist agenda was the return to the original sources of western European culture in classical Rome and Athens. The theological counterpart to this agenda was the direct return to the foundational resources of Christian theology, supremely in the New Testament. This agenda proved to be of major significance, as will be seen later (see p. 274). One of its most important consequences was a new appreciation of the foundational importance of Scripture as a theological resource. As interest in Scripture developed, it became increasingly clear that existing Latin translations of this source were inadequate. Supreme among these was the "Vulgate," a Latin translation of the Bible which achieved widespread influence during the Middle Ages. The Old Testament was written in Hebrew (although small sections are written in Aramaic); the New Testament was written in Greek. The Vulgate provided a Latin translation of these texts for the benefit of writers who knew Latin, but not Hebrew or Greek. Yet the reliability of this translation was soon called into question.

The rise of humanist scholarship would expose the distressing discrepancies between the Vulgate and the texts it purported to translate – and thus open the way to doctrinal reformation as a consequence. It is for this reason that humanism is of decisive importance to the development of medieval theology: it demonstrated the unreliability of this translation of the Bible – and hence, it seemed, of theologies based upon it. The biblical basis of scholasticism seemed to collapse, as humanism uncovered error after error in its translation. We shall explore this point further in what follows.

The literary and cultural program of humanism can be summarized in the slogan *ad fontes* – "back to the original sources." The "filter" of medieval commentaries – whether on legal texts or on the Bible – is abandoned, in order to engage directly with the original texts. Applied to the Christian church, the slogan *ad fontes* meant a direct return to the title-deeds of Christianity – to the patristic writers, and supremely to the Bible, studied in its original languages. This necessitated direct access to the Greek text of the New Testament.

The first printed Greek New Testament was produced by Erasmus of Rotterdam in 1516. Erasmus' text was not as reliable as it ought to have been: Erasmus had access to a mere four manuscripts for most of the New Testament, and only one for its final part, the Book of Revelation. As it happened, that manuscript left out five verses, which Erasmus himself had to translate into Greek from the Latin of the Vulgate. Nevertheless, it proved to be a literary milestone. For the first time, theologians had the opportunity of comparing the original Greek text of the New Testament with the later Vulgate translation into Latin.

Drawing on work carried out earlier by the Italian humanist Lorenzo Valla, Erasmus showed that the Vulgate translation of a number of major New Testament texts could not be justified. As a number of medieval church practices and beliefs were based upon these texts, Erasmus' allegations were viewed with consternation by many conservative Catholics (who wanted to retain these practices and beliefs) and with equally great delight by the reformers (who wanted to eliminate them). For example, the Vulgate translated the opening words of Jesus' ministry (Matthew 4:17) as "do penance, for the Kingdom of heaven is at hand." This translation suggested that the coming of the kingdom of heaven had a direct connection with the sacrament of penance. Erasmus, again following Valla, pointed out that the Greek should be translated as "repent, for the Kingdom of heaven is at hand." In other words, where the Vulgate seemed to refer to an outward practice (the sacrament of penance), Erasmus insisted that the reference was to an inward psychological attitude – that of "being repentant."

Such developments undermined the credibility of the Vulgate translation, and opened the way to theological revision on the basis of a better understanding of the biblical text. It also demonstrated the importance of biblical scholarship in relation to theology. Theology could not be permitted to base itself upon translation mistakes! The recognition of the vitally important role of biblical scholarship to Christian theology thus dates from the second decade of the sixteenth century. It also led to the theological concerns of the Reformation, which we shall consider in chapter 12.

Western Christianity in the Late Middle Ages

The Christianity which flourished in western Europe in the period 1350–1500 is widely regarded as having great strengths and equally great weaknesses. Historians have tended to concentrate on the weaknesses, partly to understand the development of the sixteenth century, in which the Reformation got under way. While it is important to understand the nature of these weaknesses, it must be understood that there were considerable strengths.

It is clear that the fifteenth century witnessed a remarkable growth in popular versions of Christianity. It is true that this "popular Christianity" often bore little relation to the official teachings of the church. For example, the gospel was often linked to a series of popular concerns about illness, crop failures, personal romance, and individual prosperity. Many were attracted to the cult of relics – that is, objects or personal possessions associated with the great men and women of faith, or perhaps even with Jesus himself. Thus merchants were known to carry "splinters of the cross" as they made potentially dangerous trading journeys, in much the same way as soldiers wore relics of the saints to protect them from their enemies. In countless such ways, Christianity had become deeply rooted in the popular consciousness by the end of the Middle Ages.

One particularly striking example of this is to be found in the practice of making pilgrimages. In England, a tradition developed of making a pilgrimage to the cathedral city of Canterbury, celebrated in Geoffrey Chaucer's famous work *The Canterbury Tales*. Other sites of major importance included the city of Rome, venerated as the burial place of both the apostles Peter and Paul, and the north-western Spanish shrine of Santiago de Compostela.

The growing literature of the late fifteenth and early sixteenth century listing complaints about the church – once thought by some scholars to point to a decline in the influence of religion in the period – is now thought to point to a growing ability and willingness on the part of the laity to criticize the church, with a view to reforming it. For example, the period 1450–1520 saw a considerable increase in popular religion in Germany. Just about every conceivable objective criterion – the number of masses endowed, the fashion for forming religious brotherhoods, the donations to religious charities, the building of new churches, the number of pilgrimages made, and the growth in popular religious literature – points to a remarkable growth in popular interest in religion. This was often linked with a very deep devotion to the Virgin Mary. A major cult came to center on Mary, often linked with the recitation of the rosary – a series of fifteen prayers, counted off using a string of beads as a memory aid.

A renewed interest in the Christian faith on the part of more academic individuals, linked with a perception of the need to refashion and renew it if it was to regain its vitality, is also evident from the final decade of the fifteenth century onwards. The dynanism unleashed by the remarkably sudden (and still largely unexplained) development of Spanish mysticism in the 1490s was harnessed through the Cisnerian reforms, leading to a new concern for religious education and a revival of religious vocations in Spain. The University of Alcalá and the Complutensian Polyglot (a multilingual version of the Bible) were perhaps the most tangible results of these reforms.

The church was probably the most important sponsor of the arts during this period, commissioning a series of major works – such as Michaelangelo's Sistine Chapel roof – which continue to be regarded as cultural high points. Important advances were also made in the area of spirituality. Works such as Thomas à Kempis' *Imitation of Christ* came to be regarded as a classic. Many other works of similar importance appeared, demonstrating the commitment of the church of this period to the pastoral and spiritual care of its members.

The rise of humanism led to a new concern to relate the Christian faith to the personal experience of individuals. One of the most subtle and significant developments in the self-understanding of Christianity began to take place, as a religion which had grown used to expressing and defining itself in external forms began to rediscover its appeal to the inward consciousness. The Christian writers of Renaissance recognized the need to implant the gospel firmly in the experiential world of the individual, as something which could and should be personally and inwardly appropriated. The age-old appeal of both Paul and Augustine to the introspective conscience of the individual led to these writers being reappropriated with fresh interest, whether in the sonnets of Petrarch or the new religious writings of Renaissance theologians, preachers and biblical commentators.

A generation of thinkers subsequently rose to the challenge on the eve of the Reformation. In Paris, Lefèvre d'Etaples explored the relevance of Paul's understanding of faith for the individual. At Oxford, John Colet stressed the importance of a personal encounter with the risen Christ in the Christian life. In Italy, the movement often known as "catholic evangelicalism" or "evangelism," with its stress on the question of personal salvation, became firmly established within the church, even penetrating deeply within its hierarchy, without being regarded as in any way heretical.

In the Low Countries, Erasmus won the hearts and minds of the educated elite of Europe with the reforming program outlined in the *Enchiridion* or "Handbook of the Christian Soldier," which appeared in 1503. This book was notable for its stress on a personally-assimilated and inward faith, which Erasmus contrasted unfavorably with the concern for external matters characteristic of the institutional church. The work was reprinted in 1509, and entered its third edition in 1515. From that moment onwards, it became a cult work, apparently going through twenty-three editions in the next six years. It was devoured by educated laity throughout western Europe. The work developed the radical and – to lay minds – attractive idea that the church could be reformed and renewed by its laity. The clergy may assist the laity in their understanding of their faith, but do not have any superior status. Religion is an inner spiritual affair, in which the individual believer seeks to deepen his or her knowledge of God by the reading of scripture. Significantly, the *Enchiridion* plays down the role of the institutional church, in order to emphasize the importance of the individual believer.

Despite these obvious strengths, some serious challenges to the established forms of Christianity in western Europe can be identified, which are of relevance to the increasing demands for reform within the late medieval church at the time. The following are of particular importance to understanding the important developments which followed in the sixteenth century.

The Growth in Adult Literacy

By the dawn of the sixteenth century adult literacy was increasingly common, made possible by the development of printing, the growth of the paper industry, and the growing appeal of the humanist movement. In the early Middle Ages, literacy was restricted to the clergyy. Written material took the form of manuscripts which had to be painstakingly copied out by hand, and were generally confined to the libraries of monasteries on account of their scarcity. In order to save precious parchment, words were abbreviated, making manuscripts difficult to decipher. Humanism, however, made adult literacy a social achievement, a skill which opened the way to social refinement and advancement. As the newly-emerging professional classes began to gain power in the cities, gradually wresting control from the old patrician families, they brought to their practice and interpretation of the Christian faith much the same critical acumen and professionalism they employed in their secular careers. The clerical monopoly on literacy was thus decisively broken. This development opened the way for an increasingly critical lay assessment of the abilities of the clergy, and growing lay confidence in religious matters.

The Growth of Anti-Clericalism

Among the more significant elements in our understanding of the background to the Reformation is the new contempt with which clergy were viewed by an increasingly literate and articulate laity. The phenomenon of anti-clericalism was widespread, and not specifically linked to any part of Europe. In part, the phenomenon reflects the low quality of the rank and file clergy. In Renaissance Italy it was common for parish priests to have had virtually no training; what little they knew, they gleaned from watching, helping, and imitating. Diocesan visitations regularly revealed priests who were illiterate, or had apparently permanently mislaid their breviaries. The poor quality of the parish clergy reflected their low social status: in early sixteenth-century Milan, chaplains had incomes lower than those of unskilled laborers. Many resorted to horse and cattle trading to make ends meet. In rural France during the same period, the clergy enjoyed roughly the same social status as vagabonds: their exemption from taxation, prosecution in civil courts and compulsory military service apart, they were virtually indistinguishable from other itinerant beggars of the period.

The tax privileges enjoyed by clergy were the source of particular irritation, especially in times of economic difficulty. In the French diocese of Meaux, which would become a center for reforming activists in the period 1521–46, the clergy was exempted from all forms of taxation, including charges relating to the provisioning and garrisoning of troops – which provoked considerable local resentment. In the diocese of Rouen, there was popular outcry over the windfall profits made by the church by selling grain at a period of severe shortage. Clerical immunity from prosecution in civil courts further isolated the clergy from the people.

In France, the subsistence crises of the 1520s played a major role in the consolidation of anti-clerical attitudes. In his celebrated study of Languedoc, Le Roy Ladurie pointed out that the 1520s witnessed a reversal of the process of expansion and recovery which had been characteristic of the two generations since the ending of the Hundred Years War. From that point onwards, a crisis began to develop, taking the form of plague, famine, and migration of the rural poor to the cities in search of food and employment. A similar pattern has now been identified for the period in most of France north of the Loire. This subsistence crisis focused popular attention on the gross disparity between the fate of the lower classes and the nobles and ecclesiastical establishment.

The Rise of Doctrinal Pluralism

Confusion began to emerge within the church over matters of doctrine. Indeed, it can be argued that doctrinal unclarity was of major importance in relation to the origins of the Reformation in the following century. It was far from clear who had authority to speak on behalf of the church. If a novel theological opinion developed, who was to determine whether it was consistent with the teachings of the church? And there was no shortage of new opinions in the late medieval church. The reasons for this are not difficult to understand.

The rapid expansion of the university sector throughout western Europe in the late fourteenth and fifteenth centuries led to an increased number of theology faculties, with a corresponding increase in the number of theological treatises produced as a result. Then, as now, theologians had to do something to justify their existence. These works frequently explored new ideas. But what was the status of these ideas? The general failure to draw a clear distinction between theological opinions and church teaching, between private opinion and communal doctrine, caused considerable confusion. Who was to distinguish between opinion and doctrine? The pope? an ecumenical council? a professor of theology? Failure to clarify such crucial questions contributed in no small manner to the crisis of authority in the late medieval church. In many centers in western Europe, a "long period of magnificent religious anarchy" (to use a phrase from the historian Lucien Febvre) set in.

Confusion over the official teaching of the church contributed in no small manner to the origins of Luther's program of reform in Germany. Of central importance to Luther was the doctrine of justification – the question of how an individual enters into a relationship with God. The most recent known authoritative pronouncement on the part of a recognized ecclesiastical body relating to this doctrine dated from 418, more than a millennium before the Reformation – and its confused and outdated statements did little to clarify the position of the church on the matter in 1518, eleven hundred years later. It seemed to Luther that the church of his day had lapsed into Pelagianism, an unacceptable understanding of how an individual entered into fellowship with God. The church, he believed, taught that individuals could gain favor and acceptance in the sight of God on account of their personal achievements and status, thus negating the whole idea of grace. Luther may well have been mistaken in this apprehension – but there was such confusion within the church of his day that none was able to enlighten him on the authoritative position of the church on the matter. Even within the papal sovereign enclave at Avignon, an anarchy of ideas prevailed. "Everyone has his own opinion," wrote Boniface Amerbach, who added further to the chaos during the 1520s by promoting the ideas of the "excellent doctor Martin" within this papal stronghold.

We therefore turn to consider the turmoil of the sixteenth century, which saw major divisions arise within the western church, which remain of major importance to the present day.

1 Why is "Byzantine" Christianity so called? And what are its main features?
2 Why did the Renaissance begin in Italy?
3 What were the implications of the Renaissance for the church? And for Christian theology?
4 What evidence is there for the growing political power of the papacy during the later Middle Ages? What were the consequences of this development?
5 What weaknesses did the western church show toward the end of the Middle Ages?

STUDY QUESTIONS

The Reformation of the Church, 1500–1750

The sixteenth century proved to be a period of remarkable importance, setting the scene for the development of many of the features now associated with western Christianity. One particularly important feature which can be traced back to this period and its aftermath is the rise of "denominations" – that is, distinctive types of Christians, such as Anglicans, Baptists, Lutherans, and Methodists. The period proved to be remarkably creative. Not only did the period give rise to what is loosely called "Protestantism"; it also gave birth to a theologically and spiritually renewed Catholicism. Such is the importance of this period to the emergence of modern Christianity in the west that it demands careful attention. While the terms used to refer to periods of Christian history can be misleading or controversial, there is a widespread tendency to refer to the events of this period collectively as "the Reformation."

The Reformation

The term "Reformation" is used by historians and theologians to refer primarily to the western European movement, centering upon individuals such as Martin Luther, Huldrych Zwingli, and John Calvin, concerned with the moral, theological, and institutional reform of the Christian church in that region. Initially, up to about 1525, the Reformation may be regarded as centering upon Martin Luther and the University of Wittenberg, in modern-day north-eastern Germany. However, the movement also gained strength, initially independently, in the Swiss city of Zurich in the early 1520s. Through a complex series of developments, the Zurich Reformation gradually underwent a series of political and theological developments, eventually coming to be associated primarily with the city of Geneva (now part of modern-day Switzerland, although then an independent city-state) and John Calvin. Although initially focusing on regions such as Germany and Switzerland, the Reformation had a considerable impact on most of western Europe during the sixteenth century, provoking either a positive response to at least one aspect of the movement (as, for example, in England, Holland, and Scandinavia) or a reaction against the movement resulting in a consolidation of Catholicism (as, for example, in Spain and France).

The Reformation movement was complex and heterogeneous, and concerned an agenda far broader than the reform of the doctrine of the church. It addressed fundamental social, political and economic issues, too complex to be discussed in any detail in this volume. The growing power of nationalism was unquestionably important in some regions of Europe, including England and Germany. The agenda of the Reformation varied from one country to another, with the theological issues which played major roles in one country (for example, Germany) often having relatively little impact elsewhere (for example, in England). In response to the Reformation, the Catholic church moved to put its own house in order. Prevented from calling a council at an early date due to political instability in Europe resulting from tensions between France and Germany, the pope of the day was eventually able to convene the Council of Trent. The council set itself the task of clarifying and defending Catholic thought and practice against its evangelical opponents.

The term "Reformation" is used in a number of senses, and it is helpful to distinguish them. Four elements may be involved in its definition, and each will be discussed briefly below: Lutheranism; the Reformed church (often referred to as "Calvinism"); the "radical Reformation," often still referred to as "Anabaptism"; and the "Counter Reformation" or "Catholic Reformation."

The Lutheran Reformation

The Lutheran Reformation is particularly associated with the German territories and the pervasive personal influence of one charismatic individual – Martin Luther. Luther was particularly concerned with the doctrine of justification, which formed the central point of his religious thought. The Lutheran Reformation was initially an academic movement, concerned primarily with reforming the teaching of theology at the University of Wittenberg. Wittenberg was an unimportant university, and the reforms introduced by Luther and his colleagues within the theology faculty attracted little attention. It was Luther's personal activities – such as his posting of the famous Ninety-Five Theses (31 October 1517) – which attracted considerable interest, and brought the ideas in circulation at Wittenberg to the attention of a wide audience.

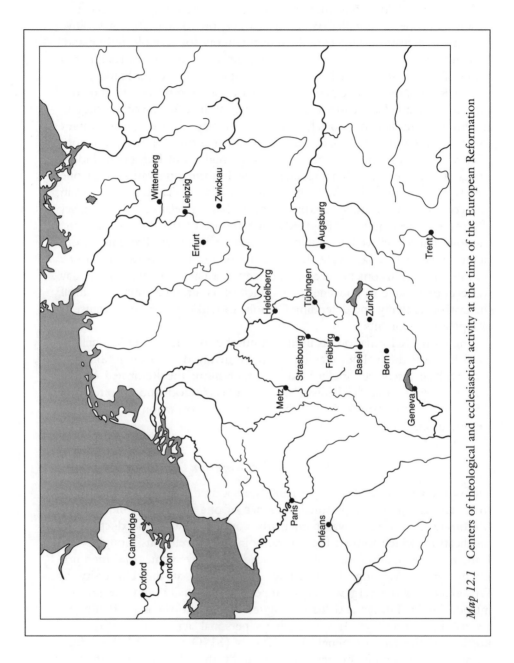

Map 12.1 Centers of theological and ecclesiastical activity at the time of the European Reformation

Strictly speaking, the Lutheran Reformation only began in 1522, when Luther returned to Wittenberg from his enforced isolation in the Wartburg. Luther had been condemned by the Diet of Worms in 1521. Fearing for his life, certain well-placed supporters removed him in secrecy to the castle known as the "Wartburg," until the threat to his safety ceased. In his absence, Andreas Bodenstein von Karlstadt, one of Luther's academic colleagues at Wittenberg, began a program of reform at Wittenberg which seemed to degenerate into chaos. Convinced that he was needed if the Reformation was to survive Karlstadt's ineptitude, Luther emerged from his place of safety, and returned to Wittenberg.

At this point, Luther's program of academic reform changed into a program of reform of church and society. No longer was Luther's forum of activity the university world of ideas – he now found himself regarded as the leader of a religious, social, and political reforming movement which seemed to some contemporary observers to open the way to a new social and religious order in Europe. In fact, Luther's program of reform was much more conservative than that associated with his Reformed colleagues, such as Huldrych Zwingli. Furthermore, it met with considerably less success than some anticipated. The movement remained obstinately tied to the German territories, and – Scandinavia apart – never gained the foreign power-bases which seemed to be like so many ripe apples, ready to fall into its lap. Luther's understanding of the role of the "godly prince" (which effectively ensured that the monarch had control of the church) does not seem to have had the attraction which might have been expected, particularly in the light of the generally republican sentiments of Reformed thinkers such as Calvin.

The Calvinist Reformation

The origins of Calvinist Reformation, which brought the Reformed churches (such as the Presbyterians) into being, lie with developments within the Swiss Confederation. Whereas the Lutheran Reformation had its origins in an academic context, the Reformed church owed its origins to a series of attempts to reform the morals and worship of the church (but not necessarily its doctrine) according to a more biblical pattern. It must be emphasized that although Calvin gave this style of Reformation its definitive form, its origins are to be traced back to earlier reformers, such as Huldrych Zwingli and Heinrich Bullinger, based at the leading Swiss city of Zurich.

Although most of the early Reformed theologians – such as Zwingli – had an academic background, their reforming programs were not academic in nature. They were directed towards the church, as they found it in the Swiss cities, such as Zurich, Berne, and Basel. Whereas Luther was convinced that the doctrine of justification was of central significance to his program of social and religious reform, the early Reformed thinkers had relatively little interest in doctrine, let alone one specific doctrine. Their reforming program was institutional, social and ethical, in many ways similar to the demands for reform emanating from the humanist movement.

The consolidation of the Reformed church is generally thought to begin with the stablization of the Zurich reformation after Zwingli's death in battle (1531) under his successor, Heinrich Bullinger, and to end with the emergence of Geneva as its power base, and John Calvin as its leading spokesman, in the 1550s. The gradual shift in power within the Reformed church (initially from Zurich to Berne, and subsequently from Berne to Geneva) took place over the period 1520–60, eventually establishing both the city of Geneva, its political system (republicanism), and its religious thinkers (initially Calvin, and after his death Theodore Beza) as predominant within the Reformed church. This development was consolidated through the establishment of the Genevan Academy (founded in 1559), at which Reformed pastors were trained.

The term "Calvinism" is often used to refer to the religious ideas of the Reformed church. Although still widespread in the literature relating to the Reformation, this practice is now generally discouraged. It is becoming increasingly clear that later sixteenth-century Reformed theology draws on sources other than the ideas of Calvin himself. To refer to later sixteenth- and seventeenth-century Reformed thought as "Calvinist" implies that it is essentially the thought of Calvin – and it is now generally agreed that Calvin's ideas were modified subtly by his successors. The term "Reformed" is now preferred, whether to refer to those churches (mainly in Switzerland, the Lowlands, and Germany) or religious thinkers (such as Theodore Beza, William Perkins or John Owen) which based themselves upon Calvin's celebrated religious textbook, *Institutes of the Christian Religion*, or church documents (such as the famous *Heidelberg Catechism*) based upon it.

Of the three constituents of the Protestant Reformation – Lutheran, Reformed or Calvinist, and Anabaptist – it is the Reformed wing which is of particular importance to the English-speaking world. Puritanism, which figures so prominently in seventeenth-century English history and is of such fundamental importance to the religious and political views of New England in the seventeenth century and beyond, is a specific form of Reformed Christianity. To understand the religious and political history of New England or the ideas of writers such as Jonathan Edwards, for example, it is necessary to come to grips with at least some of the theological insights and part of the religious outlook of Puritanism, which underlie their social and political attitudes.

The Radical Reformation (Anabaptism)

The term "Anabaptist" owes its origins to Zwingli (the word literally means "rebaptizers," and refers to what was perhaps the most distinctive aspect of Anabaptist practice – the insistence that only those who had made a personal public profession of faith should be baptized). Anabaptism seems to have first arisen around Zurich, in the aftermath of Zwingli's reforms within the city in the early 1520s. It centered on a group of individuals (among whom we may note Conrad Grebel) who argued that Zwingli was not being faithful to his own reforming principles. He preached one thing, and practiced another. Although Zwingli professed faithfulness to the *sola scriptura*, "by scripture alone," principle, Grebel argued that he retained a number of practices – including infant baptism, the close link between church and magistracy, and the participation of Christians in warfare – which were not sanctioned or ordained by Scripture. In the hands of such radical thinkers, the *sola scriptura* principle would be radicalized; reformed Christians would only believe and practice those things explicitly taught in Scripture. Zwingli was alarmed by this, seeing it as a destabilizing development which threatened to cut the reformed church at Zurich off from its historical roots and its continuity with the Christian tradition of the past.

A number of common elements can be discerned within the various strands of the movement: a general distrust of external authority, the rejection of infant baptism in favor of the baptism of adult believers, the common ownership of property, and an emphasis upon pacifism and non-resistance. To take up one of these points: in 1527, the governments of Zurich, Berne, and St Gallen accused the Anabaptists of believing "that no true Christian can either give or receive interest or income on a sum of capital; that all temporal goods are free and common, and that all can have full property rights to them." It is for this reason that "Anabaptism" is often referred to as the "left wing of the Reformation" (Roland H. Bainton) or the "radical Reformation" (George Hunston Williams). For Williams, the "radical Reformation" was to be contrasted with the "magisterial Reformation," which he broadly identified with the Lutheran and Reformed movements. These terms are increasingly being accepted within Reformation scholarship, and you are likely to encounter them in your reading of more recent studies of the movement.

The Catholic Reformation

This term is often used to refer to the revival within Roman Catholicism in the period following the opening of the Council of Trent (1545). In older scholarly works, the movement is often designated the "Counter Reformation": as the term suggests, the Roman Catholic church developed means of combating the Protestant Reformation, in order to limit its influence. It is, however, becoming increasingly clear that the Roman Catholic church countered the Reformation partly by reforming itself from within, in order to remove the grounds of Protestant criticism. In this sense, the movement was a reformation of the Roman Catholic church, as much as it was a reaction against the Protestant Reformation.

The same concerns underlying the Protestant Reformation in northern Europe were channelled into the renewal of the Catholic church, particularly in Spain and Italy. The Council of Trent, the foremost component of the Catholic Reformation, clarified Catholic teaching on a number of confusing matters, and introduced much needed reforms in relation to the conduct of the clergy, ecclesiastical discipline, religious education and missionary activity. The movement for reform within the church was greatly stimulated by the reformation of many of the older religious orders, and the establishment of new orders (such as the Jesuits). The more specifically theological aspects of the Catholic Reformation will be considered in relation to its teachings on Scripture and tradition, justification by faith, and the sacraments. As a result of the Catholic Reformation, many of the abuses which originally lay behind the demands for reform – whether these came from humanists or Protestants – were removed.

In its broadest sense, the term "Reformation" is used to refer to all four of the movements described above. The term is also used in a somewhat more restricted sense, meaning "the Protestant Reformation," excluding the Catholic Reformation. In this sense, it refers to the three Protestant movements noted above. In many scholarly works, however, the term "Reformation" is used to refer to what is sometimes known as the "magisterial Reformation," or the "mainstream Reformation" – in other words, that linked with the Lutheran and Reformed churches (including Anglicanism), and excluding the Anabaptists.

The Rise of Protestantism

Given the historical and contemporary importance of the tensions between Catholics and Protestants, it is clearly important to establish how this division came into being. The following section will deal with the rise of Protestantism in the sixteenth century; a later section (see pp. 405–15) will deal with the characteristics of each individual type of Protestantism in more detail.

The Limitations of the Term "Protestant"

The term "Protestant" is widely used to refer to the forms of Christianity which emerged in western Europe during the sixteenth century in response to medieval Christianity. The term requires some comment, in that it is not particularly helpful. It derives from the aftermath of the Diet of Speyer (February 1529), which voted to end the toleration of Lutheranism in Germany. In April of the same year, six German princes and fourteen cities protested against this oppressive measure, defending freedom of conscience and the rights of religious minorities. The term "Protestant" derives from this protest. It is therefore not strictly correct to apply the term "Protestant" to individuals prior to April 1529, or to speak of events prior to that date as constituting "the Protestant Reformation." The term "evangelical" is often used in the literature to refer to the reforming factions at Wittenberg and elsewhere (e.g., in France and Switzerland) prior to this date. Although the word "Protestant" is often used to refer to this earlier period, this use is, strictly speaking, an anachronism. The term "evangelical" is generally more accurate and helpful.

The term "evangelical" originally dates from the sixteenth century, and was used to refer to Catholic writers wishing to revert to more biblical beliefs and practices than those associated with the late medieval church. It is now generally accepted that attitudes toward the personal appropriation of salvation and the spiritual importance of the reading of Scripture which would now be called "evangelical" emerged in Italian Benedictine monasteries during the late fifteenth century. Similarly, scholars of the later Italian Renaissance have identified a major spiritual movement, which becomes particularly important amongst the Italian aristocratic laity in the 1520s, placing an emphasis on a personally-appropriated salvation. As we noted earlier, one of the most important features of the late Renaissance is the growth of lay religion, and the increased demands on the part of a Christian laity throughout western Europe for a form of Christian spirituality which was of direct relevance to their personal spiritual concerns. It is known that such evangelical attitudes were not initially regarded as a threat by ecclesiastical authorities; indeed, they were even welcomed in some areas as making an overdue and welcome contribution to the renewal of the spiritual vitality of a tired church. The Italian church in particular was deeply and positively affected by the emergence of evangelicalism during the 1530s. Several cardinals of the period were profoundly influenced by evangelical attitudes, which they did not regard as inconsistent with their senior positions within the church. It was only in the mid-1540s, when an increasingly anxious church, alert to the growing threat posed by northern European Lutheranism, condemned such attitudes as destabilizing, that evangelicalism went off-limits. What was the reason for this development? The church authorities had become convinced that to be an *evangelical* was to be a *Lutheran* – and hence to be anti-Catholic.

The term "evangelical" was especially associated with the 1520s, when the French term *évangélique* and the German *evangelisch* begin to feature prominently in the controversial writings of the early Reformation. In the 1530s, the term "Protestant" came to become more significant; increasingly, this came to be understood simply as "anti-Catholic." However, it must be appreciated this term was imposed upon evangelicals by their Catholic opponents, and was not one of their own choosing. The term "Protestant" referred originally to the "protest" of the six princes and fourteen south German cities at the second Diet of Speyer (1529) against the rescinding of the guarantee of religious freedom set out by the *first* Diet of Speyer, three years earlier. Despite the popular mythology surrounding the origins of the term, the "protest" in question was not against Rome, nor even the theology of the pre-Reformation church, but against the outcome of a specific form of political intrigue in southern Germany. Although the term "Protestant" is now widely used to refer to forms of western Christianity which do not accept the authority of the pope, the limitations of the term need to be recognized.

The Origins of Protestantism

The origins of Protestantism are enormously complex, involving social, political, economic, and theological matters. It has, for example, often been noted that Protestantism had an especial appeal to the rising middle classes of the sixteenth century, offering them opportunities and status denied to them in more traditional societies, in which the aristocracy held power. Equally, the adoption of one form of Protestantism by England's Henry VIII is partly due to Henry's desire to establish a national English church, free of interference from Rome. While it is thus not true to say that the origins of Protestantism are purely religious in nature, it is nevertheless important to appreciate that religious matters were of major importance to its emergence.

To explore the origins of Protestantism, it is probably most helpful to look at three of its leading representatives: Martin Luther (1483–1546), Huldrych Zwingli (1484–1531), and John Calvin (1509–64). Each can be seen as in some way contributing to the emergence of the movement.

Martin Luther began his career with the intention of studying law. He initially studied at the University of Erfurt, a noted stronghold of scholasticism. Following what seems to have been a traumatic experience during a violent thunderstorm, Luther decided to enter the Augustinian monastery in Erfurt, and train for the priesthood. After a period spent studing theology and serving his religious order in several capacities, Luther took up a teaching position at the recently founded University of Wittenberg in 1511. As a professor of biblical studies, he gave courses of lectures on a number of biblical works, including the Psalter, Romans, Galatians, and Hebrews. During the course of these lectures he appears to have gone through some kind of theological conversion.

The nature of this conversion is quite complex; however, it is generally agreed to focus on the doctrine of justification – the question of how human beings enter into a right relationship with God. Luther's initial position seems to have been that this right relationship can be brought into being through human achievement. In other words, people can do certain quite definite things, through their own efforts. As a result, they are put in a right relationship with God. However, Luther came to regard this understanding as seriously deficient. At some point around the year 1515 (although the precise date is disputed), Luther seems to have decided that this relationship could only be established from God's side. It is to be understood as a divine gift, rather than a human achievement. On the basis of this changed understanding of how human beings are put in a correct relationship with God, Luther embarked on a program of reform within the church.

Perhaps the most famous aspect of that program was the posting of the ninety-five theses on 31 October 1517; there related to the practice of selling indulgences. The theses caused considerable controversy, and resulted in Luther's name becoming widely known. This was followed up in 1519 by the Leipzig Disputation, in which Luther and Johann Eck entered into public debate over a number of important issues, including that of the authority of the pope. The following year saw the publication of three major reforming works, which set an agenda for the reformation and renewal of the church and its theology: *The Appeal to the German Nobility*, *The Babylonian Captivity of the Church*, and *The Freedom of a Christian*. These increased considerably the pressure on the church authorities, particularly in Germany, for a reform of some of the current practices and beliefs of the church.

It was not long before Luther's ideas were being widely discussed and debated within western Europe. A group met regularly in the English university town of Cambridge to discuss Luther's writings. Known as "the White Horse" group after the tavern in which they were prone to gather, the group included several figures who would have a major impact on the development of the Reformation in England during the 1530s.

Yet reforming movements were springing up elsewhere in Europe, including in Switzerland. The Swiss reformer Huldrych Zwingli was educated at the universities of Vienna and Basel, before taking up parish duties in eastern Switzerland. It is clear that he took a keen interest in the agenda of Christian humanism, especially the writings of Erasmus, and became committed to belief in the need to reform the church of his day. In 1519, he took up a pastoral position in the city of Zurich. Zwingli used the pulpit of the Great Minster, the chief church within the city, to propagate a program of reform. Initially, this program was primarily concerned with the reformation of the morals of the church. However, it soon extended to include criticism of the existing theology of the church, especially in relation to sacramental theology. The term "Zwinglian" is used especially to refer to the belief, associated with Zwingli, that Christ is not present at the Eucharist, which is best seen as a memorial of Christ's death.

Yet perhaps the most significant of the reformers began his work after the first wave of the Reformation had passed. John Calvin belongs to the second generation of reformers, who were more concerned with the consolidation of the ideas and practices of the Reformation. Calvin was born in Noyon, north-east of Paris, in 1509. Educated at the scholasticism-dominated University of Paris, he subsequently moved to the more humanist University of Orléans, at which he studied civil law. Although initially inclined to a career of scholarship, he underwent a conversion experience in his mid-20s, which led to his becoming increasingly associated with reforming movements in Paris, and eventually being forced into exile in Basel.

The second generation of reformers were far more aware of the need for works of systematic theology than the first. Calvin, the major figure of the second period of the Reformation, saw the need for a work which would set out clearly the basic ideas of evangelical theology, justifying them on the basis of Scripture and defending them in the face of Catholic criticism. In 1536, he published a small work entitled *Institutes of the Christian Religion*, a mere six chapters in length. For the next quarter of a century Calvin worked away at this, adding extra chapters and rearranging the material. By the time of its final edition (1559), the work had eighty chapters, and was divided into four books. The first book deals with God the creator, and his sovereignty over that creation. The second book concerns the human need for redemption, and the manner in which this redemption is achieved by Christ the mediator. The third book deals with the manner in which this redemption is appropriated by human beings, while the final book deals with the church and its relation to society. Although it is often suggested that predestination stands at the center of Calvin's system, this is not the case; the only principle which seems to govern Calvin's organization of his theological system is a concern to be faithful to Scripture on the one hand, and to achieve maximum clarity of presentation on the other.

After winding up his affairs in Noyon early in 1536, Calvin decided to settle down to a life of private study in the great city of Strasbourg. Unfortunately, the direct route from Noyon to Strasbourg was impassable, due to the outbreak of war between Francis I of France and the Emperor Charles V. Calvin had to make an extended detour, passing through the city of Geneva which had recently gained its independence from the neighboring territory of Savoy. Geneva was then in a state of confusion, having just evicted its local bishop, and had begun a controversial program of reform under the Frenchmen Guillaume Farel and Pierre Viret. On hearing that Calvin was in the city, they demanded that he stay, and help the cause of the Reformation. They needed a good teacher. Calvin reluctantly agreed.

His attempts to provide the Genevan church with a solid basis of doctrine and discipline met intense resistance. After a series of quarrels, matters reached a head on Easter Day 1538: Calvin was expelled from the city, and sought refuge in Strasbourg. Having arrived in Strasbourg two years later than he had anticipated, Calvin began to make up for lost time. In quick succession he produced a series of major theological works. As pastor to the French-speaking congregation in the city, Calvin was able to gain experience of the practical problems facing reformed pastors. Through his friendship with Martin Bucer, the Strasbourg reformer, Calvin was able to develop his thinking on the relation between the city and church.

In September 1541, Calvin was asked to return to Geneva. In his absence, the religious and political situation had deteriorated. The city appealed to him to return, and restore order and confidence within the city. The Calvin who returned to Geneva was a wiser and more experienced young man, far better equipped for the tasks awaiting him than he had been three years earlier. His experience at Strasbourg lent new realism to his theorizing about the nature of the church, which is reflected in his subsequent writings in the field. By the time of his death in 1564 Calvin had made Geneva the center of an international movement, which came to bear his name. Calvinism is still one of the most potent and significant intellectual movements in human history.

The Reformation in England

The English Reformation took a somewhat different direction than its continental counterpart. Although there was at least some degree of popular pressure for a reform within the church, the leading force for reform was Henry VIII, who ascended the throne in 1509. In 1527, Henry took the first steps to dissolve his marriage to Catherine of Aragon. This decision resulted from Henry's desire to ensure the succession to the English throne. The only child of this marriage, Mary Tudor, was female; Henry wanted a male heir. The pope refused to dissolve or annul the marriage.

It is quite improper to suggest that the English Reformation resulted from the pope's refusal to grant Henry his divorce. Nevertheless, it was a factor. Henry gradually appears to have shifted toward a policy which involved the replacement of papal authority in England with his own authority. The creation of an English national church was part of this vision. Henry seems not to have been particularly interested in matters of doctrine or theology, preferring to concentrate upon the practicalities of religious and political power. His decision to appoint Thomas Cranmer (1489–1556) as

Archbishop of Canterbury led to at least some Protestant influences being brought to bear on the English church.

When Henry died in 1547, he was succeeded by his son, Edward VI. Edward was a minor on his accession; as a result, real power was exercised by his advisors, who were generally of a strongly Protestant persuasion. Cranmer, who remained in office as archbishop during Edward's reign, was able to bring in noticably Protestant forms of public worship, and encouraged leading Protestant thinkers (such as Martin Bucer and Peter Martyr Vermigli) to settle in England, and give theological direction to the Reformation. However, Edward died in 1553, leaving the nation in a state of religious flux.

Edward was succeeded by Mary Tudor, who was strongly Catholic in sympathy. She set in motion a series of measures which suppressed Protestantism, and restored Catholicism. Some of the measures were deeply unpopular, most notably the public burning of Thomas Cranmer at Oxford in 1556. Cranmer was replaced as Archbishop of Canterbury by Reginald Pole, a moderate Catholic. At the time of her death in 1558, Catholicism had not yet been entirely re-established. When Elizabeth I succeeded to the throne, it was not entirely clear what direction her religious policies might take. In the event, Elizabeth pursued a complex policy, which seems to have been aimed at appeasing both Protestants and Catholics, while allowing the Queen to have supreme authority in matters of religion. What is usually referred to as "the Elizabethan Settlement" (1558–9) established the national English church as a reformed episcopal church, having broadly Protestant articles of faith with a more Catholic liturgy. Nobody was really entirely happy with the outcome, which was widely seen as a compromise; however, it enabled England to emerge from a period of religious tension, and avoid the serious religious conflicts which were raging elsewhere in Europe at the time.

Leading Features of Protestantism

Protestantism was, as we have noted, a remarkably diverse movement. However, examination of Protestant church practice and key documents – such as the Augsburg Confession (Lutheran, 1530); the Heidelberg Catechism (Reformed, 1562), the Thirty-Nine Articles (Anglican, 1563) – shows that a number of central themes can be seen as typical of the movement. These include the following.

1 A rejection of papal authority. Protestants regarded the authority of the pope as resting on a series of unjustifiable developments, and wished to return to simpler models of church leadership, such as those found in the New Testament. As a result, some Protestant churches retained an

episcopal system of church government, regarding this as a legitimate and biblical means of maintaining faith and order within the churches.

2 Particular emphasis was placed on the priority of the Bible. The Reformation introduced what is generally known as the "Scripture principle" – that is, the insistence that the ultimate foundation and criterion of Christian thinking is the Bible. This does not mean that Protestant writers rejected reason or tradition in their thinking; it simply means that they regarded these as playing a subordinate role to the Bible (see pp. 184–7). The English writer William Chillingworth (1602–44) gave a particularly distinctive statement of this belief in his famous declaration that "the Bible only is the religion of Protestants."

3 Protestant churches rejected the medieval sacramental system, which recognized seven sacraments. Instead, they affirmed that there were only two "sacraments of the gospel" – baptism and what was variously referred to as the Holy Communion, Lord's Supper, Mass, or Commemoration.

4 One of the most visible distinctions between Catholics and Protestants centered on the sacrament, which was variously referred to in the ways just noted. Catholic churches practiced "communion in one kind" – that is, they allowed the laity to receive only bread at the communion. (Priests were allowed to receive both bread and wine.) While the origins of this practice are not clear, it became widespread within medieval western Christianity. In contrast, Prostestant churches practiced "communion in both kinds" – that is, the laity were allowed to receive the bread and the wine.

5 In the medieval catholic church, a strong distinction was maintained between priests and laity. The sacrament of ordination was understood to confer some distinct and indelible character upon ministers, which marked them off from the laity. The distinction between clergy and laity was generally maintained within Protestantism, but understood in a rather different way. The doctrine of the "priesthood of all believers," which was widely accepted among leading Protestant thinkers, affirmed that all believers were to be regarded as priests, at least in some sense. As a result, professional ministers differed from the laity only in that they exercised specific functions within the church.

6 Protestants rejected a series of Catholic beliefs concerning purgatory (see pp. 227–8), arguing that they were without biblical foundation. The related practice of praying for the dead was also abandoned.

7 Protestants generally adopted a suspicious attitude toward Mary, seeing in her as much a potential source of idolatry as an example of Christian obedience. The practice of Marian veneration was generally rejected within Protestantism, along with a series of beliefs concerning the ability of the saints to intercede for either the living or the dead.

Many other examples of differences between Catholics and Protestants could be given; interested readers are referred to the analysis on pp. 398–415 for further discussion of differences between the various styles of Christianity. However, it is important to appreciate that there are considerable areas of agreement between Catholics and Protestants, which can easily be overlooked in the face of their obvious differences.

Further Developments in Protestantism to 1700

Three major movements to emerge within Protestantism should be noted: Orthodoxy, Puritanism, and Pietism. We shall explore each of these in what follows.

1 *Orthodoxy.* As we have seen, the initial period in the life of Protestantism was enormously dynamic. From about 1520 to 1560, the movement was concerned to conquer new territories and make new advances. Yet a change of outlook appears to have settled in at some point in the 1560s, perhaps around the time of the death of Calvin in 1564. The movement was now concerned to defend itself. Something along the lines of a siege mentality seems to have evolved. Two general themes seem to have contributed to this change of outlook.

First, following the Council of Trent, Catholicism underwent a dramatic renewal of confidence. Protestants were forced to realize that the vision of nation after nation accepting the agenda of the Reformation was unrealistic. Catholicism began to regain territories which had once been sympathetic to the Reformation, and consolidated its hold on others which had remained loyal. The task now facing Protestantism was that of maintaining its present position. Part of that defensive strategy was the formulation of rigorous theological criteria of identity, so that Protestants could distinguish themselves from Catholics. The issue of doctrinal purity or "theological correctness" became of major importance. Increasingly, Protestant theologians came to concentrate their attention on the formulation and defense of theological orthodoxy.

Second, increasing tensions developed between the two major types of Protestantism in mainland Europe – Lutheran and Reformed (or Calvinist). It had been generally assumed that those parts of Germany which were Protestant would be Lutheran. However, in the 1560s, Calvinism began to make significant inroads in Germany, increasing the tension between the Lutheran and Reformed churches in this region. Lutheran theologians now found themselves fighting on two fronts – against Catholics on the one hand, and Calvinists on the other. As a result, it became increasingly important to distinguish these two types of Protestantism. This led to a deliberate attempt to draw rigorous theological or doctrinal distinctions between them. As a result, a concern for "right doctrine" became of decisive importance.

The term "Orthodoxy" is used to refer to this period in the history of both the Lutheran and Reformed churches, which saw such an emphasis being placed on doctrinal conformity. It is associated with the rise of "Protestant scholasticism," similar in many ways to the forms of scholasticism which developed within the medieval church several centuries earlier. An emphasis came to be placed on the rational justification and defense of key doctrines, which were in turn used to justify and defend the integrity of the particular type of Protestantism in question, over and against other types of Protestantism on the one hand, and Catholicism on the other. To many observers, it seemed that this type of Christianity placed too much weight on matters of the head, and not enough on matters of the heart. It is this belief which underlies the rise of Pietism, to which we shall turn presently.

2   *Puritanism.* The term "Puritan" was originally intended to be abusive. It was used to stigmatize those members of the Church of England during the reign of Elizabeth I who wanted to adopt more Reformed beliefs and practices (such as the abolition of bishops). The University of Cambridge was a major center for Puritan activity, with Emmanuel College establishing itself as a significant seedbed of Puritan theological and pastoral thinking. Official hostility toward these trends led to the formation of small separatist congregations, which "withdrew" from the national church as a protest against its failure to reform itself completely. The most important of these separatist groups was the "Brownists," named after Robert Browne (*c.*1550–1633).

Following official harassment, the separatists initially found refuge in the Netherlands; some, however, were able to return to England later, and establish congregations in England. These groups, which may be regarded as forerunners of modern Baptists, flourished particularly during the period of the Puritan commonwealth, when it is estimated that there were 300 such congregations in England. Following the restoration of Charles II, the Baptists found themselves facing official hostility once more; it was not until the late eighteenth century that they would achieve a significant degree of acceptance and stability.

One group of particular interest should be noted. A separatist congregation was established at Scrooby, Nottinghamshire, in 1606, with John Robinson (*c.*1575–1625) as its pastor. Growing official hostility forced the congregation to move to Leiden in the Netherlands in 1609. However, the Dutch situation was still not ideal. The congregation set its sights on America, which was then being opened up to European settlers. On 6 September 1620, 102 members of the congregation set sail for America in the *Mayflower*. The resulting colony established in Massachussets would be seen as a model by many Europeans, dissatisfied with the restrictions of religious life in the region.

Despite its growing influence within the national English church, Puritanism continued to encounter strong hostility from both church and state in the early seventeenth century. However, growing popular discontent with the monarchy at the time led to Puritanism becoming identified with the forces of democracy. As the tension between king and parliament grew, Puritanism was seen as a vigorous supporter of parliamentary authority. The resulting Civil War led to the execution of Charles I, and the establishment of a Puritan Commonwealth under Oliver Cromwell during the 1650s. However, the restoration of Charles II led to the withering of Puritanism as a significant political and social force in England.

Yet Puritanism was set to exercise a major influence elsewhere. Dissatisfaction with the religious situation in England led many English Puritans to emigrate to America, taking their faith with them. Massachussets Bay became a center of Puritanism. The impact of this development on American history was considerable.

Nineteenth-century historians adopted a strongly hostile attitude toward Puritanism, depicting Puritans as religious killjoys, intellectually sterile, and devoid of any serious importance for western civilization. This stereotype is largely due to the polemical strategies of its contemporary opponents, who were understandably anxious to discredit the movement. The English high church Tory portrayal of Calvinism in these aggressively negative terms is little more than a defensive response to a movement which was perceived – rightly, as the English Civil War, culminating in a Calvinist military victory, demonstrated – as a major threat to the political and religious *status quo*. Puritanism, with its credible political vision of the City of God, proved to be a major challenge to the vested interests of English church and state in the seventeenth century. However, the twentieth century has seen something of a scholarly rehabilitation of Puritanism, due to the activities of historians such as Perry Miller and Edmund Morgan.

3 *Pietism.* As Orthodoxy became increasingly influential within mainstream Protestantism, so its defects became clear. At its best, Orthodoxy was concerned with the rational defense of Christian truth claims, and a concern for doctrinal correctness. Yet, too often, this came across as an academic preoccupation with logical niceties, rather than a concern for relating theology to the issues of everyday life. The term "Pietism" derives from the Latin word *pietas* (best translated as "piety" or "godliness"), and was initially a derogatory term used by the movement's opponents to describe its emphasis upon the importance of Christian doctrine for the everyday Christian life.

The movement is usually regarded as having been inaugurated with the publication of Philip Jakob Spener's *Pia Desideria* ("Pious Wishes," 1675).

In this work, Spener lamented the state of the German Lutheran church in the aftermath of the Thirty Years War (1618–48), and set out proposals for the revitalization of the church of his day. Chief among these proposals was a new emphasis upon personal Bible study. These proposals were treated with derision by academic theologians; nevertheless, they were to prove influential in German church circles, reflecting a growing disillusionment and impatience with the sterility of Orthodoxy in the face of the shocking social conditions endured during the war. For Pietism, a reformation of doctrine must always be accompanied by a reformation of life.

Pietism developed in a number of different directions, especially in England and Germany. Among the representatives of the movement, the following should be noted as being of particular importance.

1   Nikolaus Ludwig Graf von Zinzendorf (1700–60) founded the Pietist community generally known as the "Herrnhuter," named after the village of Herrnhut. Alienated from what he regarded as the arid rationalism and barren Orthodoxy of his time, he stressed the importance of a "religion of the heart," based on an intimate and personal relationship between Christ and the believer. A new emphasis was placed upon the role of "feeling" (as opposed to reason or doctrinal orthodoxy) within the Christian life, which may be regarded as laying the foundations of Romanticism in later German religious thought. Zinzendorf's emphasis upon a personally appropriated faith finds expression in the slogan "a living faith," which he opposed to the prevailing nominalism of Protestant Orthodoxy.

2   John Wesley (1703–91) was a founder and early leader of the Methodist movement within the Church of England, which subsequently gave birth to Methodism as a denomination in its own right. Convinced that he "lacked the faith whereby alone we are saved," Wesley paid a visit to Herrnhut in 1738, and was deeply impressed by what he found. The Pietist emphasis upon the need for a "living faith" and the role of experience in the Christian life led to his conversion experience at a meeting in Aldersgate Street in May 1738, in which he felt his heart to be "strangely warmed." Wesley's emphasis upon the experiential side of Christian faith, which contrasted sharply with the dullness of contemporary English Deism, led to a minor religious revival in England.

Despite their differences, the various branches of Pietism succeeded in making Christian faith relevant to the experiential world of ordinary believers. It is of some importance to note that the strongly anti-religious tone of the French Revolution during the eighteenth century is partly due to the absence of any real equivalent of Pietism in the region. The movement may be regarded as a reaction against a one-sided emphasis upon doctrinal orthodoxy, in favor of a faith which relates to the deepest aspects of human nature.

The Renewal of Catholicism

The evidence suggests that the Catholic church was poorly prepared to meet the challenges thrown at it by the Reformation. As a result, the new ideas of the Reformation were able to gain a considerable advantage over their Catholic rivals. Among the points of importance, the following should be noted.

1   Relatively few Catholic theologians were able or willing to write in the everyday languages of Europe, such as French or German. Luther and Calvin, by addressing audiences directly in their own languages (rather than the Latin favored by scholars) were able to outmaneuver their opponents. A particularly important example of an evangelical work to appear in a major European language is provided by the anonymous work *The Benefits of Christ*, which was published in Italian in 1543. Its author remains uncertain; its impact was, however, dramatic. According to one contemporary source, the second edition of the work, published at Venice, sold 40,000 copies over a period of six years.

Perhaps most important of all, the Bible was translated into the everyday languages of Europe, making its ideas widely available to ordinary people. One of the most influential translations was Martin Luther's *German Bible*, which had a massive influence on the shaping of the German language. William Tyndale (*c.*1494–1536) produced an English translation of the New Testament in 1526, which had a similar impact on the English language. Catholics, meanwhile, had to continue relying on the Latin translation of the Vulgate – a translation which was increasingly regarded as inaccurate and unreliable at critical points.

2   Early evangelical writers, such as Philip Melanchthon, were able to argue that the Reformation represented a return to the ideas and practices of the early church. Their Catholic opponents simply did not have enough knowledge of the writings of the period to contest this point. An excellent illustration of this point is provided by the Lausanne Disputation of October 1536, in which John Calvin responded to the suggestion that evangelicals despised the fathers (that is, the Christian writers of the first five centuries), regarding them as possessing no authority in matters of doctrine. Calvin declared that this was simply not true: not merely did the evangelicals respect the fathers more than their Catholic opponents; they also knew them better. Reeling off a remarkable chain of references to their writings, includ-

ing their location – apparently totally from memory – Calvin virtually destroyed the credibility of his opponent. Cyprian is quoted to the letter ("in the second book of his letters, the third letter"), Chrysostom even more precisely ("the twenty-first homily, about half-way through"). The dramatic effect of this intervention was considerable. Yet looking into Calvin's quotations more closely, it is clear that the fathers are generally quoted out of context, often omitting material which points to a different interpretation than that which Calvin suggested. Nevertheless, his Catholic opponents at Lausanne (and, indeed, as time would prove, elsewhere) lacked the ability to refute him.

3   The first phase of the Reformation recognized the importance of catechetical material – that is to say, material designed to make the ideas of the Reformation as accessible and intelligible as possible. A classic example of this is provided by Luther's *Short Catechism* (1527), which set out his ideas in a clear and simple format. It proved to be a long time before a Catholic equivalent was forthcoming.

4   The Habsburg–Valois conflict, which rumbled on during the critical period of the 1530s until 1544, meant that two major Catholic power blocks were engaged in fighting each other. This provided a window of opportunity for the various forms of Protestantism to expand and consolidate their influence in Germany and elsewhere. The formation of the "Schmalkaldic League" (February 1531) united Lutheran and Reformed forces in the face of a military threat from Emperor Charles V, and ensured the safety of Protestantism in the meantime.

Yet all of these proved to be temporary difficulties. It was not long before Catholic writers were producing high-quality literature in the everyday languages of Europe. As Catholics devoted more time to studying the patristic period, they became increasingly confident concerning the continuity between the early church and their own period. Catholic catechisms began to appear. And the resolution of the Habsburg–Valois conflict in 1544 allowed the armies of Charles V to turn their attention to the military defeat of Lutheranism. By the end of 1544, the Schmalkaldic League had been routed. The Religious Peace of Augsburg (1555) eventually established the principle widely known as *"cuius regio, eius religio"* (which can be roughly translated as "the region determines the religion"). This more or less fixed the boundaries of Lutheranism, the Reformed churches, and Catholicism in central Europe.

The Council of Trent

Perhaps the most important development within Catholicism during the sixteenth century was the convening of the Council of Trent. This council, which began its discussions in December 1545, was suspended at various points. In 1547, the outbreak of an epidemic at Trent forced its relocation to Bologna, followed by its suspension until 1551. A further suspension resulted in 1552, as a result of the revolt of the German princes against the authority of the emperor (which was eventually settled by the Religious Peace of Augsburg). It was not until 1562 that the Council could meet again; it concluded its work the following year.

Why did the Council of Trent not meet earlier? The most important reason relates to a war which was raging in Europe at the time. The emperor Charles V was engaged in battle with the King of France. While this war was taking place, it would have been impossible for French and German bishops to sit down at the same conference table. An attempt was made to convene a reforming council at Mantua in 1537; it has to be aborted, due to the war. Another attempt was made in 1542; once more, it failed. However, in September 1544 the Peace of Crépy brought hostilities between the French and Germans to an end. Two months later Pope Paul III issued a document convening the Council of Trent with the objectives of settling theological disputes, reforming the church, and liberating Christians from Turkish invaders. The council was scheduled to begin in March 1545, although delays crept in for a number of reasons.

The impact of the council on the development of Catholicism during the remainder of the sixteenth century and beyond was considerable. It is widely regarded as the most important church council between the Council of Nicea (325) and the second Vatican Council (1962–65). Its main achievements can be summarized as follows.

1 *The clarification of Catholic teaching.* As noted earlier, there was considerable confusion within Catholicism over what counted as the "official teaching of the church," and what was to be regarded simply as the "private opinions of individuals." This was particularly important in relation to the doctrine of justification (see pp. 278–9), which lay at the heart of Martin Luther's campaign for reform back in the late 1510s. Many traditional Catholic doctrines and practices were affirmed, including the practice of communion in one kind, the authority of the Vulgate translation of the Bible (although a revision of the translation was ordered on 1546, and completed in 1592), and the necessity of seven sacraments.

2 *The elimination of abuses within the church.* The late medieval church was plagued by a series of abuses, which did little to enhance its popular reputation. Clergy and bishops were known to be permanently absent from their parishes or dioceses; occasionally, clergy would hold several parishes in plurality, receiving a larger income without providing the

necessary pastoral care in return. Trent moved to eliminate such abuses, by laying down strict guidelines for bishops and clergy.

An important development which took place around this period was the development of the "Society of Jesus," more generally known as "the Jesuits." We shall explore the implications of this in what follows.

The Society of Jesus

The Jesuits were founded by Ignatius Loyola. Loyola was a professional soldier invalided out of service in 1521 on account of a leg wound. While convalescing he read biographies of the saints, and became convinced of the need for a tightly disciplined life of faith, modeled on military lines. The importance of discipline can be seen clearly in Loyola's most important contribution to the field of Christian spirituality – the *Spiritual Exercises,* which he drew up during the period 1522–3. These set out a four-week program of prayer, meditation and reflection, aimed at deepening the commitment of the reader to Christ.

Loyola and six colleagues constituted the original nucleus of the society, founded in Paris in 1534, which was given papal approval by Paul III in 1540. From that point onward it expanded rapidly. The constitution of the order was unusual in that it added a fourth vow to the traditional list of three vows associated with religious orders. In addition to vows of poverty, chastity and obedience, Jesuits were required to give an oath of absolute obedience to the pope. In effect, the Jesuits became a spiritual elite, personally and directly responsible to the pope, who was free to use them in whatever way he thought best for the defense of the Christian faith and the Christian church. Although the Jesuits were not founded with the religious controversies of the Reformation period in mind, it is clear that combating Protestantism soon became one of the central goals pursued by the Jesuits, especially after the final session of the Council of Trent.

By 1556, the year of Loyola's death, there were more than a thousand members of the order, which became a significant presence in Italy, Spain, and Portugal. Their influence was felt especially in the fields of missionary work and education. Jesuit missions were established during the sixteenth century in areas as diverse as Brazil, China, India, Japan, and Malaya. In the field of education the Jesuits established a rigorous program of studies, designed to ensure the intellectual excellence of the order. The "Ratio Studiorum" ("Method of Studies") issued in 1599 focused on literature, philosophy and theology, and went some considerable way toward establishing the pre-eminence of Jesuits in the theological and cultural debates of the time. The legacy of this educational development can still be seen, particularly in the United States.

The Renewal of Spirituality

It is widely accepted that one of the more significant developments within the sixteenth-century Catholic church relates to the renewal of spirituality, especially in Spain. We have already noted the importance of Ignatius Loyola's *Spiritual Exercises*. Two other major writers should also be noted. Teresa of Avila (1515–82) was a Carmelite nun with a particular concern for evangelism and the pursuit of reconciliation with Protestants. Her best-known work of spirituality is entitled *The Interior Castle*, which emphasizes the importance of a profound and direct personal experience of God. This may be contrasted with the somewhat dry and detached approach, characteristic of medieval scholastic theology. In many ways, there is a parallel to be drawn between the relation of medieval scholasticism and Spanish mysticism and the relation of Protestant Orthodoxy and Pietism (see pp. 296–7). John of the Cross (1542–91) was also a Carmelite with a link with the town of Avila, where he served during the period 1572–77. In a series of writings, such as *The Dark Night of the Soul* and *The Ascent of Mount Carmel*, John stressed the need for believers to achieve a mystical union with God.

The Wars of Religion

The rise of Protestantism and the renewal of Catholicism inevitably caused political and social tensions to rise throughout Europe. The emperor Charles V had felt the force of these tensions, and was eventually obliged to establish an uneasy truce through the 1555 Religious Peace of Augsburg, which put an end to the longstanding conflicts between the Lutheran princes and the Catholic emperor. Yet it was not long before conflict broke out elsewhere.

The first major European war which can be shown to be directly due to religious issues broke out in France. The specific tension in this case was between Catholics and Calvinists (the term "Huguenots" was used locally to refer to the latter). Earlier, we noted that Calvin was French. Calvin appears to have seen part of his mission in life as being to convert his native country to the Reformed faith, using Geneva as a base. In April 1555, Genevan records document several agents sent out from Geneva to evangelize parts of France likely to be fertile ground for Calvinism. Others followed rapidly, in response to requests for help from French Calvinist congregations.

The whole affair was cloak-and-dagger. Secrecy was essential to the entire operation, at both the Genevan and French ends. Safe houses, complete with hiding places, were established, a day's journey apart. An underground network, similar to that employed by the French Resistance during the Second World War, allowed men from Geneva to slip undetected into France. By 1560, Calvinism was firmly established in many leading French cities, and gaining influential converts. There had been an explosion in the growth of Calvinist congregations and influence; the complete reformation of France seemed a real possibility. Perhaps one-third of the nobility had signalled their acceptance of Calvin's religious ideas.

According to a list prepared for Admiral de Coligny in March 1562, there were 2,150 Huguenot churches in France at that point. It is difficult to verify these figures; it would, however, seem reasonable to suggest that there were at least 1,250 such churches, with a total membership in excess of 2,000,000 out of a national population of 20,000,000. Tensions rose. In 1562, war broke out. The issue was only settled through the Edict of Nantes (1598), which guaranteed the rights of French Protestants. However, it was widely ignored by subsequent French monarchs, and was finally revoked by Louis XIV in 1685, resulting in a substantial exodus of Protestants from the country.

Other religious conflicts erupted in the region. The Dutch War of Independence (1560–1618) had strongly religious dimensions. An increasingly Calvinist Dutch population wished to rid themselves of a Catholic Spanish colonial power. In England, the Civil War (1642–9) clearly had religious aspects, reflecting deep-seated disagreements between Royalists and Puritans over the manner of government and the doctrines of the national Church of England.

By far the most important religious conflict, however, was the Thirty Years War, which rumbled on from 1618 to 1648. The context within which this war emerged was the tension after the Peace of Augsburg (1555). The Peace did not take account of Calvinism, which became a major presence in the region from 1560. As a result, Calvinism was given no official protection, in contrast to both Lutheranism and Catholicism. As Calvinism continued to expand, tensions increased. The trigger for the conflict was the outbreak of anti-Protestant riots in Bohemia, partly reflecting the vigorous Catholicism of Ferdinand II. The Bohemian nobles protested to the emperor over these developments. On failing to receive any satisfactory assurances for their safety, they revolted, and demanded to be ruled by a local Calvinist prince instead.

The revolt sparked a wider conflict, drawing in surrounding states and principalities. Its impact on the German economy was disastrous. When the war was finally resolved through the Peace of Westphalia (1648), any remaining enthusiasm for religious warfare had evaporated. People had had enough. A yearning for peace led to a new emphasis on toleration, and growing impatience with religious disputes. The scene was set for the Enlightenment insistence that religion was to be a matter of private belief, rather than state policy. Our attention now turns to the curious cultural climate, which amalgamated rationalism, revival and revolution, which gained the ascendancy in the eighteenth century.

STUDY QUESTIONS

1 What does the term "Reformation" mean?
2 What are the leading features of "Protestantism"? Is the term itself useful?
3 What was Pietism? What weaknesses within Protestantism does its emergence suggest?
4 What were the achievements of the Council of Trent?
5 What was the importance of the Society of Jesus?

Christianity in the West, 1750 to the Present

During the second half of the fifteenth century, Christianity became increasingly a European religion. Islam had launched a *jihad* ("holy war") against Christianity several centuries earlier. By about 1450, as a direct result of its military conquests, Islam was firmly established in the south-western and south-eastern parts of Europe. Although Christian communities continued to exist outside Europe (most notably in Egpyt, Ethiopia, India, and Syria), Christianity was becoming geographically restricted. Its future seemed insecure.

One of the most dramatic developments to take place during the last few centuries has been the recovery of Christianity from this crisis. By the twentieth century, Christianity was firmly established as the dominant religion in the Americas, Australasia, southern Africa, and throughout many of the island nations of the South Pacific. Despite this dramatic expansion outside Europe, however, Christianity suffered a series of internal setbacks in Europe. The present chapter aims to explore developments in Christianity in the west during the modern period; the chapter which follows will consider its expansion into the developing world.

The Rise of Indifference to Religion in Europe

With the ending of the European Wars of Religion, a degree of stability settled upon the continent. Although religious controversy continued intermittently, it became generally accepted that certains parts of Europe were Lutheran, Catholic, Orthodox, or Reformed. The sense of weariness which had been created by the Wars of Religion led to a new interest in religious toleration. The classic argument for toleration of diversity in matters of religion may be found in John Locke's *Letter Concerning Toleration*. Locke argues for religious toleration on the basis of three general considerations, as follows.

First, it is impossible for the state to adjudicate between competing religious truth-claims. This does not mean that there is no truth in matters of religion, or that all religions are equal in terms of their insights into reality. The modern view, associated with writers such as John Hick, that all religions are equally valid is simply the improper extrapolation of a political judgment to a metaphysical plane. Instead, Locke points out that no earthly judge can be brought forward to settle the matter. For this reason, religious diversity is to be tolerated.

Second, Locke argues that, even if it could be established that one religion was superior to all others, the legal enforcement of this religion would not lead to the desired objective of that religion. Locke's argument here is based upon the notion that "true and saving religion consists in the inward persuasion of the mind, without which nothing is acceptable to God. And such is the nature of the understanding, that it cannot be compelled to the belief of any thing by outward force." (It is interesting to note that Locke's argument here is shaped by the Christian conception of salvation; a religion which demanded external conformity to a set of regulations would not fit in to his analysis.)

Third, Locke argues, on pragmatic grounds, that the results of trying to impose religious uniformity are far worse than those which result from the continuing existence of diversity. Religious coercion leads to internal discord, or even civil war. Locke thus argues that religious truth cannot be established with certainty. Even if it could be established with certainty, its imposition would not lead to inward faith. And if it were imposed, the negative results would far outweigh the advantages gained.

Yet Locke does not see this toleration of religious diversity as leading to moral diversity. Theological disputations may be tolerated, precisely because they do not, in Locke's view, have any impact upon the core moral agreement which his commonwealth persupposes. Indeed, at several points, Locke suggests that the religions – Jewish, Christian, and Muslim – are consistent with, and supportive of, public morality. Alexis de Tocqueville provided much support for this view, with his observation that, although there is "an innumerable multitude of sects in the United States," there was nevertheless agreement concerning duty and morality.

Locke's analysis can be seen as leading to the view that religion is a private matter of public indifference. What individuals believe should be regarded as private, with no relevance to the public field. This approach at one and the same time upheld religious toleration, while indicating that religion was a purely private matter. This perception was strengthened by the rise of the Enlightenment, which regarded the religions as different expressions of the same ultimate reality, which could be known through reason.

The notion of religious toleration was of especial importance in relation to the emergence of the United States of America during the eighteenth century. We shall explore this issue now.

Christianity in America: the Great Awakening and the American Revolution

The United States of America is today widely regarded as the most important Christian nation. Christianity plays a major role in the national and international politics of this superpower. It is therefore of importance to appreciate how Christianity came to be of such importance to the life of this nation. As we noted earlier, Christianity was brought to North America largely by refugees seeking to escape from religious persecution then endemic in Europe. As a result, the first settlers in North America were generally deeply committed to their Christian beliefs. Most early settlers were English-speaking Protestants; an important exception to this is found in the case of Maryland, which was a Catholic enclave for a period during the 1630s. (It was not until the nineteenth century that large numbers of Catholic immigrants from Ireland and Italy would swell the numbers of Catholics in the region.)

The Great Awakening

A renewed interest in the Christian faith resulted from the "Great Revival," which broke out in Massachussets during the 1730s, and initially centered on the ministry of Jonathan Edwards (1703–58). To understand the importance of this Revival, it is necessary to explore the early history of Christianity in America. In 1620 the Pilgrim Fathers sailed from Plymouth. Between 1627 and 1640 some 4,000 individuals made the hazardous crossing of the Atlantic Ocean, and settled on the coastline of Massachussets Bay. For them, America was the promised land, and they were the chosen people. Expelled from their Egypt by a cruel Pharaoh, they had settled in a land flowing with milk and honey. They would build a new Jerusalem, a city upon a hill, in this strange land. They might be far from the country of their birth, but they were close to God.

By the end of the first quarter of the eighteenth century, however, it seemed to many that Christianity had lost its way in the New World. In the early seventeenth century New England churches would only admit to full membership individuals who could testify to a personal experience of conversion. As the century progressed, fewer and fewer individuals could testify to such an experience. Yet most individuals wanted some kind of connection with the church – for example, to have their children baptized, or to have a

Christian burial service. From about 1660 onwards, a "half-way" member-ship was recognized: anyone who was prepared to accept the truth of Christianity and the moral discipline of the church could have his or her children baptized.

The result of this was inevitable: by the beginning of the eighteenth century a large proportion of church members were "nominal" or "half-way." They might attend church, and learn from the preaching of the word of God; they might have their children baptized; they might recognize Christianity as true and morally helpful – but they were, in the final resort, unconverted. Christianity and church membership were viewed as just an-other part of American society. Being baptized and attending church were one aspect of being a good citizen.

Growing material prosperity brought with it an indifference to faith, which soon became reduced to morality. The future of Christianity in the New World seemed to be in doubt. A sense of listlessness, of despondency, appears in many Christian writings of the period. The sense of purpose which pervaded the lives and writings of earlier generations of Christians in North America began to fade away. Older Christians began to become intensely nostalgic, longing for the old days of their youth. What would happen next?

The first clues began to be noticed in 1727. Theodore Freylinghausen, a Dutch pastor ministering to a congregation in the Raritan Valley of New Jersey, began to notice signs of a revival. Like a forest fire fanned by the wind, the revival began to spread, through the agency of individuals such as Gilbert Tennent. From New Jersey it found its way to Pennsylvania and Virginia. But it was in 1734 that the smouldering revival exploded into flame, to become what is now generally known as "the Great Awakening." An extraordinary series of events took place in Northampton, Mas-sachussets, in response to the preaching of Jonathan Edwards.

Edwards was born at East Windsor, Connecticut, on 5 October 1703. His father was a local pastor, under whose ministry a series of revivals would take place in the 1720s. In September 1716 Edwards entered Yale College, New Haven (now Yale University), where he later served as tutor from 1724 to 1726. When he was around seventeen years of age, Edwards underwent a conversion experience, and resigned his post at Yale in order to take up a pastoral position in the town of Northampton. Reflecting on the events of those two years, Edwards noted an absence of any general interest in religion: Northampton, like virtually all of colonial North America, "seemed to be at that time very insensible of the things of religion, and engaged in other cares and pursuits."

That situation changed at Northampton, radically and suddenly, in the winter of 1734–5. The final weeks of 1734 witnessed a spate of conversions. The revival continued into the new year, reaching its peak during the months of March and April 1735. There was hardly a household in the town that was not affected. Edwards published accounts of the events at North-ampton in the form of a book, *A Faithful Narrative of the Surprising Work of God*, which drew international attention to the awakening. Between 1737 and 1739 the book went through three editions and twenty printings. As evangelical revival gathered momentum in North America and England, the happenings at Northampton were seen as the harbingers of that dawn.

As the revival continued in New England, it was given a new sense of direction by George Whitefield (1714–70), recently arrived from England. In 1740, he undertook a preaching tour of the colonies, from Georgia in the south to Maine in the north. The tour of New England, undertaken in the fall of that year, caused a sensation. Crowds of up to 8,000 people came to hear him preach every day for the best part of a month. Benjamin Franklin heard Whitefield preach in Philadelphia, and was amazed both by the size of the crowd which had gathered to hear him, and the quality of his voice.

The revival had a lasting impact on American Christianity. It established the role of wandering preachers, unattached to any particular church. It undermined the authority of the clergy of established churches, who felt their positions to be deeply theatened by the upsurge in popular religious interest. The foundations of a mass popular culture were laid, in which Christianity was not the preserve of a clerical elite committed to the preser-vation of the existing social order, but a popular movement with a direct appeal to the masses. The established clergy refused to allow Whitefield to preach in their churches; he responded by preaching in the fields around towns, and attracting vast audiences which could never have been contained within the churches from which he was barred. Perhaps the group to be most deeply threatened by this development was the colonial clergy of the Church of England – the guardians of the existing social order. It is no exaggeration to say that the roots of the American Revolution lay in the growing religious alienation between the new popular American religion and the established religion of England. Within a generation of the Great Awakening, the colonies were in revolt.

The American Revolution

The causes of the American Revolution are complex, involving a number of interrelated issues. Perhaps the dominant theme is that of a desire to break free from the influence of England, which was increasingly seen as paternalist, oppressive, and exploitative. This desire for freedom expressed itself in the political, economic, and religious arenas. The Church of Eng-land was increasingly viewed as the religious dimension of British colonial-ism. During the 1760s, vigorous efforts were made by American Protestants to resist the expansion of the Church of England's authority in the region.

The Church of England was established by law in all the southern colonies, and its influence seemed destined to increase still further. The Quebec Act of 1774, which established Catholicism in French-speaking regions of Canada, was seen as particularly provocative. If Britain could decide what was the established religion in Canada, what would it do in America? Suspicion and hostility grew unchecked.

The imposition of the Stamp Tax (1764) brought cries for "no taxation without representation." The 1773 decision of the British parliament to give the East India Company exclusive rights to sell tea in North America led to the "Boston Tea Party," and widespread unrest in Massachussets. British troops were sent to restore order; this action was interpreted as an act of war by the colonists. A series of battles were fought in 1775, leading to the Declaration of Independence on 4 July 1776. A full-scale war of independence ensued, in which church pulpits often served as rallying points for revolutionary activity. In effect, the Revolution united Christian groups of more or less all persuasions in the service of a greater goal. The Church of England was isolated, and would lose any privileges it once possessed.

The First Amendment to the Constitution declared that "Congress shall make no law respecting an establishment of religion or restricting the free exercise thereof." The Constitution thus prevented the formal establishment of religion, meaning that no Christian church (such as the Church of England) was to be given a favored legal status by the state. Although some modern constitutional theorists argue that this was intended to remove religion from American public life, or that it justifies this practice today, it is clear that the intention of the Constitution was simply to avoid giving legal or social precedence to any specific Christian grouping.

The American Revolution led to the consolidation of Christianity in the United States. However, on the continent of Europe, another revolution was about to break out. In this case, the consequences were more far reaching and negative.

The Watershed in Europe: the French Revolution

The French Revolution is usually singled out as marking the high point of anti-religious feeling in Europe. In 1789, the established social structure in France was shaken to its foundations by a popular uprising, which eventually led to the ending of the monarchy and the establishment of a secular republic. The church and the monarchy were the two pillars of this established order (usually referred to as the *ancien régime*). What began as an attempt to reform both institutions ended up as a revolution, in which power was decisively transferred from the old feudal aristocracy to the rising middle classes.

There was little to indicate that such a radical shake-up was on the way. There was a parallel to be drawn with the American revolution of the previous decade, which had led to the consolidation of the influence of various forms of Protestant Christianity in the region. While the established religion of the area (the religion of the colonial power – the Church of England) suffered a serious setback, other forms of Christianity strengthened their position. The disestablishment of Christianity in the region is widely regarded as contributing to its future success. Yet the situation in France proved to be very different.

It was clear that both the pillars of traditional French society – the monarchy and the church – needed reform. Even late in the summer of the momentous year 1789, the general feeling was that the French monarch had allowed a series of measures which would abolish feudalism and remove some of the grievances felt by ordinary people against the power and privileges of the church. On 2 November, it was agreed that all church lands should be nationalized, with a basic minimum wage for priests being set in place, guaranteed by the state. The Civil Constitution of the Clergy (July 1790) rejected the authority of the pope, and reorganized and slimmed down the dioceses and the cathedral clergy. Although radical, the measures were not anti-Christian. The clergy split into a group which wished to remain loyal to Rome, and another wishing to comply with the new civil authority.

All changed soon afterwards. A more radical revolutionary faction, headed by Robespierre, gained power, and launched its celebrated "Reign of Terror." Louis XVI was publicly guillotined on 21 January 1793. A program of dechristianization was put in place during the period 1793–4. The cult of the Goddess Reason was given official sanction. The old calendar was replaced by a republican calendar which eliminated Sundays and Christian festivals, replacing them with secular alternatives. Priests were placed under pressure to renounce their faith. A program of church closure was initiated. Although the impact of these measures seems to have been felt mostly in urban areas, they caused considerable disruption and hardship to the church throughout France.

The religious policies of the French Revolution were soon extended to neighboring regions. In November 1792, French revolutionary armies embarked on a campaign of conquest in the region. By 1799, six satellite republics had been established, embracing areas such as the Netherlands, Switzerland, parts of northern Italy, and areas of the Rhineland. In February 1798, the papal states were occupied, and the pope was deported to France, where he died six months later. The French Revolution, it seemed to many, had destroyed not only the French church, but also the papacy.

On the eve of the nineteenth century, the future of Christianity in Europe thus seemed remarkably fragile. Many saw it as linked with the politics of a bygone era, an obstacle to progress and liberty. Its faith and its institutions seemed to be in irreversible decline. In fact, this would prove to be a false perception. The revolutionary experimentation with a secular state eventually fizzled out. Under Napoleon, relations with the pope were re-established, although on very different terms to those in operation before the Revolution. The Bourbon monarchy was restored. In 1814, Louis XVIII returned to claim the throne of France, and re-established Catholicism. The situation was never easy, and real tensions between church and state continued unabated throughout most of the nineteenth century. Nevertheless, the church was able to regain at least some of its lost influence, prestige, and clergy. The period 1815–48 witnessed a series of popular revivals (usually referred to as "le Réveil") in French-speaking Europe.

It is clear that the French Revolution drew at least some of its strength from the rationalist worldview which pervaded the writings of leading French writers of the period – such as Denis Diderot (1713–84), Jean-Jacques Rousseau (1712–78) and Voltaire (1694–1778). This leads us to consider some of the worldviews which dominated western thinking in the modern period, and their impact on Christianity.

The Intellectual Context of Western Christianity

Western Christianity has been deeply influenced by its general cultural climate. For example, many writers of the patristic period were deeply influenced by Platonic ideas (whether they agreed with them or reacted against them). In much the same way, many medieval theologians were influenced by Aristotelianism, either by incorporating some of its ideas into their thinking, or by reacting against them. The same pattern can be seen in the way Christianity related to three major movements in modern western thought, which we shall consider in the present section: rationalism, romanticism, and Marxism. In every case, the same general pattern can be seen emerging. The rise of these movements posed a challenge to Christianity in several respects, while at the same time providing a stimulus for Christianity to explore parts of its own heritage more deeply. For example, the rise of Marxism can be shown to have encouraged Christians to rediscover the social teachings of the Old Testament, and apply them to the social situations of their own day.

Rationalism

The movement which is now generally known as "the Enlightenment" ushered in a period of considerable uncertainty for Christianity in western Europe and north America. The trauma of the Reformation and the resulting Wars of Religion had barely subsided on the continent of Europe, before a new and more radical challenge to Christianity arose. If the sixteenth-century Reformation challenged the church to rethink its external forms and the manner in which it expressed its beliefs, the Enlightenment saw the intellectual credentials of Christianity itself (rather than any one of its specific forms) facing a major threat on a number of fronts. The origins of this challenge may be traced back to the seventeenth century, with the rise of Cartesianism on the continent of Europe, and the growing influence of Deism in England. The growing emphasis upon the need to uncover the rational roots of religion had considerable negative implications for Christianity, as subsequent events were to prove.

The Enlightenment criticism of traditional Christianity was based upon the principle of the omnicompetence of human reason. A number of stages in the development of this belief may be discerned. First, it was argued that the beliefs of Christianity were rational, and thus capable of standing up to critical examination. This type of approach may be found in John Locke's *Reasonableness of Christianity* (1695), and within the early Wolffian school in Germany. Christianity was a reasonable supplement to natural religion. The notion of divine Revelation was thus maintained.

Second, it was argued that the basic ideas of Christianity, being rational, could be derived from reason itself. There was no need to invoke the idea of divine revelation. As this idea was developed by John Toland in his *Christianity not Mysterious* (1696) and Matthew Tindal's *Christianity as Old as Creation* (1730), Christianity was essentially the republication of the religion of nature. It did not transcend natural religion, but was merely an example of it. All so-called "revealed religion" is actually nothing other than the reconfirmation of what can be known through rational reflection on nature. "Revelation" was simply a rational reaffirmation of moral truths already available to enlightened reason.

Third, the ability of reason to judge revelation was affirmed. As critical reason was omnicompetent, it was argued that it was supremely qualified to judge Christian beliefs and practices, with a view to eliminating any irrational or superstitious elements. This view placed reason firmly above revelation, and may be seen as symbolized in the enthronement of the Goddess of Reason in Notre-Dame de Paris in 1793, in the aftermath of the French Revolution.

The Enlightenment was primarily a European and American phenomenon, and thus took place in cultures in which the most numerically significant form of religion was Christianity. This historical observation is of importance: the Enlightenment critique of religion in general was often particularized as a criticism of Christianity in general. It was Christian doctrines which were subjected to a critical assessment of a vigour without any precedent. It was Christian sacred writings – rather than those of Islam or Hinduism – which were subjected to an unprecedented critical scrutiny, both literary and historical, with the Bible being treated "as if it were any other book" (Benjamin Jowett). It was the life of Jesus of Nazareth which was subjected to critical reconstruction, rather than that of Muhammed or Buddha.

The Enlightenment attitude to religion was subject to a considerable degree of regional variation, reflecting a number of local factors peculiar to different situations. One of the most important of such factors is Pietism, perhaps best known in its English and American form of Methodism. As noted earlier, this movement placed considerable emphasis upon the experiential aspects of religion (for example, see John Wesley's notion of "experimental religion"). This concern for religious experience served to make Christianity relevant and accessible to the experiential situation of the masses, contrasting sharply with the intellectualism of, for example, Lutheran Orthodoxy, which was perceived to be an irrelevance. Pietism forged a strong link between Christian faith and experience, thus making Christianity a matter of the heart, as well as of the mind.

As noted earlier, Pietism was well established in Germany by the end of the seventeenth century, whereas the movement only developed in England during the eighteenth century, and in France not at all. The Enlightenment thus preceded the rise of Pietism in England, with the result that the great evangelical revivals of the eighteenth century significantly blunted the influence of rationalism upon religion. In Germany, however, the Enlightenment followed after the rise of Pietism, and thus developed in a situation which had been significantly shaped by religious faith, even if it would pose a serious challenge to its received forms and ideas. (Interestingly, English Deism began to become influential in Germany at roughly the same time as German Pietism began to exert influence in England.) The most significant intellectual forces in the German Enlightenment were thus directed towards the reshaping (rather than the rejection or demolition) of the Christian faith.

In France, however, Christianity was widely perceived as both oppressive and irrelevant, with the result that the writers of the French Enlightenment were able to advocate the total rejection of Christianity as an archaic and discredited belief system. In his *Treaty on Tolerance*, Denis Diderot argued that English Deism had compromised itself, permitting religion to survive where it ought to have been eradicated totally.

Yet rationalism itself was soon realized to have its limits, as the rise of Romanticism was to prove. We may turn to consider this development in what follows.

Romanticism

In the closing decade of the eighteenth century, increasing misgivings came to be expressed concerning the arid quality of rationalism. Reason, once seen as a liberator, came increasingly to be regarded as spiritually enslaving. These anxieties were not expressed so much within university faculties of philosophy, as within literary and artistic circles, particurly in the Prussian capital, Berlin, where the Schlegel brothers became particularly influential.

"Romanticism" is notoriously difficult to define. The movement is perhaps best seen as a reaction against certain of the central themes of the Enlightenment, most notably the claim that reality can be known to the human reason. This reduction of reality to a series of rationalized simplicities seemed, to the Romantics, to be a culpable and crude misrepresentation. Where the Enlightenment appealed to the human reason, Romanticism made an appeal to the human imagination, which was capable of recognizing the profound sense of mystery that arises from realizing that the human mind cannot comprehend even the finite world, let alone the infinity beyond this. This ethos is expressed well by the English poet William Wordsworth, who spoke of the human imagination in terms of transcending the limitations of human reason, and reaching beyond its bounds to sample the infinite through the finite. Imagination, according to Wordsworth,

> Is but another name for absolute power
> And clearest insight, amplitude of mind,
> And Reason in her most exalted mood.

Romanticism thus found itself equally unhappy with both traditional Christian doctrines and the rationalist moral platitudes of the Enlightenment: both failed to do justice to the complexity of the world, in an attempt to reduce the "mystery of the universe" – to use a typically Romantic phrase found in the writings of August William Schlegel – to neat formulae.

A marked limitation of the competence of reason may be discerned in such sentiments. Reason threatens to limit the human mind to what may be deduced; the imagination is able to liberate the human spirit from this self-imposed bondage, and allow it to discover new depths of reality – a vague and tantalizing "something" which can be discerned in the world of everyday realities. The infinite is somehow present in the finite, and may be known through feeling and the imagination. As John Keats put it, "I am certain of nothing except that holiness of the heart's affections, and the truth of the imagination."

The reaction against the aridity of reason was thus complemented by an emphasis upon the epistemological significance of human feelings and emotions. Under the influence of Novalis (Friedrich von Hardenberg), German Romanticism argued that 'feeling" has to do with the individual subjective thinker, who becomes aware of his or her subjectivity and inward individuality. Rationalism may have made its appeal to individual reason; Romanticism retained the emphasis upon the individual, but supplanted a concern with reason by a new interest in the imagination and personal feeling. The Enlightenment looked inward to human reason; Romanticism looked inward to human feelings, seeing in these "the way to all mysteries" (Novalis). This "feeling" was also understood to be orientated towards the infinite and eternal, providing the key to these higher realms. It is for this reason, Novalis declares, that the Enlightenment proscribed the imagination and feeling as "heretical," in that they offered access to the "magical idealism" of the infinite; by its wooden appeal to reason alone, the Enlightenment attempted to suppress knowledge of these higher worlds through an appeal to the aridities of philosophy. Human subjectivity and inwardness were now seen as a mirror of the infinite. A new emphasis came to be placed upon music as a "revelation of a higher order than any morality or philosophy" (Bettina von Arnim).

The development of Romanticism had considerable implications for Christianity in Europe. Those aspects of Christianity (especially Roman Catholicism) which rationalism found distasteful came to captivate the imaginations of the Romantics. Rationalism was seen to be experientially and emotionally deficient, incapable of meeting real human needs, traditionally addressed and satisfied by Christian faith. As F. R. de Châteaubriant remarked of the situation in France in the first decade of the nineteenth century, "there was a need for faith, a desire for religious consolation, which came from the very lack of that consolation for so long." Similar sentiments can be instanced from the German context in the closing years of the eighteenth century.

That rationalism had failed to undermine religion is evident from developments in England, Germany, and North America. The new strength evident in German Pietism and English evangelicalism in the eighteenth century is evidence of the failure of rationalism to provide a cogent alternative to the prevailing human sense of personal need and meaning. Philosophy came to be seen as sterile, academic in the worst sense of the word, in that it was detached from the outer realities of life and the inner life of the human consciousness.

Marxism

Marxism, probably one of the most significant worldviews to emerge during the modern period, has had a major impact upon Christianity during the twentieth century. "Marxism" is usually understood to refer to the ideas associated with the German writer Karl Marx (1818–83). Until about 1989, the term also referred to a state ideology, characteristic of a number of states in eastern Europe and elsewhere, which regarded Christianity and other religions as reactionary, and adopted repressive measures to eliminate them.

The notion of materialism is fundamental to Marxism. This is not some metaphysical or philosophical doctrine which affirms that the world consists only of matter. Rather, it is an assertion that a correct understanding of human beings must begin with material production. The way in which human beings respond to their material needs determines everything else. Ideas, including religious ideas, are responses to material reality. They are the superstructure which is erected upon a socioeconomic substructure. In other words, ideas and belief-systems are a response to a quite definite set of social and economic conditions. If these are radically altered (for example, by a revolution), the belief systems which they generated and sustained will pass away with them.

This first idea flows naturally into the second – alienation of humanity. A number of factors bring about alienation within the material process, of which the two most significant are the division of labor and the existence of private property. The former causes the alienation of the worker from his product, whereas the second brings about a situation in which the interests of the individual no longer coincide with that of society as a whole. As productive forces are owned by a small minority of the population, it follows that societies are divided along class lines, with political and economic power being concentrated in the hands of the ruling class.

If this analysis is correct, Marx believed that the third conclusion naturally followed. Capitalism – the economic order just described – was inherently unstable, due to the tensions arising from productive forces. As a result of these internal contradictions, it will break down. Some versions of Marxism present this breakdown as happening without any need for assistance. Others present it as the result of a social revolution, led by the working class. The closing words of the *Communist Manifesto* (1848) seem to suggest the latter: "Workers have nothing to lose but their chains. They have a world to gain. Workers of the world, unite!"

So how do these ideas relate to Christian theology? In his 1844 political and economic manuscripts, Marx develops the idea that religion in general (he does not distinguish the individual religions) is a direct response to social and economic conditions. Religion has no real independent existence. It is a reflection of the material world, a spiritual superstructure built upon an economic and social substructure. "The religious world is but the reflex of the real world." There is an obvious and important allusion here to Feuerbach's critique of religion, which we shall consider in a later section. Thus Marx argues that "religion is just the imaginary sun which seems to man to revolve around him, until he realizes that he himself is the centre of his own revolution." In other words, God is simply a projection of human concerns. Human beings "look for a superhuman being in the fantasy reality of heaven, and find nothing their but their own reflection."

But why should religion exist at all? If Marx is right, why should people continue to believe in such a crude illusion? Marx's answer centers on the notion of alienation. "Humans make religion; religion does not make humans. Religion is the self-consciousness and self-esteem of people who either have not found themselves or who have already lost themselves again." Religion is the product of social and economic alienation. It arises from that alienation, and at the same time encourages that alienation by a form of spiritual intoxication which renders the masses incapable of recognizing their situation, and doing something about it. Religion is a comfort, which enables people to tolerate their economic alienation. If there were no such alienation, there would be no need for religion. The division of labor and the existence of private property introduce alienation and estrangement into the economic and social orders.

Materialism affirms that events in the material world bring about corresponding changes in the intellectual world. Religion is thus the result of a certain set of social and economic conditions. Change those conditions, so that economic alienation is eliminated, and religion will cease to exist. It will no longer serve any useful function. Unjust social conditions produce religion, and are in turn supported by religion. "The struggle against religion is therefore indirectly a struggle against *the world* of which religion is the spiritual fragrance."

Marx thus argues that religion will continue to exist, as long as it meets a need in the life of alienated people. "The religious reflex of the real world can . . . only then vanish when the practical relations of everyday life offer to man none but perfectly intelligible and reasonable relations with regard to his fellow men and to nature." In other words, a shake-up in the real world is needed to get rid of religion. Marx thus argues that when a non-alienating economic and social environment is brought about through communism, the needs which gave rise to religion will vanish. And with the elimination of those material needs, spiritual hunger will also vanish.

In practice, Marxism had virtually no influence until the period of the First World War. This can be put down partly to some internal problems, and partly due to the lack of any real opportunities for political expansion. The internal problems are especially interesting. The suggestion that the working class could liberate itself from its oppression, and bring about a political revolution, soon proved to be illusory. It rapidly became clear that Marxists, far from being drawn from the ranks of the politically conscious working class, were actually depressingly middle class (like Marx himself). Aware of this problem, Lenin developed the idea of a "vanguard party." The workers were so politically naïve that they needed to be led by professional revolutionaries, who alone could provide the overall vision and practical guidance that would be needed in bringing about and sustaining a world revolution.

The Russian Revolution gave Marxism the break it needed. However, although Marxism established itself in a modified form (Marxism–Leninism) within the Soviet Union, it proved unsuccessful elsewhere. Its successes in eastern Europe after the Second World War can be put down mainly to military strength and political destabilization. Its successes in Africa were largely due to the seductive appeal of Lenin's carefully devised concept of "imperialism," which allowed alienated elements in certain African and Asian countries to put their backwardness down to their ruthless and systematic exploitation by the external agency of western capitalism, rather than any inherent deficiencies.

The economic failure and political stagnation which resulted when such countries experimented with Marxism in the 1970s and 1980s soon led to disillusionment with this new philosophy. In Europe, Marxism found itself locked into a spiral of decline. Its chief advocates increasingly became abstract theoreticians, detached from working-class roots, with virtually no political experience. The idea of a socialist revolution gradually lost its appeal and its credibility. In the United States and Canada, Marxism had little, if any social appeal in the first place, although its influence upon the academic world was more noticeable. The Soviet invasion of Czechoslovakia in 1968 resulted in a noticeable cooling in enthusiasm for Marxism within western intellectual circles. However, Marx's ideas have found their way, suitably modified, into modern Christian theology. Latin American liberation theology (see pp. 338–40) can be shown to have drawn appreciatively on Marxist insights, even if the movement cannot really be described as "Marxist" as a result.

The Development of Catholicism

After the trauma of the French Revolution, Catholicism began to regain something of the confidence it had known in earlier periods. The rise of Romanticism had a powerful effect on the reawakening of interest in Catholicism, particularly in Germany and France. Châteaubriand's *Génie du Christianisme* ("Genius of Christianity"), which appeared in 1802, did much to develop this new interest in the Christian faith, which can be seen reflected in many aspects of nineteenth-century culture. Other writers who drew on Romanticism in their defense of Catholicism included Allessandro Manzoni (1785–1873) in Italy and Friedrich von Stohlberg (1750–1819) in Germany. Rationalism was widely regarded as having led to the catastrophes of the past; there was a new sympathy for the view that Christianity was a major source of artistic inspiration and cultural excellence.

There can be no doubt that Catholicism needed to renew itself after the trauma of the French Revolution and its aftermath. It is helpful to reflect on the extent of Catholicism after the end of the Napoleonic era in 1814. Although Catholic missions had led to the establishment of Catholic communities in regions such as South America, Japan and India, Catholicism was largely a European religion at this stage, bounded by the new nation of Belgium in the north-west, Spain in the south-west, Austria in the north-east, and Italy in the south-east. Most of the 100 million European Catholics were to be found in the Habsburg Empire, Italy and France. It fell to Pius VII to renew his church after his return to Rome in May 1814. The task seemed enormous; nevertheless, he proved equal to the task. The groundwork for this task was laid down by the papal Secretary of State, Consalvi, who negotiated concordats with a series of states during the Congress of Vienna (1815). The Congregation for Extraordinary Ecclesiastical Affairs was established in 1814, with the objective of rebuilding Catholicism throughout Europe. The success of these measures can be seen in a traditionally strongly Protestant nation such as England, in which the Catholic hierarchy was re-established in 1850.

Catholicism became a major influence in the United States during this period. Although revolutionary America was dominated by Protestantism, waves of immigrants from Ireland and Italy began to alter the religious balance of power decisively as the nineteenth century progressed. Archbishop John Carroll (1735–1815) did much to encourage the social acceptance of Catholicism at a time during which its numbers were rapidly increasing. During the 1840s, it is estimated that 2.5 million Irish Catholics emigrated to the east coast of the United States, with dramatic demographic consequences for eastern cities such as Boston and New York. The emergence of American Catholicism as a major force in the life of the nation was partly due to the ethnic loyalty of its adherents, who saw Catholicism as an integral aspect of their identity. Their European origins thus served to mold the religious views of American immigrants at this critical period in the history of the nation. The founding of major Catholic educational institutions, such as the University of Notre-Dame in 1842, laid the foundations for the emergence of Catholicism as a significant intellectual force in the life of the nation.

The re-emergence of the pope as a major figure within Catholicism during the nineteenth century can be attributed, at least in part, to the aftermath of the Napoleonic wars. In the decades prior to the French Revolution, the pope seems to have been largely ignored by the Catholic faithful, who regarded him as isolated and distant. However, Napoleon's fairly vicious treatment of the pope caused him to regain his prestige in the eyes of both the faithful and European governments. Even in France, the heartland of movements which advocated nationally-governed churches, there was a new respect for the pope. The scene was set for the re-emergence of the papacy as a leading institution within Catholicism and beyond. The movement which advocated increased papal authority was known as "ultramontanism," and merits further attention in its own right.

Ultramontanism

The term "ultramontanism" derives from two Latin words bearing the sense of "beyond the mountains." The mountains in question are the Alps, and the issue at stake is the extent to which the pope had authority "beyond the Alps" – that is to say, beyond Italy into Europe itself. There was considerable sympathy for this view in the 1820s, partly due to the influence of Joseph de Maistre (1754–1821), whose *Du pape* ("On the Pope") appeared in 1819. The rise of revolutionary movements in France, Italy, and Germany during the late 1840s led to increased concern over the political stability of Catholic countries, and particularly the position of the pope himself. Faced with the prospect of steadily decreasing political power, culminating in his unhappy eviction from many of his former possessions in 1870, Pius IX (pope from 1846–78) concentrated on establishing his spiritual authority within the church.

The most significant aspect of this program is widely agreed to be the opening of the First Vatican Council in 1869. This council can be seen as marking a decisive confrontation between liberal Catholics on the one hand, and ultramontanists on the other. The issue which brought this controversy to sharp focus was the location of supreme authority within the church. Was supreme authority invested in the great Councils of the church, or in the papacy itself? In the end, the outcome was a decisive victory for the ultramontanists. This was given formal expression in the famous dogma of papal infallibility, promulgated on 13 July 1870. This affirmed that the pope, when speaking *ex cathedra* (that is, in his formal capacity as teacher and defender of the faith), is infallible. This dogma caused some concern, particularly in Germany. Otto von Bismarck (1815–98) was appointed Chancellor of Prussia in 1864. He embarked on a policy of German unification, which was pursued with increasing vigor after the end of the Franco-Prussian war in 1871. Bismarck regarded the dogma as an insult to German Protestants, and a potential threat to the emerging authority of the German state. As a result, Bismark embarked on a policy of discrimination against German Catholics during the 1870s. This *Kulturkampf* ("Culture-War") eventually fizzled out in 1886. Yet anti-religious feeling was growing else-where in Europe, most notably in France, where the 1901 Association Law and the 1905 Separation Law virtually eliminated religion from public life, including education.

In Italy, the position of the pope became difficult following the rise to power of Victor Emmanuel (1820–78), who in effect stripped the pope of all his territories except for the Vatican, the Lateran and Castel Gandolfo. While the Law of Papal Guarantees ensured his independence and safety, it nevertheless placed restrictions on his rights. This was eventually replaced by the Lateran Treaty of 1929, which was more favorable to the pope.

The dogma of papal infallibility should be seen against the broader background of the emergence of more liberal or modern ways of thinking within western society in general, and the church in particular. A threat seemed to be posed to traditional Catholic teachings through the rise of modernism, which was shall consider in what follows.

The Rise of Catholic Modernism

The term "modernist" was first used to refer to a school of Catholic theologians operating toward the end of the nineteenth century, who adopted a critical and skeptical attitude toward traditional Christian doctrines. The movement adopted a positive attitude toward radical biblical criticism, and stressed the ethical, rather than the more theological, dimensions of faith. In many ways, modernism may be seen as an attempt by writers within the Roman Catholic church to come to terms with the outlook of the Enlightenment which had, until that point, largely been ignored by that church.

"Modernism" is, however, a loose term, which should not be understood to imply the existence of a distinctive school of thought, committed to certain common methods or indebted to common teachers. It is certainly true that most modernist writers were concerned to integrate Christian thought with the spirit of the Enlightenment, especially the new understandings of history and the natural sciences that were then gaining the ascendency. Equally, some modernist writers drew inspiration from writers such as Maurice Blondel (1861–1949), who argued that the supernatural was intrinsic to human existence, or Henri Bergson (1859–1941), who stressed the importance of intuition over intellect. Yet there is not sufficient commonality between the French, English and American modernists, nor between Roman Catholic and Protestant modernism, to allow the term to be understood as designating a rigorous and well-defined school.

Among Roman Catholic modernist wristers, Alfred Loisy (1857–1940) and George Tyrrell (1861–1909) stand out as being of especial importance. During the 1890s, Loisy established himself as a critic of traditional views of the biblical accounts of creation, and argued that a real development of doctrine could be discerned within scripture. His most significant publication. *L'évangile et l'église* ("The Gospel and the Church"), appeared in 1902. This important work was a direct response to the views of Adolf von Harnack, published two years earlier as *What is Christianity?*, on the origins and nature of Christianity. Loisy rejected Harnack's suggestion that there was a radical discontinuity between Jesus and the church; however, he made significant concessions to Harnack's liberal Protestant account of Christian origins, including an acceptance of the role and validity of biblical criticism in interpreting the gospels. As a result, the work was placed upon the list of prohibited books by the Roman Catholic authorities in 1903.

The British Jesuit writer George Tyrrell followed Loisy in his radical criticism of traditional Catholic dogma. In common with Loisy, he criticized Harnack's account of Christian origins in *Christianity at the Crossroads* (1909), dismissing Harnack's historical reconstruction of Jesus as "the reflection of a Liberal Protestant face, seen at the bottom of a deep well." The work also included a defense of Loisy's work, arguing that the official Roman Catholic "hostility to the book and its author have created a general impression that it is a defense of Liberal Protestant against Roman Catholic positions, and that 'Modernism' is simply a protestantizing and rationalizing movement."

In part, this perception may be due to the growing influence of modernist attitudes within the mainstream Protestant denominations. In England, the Churchmen's Union was founded in 1898 for the advancement of liberal religious thought; in 1928, it altered its name to the Modern Churchmen's Union. Among those especially associated with this group was Hastings Rashdall (1858–1924), whose *Idea of Atonement in Christian Theology* (1919) illustrates the general tenor of English modernism. Drawing somewhat uncritically upon the earlier writings of liberal Protestant thinkers such as Ritschl, Rashdall argued that the theory of the atonement associated with the medieval writer Peter Abelard was more acceptable to modern thought forms than traditional theories which made an appeal to the notion of a substitutionary sacrifice. This strongly moral or exemplarist theory of the atonement, which interpreted Christ's death virtually exclusively as a demonstration of the love of God, made a considerable impact upon English, and especially Anglican, thought in the 1920s and 1930s. Nevertheless, the events of the Great War (1914–18), and the subsequent rise of fascism in Europe in the 1930s, undermined the credibility of the movement. It was not until the 1960s that a renewed modernism or radicalism became a significant feature of English Christianity.

The rise of modernism in the United States follows a similar pattern. The growth of liberal Protestantism in the late nineteenth and early twentieth centuries was widely perceived as a direct challenge to more conservative evangelical standpoints. Newman Smyth's *Passing Protestantism and Coming Catholicism* (1908) argued that Catholic modernism could serve as a mentor to American Protestantism in several ways, not least in its critique of dogma and its historical understanding of the development of doctrine. The situation became increasingly polarized through the rise of fundamentalism in response to modernist attitudes.

The Great War ushered in a period of self-questioning within American modernism, which was intensified through the radical social realism of writers such as H. R. Niebuhr. By the mid-1930s, modernism appeared to have lost its way. However, the movement gained new confidence in the post-war period, and arguably reached its zenith during the period of the Vietnam War.

The Second Vatican Council

The 1960s are now widely regarded as marking the high watermark of a period of secular optimism in western culture. The question of the relevance of Christianity within such a context become of considerable importance. Sensitive to a whole range of issues, John XXIII (pope from 1958–63) summoned the Second Vatican Council to deal with the issue of "updating" the agenda of the church. The Council began its meetings in October 1962. In four sessions, spread over the fall of each year during the period 1962–5, more than 2,450 bishops from all over the world met at Rome to discuss the future direction of the Catholic church. The death of John XXIII on 3 June 1963 did not interrupt the work of the Council, which was continued by his successor Paul VI (pope from 1963–78).

The agenda set before the council was enormous. In general terms, the council considered the place of the Christian faith in the modern world, particularly the relation between Christians and non-Christians, and between Catholics and other Christians. The importance of evangelism was affirmed, within a context of respecting the identities and integrities of non-Christians. Particular attention was paid to the nature of the church itself, and the relation of the bishops and pope.

After Vatican II, the Catholic church increasingly came to see itself more as a community of believers than as a divinely ordained and hierarchically-ordered society. The laity was given an increasingly important place in the life of the church. The importance of ecumenism – that is, the program of relating to and increasing understanding between different styles of Christianity – was recognized. The council also followed the example of Leo XIII in stressing the social aspects of the Christian faith, including its implications for human rights, race relations, and social justice. Within the church, the idea of "collegiality" became of increasing importance. This expresses the notion that the church is itself a community of member churches, with authority dispersed to some extent among its bishops, rather than concentrated in the pope.

Vatican II is a landmark in the history of Catholicism. It remains to be seen how it will influence the development of Christianity into the next millennium. While many Catholics welcomed the new atmosphere which it introduced, others felt that it had betrayed many central concerns of tradi-

The opening session of the Second Vatican Council in St Peter's Basilica on 2 October 1962. The Pope can be seen as the central figure on the elevated section at the far end of the basilica. Popperfoto.

tional Catholic teaching and practice. Traces of this tension remain in the modern Catholic church. It is, however, a creative tension, and can be expected to lead to a healthy process of self-examination in the future.

Other tensions have emerged as significant within post-Vatican II Catholicism. Increasingly, Christianity is becoming a religion of the developing world, with its numerical center of gravity moving away from the western world toward the emerging nations of Africa and Asia. Much the same pattern is reflected in other Christian churches. This means that the agenda of the developing world is increasingly coming to dominate Catholicism, as the traditional agenda of the west becomes of lesser importance. For many observers, the ultimate confirmation of this trend would be the election of a non-western Catholic as pope. This development, which is now widely seen as inevitable, would mark the final stage in the rebirth of Catholicism since the disaster of the 1790s. It would have moved decisively from being a western European faith to a global faith.

The Development of Protestantism

Protestantism has undergone considerable development during the last two centuries. In what follows, we shall consider some of the most important movements to have arisen within it, and assess their significance.

Liberal Protestantism

Liberal Protestantism is unquestionably one of the most important movements to have arisen within modern western Protestant Christianity. Its orgins are complex. However, it is helpful to think of it as having arisen in response to the theological program set out in the early nineteenth century by the German writer F. D. E. Schleiermacher, especially in relation to his emphasis upon human "feeling," and the need to relate Christian faith to the human situation. Classic liberal Protestantism had its origins in the Germany of the mid-nineteenth century, amidst a growing realization that Christian faith and theology alike require reconstruction in the light of modern knowledge. In England, the increasingly positive reception given to Charles Darwin's theory of natural selection (popularly known as the "Darwinian theory of evolution") created a climate in which some traditional Christian theology (such as the doctrine of the seven days of creation) seemed to be increasingly untenable. From its outset, liberalism was committed to bridging the gap between Christian faith and modern knowledge.

Liberalism's program required a significant degree of flexibility in relation to traditional Christian teachings. Its leading writers argued that the reconstruction of Christian belief in the light of modern thought-forms was essential if Christianity was to remain a serious option in the modern world. For this reason, they demanded a degree of freedom in relation to the doctrinal inheritance of Christianity on the one hand, and traditional methods of biblical interpretation on the other. Where traditional ways of interpreting Scripture, or traditional beliefs, seemed to be compromised by developments in human knowledge, it was imperative that they should be discarded or reinterpreted to bring them into line with what was now known about the world.

The implications of this shift in direction were considerable. A number of Christian beliefs came to be regarded as seriously out of line with modern cultural norms; these suffered one of two fates:

1 They were abandoned, because they were argued to be grounded on outdated or mistaken presuppositions. The doctrine of original sin is a case in point; this was put down to a misreading of the New Testament in the light of the writings of St Augustine, whose judgment on these matters had become clouded by his overinvolvement with a fatalist sect (the Manichees).

2 They were reinterpreted, in ways which were sympathetic to the spirit of the age. A number of central doctrines relating to the person of Jesus Christ may be included in this category, including his divinity (which was reinterpreted as an affirmation of Jesus exemplifying qualities which humanity as a whole could hope to emulate).

Alongside this process of doctrinal reinterpretation may be seen a new concern to ground Christian faith in the world of humaity – above all, in human experience and modern culture. Sensing potential difficulties in grounding Christian faith in an exclusive appeal to Scripture or the person of Jesus Christ, liberalism sought to anchor that faith in common human experience, and interpret in ways that made sense within the modern worldview.

Liberalism was inspired by the vision of a humanity which was ascending upwards into new realms of progress and prosperity. The doctrine of evolution gave new vitality to this belief, which was nurtured by strong evidence of cultural stability in western Europe in the late nineteenth century. Religion came increasingly to be seen as relating to the spiritual needs of modern humanity, and giving ethical guidance to society. The strongly ethical dimension of liberal Protestantism is especially evident in the writings of the leading German liberal thinker, Albrecht Benjamin Ritschl (1822–89). For Ritschl, the idea of the "kingdom of God" was of central importance. Ritschl tended to think of this as a static realm of ethical values, which would undergird the development of German society at this point in its history. History, it was argued, was in the process of being divinely guided toward perfection. Civilization is seen as part of this process of evolution. In the course of human history, a number of individuals appear who are recognized as being the bearers of special divine insights. One such individual was Jesus. By following his example and sharing in his inner life, other human beings are able to develop. The movement showed enormous and unbounded optimism in human ability and potential. Religion and culture were, it was argued, virtually identical. Later critics of the movement dubbed it "culture Protestantism" on account of their belief that it was too heavily dependent upon accepted cultural norms.

Many critics – such as Karl Barth in Europe and Reinhold Niebuhr in North America – regarded liberal Protestantism as based upon a hopelessly optimistic view of human nature. They believed that this optimism had been destroyed by the events of the First World War, and that liberalism would henceforth lack cultural credibility. This has proved to be a considerable misjudgment. At its best, liberalism may be regarded as a movement committed to the restatement of Christian faith in forms which are acceptable within contemporary culture. Liberalism has continued to see itself as a mediator between two unacceptable alternatives: the mere restatement of traditional Christian faith (usually described as "traditionalism" or "fundamentalism" by its liberal critics), and the rejection of Christianity in its totality. Liberal writers have been passionately committed to the search for a middle road between these two stark alternatives.

Perhaps the most developed and influential presentation of liberal Protestantism is to be found in the writings of Paul Tillich (1886–1965), who rose to fame in the United States in the late 1950s and early 1960s, toward the end of his career, and who is widely regarded as the most influential American theologian since Jonathan Edwards. Tillich's program can be summarized in the term "correlation." By the "method of correlation," Tillich understands the task of modern theology to be to establish a conversation between modern human culture and Christian faith. Tillich reacted with alarm to the theological program set out by Karl Barth (pp. 328–9), seeing this as a misguided attempt to drive a wedge between theology and culture. For Tillich, existential questions – or "ultimate questions," as he often terms them – are thrown up and revealed by human culture. Modern philosophy, writing, and the creative arts point to questions which concern humans. Christianity then provides anwers to these questions, and by doing so, correlates the gospel to modern culture. The gospel must speak to culture, and it can do so only if the actual questions raised by that culture are heard.

Liberalism probably reached its zenith in North America during the late 1970s and early 1980s. Although continuing to maintain a distinguished presence in seminaries and schools of religion, it is now widely regarded as a waning force both in modern theology and in church life in general.

Neo-Orthodoxy

The First World War witnessed a disillusionment with, although not a final rejection of, the liberal theology which had come to be associated with Schleiermacher and his followers. A number of writers argued that Schleiermacher had, in effect, reduced Christianity to little more than religious experience, thus making it a human-, rather than God-centered, affair. The First World War, it was argued, destroyed the credibility of such an approach. Liberal theology seemed to be about human values – and how could these be taken seriously, if they led to global conflicts on such a massive scale? By stressing the "otherness" of God, writers such as the Swiss theologian Karl Barth (1886–1968) believed that they would escape from the doomed human-centered theology of liberalism. There ideas were given systematic exposition in Karl Barth's *Church Dogmatics* (1936–69), probably the most significant theological achievement of the twentieth century.

Perhaps the most distinctive feature of Barth's approach is his "theology of the Word of God." According to Barth, theology is a discipline which seeks to keep the proclamation of the Christian church faithful to its foundation in Jesus Christ, as he has been revealed to us in Scripture. Theology is not a response to the human situation or to human questions; it is a response to the word of God, which demands a response on account of its intrinsic nature.

Neo-Orthodoxy became a significant presence on the North American scene during the 1930s, especially through the writings of Reinhold Niebuhr and others, which criticized the optimistic assumptions of much liberal Protestant social thinking of the time. Yet the reaction against liberalism in North America in the 1920s soon came to be associated with another movement, to which we may now turn.

The Rise of Fundamentalism

In 1910, the first of a series of twelve books appeared from a small American publishing house. The series was unremarkably entitled *The Fundamentals*. By a series of historical accidents, the term "fundamentalist" took its name from this series of works. Fundamentalism arose as a religious reaction within American Protestantism to the rise of a secular culture during the period 1920–40. Initially, the term "fundamentalism" was devoid of the overtones of obscurantism, anti-intellectualism, and political extremism now associated with it. Yet these were not long in developing.

Fundamentalists initially saw themselves simply as returning to biblical orthodoxy. Yet the context in which the fundamentalist protest took place inevitably had an influence in shaping the movement's response to the challenges facing it. In at least one sense, fundamentalism is a deliberate and considered reaction to developments in the twentieth century, and is thus, in one sense of the word, thoroughly "modern." It was from its outset, and has remained, a counter-cultural movement, using central doctrinal affirmations as a means of defining cultural boundaries. Whereas most nineteenth-century forms of American evangelicalism were culturally centralist, committed to engaging with culture in order to transform it through the gospel, the fundamentalist reaction against "modernity" carried with it, as part of its religious package, a separatist attitude to culture. Certain central doctrines (most notably, the absolute literal authority of Scripture and the premillennial return of Christ) were treated as barriers, intended as much to alienate secular culture as to give fundamentalists a sense of identity and purpose. A siege mentality rapidly became characteristic of the movement; fundamentalist counter-communities viewed themselves as walled cities, or (to evoke the pioneer spirit) circles of wagons, defending their distinctiveness against an unbelieving culture. "Oppositionalism" became a leading characteristic of a fundamentalist *mentalité*.

The negative consequences of this polarization can be seen especially from the painful history of the Presbyterian church in the United States. In 1922, an ill-tempered controversy broke out, which is widely regarded as having marked the beginning of the spiral of numerical decline within that church, laid the foundations of schism within it, and ultimately caused a radical loss of theological vision which eroded its distinctiveness within the American situation. The row centered on whether traditional doctrines should be modified in the light of modern scientific and cultural knowledge. Presbyterians were forced to decide whether they were, to use the categories of the protagonists, "unbelieving liberals" or "reactionary fundamentalists." The church was shattered. There were other options, and saner voices; yet the climate of opinion made it impossible for them to gain a hearing. "Oppositionalism" led to the issue being perceived in crystal-clear terms: either an unbelieving culture would win, or victory would go to the gospel. There were no alternatives.

One of the consequences of this was a growing demand within fundamentalist circles for separation from allegedly corrupt denominations. If it proved impossible to reform denominations from within, the only course open was to break away from the denomination, and form a new yet doctrinally pure church body. For some fundamentalist writers, the only way of safeguarding the "fundamentals of faith" was to separate. The fundamentalist war against modernity led to a closed, cautious, and defensive attitude on the part of fundamentalists towards what they regarded as a secular culture and largely apostate churches. Separatism seemed the only way ahead. If culture and mainline denominations could not be converted or reformed, there was no option but to become a voice in the wilderness.

One of the most significant results of this shake-up within the Presbyterian Church in the United States was the departure of four members of the Princeton Theological Seminary faculty to form Westminster Theological Seminary, Philadelphia. Convinced that Princeton had abandoned its commitment to the "old theology," J. Gresham Machen and three Princeton colleagues (including Cornelius van Til) became the nucleus of the faculty of the new seminary, dedicated to maintaining the tradition from which Princeton now seemed to have departed. They took with them some of the Seminary's most promising students, including Carl McIntyre and Harold J. Ockenga, both of whom proved to be of considerable significance to the later development of evangelicalism. By separating from Princeton, Machen and his colleagues believed that they could reclaim the classical evangelical heritage which Princeton seemed to them to be bent on abandoning in its rush toward embracing modernism.

"Oppositionalism" rapidly proved, however, to be of limited value in constructing a movement to face the future. Despite its apparent successes, most historians regard fundamentalism as never having recovered its credibility in the aftermath of the Scopes "monkey" trial of 1925. In May 1925, John T. Scopes, a young high-school science teacher, fell foul of a recently adopted statute which prohibited the teaching of evolution in Tennessee's public schools. He was taken to court. This proved to be the biggest public relations disaster of all time for fundamentalism. Fundamentalists came to be seen as intolerant, backward, and ignorant dolts who stood outside the mainstream of American culture. From that moment onward, fundamentalism became as much a cultural stereotype as a religious movement. It could not hope to win support among the educated and cultural elites within mainline Protestantism. The damage inflicted would never be undone. It was only with the emergence of a new form of evangelicalism after the Second World War that momentum and credibility were regained. We may turn to consider this development in what follows.

The Emergence of Evangelicalism

The term "evangelical" dates from the sixteenth century, and was then used to refer to Catholic writers wishing to revert to more biblical beliefs and practices than those associated with the late medieval church. It is used especially in the 1520s, when the terms *évangélique* and *evangelisch* come to feature prominently in polemical writings of the early Reformation. The term is now used widely to refer to a transdenominational trend in theology and spirituality, which lays particular emphasis upon the place of Scripture in the Christian life. Most evangelicals and well-informed observers of the movement would suggest that it finds its identity in relation to a series of central themes and concerns, including the following:

1   The identification of Scripture as the ultimate authority in matters of spirituality, doctrine and ethics;
2   A focus on the saving death of Jesus Christ on the cross as the only source of redemption and hope;
3   An emphasis upon conversion or a "new birth" as a life-changing religious experience;
4   A concern for sharing the Christian faith, especially through evangelism.

All other matters have tended to be regarded as "matters of indifference," upon which a substantial degree of pluralism may be accepted.

Of particular importance is the question of ecclesiology, or the understanding of the nature of the church associated with evangelicalism. Historically, evangelicalism has never been committed to any particular theory of the church, regarding the New Testament as being open to a number of interpretations in this respect, and treating denominational distinctions as of secondary importance to the gospel itself. This most emphatically does not mean that evangelicals lack commitment to the church, as the body of Christ; rather, it means that evangelicals are not committed to any one theory of the church. A corporate conception of the Christian life is not understood to be specifically linked with any one denominational understanding of the nature of the church. In one sense, this is a "minimalist" ecclesiology; in another, it represents an admission that the New Testament itself does not stipulate with precision any single form of church government, which can be made binding upon all Christians. This has had several major consequences, which are of central importance to an informed understanding of the movement.

1 Evangelicalism is transdenominational. It is not confined to any one denomination, nor is it a denomination in its own right. There is no inconsistency involved in speaking of "Anglican evangelicals," "Presbyterian evangelicals," "Methodist evangelicals," or even "Roman Catholic evangelicals."
2 Evangelicalism is not a denomination in itself, possessed of a distinctive ecclesiology, but is a trend within the mainstream denominations.
3 Evangelicalism itself represents an ecumenical movement. There is a natural affinity amongst evangelicals, irrespective of their denominational associations, which arises from a common commitment to a set of shared beliefs and outlooks. The characteristic evangelical refusal to allow any specific ecclesiology to be seen as normative, while honoring those which are clearly grounded in the New Testament and Christian tradition, means that the potentially divisive matters of church ordering and government are treated as of secondary importance.

An essential question which needs to be clarified at this point is the relation between fundamentalism and evangelicalism. As we have seen, fundamentalism arose during the 1920s as a reaction within some of the American Protestant churches to the rise of a secular culture. It was from its outset, and has remained, a counter-cultural movement, using central doctrinal affirmations as a means of defining cultural boundaries. Disquiet became obvious within American fundamentalism during the late 1940s and early 1950s. Neo-evangelicalism (as it has subsequently come to be known) began to emerge, committed to redressing the unacceptable situation created by the rise of fundamentalism. Fundamentalism and evangelicalism can be distinguished at three general levels.

1   Biblically, fundamentalism is totally hostile to the notion of biblical criticism, in any form, and is committed to a literal interpretation of Scripture. Evangelicalism accepts the principle of biblical criticism (although insisting that this be used responsibly), and recognizes the diversity of literary forms within Scripture.

2   Theologically, fundamentalism is narrowly committed to a set of doctrines, some of which evangelicalism regards as at best peripheral (such as those specifically linked with Dispensationalism), and at worst an utter irrelevance. There is an overlap of beliefs (such as the authority of Scripture), which can too easily mask profound differences in outlook and temperament.

3   Sociologically, fundamentalism is a reactionary counter-cultural movement, with tight criteria of membership, and is especially associated with a "blue-collar" constituency. Evangelicalism is a cultural movement with increasingly loose criteria of self-definition, which is more associated with a professional or "white-collar" constituency. The element of irrationalism often associated with fundamentalism is lacking in evangelicalism, which has produced significant writings in areas of the philosophy of religion and apologetics.

The break between fundamentalism and neo-evangelicalism in the late 1940s and early 1950s changed both the nature and the public perception of the latter. Billy Graham, perhaps the most publicly visible representative of this new evangelical style, became a well-known figure in many western societies, and a role model for a younger generation of evangelicals. The public recognition in America of the new importance and public visibility of evangelicalism dates from the early 1970s. The crisis of confidence within American liberal Christianity in the 1960s was widely interpreted to signal the need for the emergence of a new and more publicly credible form of Christian belief. In 1976, America woke up to find itself living in the "Year of the Evangelical," with a born-again Christian (Jimmy Carter) as its President, and an unprecedented media interest in evangelicalism, linked with an increasing involvement on the part of evangelicalism in organized political action.

A number of evangelical theologians have emerged as significant within the movement since the Second World War. Carl F. H. Henry (born 1913) is noted for his six-volumed *God, Revelation and Authority* (1976–83), which represents a vigorous defense of traditional evangelical approaches to biblical authority. Donald G. Bloesch (born 1928) maintains this emphasis, especially in his *Essentials of Evangelical Theology* (1978–9), setting out an evangelical theology which is distinguished from liberalism on the one hand, and fundamentalism on the other. James I. Packer (born 1926) has also maintained an emphasis on the importance of biblical theology, while

The evangelist Billy Graham speaking at the Olympic Stadium in Berlin, 28 June 1954. Popperfoto.

pioneering the exploration of the relation between systematic theology and spirituality in his best-selling *Knowing God* (1973). One of evangelicalism's most significant areas of theological activity is the field of apologetics, in which writers such as Edward John Carnell (born 1919) and Clark H. Pinnock (born 1939) have made considerable contributions. Yet despite the growing theological renaissance within the movement, evangelicalism has yet to make a significant impact on mainline theology. This situation is certain to change, especially if postliberalism continues to expand its influence within North America and beyond. Despite major differences between the two movements, it is becoming increasingly clear that there are also significant convergences, thus facilitating an evangelical contribution to the mainline discussion.

The Rise of Charismatic and Pentecostal Movements

In the last few decades, the term "charismatic" has become widely used to refer to strongly experiential types of Christianity which place an emphasis on the presence and power of the Holy Spirit in the lives of Christians. The rediscovery of spiritual gifts is linked with the movement known as Pentecostalism, generally regarded as the first modern movement to demonstrate clearly charismatic inclinations. Although this movement can be argued to have long historical roots, its twentieth-century development is generally traced back to the ministry of Charles Fox Parham (1873–1929), and events at the Azusa Street Mission, Los Angeles, in 1906–8. The impact of the charismatic movement within mainline Christianity is generally thought to date from the 1960s, and is especially associated with the United States. The incident which brought it to public attention took place in Van Nuys, California. The rector of the local Episcopalian church, Dennis Bennett, told his congregation that he had been filled with the Holy Spirit and had spoken in tongues. Reaction varied from bewilderment to outrage; the local Episcopalian bishop promptly banned speaking in tongues from his churches. However, it soon became clear that others had shared Bennett's experience, and that the phenomena were not restricted to Protestant Christians. Many Roman Catholics began to report similar experiences. The theme of "renewal in the Spirit" began to emerge as significant across a wide range of Christian bodies. Although there were initially indications that a separate charismatic denomination might emerge, the general pattern to develop was that of charismatic renewal within the mainline churches.

More recent developments within the charismatic movement have proved controversial. The ministry of John Wimber and the Vineyard Christian Fellowship (Anaheim, California) is a case in point. In his study of the development of charismatic movements in the twentieth century, C. Peter Wagner, Professor of church growth at Fuller Seminary, distinguishes three "waves." The first wave was classic Pentecostalism, which arose in the early 1900s, and was characterized by its emphasis upon speaking in tongues. The second wave took place in the 1960s and 1970s, as noted above, and took place mainly within mainline denominations as they appropriated spiritual healing and other charismatic practices. The third wave, exemplified by Wimber, places emphasis upon "signs and wonders," seen as a new wave of supernatural power unleashed upon the churches. Controversy has centered on this "third wave." Wimber and Wagner ran Fuller Seminary's class MC510, known as "Signs and Wonders" from 1982, until faculty and trustee controversy closed it down for a year in 1986; it was reinstated, with a lower profile, a year later.

The charismatic movement has led to a rediscovery of the New Testament emphasis upon the need for spiritual gifts and discernment, which is some-times linked with matters of church life such as speaking in tongues, and a demand that these gifts and practices should find their way back into a church which would be impoverished without them. Yet the new awareness and experience of the presence of the Holy Spirit in the modern church has raised a series of debates over the nature of baptism of the Spirit, and which of the various "spiritual gifts (*charismata*)" are of greatest importance in relation both to personal faith and spirituality, and to the upbuilding of the church as a whole. It is virtually impossible to be an active participant in

Christianity at the moment without having at least some awareness of these kinds of debates.

Charismatic forms of Christianity have had a particular influence recently on the expansion and consolidation of Christianity in the developing world. In chapter 14, we shall consider this development in more detail, focusing particularly on its impact on Latin American Christianity.

STUDY QUESTIONS

1 What was the impact of the European Wars of Religion on contemporary European society, to judge by the response of John Locke?
2 What was the "Great Awakening"? What were its consequences?
3 What were the implications of the rise of Marxism for Christianity?
4 What was "ultramontanism"? How is the development of this movement linked with the political situation in Europe at the time?
5 What were the achievements of Vatican II?
6 What is distinctive about the "charismatic movement"?

The Rise of Christianity in the Developing World

Although Christianity had its origins in Palestine, it rapidly spread through-out the Mediterranean world. Although many of its initial regions of influ-ence were subsequently subjected to a process of Islamization as a result of the Arab invasions of the seventh century and beyond, Europe remained Christian. Even Turkey, the most Islamic nation in Europe, retained a significant Christian presence (largely in the form of Armenian Christians) until a program of genocide by the Islamic government led to the virtual elimination of Christianity in the region by the end of the First World War. As the great European powers – such as England, France, Portugal, and Spain – began to expand their spheres of influence, so Christianity began its process of transformation from a primarily European to a global faith.

The establishment by the Catholic church of the commission *de propa-ganda fide* ("for the spreading of the faith") in the second half of the sixteenth century is to be regarded as a landmark in this process. It reflected the Catholic church's awareness of large populations in newly-discovered territories outside Europe, and the need to create missionary and pastoral agencies to deal with territories in which there was no formally established system of church administration.

Protestants were much slower to meet the challenge of the newly-discovered territories, such as the Americas. Although a Calvinist missionary is known to have been active in Brazil during the sixteenth century, the general picture is that of a missionary situation dominated by the Catholic church, with a particularly important role being played by the Society of Jesus. The evangelical revival in England during the eighteenth century led to a dramatic increase in the number of evangelical missionaries active in regions in which Britain had political or economic interests. A missionary enterprise of major proportions began in southern Africa, India, and the vast sprawling island territories of the southern Pacific.

The outcome of this transformation can be clearly seen from a simple statistic. In the early nineteenth century, the vast majority of Christians lived in the northern hemisphere, and were primarily concentrated in Europe. By the middle of the twentieth, the balance had shifted decisively. Most Christians now live in the southern hemisphere. It is no longer Europe or North America which constitutes the numerical center of gravity of the Christian faith. That center has shifted decisively to South America, southern Africa, and parts of Asia.

So how did Christianity come to be present in such societies? In what follows, we shall explore the origins and development of Christianity in several significant regions of the world, beginning with the case of South America.

Latin America

The colonial powers in South America were Spain and Portugal. During the sixteenth century, these two nations established their presence in the region. This was consolidated during the following centuries. Mission settlements were developed, particularly by the Jesuits. The missionaries moved north from their Latin American bases, establishing missions in what is now northern California, New Mexico, Texas, and Arizona. Although territorial disputes between Spain and Portugal often hindered missionary work, South America had been extensively Christianized by the end of the eighteenth century.

It is more recent developments which have been of particular interest, and we may turn to consider two of these – Latin American liberation theology, and the rise of evangelical and charismatic movements – in what follows.

The term "liberation theology" could, in theory, be applied to any theology which is addressed to or deals with oppressive situations. However, in practice, the term is used to refer to a quite distinct form of theology, which has its origins in the Latin American situation in the 1960s and 1970s. In 1968, the Catholic bishops of Latin America gathered for a congress at Medellín, Colombia. This meeting – often known as CELAM II – sent shock waves throughout the region, by acknowledging that the church had often sided with oppressive governments in the region, and declaring that in future it would be on the side of the poor.

This pastoral and political stance was soon complemented by a solid theological foundation. In his *Theology of Liberation* (1971), the Peruvian theologian Gustavo Gutiérrez introduced the characteristic themes that would become definitive of the movement, and which we shall explore presently. Other writers of note include the Brazilian Leonardo Boff, the

Uruguayan Juan Luis Segundo, and the Argentinian José Miguel Bonion. This last is unusual in one respect, in that he is a Protestant (more precisely, a Methodist) voice in a conversation dominated by Catholic writers.

The basic themes of Latin American liberation theology may be summarized as follows.

1   Liberation theology is orientated towards the poor and oppressed. "The poor are the authentic theological source for understanding Christian truth and practice" (Sobrino). In the Latin American situation, the church is on the side of the poor. "God is clearly and unequivocally on the side of the poor" (Bonino). The fact that God is on the side of the poor leads to a further insight: the poor occupy a position of especial importance in the interpretation of the Christian faith. All Christian theology and mission must begin with the "view from below," with the sufferings and distress of the poor.

2   Liberation theology involves critical reflection on practice. As Gutiérrez puts it, theology is a "critical reflection on Christian praxis in the light of the word of God." Theology is not, and should not be, detached from social involvement or political action. Whereas classical western theology regarded action as the result of reflection, liberation theology inverts the order: action comes first, followed by critical reflection. "Theology has to stop explaining the world, and start transforming it" (Bonino). True knowledge of God can never be disinterested or detached, but comes in and through commitment to the cause of the poor. There is a fundamental rejection of the Enlightenment view that commitment is a barrier to knowledge.

At this point, the indebtedness of liberation theology to Marxist theory becomes evident. Many western observers have criticized the movement for this reason, seeing it as an unholy alliance between Christianity and Marxism. Liberation theologians have vigorously defended their use of Marx, on two major grounds. First, Marxism is seen as a "tool of social analysis" (Gutiérrez), which allows insights to be gained concerning the present nature of Latin American society, and the means by which the appalling situation of the poor may be remedied. Second, it provides a political program by which the present unjust social system may be dismantled, and a more equitable society created. In practice, liberation theology is intensely critical of capitalism and affirmative of socialism. Liberation theologians, noting the way in which the medieval scholastic writer Thomas Aquinas used Aristotle in his writings, argued that they were merely doing the same thing – using a secular philosopher to give substance to fundamentally Christian beliefs. For, it must be stressed, liberation theology declares that

God's preference for and commitment to the poor is a fundamental aspect of the gospel, not some bolt-on option arising from the Latin American situation or based purely in Marxist political theory.

It will be clear that liberation theology is of major significance to recent theological debate. For example, Scripture is read as a narrative of liberation. Particular emphasis is laid upon the liberation of Israel from bondage in Egypt, the prophet's denunciation of oppression, and Jesus' proclamation of the gospel to the poor and outcast. Scripture is read, not from a standpoint of wishing to understand the gospel, but out of a concern to apply its liberating insights to the Latin American situation. Western academic theology has tended to regard this approach with some impatience, believing that it has no place for the considered insights of biblical scholarship concerning the interpretation of such passages.

Liberation theology has also important concerns relating to the nature of salvation. It often seems to equate salvation with liberation, and stresses the social, political, and economic aspects of salvation. The movement had laid particular emphasis upon the notion of "structural sin," noting that it is society, rather than individuals, who are corrupted and require redemption. To its critics, liberation theology has reduced salvation to a purely worldly affair, and neglected its transcendent and eternal dimensions. This aspect of the movement is probably the rapid growth of forms of Christianity (such as the charismatic movement) which stress the transcendent and spiritual aspects of life. We shall consider these in what follows.

Since the colonization of South America by Spain and Portugal during the sixteenth century, it has been generally assumed that the form of Christianity which dominated the region was Catholicism. One of the most remarkable developments within the region since the 1960s has been the explosion of evangelical and pentecostal groups. The extent of this change can be seen by comparing the evangelical populations of key countries in Latin America in 1960 and 1985 (see table 14.1).

Table 14.1 Evangelical growth in Latin America

Country	Evangelicals (as percentage of total population)		Growth factor
	1960	*1985*	
Bolivia	1.27	6.51	5.1
Brazil	4.40	15.95	3.6
Chile	11.71	21.57	1.8
El Salvador	2.45	12.78	5.2
Guatemala	2.81	8.92	6.7

It can be seen that where evangelicalism was relatively well established in 1960, growth has been steady but not spectacular. However, in other regions, there has been a dramatic growth, with evangelicalism rapidly becoming a significant presence in the region. So how is this to be explained?

In part, this development reflects growing disillusionment within Latin America concerning the government of the region. Liberation theology offered one means of meeting this challenge; evangelical groups offered another, which proved to be more attractive to many. Part of the appeal of evangelicalism to Latin Americans is its association with the political and economic policies of the United States of America. The adoption of evangelicalism was seen as one aspect of a more general cultural shift toward the democratic culture of the United States.

Nevertheless, it is clear that other factors are of importance in understanding the rapid growth of charismatic and evangelical groups in this region. One of them is the evangelical insistence that it is not necessary to be a member of a specific denomination in order to be saved; it is necessary only to repent of one's sins, and believe the true gospel. The Catholic church, however, generally remains committed to the more restricted idea that it is necessary to be a member of the "true church" – which, historically, it has identified as itself – in order to be saved. Although the Second Vatican Council softened this position significantly, the maxim "outside the church there is no salvation (*extra ecclesiam nulla salus*)" continues to have a deep impact on Catholic reflection. Evangelicalism rejects the idea that the "church" can in any way be equated with one ecclesiastical body. The true church is found wherever the gospel is truly preached and truly received.

Evangelicals who get fed up with their pastors thus start their own churches, which is how the rapidly growing number of Latin American denominations began. This free-enterprise, leveling form of ministry is quite a contrast to the authority structure of the Catholic Church, whose origin in the Roman Empire makes it the oldest bureaucracy in the world. Whereas evangelical structures provide ample room for the power of personal charisma, enabling new leaders to organize their own, equally legitimate churches, the Catholic structure of appointment from above is calculated to keep charisma under strict control, if not stifle it altogether. It is not hard to work out which of these two approaches will flourish in a cultural situation which encourages the rupture of old social bonds and encourages personal initiative. Evangelicals can break away and remain evangelical, but Catholics who reject the authority of their clergy may well become evangelicals.

A further issue of importance here is the way in which Pentecostalism links up with the popular folk culture of Latin America. Pentecostalism allowed important bridges to be built with significant elements of popular Latin American culture – such as a pervasive belief in spirits. The Pentecostal worldview, which includes elements such as the exorcism of demons, related easily and naturally to the folk religion of the region. In addition, it offered a conversion experience which might not change the social order (the vision of Liberation Theology), but which certainly transformed the personal world of the individual believer. As belief in the possibility of positive political change in the region began to falter, the attraction of changing the private world of individuals seemed much more attractive, as well as being much more realistic.

This development has had significant political and social implications. Traditionally, South American nations generally assumed a close working alliance between the Catholic church and the state. Exceptions can certainly be provided: the anticlericalism which flourished until recently in Mexico reflects the fact that the church backed the losing side in a power struggle earlier this century. However, in general terms, it was assumed until very recently that, for example, a good and loyal Brazilian would be a Catholic. The implications of this assumption are clear: evangelical or charismatic Christians are not loyal. Yet with the upsurge in evangelical and charismatic forms of Christianity in the region, a radical change in the assumptions which had traditionally undergirded the politics of the region seem inevitable. In particular, the dominant role of the Catholic church in society and government no longer seems assured. It is unclear what the future holds; nevertheless, it is also clear that this region is going to be the center of some very dynamic and active forms of Christianity in the next few decades.

South-East Asia

In 1521, the great Spanish explorer Ferdinand Magellan discovered a group of some 3,141 islands. The islands, now known as "the Philippines," became a Spanish colony. Under Spanish rule, a program of evangelization was undertaken by various religious orders, especially the Franciscans and Dominicans. The islands came under American rule in 1898. The Philippines are unusual, in that they constitute the only predominantly Christian country in south-east Asia. Although Catholicism is the dominant form of Christianity in the region at present, many Protestant missionary societies established a presence following the end of Spanish rule. While various forms of Protestantism are now firmly rooted in the region, they constitute a minority.

Elsewhere in south-east Asia, Christianity is best described as a growing minority presence. In Japan, Christianity first gained a presence in 1549, when the Jesuit missionary Francis Xavier landed at Kagoshima. The small church in the country experienced a long period of isolation from the west during the Tokugawa shogunate. It was only in 1865 that Japan opened its doors to the west, revealing the continuing presence of about 60,000 Christian believers in the country. During the Meiji period (1868–1912), Christianity gained a growing following in the country. However, it has never achieved the substantial levels of growth seen in China or Korea in recent years. For many Japanese, Christianity, like butter, is seen as a western import. This is evident from the colloquial Japanese term for Christianity, which can be translated as "it tastes of butter."

Perhaps the most interesting developments in south-east Asia are to be found in China and Korea. It is known that Christianity established a presence in China in 1294, when Franciscan missionaries reached the country. There is, however, evidence that Christianity reached China much earlier. The Sigan-Fu Tablet, generally thought to date from 781, refers to a Nestorian missionary who had arrived in the region 146 years earlier, pointing to the strong missionary activity of this eastern form of Christianity around this time. However, the church never achieved any great success in conversions. One of the many effects of the Opium War of the 1840s was to open the "Middle Kingdom" up to at least some western attitudes. China chose to remain isolated from the west until the nineteenth century, when growing interest in commerce opened up the region to western missionaries. Of these, James Hudson Taylor (1832–1905) may be singled out for special comment.

Hudson Taylor was initially a missionary with the Chinese Evangelization Society. Dissatisfaction with this organization led him to found the China Inland Mission in 1865. This Mission was unusual in several aspects, not least its willingness to accept single women as missionaries and its interdenominational character. Hudson Taylor showed an awareness of the cultural barriers facing Christian missionaries in China, and did what he could to remove them – for example, he required his missionaries to wear Chinese, rather than western, dress.

Nevertheless, western attempts to evangelize Christianity were of very limited value. Christianity was seen as something western, and hence un-Chinese. The defeat of China by Japan in an ill-fated war during the years 1894–95 was widely regarded as a direct result of the presence of foreigners in the country. This led to the I Ho Ch'uan crusade of 1899–1900, with its fanatical opposition to foreign investment and religious activity. With the establishment of the Republic of China in 1911, Christianity received a degree of official toleration. This ended abruptly in 1949, with the communist victory which led to the foundation of the Peoples' Republic of China, and the ejection of all western missionaries from the country. The "cultural revolution" of the 1960s involved the forcible suppression of Christianity. It was far from clear what was happening to Christians; many came to the conclusion that Christianity had been eradicated.

In 1979, the horrors of the cultural revolution came to an end. It became clear that Christianity had survived the revolution. In broad terms, three main strands can be discerned within modern Chinese Christianity.

1 The Three Self Patriotic Movement, founded in 1951, is the "official" church. The phrase "Three Self" refers to the three principles of self-supporting, self-administering, and self-propagating. The general idea was to ensure that the church was totally independent of any foreign influence. However, it is also clear that the state exercises considerable control over this church.

2 The Catholic church remains important within China. The government insistence that churches shall not be dependent on or obedient to foreign agencies clearly causes some difficulties for Catholics, on account of their loyalty to the pope. In general terms, there seem to be two groups within modern Chinese Catholicism, one of which is independent of the Vatican (the "Catholic Patriotic Association"), the other which is not. The former group seems to be in the ascendancy.

3 The house church movement is now the most important Christian movement within China. Strongly charismatic in orientation, the movement has witnessed spectacular numerical gains, particularly in the rural areas of China. While it is impossible to obtain reliable figures, there are indications that possibly as many as 50 million Chinese belong to such churches.

Outside mainland China, Christianity has made considerable inroads into Chinese expatriate communities in Singapore and Malaysia. A similar picture emerges in Chinese communities in large western cities, such as Los Angeles, Vancouver, Toronto, and Sydney.

The situation in Korea is of importance to the future of Christianity in the region. The Christian population in Korea prior to 1883 was miniscule. However, in 1883, the Korean government ended a long period of international isolation by signing the Korean–American treaty. This led to the establishment of American Presbyterian missions in the country in 1884. Initial evangelistic efforts centered on women and other marginalized groups, and stressed the importance of training native Korean evangelists. The evangelistic campaign of 1909–11 met with a considerable response. In 1910, however, Japan annexed Korea as a colony, and eventually forcibly imposed Shintoism on the population. With the liberation of Korea after the Second World War, Christianity enjoyed massive growth in the region. At present, some 30 percent of the Korean population are Christians, predominantly Presbyterians. One of the factors which may help explain the growth of Christianity is that western culture was not seen as oppressive (as in China), but as liberating (particularly in the war with Japan).

Africa

Christianity became established in North Africa during the first centuries of the Christian era. Churches were established along much of the North African coast, in the areas now known as Algeria, Tunisia, and Libya. A particularly strong Christian presence developed in Egypt, with the city of Alexandria emerging as a leading center of Christian thought and life. Much of this Christian presence was swept away through the Arab invasions of the seventh century. Christianity survived in Egypt, although as a minority faith. Only the small kingdom of Ethiopia (which designates a territory much smaller than the modern nation of the same name) can be said to have remained a Christian nation. At the opening of the sixteenth century, Africa was dominated by Islam in its north, and by native forms of religion in the south. Apart from the isolated case of Ethiopia, there was no significant Christian presence whatsoever.

The situation began to change gradually during the later sixteenth century. Portuguese settlers occupied previously uninhabited islands off the west African coast, such as the Cape Verde Islands. However, such settlement had little impact on the mainland of Africa. The coming of Christianity to southern Africa is to be dated from the eighteenth century, and is closely linked with the great evangelical awakening in England at this time.

Major British missionary societies which were active in Africa during the late eighteenth or early nineteenth century include the Baptist Missionary Society (founded 1792, and initally known as "The Particular Baptist Society for the Propagation of the Gospel"); the London Missionary Society (founded 1795, and initially known as "The Missionary Society"); and the Church Missionary Society (founded 1799, and originally known as "The Church Missionary Society for Africa and the East"). Each of these societies developed a particular focus on specific regions: the BMS focused on the Congo basin, the LMS on southern Africa (including Madagascar), and the CMS on west and east Africa. All of these societies were Protestant, and generally strongly evangelical in their outlook. It was not until the middle of the nineteenth century that Catholic mission groups began to become seriously involved in the region. The trauma of the French Revolution (1789) and its aftermath had severely shaken the Catholic church. Only after the Congress of Vienna (1815) had settled the future shape of Europe could the church turn its attention to evangelism.

The dominant feature of sub-Saharan Africa in the nineteenth century is the growing importance of colonialism. Belgium, Britain, France, and Germany had all established colonies in this region during the period. The forms of Christianity dominant in these European nations varied considerably, with the result that a considerable diversity of churches became established in Africa. Anglicanism, Catholicism, and Lutheranism were all well established by the end of the century; in South Africa, the Dutch Reformed church had a particularly strong influence among European settlers. It must, however, be stressed that other missionaries from radically different backgrounds were also active in the region. For example, at least 115 black American missionaries are known to have been present and active in Africa during the period 1875–99.

African Christians of this period can be broadly divided into two categories: expatriate Europeans, and indigenous Africans. The former tended to maintain as much of the Christian life of their homeland as possible, often for sentimental or cultural reasons. Thus the external trappings of the Church of England found themselves replicated to various extents in the many British colonies to spring up in southern Africa during this period. More significant, however, was the gradual adoption of Christianity by native African people. The early converts to Christianity were often those who were on the margins of traditional African societies – such as slaves, women, and the poor. In several areas in which missionaries were active, the number of Christian women became far greater that the number of Christian men, causing severe difficulties. How were they to find Christian husbands? It is clear that the most successful missionaries here were not Europeans, but Africans themselves. The dramatic growth in African Christianity is mainly subsequent to the establishment of African Christian communities, which provided catechists and pastors to the growing number of converts which they attracted.

Despite this, the names of several European missionaries stand out as being of particularly important; David Livingstone (1813–73) is a case in point. Livingstone was convinced of the importance of commerce in relation to the Christianization of Africa. He declared his intention to go to Africa "to make an open path for commerce and Christianity." Exploiting the British government's interest in replacing the banned slave trade with more legitimate forms of commerce, Livingstone obtained government backing for an expedition to explore the Zambezi river as a potential gateway to the interior. He believed that the interior would be capable of commercial exploitation (such as the growing of cotton, then greatly in demand by the cotton mills of Lancashire). Although the expedition was a commercial failure, it opened up the interior to missionary activity.

The case of South Africa is of particular interest, given the difficulties experienced by the country in the second half of the twentieth century. A European presence was established in 1658 by the Dutch East India Company in the Cape of Good Hope region. The region became a British colony in 1795, with a polarization developing between Dutch- and English-speaking populations which would eventually reach a climax in the Boer War at the end of the nineteenth century. Christianity (although in very different forms) was integral to the identity of both European communities. Missionary work in the 1790s led to the establishment of small Christian communities amongst native tribes, particularly the Khoi. Gradually, surrounding tribes began to convert to Christianity. Here, as in many other situations, the motivation for conversion varied considerably. Some conversions clearly reflect a deep spiritual experience; others reflect a conviction of the truth of the Christian gospel; other conversions may reflect a belief that Christianity would make the benefits of western civilization more widely available to African culture. This is particularly clear in the case of the Ganda tribe of east Africa, where the decision to convert to Christianity (rather than Islam) seems to have been partly influenced by the superiority of British technology.

Enormous difficulties were experienced at the level of communication of ideas. How could the distinctive ideas of Christianity be explained to peoples who had no understanding of any of its concepts? It was all very well for English evangelical missionaries to urge their African audiences to be "washed in the blood of the Lamb" (a reference to receiving forgiveness through the death of Christ); the evidence suggests that this bewildered many potential converts.

Christianity also caused tensions to arise within traditional African societies. Western Christianity was strongly monogamist; African culture had long recognized the merits of polygamy. Increasingly, the European Christian insistence upon a man having only one wife was seen as a western import, having no place in traditional African society. The United African Methodist Church, an indigenous church which recognized polygamy, traces its origins back to a meeting of the Methodist Church in Lagos, Nigeria, in 1917, when a large group of leading lay people were debarred from the church on account of polygamy. They responded by forming their own Methodist church, which adopted native African values frowned on by the European missionaries.

In several cases, these tensions led to bloodshed. A case in point is provided by the Baganda people, who lived in a region which is now incorporated into modern-day Uganda. The persecution of Christians by the Baganda king Mwanga in 1886 is an important example, as it points to the threat posed by the growing influence of Christianity to more traditional power structures in the region. The occasion for the massacre was the refusal of some court pages to take part in homosexual activities on the basis of their Christian faith. The issue was not so much whether homosexuality was right or wrong, as whether the pages would obey the king or their Christian beliefs. It was clear that Christianity was threatening traditional tribal loyalties. It is thought that about 100 were executed, including 31 who were burned alive. All were native Africans; no expatriate missionaries were affected. The persecution simply increased the determination of the Christians to persevere in their faith. By 1911, slightly less than half of the population of the region was Christian.

In the period following the First World War Christianity underwent significant transformation and development. The most obvious of these is the growing numerical strength of Christianity in the region, which is having major effects on the politics of the region. Of particular importance is the Islam–Christianity interface, which is potentially the case of considerable conflict in the region. For example, the southern part of Nigeria is predominantly Christian, and the north predominantly Muslim. This raises the question of whether Nigeria can survive as a single nation, or whether some form of partition – such as that introduced between predominantly Muslim Pakistan and predominantly Hindu India in 1947 – will be necessary in future.

Yet other issues are of importance. Two related developments may be singled out as being of particular interest. The period after the Second World War saw the end of colonialism. The colonial powers – such as Belgium, France, and Great Britain – gradually withdrew from the region, leaving behind independent nation states. Accompanying this transition to independence, the churches in the region gradually cast off their dependence on their mother churches in Europe. For example, the Anglican churches in regions such as South Africa, Uganda, and Zimbabwe originally depended on expatriate Britons to assume senior positions of leadership – such as bishops, deans of cathedrals, and heads of seminaries. These positions are now being filled by native Africans. Although many of these senior clergy have been educated in Britain, it is clear that the churches in the region now regard themselves as self-sufficient in terms of personnel and resources.

A related development concerns the rise of African Independent Churches, a term which refers to a very broad range of Christian churches which place an emphasis on retaining a traditional African heritage within the context of their Christian faith. These churches are often strongly charismatic, placing an emphasis on the importance of spiritual healing, exorcism, the interpretation of dreams, and prophetic guidance. Reacting against the word-based culture of the nineteenth-century west, these churches place an emphasis on experience and symbolism. A further factor of importance here is the racism of some white churches, particularly in South Africa under the apartheid regime. The Zionist churches of this region can be seen as a celebration and affirmation of black African identity in the face of such official hostility. In the last few decades, these churches have often been influenced by the charismatic movement, which has proved to be an important catalyst for further growth in the region. In 1967, a reliable survey suggested that there were at least five thousand independent churches of this kind, with seven million members drawn from 290 tribes across 34 countries. Substantial further growth has taken place subsequently.

India

Christianity became established in the Indian subcontinent at a relatively early stage. Traditionally, it is believed that the apostle Thomas founded the Indian Mar Thoma church in the first century; even allowing for a degree of pious exaggeration here, there are excellent reasons for believing that Christianity was an indigenous element of the Indian religious scene by the fourth century. It seems likely that western merchants discovered the existence of the Palghat gap at an early stage, thus facilitating trade with southern India. European travellers reaching India by land, prior to the opening of the ocean trading tour by the Portuguese navigator Vasco da Gama in May 1498, regularly reported the presence of Christians in the region.

The arrival of the Portuguese may be taken to signal the opening of a significant new period in Indian Christianity, in which indigenous Christian traditions were supplemented by imported versions of the gospel, each reflecting aspects of its European context. The papal Bull *Aeternia regis clementia* (21 June 1481) gave the Portuguese monarch the authority to trade with hitherto undiscovered lands, as well as investing him with "spiritual power and authority from Capes Bojador and Nam as far as the Indies." The Bishopric of Goa was established as the potential base for a campaign of Portuguese evangelization of the interior.

The importance of this settlement was considerably enhanced through the arrival of Francis Xavier on 6 May 1542. A mere two years after having been formally recognized by the Pope, the Society of Jesus was thus established in India. Xavier organized an extensive missionary enterprise, including the translation of Christian works into Tamil. As time went on, Dutch, English, and French settlers moved into India, bringing their own versions of Christianity with them.

Initially, evangelization was seen as peripheral to the more serious business of trading. The first Anglican clergy in India, for example, were ships' chaplains, appointed by the English East India Company to provide pastoral care and spiritual support for the crews of their ships. However, a growing European presence in the region brought with it the tensions of the European religious situation of the seventeenth century, in which Protestantism and Catholicism were viewed as mutually incompatible and radically divergent versions of Christianity. The establishment of Christianity in Europe inevitably meant that the political interests of Protestant and Catholic nations, such as England and France, were seen as possessing strongly religious dimensions. Religion was one aspect of a broader struggle for political and economic supremacy. As a result, evangelization became increasingly imperative.

Humphrey Prideaux, an Anglican dean of Norwich (1684–1724), may be regarded as indicative of this spirit of evangelistic adventurism. In his *Account of the English Settlements in the East Indies, together with some proposals for the propagation of Christianity in those parts of the world*, Prideaux pointed to the need to train people for the specific work of evangelism. Prideaux's idea was prophetic: a "seminary" was to be established in England, with a view to prepare mission workers, until such time as the work could be handed over to agencies based in India itself. In this proposal may be seen the basis of the missionary movement, which was destined to exercise a significant impact over Indian Christianity.

Among the major contributions to European missionary work in India, the following may be singled out for special mention. The first major Protestant mission to India was based at Tranquebar on the Coromandel Coast, about 200 kilometers south of Madras. Among the German Lutheran missionaries of note were Bartholomäus Ziegenbalg (who directed the mission from its founding in 1706 to 1719) and Christian Frederick Schwartz (director from 1750 to 1787). However, the growing political power of Britain in the region inevitably favored the activities of British missionaries, the first of which (the Baptist, William Carey) began work in Bengal in 1793. This was assisted to no small extent by the decision of Clement XIV to suppress the Society of Jesus. The bull *Dominus ac Redemptor* (21 July 1773) formally terminated "all and every one of its functions and ministries." The missionary activity of the Jesuits in India and elsewhere was thus terminated. Nevertheless, at least 50 Jesuits are known to have continued missionary work in India after the suppression of their order, despite the efforts of the Portuguese to repatriate them.

British missionary societies and individuals were thus able to operate in India without any major opposition from other European agencies. Nevertheless, they received no support from the British authorities; The East India Company, for example, was opposed to their activities, on the grounds that they might create ill-will amongst native Indians, and thus threaten the trade upon which it depended. However, the Charter Act (passed by the British parliament on 13 July 1813), revised the conditions under which the Company was permitted to operate in: the new charter gave British missionaries protected status, and a limited degree of freedom to carry out evangelistic work on the Indian subcontinent. The result was inevitable: "since 1813, Christian missions have never been wholly free from the stigma of undue dependence on government" (Stephen Charles Neill). The new Charter also made provision for the establishment of an Anglican bishopric at Calcutta. Under Reginald Heber (1783–1826; bishop of Calcutta from

1823–6), missionary work was expanded considerably, and restricted to Anglicans (Lutheran missionaries being obliged to be re-ordained to allow them to continue operating in the region). Further revisions to the East India Company's charter in 1833 removed some of the restrictions imposed earlier upon missionary work.

It was inevitable that religious tensions would develop. In 1830, the Dharma Sabha was formed, apparently as a reaction against intrusive forms of westernization in Bengal. The uprising of 1857 (generally referred to as "the Indian Mutiny" by contemporary English writers) is often regarded as the outcome of this growing resentment at westernization. It is therefore of importance to note the development of indigenous Indian approaches to Christianity, rather than theologies of essentially European provenance in the region. In its initial phases, such a theology tended to arise through Hindus assimilating Christianity to their own worldview. Rammohun Roy (1772–1833) was born of a Brahman family in Bengal. His early contacts with Islam (and particularly the mystical tradition of the Sufis) led him to conclude that his Hindu religion was corrupted, and required to be re-formed. In 1815 he founded the Atmiya Sabha, a movement dedicated to the reform of Hinduism, which advocated the abolition of _sati_ (often spelled "_suttee_": the practice of burning Hindu widows alive on their husband's funeral pyre). His growing alienation from orthodox Hinduism led to an increasing interest in Christianity, which he came to regard as embodying a moral code which would be acceptable to right-thinking Hindus. This idea, which he promoted in his _Precepts of Jesus_ (1820), attracted considerable attention.

It also provoked considerable criticism from within European Christian circles, most notably from the more conservative Protestants, such as the Lutheran pastor Deocar Schmidt. Schmidt argued that the moral precepts of Christ could not be separated from the theological question of the identity of Christ, and the subsequent implications of this for a Trinitarian concept of God. Rammohun Roy replied that it was impossible for a Hindu to accept a Trinitarian concept of God; nevertheless, a Unitarian understanding of God, linked with an emphasis upon the gospel as a moral code, might well prove acceptable. It was possible for sins to be forgiven without the need for the atonement of Christ, an idea which he regarded as utterly alien to Hinduism (Brahmo theism, for example, rejects both the ideas of revelation and atonement). In 1829, he founded the Brahmo Samaj, a theistic society which drew upon ideas derived from both Hinduism and Christianity; among the ideas derived from the latter was the practice of regular congregational worship, then unknown in Hinduism. Under his successor Devendranath Tagore, however, the Samaj moved in a more definitely Hindu direction. However, aspects of Rammohun Roy's understanding of the relation between Christianity and Hinduism were criticized by other

Hindus who had converted to Christianity. Thus the Bengali writer Krishna Mohan Banerjee argued that there were close affinities between the Vedic idea of Purusha sacrifice and the Christian doctrine of atonement, thus challenging Rammohun Roy's view that there were radical differences at this point.

A highly influential approach to understanding the relation between Christianity and Hinduism was developed by Keshub Chunder Sen (1838–84), who argued that that Christ brought to fulfillment all that was best in Indian religion. This approach bears a direct resemblance to the western European idea, associated with writers as diverse as Thomas Aquinas and John Calvin, that Christianity brings to fulfillment the aspirations of classic antiquity, as expressed in the culture of ancient Greece and Rome. Unlike Rammohun Roy, however, Keshub embraced the doctrine of the Trinity with enthusiasm. He argued that although *Brahman* was indivisible and indescribable, it could nevertheless be considered in terms of its inner relations of *Sat* ("being"), *Cit* ("reason") and *Ananda* ("bliss"). These three relations paralleled the Christian understanding of God the Father as "Being," God the Son as "Word," and God the Holy Spirit as "comforter" or "bringer of joy and love." This approach was developed by Nehemiah Goreh (1825–95), who stressed the facility with which it was possible to move from a Hindu notion of God to that now offered by Christianity. A related idea has been developed more recently by Raimundo Panikkar in his *Unknown Christ of Hinduism*, in which he argued for the hidden presence of Christ in Hindu practice, especially in relation to matters of justice and compassion.

A similar approach was developed, but with considerably greater acumen, by Brahmabandhab Upadhyaya (1861–1907), based on an analysis of the relation of the Christian faith and its articulation in terms of non-Christian philosophical systems (as in Thomas Aquinas' use of Aristotelianism as a vehicle for his theological exposition). Why should Indian Christians not be at liberty to draw upon indigenous Indian philosophical systems, in undertaking a similar task? Why should not Vedanta be used in the expression of Christian theology, and the Vedas be regarded as the Indian Old Testament? Increasingly, the issue of an authentically Indian Christian theology came to be seen as linked with that of independence from Britain: theological and political self-determination came to be seen as inextricably linked.

The move toward independence in 1947 resulted in Christianity finding itself in competition with rival ideologies: Gandhism and Marxism. A particularly important participant in this debate is Madathiparamil Mammen Thomas (b. 1916). From a Mar Thoma Christian background, M. M. Thomas has come to be regarded as a leading representative of an authentically Indian voice in modern theology. Thomas' critique of Gandhism is of especial interest. In the first, Thomas was himself a Gandhian, only to become disillusioned with what he regarded as its inadequacies and fallacies. In the second, it represents an Indian Christian response to a distinctively Indian ideology. Thomas regards Gandhi has having reduced Christianity to little more than a moral code or set of principles, and quotes with approval the letter to Gandhi from E. Stanley Jones: "I think you have grasped certain principles of the Christian faith. You have grasped the principles but missed the person." A similar criticism is directed against Indian Marxist writers.

Other issues have come to be of major importance within the Indian context in recent years, most notably the relation of the Christian gospel to the poor. It seems, however, that the continuing exploration of the relationship between Christianity and Hinduism is likely to remain a significant feature of Indian Christian theology for some time. For example, the relation between the Christian doctrine of incarnation and the Hindu notion of *avatar* has emerged as a significant debate within Indian Christian thought.

One final development should be noted in relation to Indian Christianity. On 27 September 1947, shortly after independence, several major Christian denominations in the region agreed to form a single body, known as the "Church of South India." The original pressure which led to this development was an awareness that Christian mission in the region was being hindered by denominational rivalry. Other denominations subsequently joined the body, which is regarded by some western Christians as a model for future cooperation between the churches in their region.

The South Pacific

The term "Oceania" is now generally used to refer to the 1500 or so islands in the Pacific Ocean. This is further subdivided into three general regions. *Polynesia* designates the group of islands stretching from Hawaii (known as the "Sandwich Islands" in earlier centuries) in the north to New Zealand in the south, including Tahiti and Pitcairn Island. *Micronesia* refers to the group of small islands between Hawaii and the Philippines, including the Caroline, Gilbert and Marshall Islands. *Melanesia* refers to the group of islands south of Micronesia and north of Australia, including Fiji, the Solomon Islands and the New Hebrides. The population of this vast and dispersed region is relatively small; however, it was considered to be of major importance by Christian missionaries in the nineteenth century.

Interest in the region was first awakened by reports of the voyages of Captain Cook during the eighteenth century. In 1795, the London Missionary Society was founded with the primary objective of sending missionaries to "the islands of the South Sea." The first major missionary expedition to the region set off in August 1796, when 30 missionaries set sail for Tahiti. Although this mission faced considerable difficulties – not least of which related to the very different sexual mores of England and Tahiti – it can be seen as marking the beginning of a sustained effort to establish Christianity in the region.

The geographical nature of the region made one of the most reliable means of evangelization – the establishment of mission stations – impossible. The populations of the islands were generally too small to justify the building and maintenance of such settlements. The most successful strategy to be adopted was the use of missionary vessels, which allowed European missionaries to direct and oversee the operations of native evangelists, pastors and teachers in the region.

The most significant Christian missions in the region were located in Australia and New Zealand, which eventually came to serve as the base for most missionary work in the region. Christianity came to Australia in 1788. The circumstances of its arrival were not entirely happy. The fleet that arrived in New South Wales was transporting convicts to the penal settlements which were being established in the region. At the last moment, William Wilberforce persuaded the British naval authorities to allow a chaplain to sail with the fleet. With the dramatic increase in immigration to the region from Britain in the following century, the various forms of British Christianity became established in the region. The formation of the "Bush Brotherhoods" in 1897 laid the basis for the evangelization of the interior of the continent.

The first missionaries arrived in New Zealand in 1814. The consolidation of Christianity in the region was largely due to Bishop George Selwyn (1809–78), who was appointed missionary bishop of New Zealand in 1841. During his time in the region, he had a marked impact on the development of Christianity, particularly in relation to education. He returned to England in 1867.

Throughout the south Pacific region, a major issue has concerned the relation of Christianity to the native peoples of the region, particularly the Australian Kuri (often still inappropriately referred to as "Aborigines") and New Zealand Maori peoples. For some, Christianity is a western colonial phenomenon, which is to be rejected as destructive of indigenous culture; for others, Christianity has no necessary connection with western culture or power, and can be put at the service of indigenous peoples and cultures.

Even on the basis of this very brief analysis, it will be clear that Christianity has become a global religion of considerable importance. A religion which was once virtually confined to a small region of western Europe has now become the world's largest religion. So in what ways does being a Christian affect people? In the closing section of this work, we shall explore some aspects of Christian living.

STUDY QUESTIONS

1   What is "liberation theology"? How significant has it been in relation to the Latin American situation?
2   In what ways is the spread of Christianity in the developing world linked with colonialism?
3   To what extent was Christianity regarded as a western import by the cultures of the developing world during the nineteenth and early twentieth centuries?
4   How has African traditional religious life affected the evolution of Christianity in the region?
5   What are the implications of the gradual shift in the numerical center of gravity of Christianity from the west to the developing world?

The Christian Way

In earlier parts of this work, we have explored several aspects of Christianity, focusing particularly on its teachings and history. This may create the impression that Christianity is simply a set of ideas. While it is certainly true that Christianity is based on a set of core beliefs, it is essential to appreciate that these beliefs have a significant effect on the personal lives and values of individual Christians, on the way in which Christian communities behave and worship, and the cultures in which Christianity has secured a presence.

The final part of this work aims to explore Christian life in the modern world. It is intended particularly for those who, though not Christians, need at least a basic understanding of Christianity as a major force in modern global culture. Many people experience Christianity as a living presence in the world, rather than as a set of ideas. This part of the work aims to explore the nature of that presence, wherever possible explaining the beliefs underlying Christian customs, values, and activity in the modern world.

The approach adopted in this final section of the work is as follows. Chapter 15 introduces various aspects of Christian life; it explains the structure of the Christian year, focusing both on the religious significance of major Christian festivals, and the customs which have come to be attached to them. Anyone wishing to understand Christianity needs to know that, for Christians, Christmas is most emphatically not just about giving people presents, nor is Easter just about giving people eggs. Considerable care is taken to ensure that the Christian understanding of the significance of all major festivals is accurately described.

This is followed by chapter 16, which deals with the three main forms of Christianity encountered in the modern world – Catholicism, Orthodoxy, and Protestantism. The differences between them will be noted, as well as the potential areas of tension which may result. Although due note will be taken of differences in beliefs between the various forms of Christianity, the purpose here is primarily to describe how these forms of Christianity would be experienced in the modern world.

Finally, the way in which Christianity has impacted – and continues to impact – on culture is explored.

CHAPTER 5

The Christian Life

At the heart of the Christian life is a worshipping community. Those who are encountering Christianity from the outside are most likely to experience it through various forms of worship. That worship takes an incredible variety of styles – from the sumptuous, ornate, and elaborate worship of Russian Orthodoxy within a gilded cathedral to the informal, laid-back, and guitar-led worship of Latin American pentecostalism, packed inside a makeshift church. It is therefore of considerable importance to explore the nature of Christian worship, and the way in which it has evolved down the ages, and is encountered today.

Christian Worship

The New Testament tends to use the word "church (Greek: *ekklesia*)" to refer to a gathering of people rather than a building. Indeed, the threat of persecution was such that the early church tended to meet in secret, "borrowing" buildings which were normally used for other purposes in order to avoid drawing attention to their activities. The strong element of secrecy associated with early Christian worship led to all kinds of rumors concerning what Christians did during their worship. The accusation of cannibalism, widespread in the late first century, appears to reflect a misunderstanding of the idea of eating the body and drinking the blood of Jesus Christ (see p. 371); that of orgies seems to rest on the early Christian love-feast, or *agape*, which was fundamentally a celebration of the love of Jesus Christ for his people, and the mutual love of Christians.

There are clear indications of an emerging style of worship within the New Testament. The Acts of the Apostles records that the first Christians met regularly, and "devoted themselves to the apostles' teaching and to the fellowship, to the breaking of bread and to prayer" (Acts 2:42). In addition to the "breaking of the bread," the New Testament also highlights the importance of baptism as a sign of presonal commitment to Jesus Christ, and of entrance into the Christian community. The importance of singing and thanksgiving can be seen from a number of passages: "Speak to one another with psalms, hymns and spiritual songs. Sing and make music in your heart to the Lord, always giving thanks to God the Father for everything, in the name of our Lord Jesus Christ" (Ephesians 5:19–20). The styles of Christian worship which will be encountered today can all be traced back, in different ways, to the New Testament.

Christian worship is particularly associated with one day of the week – Sunday. It is clear that Christians regarded the first day of the week as being of especial importance, as it was the day on which Jesus rose again from the dead. Whereas Jewish worship was particularly associated with the seventh day of the week (the Sabbath, or Saturday), the first Christians did not retain this traditional Jewish custom. Sunday was seen as the first day of God's new creation, and therefore was the day appropriate for all major public Christian worship. Justin Martyr, writing *c.*165, is an important witness to this tradition:

> On the day which is called Sunday, all who live in the cities or in the countryside gather together in one place. And the memoirs of the apostles or the writings of the prophets are read, so long as there is time. Then, when the reader has finished, the president delivers a discourse in which he encourages the people to follow the examples of virtue which these provide. Then we all stand up together and offer some prayers. And when we have finished these prayers, bread and wine mixed with water are presented. The president then offers prayers and a thanksgiving, according to his ability, and the people indicate their assent by saying "Amen". The elements for which thanks has been given are then distributed and received by all present, and are taken to those who are not present by the deacons.

All generalizations are dangerous, and must be treated with a degree of caution. However, they are also useful to those who are trying to gain an understanding of an exceptionally complicated matter. What follows is a listing of the various elements which will be encountered in Christian worship. The types of Christian worship vary considerably, and not all of the elements to be discussed below will be found in all types of worship. They are, nevertheless, useful as a starting point for exploring modern worship. However, the reader who is approaching Christianity from outside must be warned that it is of very limited value simply to read about Christian worship; worship is something which demands to be experienced. You are strongly recommended to supplement your reading with involvement with the worshipping life of a local Christian church, and gain an appreciation of its structures, rhythms, and appeal.

Prayer

Prayer is an integral element of all forms of Christian worship. It could be defined as "a covenant relationship between God and humanity in Christ . . . In the New Covenant, prayer is the living relationship of the children of God with their Father who is good beyond measure, with his Son, Jesus Christ, and with the Holy Spirit" (*Catechism of the Catholic Church*). Prayer takes a variety of forms. A distinction is made between the *private* prayers of individuals, and the *public* prayer of the church. Prayer can also take the form of *thanksgiving*, in which thanks are offered to God for blessings which have been received, whether by individuals or by the church as a whole. Perhaps the most important is *petitionary* prayer, in which the congregation, or individuals within that congregation, make specific requests of God. This type of prayer can be illustrated from the teaching of Jesus, who compared this type of prayer to human requests.

Jesus on Petitionary Prayer

Matthew 7:7–11
Ask and it will be given to you; seek and you will find; knock and the door will be opened to you. For everyone who asks receives; he who seeks finds; and to him who knocks, the door will be opened. Which of you, if his son asks for bread, will give him a stone? Or if he asks for a fish, will give him a snake? If you, then, though you are evil, know how to give good gifts to your children, how much more will your Father in heaven give good gifts to those who ask him!

STUDY PANEL 40

Reading Scripture

The public reading of the Bible is an integral element of Christian worship. Many churches use a structured program of Bible readings (often referred to as a "Lectionary"), which aims to ensure that the Bible is read in its totality throughout the course of the regular worship of the church. Others allow individual ministers to determine what biblical passages shall be read at any given time. The principle, however, remains the same. Part of Christian worship is the hearing and responding to the word of God. Sometimes that response may take the form of believing certain doctrines; at others, it may involve the recognition of the need to behave in certain ways, to do certain things.

In the early church, priority was given to the reading of a passage from the gospels. This was seen as a public declaration of the words and deeds of Jesus Christ. Many churches adopted the practice of standing in order to hear the gospel reading, as a way of demonstrating that the good news of Jesus Christ was central to the life and worship of the church and its individual members. This practice gradually developed into that of having two or three readings, typically arranged sequentially as: a reading from the Old Testament; a reading from one of the New Testament letters; a reading from one of the gospels. In many churches, the public reading of Scripture is followed by the explanation or application of the passage of Scripture through a sermon. We shall explore this in what follows.

Preaching

Many Christian services include a sermon. The word "sermon" derives from the Latin term *sermo*, literally meaning "a word." A sermon is fundamentally a statement or application of the Christian faith, and often takes the form of the exegesis (literally, "the drawing out") of a biblical passage (for example, the passage chosen or set for the day), a biblical theme, or an article of the creed. Collections of excellent or reliable sermons were in circulation within Christianity by an early stage. The Latin term *homilarium* is used to refer to books of sermons, such as those assembled by Paul the Deacon (*c*.790) or Alan of Farfa (died 770). Styles of sermon vary considerably, with some preachers seeing the sermon as primarily catechetical (that is, aimed at teaching the congregation more about their faith), and others as exhortatory (that is, aimed at encouraging their audience to lead better lives as Christians, or to take to heart some basic Christian teaching or principle).

Although preaching is a regular part of the worship of many Christian traditions, it was given an especially important role at the time of the Reformation. The new emphasis on the importance of the Bible, and particularly the Reformation emphasis on the "priesthood of all believers," made the creation of a biblically-literate laity of considerable importance. The especial emphasis placed by writers such as John Calvin on the importance of Bible-based preaching reflects these concerns.

The Reciting of the Creeds

Many more formal Christian services or worship involve reciting one of the creeds – usually the Apostles' Creed or the Nicene Creed. These creeds are intended to remind believers of the basic themes of their faith, and enable them to avoid false teachings as a result. The recitation of the creeds also establishes a strong sense of "belonging," in that it affirms the basic continuity between the Christian communities of today and those of the classic period.

The creeds are statements of faith which are common to all Christians, whether Protestant, Orthodox or Catholic. They are regarded as possessing a universal significance for all Christians, which transcends the particular importance of individual statements of faith of certain historic churches. Thus, for example, Anglicans might regard the Thirty-Nine Articles as having considerable importance in defining their specifically Anglican beliefs, just as Presbyterians might feel similarly about the Westminster Confession. But these two documents would never be incorporated into the public worship of these churches, in that they are seen to lack the *universal* authority of the creeds.

The Sacraments

In general terms, a sacrament may be thought of as an external rite or sign, which in some way conveys or represents the grace of God to believers. A minimalist definition of a sacrament might take the form of "an external physical sign of an interior spiritual grace." The New Testament does not actually make use of the specific term "sacrament." Instead, we find the Greek word *mysterion* (which is probably best translated as "mystery") used to refer to the saving work of God in general. This Greek word is never used to refer to what would now be regarded as a sacrament (for example, baptism). However, it is clear from what we know of the history of the early church that a connection was made at an early stage between the "mystery" of God's saving work in Christ and the "sacraments" of baptism and the eucharist.

Perhaps the most significant advances in sacramental theology took place in Roman North Africa during the third and fourth centuries, and can be seen in the writings of Tertullian, Cyprian of Carthage, and Augustine. It is interesting to ask why these developments are associated with this specific region of the church. One possible factor is that the church in this region was subjected to particularly difficult circumstances, including persecution. (It must be remembered that Cyprian would die as a martyr at the hands of the Roman authorities.) The church in North Africa was thus characterized by a strong sense of solidarity in the face of these difficult conditions. As a result, the African church placed considerable emphasis on solidarity of the faithful, and the means by which this solidarity could be maintained and enhanced. The sacraments were one vital aspect of this strategy.

Tertullian's contribution to the development of sacramental theology can be summarized in terms of three issues.

1 The use of the Latin term sacramentum (now familiar to us in its English form "sacrament") to translate the Greek word *mysterion*. It is quite possible that this translation was already familiar to him through existing Latin translations of the New Testament. However, Tertullian was noted for his ability to invent new Latin words for Greek theological terms, and it is entirely possible that this development was his own idea.

2 The use of the word "sacrament" in the plural. The New Testament spoke of a mystery in the singular. As we have just noted, Tertullian translated this as "sacrament," referring to this mystery – but also used the word in the plural to refer to the individual sacraments which were linked with this mystery. Tertullian thus uses the Latin word *sacramentum* in two different, though clearly related, senses: first to refer to the mystery of God's salvation; and second, to refer to the symbols or rites which were associated with this salvation in the life of the church.

3 The exploitation of the theological signifance of the parallel between sacraments and military oaths. Tertullian pointed out that, in normal Latin use, the word *sacramentum* meant "a sacred oath," referring to the oath of allegiance and loyalty which was required of Roman soldiers. Tertullian used this parallel as a means of bringing out the importance of sacraments in relation to Christian commitment and loyalty within the church. This theme would become of fundamental importance in the sacramental theology of the Swiss reformer Huldrych Zwingli, as we shall see later (p. 374).

The theology of the sacraments would be developed further by Augustine during the Donatist contoversy (see pp. 254–5). A central theme of his reflections is the relation between a sign and the thing which it signifies. For Augustine, the world contains many signs which point to different realities – for example, smoke as a sign of fire, or words as a sign of that to which they refer. However, there are also "sacred signs" which bridge the gap between God and ourselves, in that they serve as physical doorways or gates to spiritual realities.

Augustine uses many definitions of sacraments to express this point; perhaps the most famous of these is the idea of sacraments as "visible forms of invisible grace." Yet Augustine is clear that sacraments do not merely signify grace; in some way, they evoke or enable what they signify. In one sense, the subsequent development of sacramental theology may be said to concern the way in which the sign and thing signified relate to each other. Augustine is generally regarded as having laid down two general principles relating to the definition of sacraments. These principles are as follows.

1 A sacrament is a *sign*. "Signs, when applied to divine things, are called sacraments."
2 The sign must bear some relation to the thing which is signified. "If sacraments did not bear some resemblance to the things of which they are the sacraments, they would not be sacraments at all."

These definitions are still imprecise and inadequate. For example, does it follow that every "sign of a sacred thing" is to be regarded as a sacrament? As time developed, it became increasingly clear that the definition of a sacrament simply as "a sign of a sacred thing" was inadequate. It was during the earlier Middle Ages that further clarification took place. In the first half of the twelfth century, the Paris theologian Hugh of St Victor revised the definition, as follows:

> Not every sign of a sacred thing can properly be called a sacrament. After all, the letters in sacred writings, or statues and pictures, are all "signs of sacred things", but cannot be called sacraments for that reason . . . Anyone wanting a fuller and better definition of a sacrament can define it as follows: "a sacrament is a physical or material element set before the external senses, representing by likeness, signifying by its institution, and containing by sanctification, some invisible and spiritual grace".

There are thus four essential components to the definition of a sacrament:

1 There must be a "physical or material" element involved – such as the water of baptism, the bread and wine of the eucharist, or the oil of extreme unction. ("Extreme unction" is the practice of anointing those who are terminally ill with consecrated olive oil.)
2 A "kind of likeness" to the thing which is signified, so that it can represent the thing signified. Thus the eucharistic wine can be argued to have a "kind of likeness" to the blood of Christ, allowing it to represent that blood in a sacramental context.
3 "Institution through which it is ordered to signify this thing." In other words, there must be a good reason for believing that the sign in question is authorized to represent the spiritual reality to which it points. An example – indeed, the primary example – of the "authorization" in question is institution at the hands of Jesus Christ himself.

4 An efficacity, by which the sacrament is capable of conferring the benefits which it signifies to those who partake in it.

However, Hugh of St Victor's definition of a sacrament remained unsatisfactory. By this time, there was general agreement that there were seven sacraments – baptism, confirmation, the eucharist, penance, marriage, ordination, and extreme unction. But by Hugh's definition, penance could not be a sacrament. It contained no material element. The theory and practice of the church on this question were thus seriously out of line.

The final touches were put to the definition by Peter Lombard, who – by omitting one vital aspect of Hugh's definition – was able to bring theory into line with practice. Peter's achievement was to omit reference to any "physical or material element" in his definition, which takes the following form:

> A sacrament is precisely defined as a sign of the grace of God, and a form of invisible grace, which is such that it bears its likeness and exists as its cause.

This definition fits each of the seven sacraments noted above, and excludes such things as the creed.

The Reformation witnessed a significant challenge to this viewpoint. Martin Luther restricted the concept of a sacrament to baptism and the communion or Lord's Supper through his more restricted definition:

> It has seemed right to restrict the name of sacrament to those promises of God which have signs attached to them. The remainder, not being connected to signs, are merely promises. Hence, strictly speaking, there are only two sacraments in the church of God – baptism and the bread. For only in these two do we find the divinely instituted sign and the promise of the forgiveness of sins.

According to Luther, the two essential characteristics of a sacrament were:

1 the Word of God;
2 an outward sacramental sign (such as water in baptism, and bread and wine in the eucharist).

The only true sacraments of the New Testament church were thus baptism and eucharist; penance, having no external sign, can no longer be regarded as a sacrament. Luther was followed in this by Protestant theologians, with the Council of Trent reaffirming the traditional list of seven sacraments.

The Sacraments of the Christian Church

Catholic and Orthodox
Baptism
Eucharist
Penance
Confirmation
Marriage
Ordination
Extreme Unction

Protestant
Baptism
Eucharist

For the difficulties in naming the sacrament here referred to as "the eucharist," see pp. 372–3. Note that some Protestant writers prefer to use the term "ordinance" rather than "sacrament."

Baptism

The word "baptism" comes from the Greek word *baptizein*, meaning "to wash" or "to cleanse." In the New Testament, the term refers initially to the baptism offered by John the Baptist in the River Jordan as a sign of repentance. Jesus himself was baptized by John. For Christians, the necessity of baptism is partly grounded in the command of the risen Christ to the disciples to baptize people everywhere in the name of the Father, Son and Holy Spirit (Matthew 28:17–20). In the New Testament, baptism is clearly understood as both a condition for, and a sign of membership of, the Christian community. The Acts of the Apostles records Peter ending an early sermon with the following words, addressed to those who wanted to know what to do if they were to be saved: "Repent and be baptized, every one of you, in the name of Jesus Christ for the forgiveness of your sins. And you will receive the gift of the Holy Spirit" (Acts 2:38). In the writings of Paul, baptism is affirmed as a practice, and interpreted theologically, both in terms of dying and rising with Christ (Romans 6:1–4), and in terms of "being clothed with Christ." "You are all sons of God through faith in Christ Jesus, for all of you who were baptized into Christ have clothed yourselves with Christ" (Galatians 3:26–27).

Although the New Testament seems to indicate that baptism was administered to adults, it was not long before young children were being baptized as well. The origins of this practice are not clear. The New Testament refers to both individuals and entire households being baptized; it is possible that the baptism of households extended to include infants (Acts 16:15, 33; 1

Corinthians 1:16). Paul treats baptism as a spiritual counterpart to circumcision (Colossians 2:11–12), suggesting that the parallel may extend to its application to infants. The early church saw a clear link between baptism under the New Covenant and circumcision under the Old Covenant. There are hints of this idea in the New Testament itself. The early church argued that, just as circumcision was a covenantal sign, demonstrating that someone belonged to the people of Israel, so baptism was a sign of belonging to the covenant community of the church. Since Israel circumcised infant boys, why should not the church baptize infants? More generally, there seems to have been a pastoral need for Christian parents to celebrate the birth of a child within a believing household. Infant baptism may well have had its origins partly in response to this concern. However, it must be stressed that there is genuine uncertainty concerning both the historical origins and the social or theological causes of the practice.

It is clear, however, that the practice of infant baptism was widespread by the end of the second century. In the second century, Origen treats infant baptism as a universal practice, which he justifies on the basis of a universal human need for the grace of Christ. A similar arguments would later be deployed by Augustine: in that Christ is the savior of all, it follows that all require redemption – including infants – which baptism confers, at least in part. Opposition to the practice can be seen in the writings of Tertullian, who argued that the baptism of children should be deferred until such time as they "know Christ."

Three major approaches to the question of infant baptism can be discerned within the Christian tradition.

1   *Infant baptism remits the guilt of original sin.* This position owes its origins to Cyprian of Carthage, who declared that infant baptism procured remission of both sinful acts and original sin. The final steps in the theological justification of the practice are due to Augustine of Hippo. Noting that the Apostles' Creed affirmed that there was "One baptism for the forgiveness of sins," he argued that it therefore followed that infant baptism remitted original sin. This raised a question of potential difficulty. If original sin was remitted by baptism, why did the infants in question behave in a sinful manner in later life? Augustine met this objection by distinguishing between the guilt and the disease of original sin. Baptism remitted the guilt of original sin, but did nothing to get rid of its effects, which could only be eliminated by the continuing work of grace within the believer.

One major implication of this approach relates to the fate of those who die without being baptized. What happens to those who die without having been baptized, whether in infancy or later in life? If baptism remits the guilt of original sin, a person who dies without being baptized remains guilty. So what happens to them? Augustine's position demands that such people cannot be saved. This position was modified in the light of popular pressure, apparently based upon a belief that his doctrine was unjust. Peter Lombard argued that unbaptized infants received only "the penalty of being condemned" and do not receive the more painful "penalty of the senses." Although they are condemned, that condemnation does not include the experience of the physical pain of hell. This idea is often referred to as "limbo," although this has never become part of the official teaching of any Christian body. It is reflected in Dante's description of hell, which we considered earlier (p. 228).

2 *Infant baptism is grounded in the covenant between God and the church.* Many Protestant writers have sought to justify the practice of infant baptism by seeing it as a sign of the covenant between God and his people. The baptism of infants inside the church is regarded as a direct counterpart to the Jewish rite of circumcision. Although this idea can be found in the patristic period, the approach is developed most rigorously by the Swiss reformer Huldrych Zwingli. Zwingli argued that the Old Testament stipulated that male infants born within the bounds of Israel should have an outward sign of their membership of the people of God. The outward sign in question was circumcision – that is, the removal of the foreskin. Infant baptism was thus to be seen as analogous to circumcision – a sign of belonging to a covenant community. Zwingli argued that the more inclusive and gentle character of Christianity was publicly affirmed by the baptism of both male and female infants; Judaism, in contrast, recognized only the marking of male infants. The more gentle character of the gospel was publicly demonstrated by the absence of pain or the shedding of blood in the sacrament. Christ suffered – both in being circumcised himself, in addition to his death on the cross – in order that his people need not suffer in this manner.

3 *Infant baptism is unjustified.* The rise of the radical reformation in the sixteenth century, and subsequently Baptist churches in England during the seventeenth century, witnessed a rejection of the traditional practice of baptizing infants. Baptism was to be administered only when an individual showed signs of grace, repentance or faith. According to this approach, the silence of the New Testament on the matter is to be taken as indicating that there is no biblical warrant for the practice whatsoever.

In part, this position rests upon a particular understanding of the function of sacraments in general, and baptism in particular. A long-standing debate within the Christian tradition centers on whether sacraments are causative or declarative. In other words, does baptism cause forgiveness of sin? Or does it signify or declare that this forgiveness has already taken place? The practice of "believer's baptism" rests upon the assumption that baptism represents the public declaration of faith upon the part of a converted individual.

Conversion has already occurred; baptism represents the public declaration that this has taken place. There are parallels between this position and that of Zwingli, noted above; the essential difference between Zwingli and this Baptist position is that the event which baptism publicly declares is interpreted differently. Zwingli understands the event in question to be birth into a believing community; more Baptist writers understand it to be the dawn of a personal faith in the life of an individual.

James Robinson Graves (1820–93), probably the most significant intellectual force in the early period of the Southern Baptist Convention, sets out three essential characteristics of baptism: the proper subject (a believing Christian); a proper mode, which is total immersion and baptism in the name of the Trinity; and a proper administrator, who must be "an immersed believer, acting under the authority of a gospel church."

In more recent times, infant baptism has been subjected to intense negative criticism in the writings of the twentieth-century Swiss theologian Karl Barth, who directs three major lines of criticism against the practice, as follows.

1   It is without biblical foundation. All the evidence points to infant baptism having become the norm in the postapostolic period, not the period of the New Testament itself.
2   The practice of infant baptism has led to the disastrous assumption that individuals are Christians as a result of their birth. Barth argues, in terms which remind many of Dietrich Bonhoeffer's idea of "cheap grace," that baptism devalues the grace of God, and reduces Christianity to a purely social phenomenon.
3   The practice of infant baptism weakens the central link between baptism and Christian discipleship. Baptism is a witness to the grace of God, and marks the beginning of the human response to this grace. In that infants cannot meaningfully make this response, the theological meaning of baptism is obscured.

The practice of infant baptism – in, for example, the Catholic church – leads to the process of Christian initiation having at least two phases. First, the person is baptized as an infant. The infant has no faith, but relies upon the faith of the church and the commitment of the parents to bring the infant up within a Christian environment, and teach and embody the Christian faith in the home. Second, at confirmation, when the child is able to affirm the Christian faith in his or her own right. Within the Catholic tradition, baptism is carried out by a local priest, whereas confirmation is carried out by the bishop, as a representative of the whole church. However, the Orthodox church has always insisted on the continuity between baptism and confirmation (known as "chrismation," on account of the use of oil to anoint the person being confirmed in this way), and thus aims to allow the same priest to baptize and confirm a given person.

The Eucharist

The origins of the Christian practice of using bread and wine in public worship goes directly back to Jesus. It is clear from the New Testament witness that Jesus expected his church to continue to use bread and wine in remembrance of him.

The Eucharist in the New Testament

1   Jesus' Institution of the Eucharist (Luke 22:14–20)

And when the hour came, [Jesus] sat at table, and the apostles with him. And he said to them, "I have earnestly desired to eat this passover with you before I suffer; for I tell you I shall not eat it until it is fulfilled in the kingdom of God." And he took a cup, and when he had given thanks he said, "Take this, and divide it among yourselves; for I tell you that from now on I shall not drink of the fruit of the vine until the kingdom of God comes." And he took bread, and when he had given thanks he broke it and gave it to them, saying, "This is my body which is given for you. Do this in remembrance of me." And likewise the cup after supper, saying, "This cup which is poured out for you is the new covenant in my blood."

2   Paul's Reference to the Eucharist at Corinth, c.52
(1 Corinthians 11:23–6)

For I received from the Lord what I also delivered to you, that the Lord Jesus on the night when he was betrayed took bread, and when he had given thanks, he broke it, and said, "This is my body which is for you. Do this in remembrance of me." In the same way also the cup, after supper, saying, "This cup is the new covenant in my blood. Do this, as often as you drink it, in remembrance of me." For as often as you eat this bread and drink the cup, you proclaim the Lord's death until he comes.

STUDY PANEL 42

It is clear that Christians obeyed this explicit command of Jesus from the earliest of times. The Acts of the Apostles reports that the disciples were "breaking bread" within weeks of the death and resurrection of Jesus. Paul's first letter to the Corinthians explicitly refers to the practice in the most solemn of terms, making it clear that Paul is passing on something of the utmost importance to his readers. Justin Martyr, writing about 165, indicates that the normal practice had by then been established as reading and expounding the Bible, followed by giving thanks and distributing the bread and the wine (see p. 360). Note that the wine in question was always mixed with water. The reason for this practice is unclear; it may have been a practical measure designed to avoid dehydration on the part of those receiving the wine. Theological explanations of the practice soon developed, including the idea that the mingling of the wine and water symbolized the mingling of Jesus Christ and his people.

This fundamental pattern, in a wide variety of forms, has passed into modern Christian practice. One major difference between Christians should, however, be noted at this point. As a general rule, Catholics have taught that only priests are permitted to receive *both* the bread and the wine at communion; Protestant churches permit both priests and laity to receive both bread and wine. The origins of the Catholic practice of denying the wine to the laity remains uncertain; it may represent the outcome of a practical desire to avoid spillage. Although the Second Vatican Council clearly wished to encourage the laity to receive the wine as well as the bread, this remains the exception rather than the rule. In the Orthodox church, both priests and laity are permitted to receive both bread and wine, although the general practice is for the communion to be received from a spoon, which contains the bread to which a few drops of wine have been added. The more general western custom is the direct handing of the bread to the communicant.

STUDY PANEL 43

Eucharist, Mass, or Supper: What's in a Name?

Christians have proved unable to agree on the best way to refer to the sacrament which focuses on the bread and wine. The main terms used to refer to it are the following. Note the specific associations of each word with particular Christian traditions.

The Mass
This term derives from the Latin word *missa*, which really just means "a service of some sort." As the main service of the western church in the classic period was the breaking of the bread, the term came to refer to this one service in particular. The term "mass" is now especially associated with the Catholic tradition.

Study Panel 43 Continued

Eucharist
This term derives from the Greek verb *eucharistein*, and means "a thanksgiving." The theme of thanksgiving is an important element of the breaking of the bread, making this an entirely appropriate term for the service in question. The term "eucharist" is particularly associated with the Greek Orthodox tradition, but has found acceptance beyond this.

Holy Communion
The phrase "holy communion" points to the idea of "fellowship" or "sharing." It highlights both the bond of fellowship between Jesus and the church, and also between individual Christians. The term is used in more Protestant circles, particularly in churches tracing their origins back to the English Reformation.

Lord's Supper
This phrase picks up the theme of the breaking of the bread as a memorial of the last supper. To share in the "Lord's Supper" is to recall with thanks all that Jesus achieved for believers though his death on the cross. The term is used in more Protestant circles, particularly in churches tracing their origins back to the English Reformation. This is sometimes abbreviated to the simple term "supper."

What happens at the eucharist? In what way do the eucharistic bread and wine change, if any, as a result of being used in this service? A number of approaches to the question have been explored during the centuries, of which the following are of especial importance.

1 *Transubstantiation.* This doctrine, formally defined by the Fourth Lateran Council (1215), rests upon Aristotelian foundations – specifically, on Aristotle's distinction between "substance" and "accident." The substance of something is its essential nature, whereas its accidents are its outward appearances (for example, its color, shape, smell and so forth). The theory of transubstantiation affirms that the accidents of the bread and wine (their outward appearance, taste, smell, and so forth) remain unchanged at the moment of consecration, while their substance changes from that of bread and wine to that of the body and blood of Jesus Christ.

This approach was criticized by Protestant theologians, especially at the time of the Reformation, for introducing Aristotelian ideas into theology. It was not until 1551 that the Council of Trent finally set forth the positive position of the Roman Catholic church in the "Decree on the most holy sacrament of the eucharist." Up to this point, Trent had merely criticized the reformers, without putting forth a coherent alternative position. This deficiency was now remedied. The decree opens with a vigorous affirmation of the real substantial presence of Christ: "After the consecration of the bread and wine, our Lord Jesus Christ is truly, really and substantially contained in the venerable sacrament of the holy eucharist under the appearance of those physical things." The council vigorously defended both the doctrine and the terminology of transubtantiation. "By the consecration of the bread and wine a change is brought about of the whole substance of the bread into the substance of the body of Christ and of the whole substance of the wine into the blood of Christ. This change the Holy Catholic church properly and appropriately calls transubstantiation."

2   *Consubstantiation*. This view, especially associated with Martin Luther, insists upon the simultaneous presence of both bread and the body of Christ at one and the same time. There is no change in substance; the substance of both bread and the body of Christ are present together. The doctrine of transubstantiation seemed to Luther to be an absurdity, an attempt to rationalize a mystery. For Luther, the crucial point was that Christ was really present at the eucharist – not some particular theory as to how he was present. Luther deploys an image borrowed from Origen to make his point: if iron is placed in a fire and heated, it glows – and in that glowing iron, both the iron and heat are present.

3   *A Real Absence: Memorialism*. This understanding of the nature of the eucharist is especially associated with Huldrych Zwingli. The eucharist is "a memorial of the suffering of Christ, and not a sacrifice." Zwingli insists that the words of Jesus "this is my body" cannot be taken literally, thus eliminating any idea of the "real presence of Christ" at the eucharist. Just as a man, on setting off on a long journey from home, might give his wife his ring to remember him by until his return, so Christ leaves his church a token to remember him by until the day on which he should return in glory.

The Christian Year

Christianity is not just a set of ideas; it is a way of life. Part of that life is a richly structured yearly pattern of life, in which various aspects of the

Christian faith are singled out for particular attention during the course of a year. The two such festivals which are most familiar outside Christian circles are Christmas and Easter, celebrating the birth and resurrection of Jesus respectively. This section will focus on the major festivals of the Christian year, explaining their religious basis and noting some of the customs which have come to be attached to them in parts of the Christian world.

It should be noted that there are major variations within the Christian world over the festivals of the Christian faith. In general terms, evangelical and charismatic Christians tend to place a relatively low value on such festivals, whereas Catholic and Orthodox Christians tend to place a considerably greater emphasis upon them. Indeed, the importance attached by Christians to festivals such as Advent and Lent is generally a useful indication of the type of Christianity which they have adopted. Festivals tend to fall into a number of different categories.

A major distinction is drawn between *fixed and moveable feasts*. A "fixed feast" refers to a festival which takes place on the same date each year. Thus in the western church, Christmas Day is invariably celebrated on 25 December. Other feasts are determined with reference to events whose dates vary from year to year. For example, the date of Easter is determined in relation to the full moon, and could fall at any point between 21 March and 25 April. A series of other festivals is dependent on the date of Easter, as follows:

Ash Wednesday, which falls forty weekdays before Easter Day.
Maundy Thursday, which is the Thursday before Easter Day.
Good Friday, which is the Friday before Easter Day.
Ascension Day, which is the fortieth day after Easter Day (and thus always falls on a Thursday).
Pentecost, which is the fiftieth day after Easter Day (and thus always falls on a Sunday).
Trinity Sunday, which is the Sunday following Pentecost.

Other festivals focus on individual saints, some of which have particular regional or professional associations. Examples of these associations include:

St David, patron saint of Wales, whose feast is observed on 1 March.
St Patrick, patron saint of Ireland, whose feast is observed on 17 March.
St Cecilia, patron saint of church music, whose feast is observed on 22 November.
St Christopher, patron saint of travellers, whose feast is celebrated in some parts of the church on 25 July.

In each case, the association of saints with a particular profession is usually linked with events in their lives. Other saints have developed associations with no apparent connection with their original figure. For example, St Valentine is thought to have been a Roman Christian who was martyred at Rome in the third century. His feast day, which is celebrated on 14 February, now has strong associations with personal romance in some western societies.

In addition to festivals, two periods are often observed as times of fasting or penitence – Advent and Lent. While many Christians no longer observe the tradition of fasting once associated with these periods, particularly during the Middle Ages, some continue to regard these as being of importance as times of personal reflection or penitence.

In what follows, we shall explore the highlights of the western Christian year, which have a major impact on the way in which many Christian churches worship and pray, and which often percolate into society as a whole. In each case, the foundation of the festival or season will be noted, and some of the customs which have come to be associated with it noted. The order in which the festivals will be discussed is chronological rather than alphabetical. However, it is important to make the point that the Orthodox church follows a somewhat different understanding of the Christian year, which will be set out briefly in what follows.

The Orthodox church follows a liturgical year which is broadly divided into three parts, focusing on Easter. These three parts are the *triodion*, the *pentecostarion*, and the *octoechos*. We shall explore each of these briefly. The "triodion" refers to the ten weeks prior to Easter; which can be seen as a preparation for this great festival. The "pentecostarion" refers to the entire Easter period, which is understood to embrace the period between Easter and the Sunday after Pentecost (in the western church, this final date is often celebrated as "Trinity Sunday"). The "octoechos" refers to the remainder of the year. However, our attention focuses particularly on the western Christian calendar. The western Christian year opens with the time of advent, to which we now turn.

Advent

The term "Advent" derives from the Latin word *adventus*, meaning "coming" or "arrival." It refers to the period immediately before Christmas, during which Christians recall the background to the coming of Jesus. Traditionally, four Sundays are set apart in order to prepare for the full appreciation of Christmas, of which the first is referred to as "Advent Sunday," and the final as the "Fourth Sunday in Advent." This period of four Sundays is often observed by the making of "advent crowns," consisting of four candles in a wooden or metal frame. A candle is then lit for each of the four Sundays in Advent. Some churches use purple clerical clothing at this time as a symbol of the need for penitence (a custom which also applies to Lent, which also has a penitential character).

Strictly speaking, Advent is intended to focus on the relationship of two "advents" or "comings" of Jesus: his first coming in humility, during his time on earth (which is especially associated with Christmas); and his second coming in glory as judge, which will take place at the end of time.

A Special Prayer for Advent

Almighty God,
give us grace to cast away the works of darkness,
and to put on the armor of light,
now in the time of this mortal life,
in which your Son Jesus Christ came to us in great humility,
so that on the last day, when he will come again in his glorious majesty
to judge the living and the dead,
we may rise to eternal life.

STUDY PANEL 44

Christmas

Christmas is a fixed or immoveable feast, and is always celebrated on 25 December. It must be stressed that this has never been understood to mean that Christians believe that Jesus was born on this date; rather, this date was chosen for the celebration of the birth of Jesus, irrespective of the precise date of that birth. It is likely that the date was chosen at Rome during the fourth century to provide a Christian alternative to a local pagan festival. The date of the festival is actually something of an irrelevance, despite the association with the imagery of winter and snow found in many Christian writings originating in the northern hemisphere.

The central theme of Christmas is the birth of Jesus, which is often commemorated in special carol services. Of these, the most famous is widely regarded as the "Service of Nine Carols and Lessons" associated with King's College, Cambridge. The nine lessons (that is, readings from the Bible) are designed to trace the steady progress of God's work of redemption in the world, beginning with the call of Israel, and culminating in the coming of Jesus Christ.

Many customs have come to be associated with Christmas, the more famous of which have their origins in the nineteenth century. "Santa Claus" is an American corruption of the Dutch form of "Saint Nicolas," the patron saint of children. This saint was celebrated on 6 December by the giving of gifts to children. Dutch settlers in New Amsterdam (later renamed "New York") brought this custom to the New World, where it became firmly established, and became merged into the festival of Christmas itself. The practice of bringing a Christmas tree into houses and decorating it had its origins in Germany, and was brought to England in the 1840s by Queen Victoria's husband, Prince Albert. The origins of this custom in Germany go back to the dawn of its Christian history, when missionaries were confronted with pagan beliefs concerning tree-gods.

Epiphany

The unusual name of this festival derives from the Greek word *epiphaneia*, which literally means "manfestation" or "making known." The festival takes place on 6 January. In the eastern church, the festival is specifically linked to the baptism of Jesus. In the western church, however, it is linked with the visit of the "wise men" or "Magi" to the infant Jesus. The festival is understood to mark the beginning of the long process by which the identity and significance of Jesus was "made known" to the world. The visit of the Magi (described in Matthew 2:1–11) is here seen as an anticipation of the recognition and worship that would subsequently be associated with the ministry of Jesus in Galilee and Judea, which culminated in the resurrection.

Lent

The period of Lent begins with Ash Wednesday, which falls in the seventh week before Easter. The term "Ash Wednesday" needs explanation. The Old Testament occasionally refers to putting ashes on one's face or clothing as a symbol of repentance or remorse (e.g., Esther 4:1; Jeremiah 6:26). Lent is seen as a period of repentance; the wearing of ashes was therefore seen as a proper external sign of an inward attitude of remorse or repentance. In earlier periods in the history of the church, particularly during the Middle Ages, the first day of Lent was therefore marked by imposing ashes on the heads of the clergy and people. In more recent years, the ashes in question are made by burning the palm crosses handed out on Palm Sunday during the previous Lent. The theme of repentance is also symbolized in some churches in purple clerical dress during this season.

Lent is widely regarded as a time of preparation for Easter, and in the past

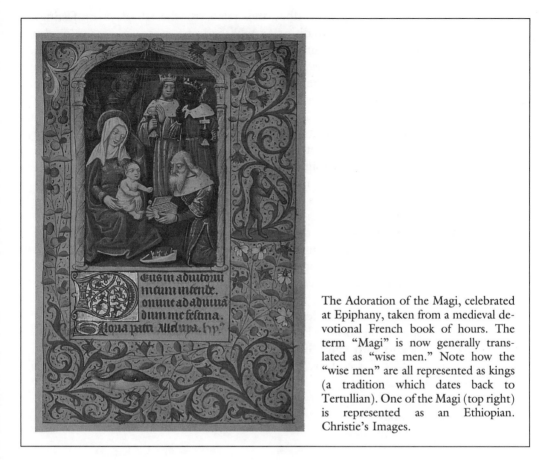

The Adoration of the Magi, celebrated at Epiphany, taken from a medieval devotional French book of hours. The term "Magi" is now generally translated as "wise men." Note how the "wise men" are all represented as kings (a tradition which dates back to Tertullian). One of the Magi (top right) is represented as an Ethiopian. Christie's Images.

was widely associated with a period of fasting. Lent is based on the period of forty days spent by Jesus in the wilderness before the beginning of his public ministry in Galilee (see pp. 89–90). Just as Jesus fasted for forty days, so his followers were encouraged to do the same thing. A period of forty days of fasting before Easter was thus encouraged. The origins of this seem to go back to the fourth century. In earlier periods, a shorter period of fasting was recommended (two or three days). The precise nature of the "fasting" varied from one location and period to another. In general terms, the western church has understood "fasting" primarily in terms of a reduced intake of food, and eating fish rather than meat. The emphasis has generally been placed on devotional reading or attendance at church rather than fasting.

An issue which needs to be noted at this point concerns the length of Lent. The period intervening between Ash Wednesday and Easter Day is actually 46 days. So how does this relate to the 40 days of fasting? The answer lies in the tradition, established at a very early stage in the development of Christianity, that every Sunday was to be regarded as a celebration of the resurrection of Christ. For this reason, fasting was forbidden on Sundays. The period of 46 days thus consists of 40 days of fasting, plus the six Sundays which fall between Ash Wednesday and Easter Day.

One of the most interesting customs linked with Lent concerns the day before Lent begins. As noted above, Lent begins on a Wednesday. The day before this therefore signified the last day before this official period of fasting began. In England, this day was called "Shrove Tuesday," although it is more widely known as "Pancake Tuesday." The origins of this name lie in the practice of clearing out larders immediately before Lent. The simplest way of using up the accumulation of eggs, flour and milk and other ingredients was to make pancakes. The same day is referred to as "Mardi Gras" in some European countries and their colonies, and is marked by major carnivals, such as that now associated with Rio de Janiero in Brazil.

The final week of Lent, leading up to Easter Day itself, should be singled out for special mention. This period, which is generally known as "Holy Week," begins with Palm Sunday (the Sunday before Easter) and ends on the day before Easter Day. It includes four days which are worth special mention. These are:

Palm Sunday
Maundy Thursday
Good Friday
Holy Saturday

(Note that Easter Day – which is always a Sunday – follows immediately after Holy Saturday. However, Easter Day is seen as lying outside the season of Lent, and marks the end of the period of fasting.) We shall consider each of these four days within Holy Week separately.

Palm Sunday refers to the Sunday immediately before Easter. It commemorates the triumphal entry of Jesus into Jerusalem, during which the crowds threw palm fronds into his path (see Matthew 21: 1–11). This day, which marks the beginning of Holy Week, is now widely marked by the distribution of crosses made from palm fronds to congregations.

Maundy Thursday focuses on one of the final acts concerning Jesus to be related in John's Gospel – the washing of the disciples' feet by Jesus (John 13:1–15). The ceremony of the "washing of the feet" of members of the congregation came to be an important part of the liturgy of the medieval church, symbolizing the humility of the clergy, in obedience to the example of Christ. The unusual term "Maundy" is related to this medieval practice. In the Middle Ages, church services were held in Latin. The opening words of a typical service on this day are based on the words of Jesus recorded in John 13:34): "A new command I give you: Love one another. As I have loved you, so you must love one another." In Latin, the opening phrase of this sentence is "*mandatum novum do vobis.*" The word "Maundy" is a corruption of the Latin word "mandatum" ("command").

In England, a particularly interesting ceremony has come to be associated with this day. As an affirmation of humility, the monarch would wash the feet of a small number of his or her subjects. This has now been replaced by the ceremony of the "Maundy Money," in which the monarch distributes specially minted coins to the elderly at cathedrals throughout England.

Good Friday is marked as the day on which Jesus died on the cross. It is the most solemn day in the Christian year, and is widely marked by the removal of all decorations from churches. In Lutheran churches, the day was marked by the reading of the passion narrative in a gospel, a practice

The traditional Maundy Service, showing Queen Elizabeth II distributing the Maundy Money to pensioners at Norwich Cathedral on 4 April 1996. Popperfoto.

which lies behind the "passions" composed by Johann Sebastian Bach (1685–1750). Both the St Matthew Passion and the St John Passion have their origins in this observance of Good Friday. The practice of observing a period of three hours' devotion from 12.00 midday to 3.00 p.m. on Good Friday has its origins in the eighteenth century. The "Three Hours of the Cross" often take the form of an extended meditation on the "Seven Last Words from the Cross," with periods of silence, prayer, or hymn-singing.

The events of Good Friday are also marked dramatically in various ways throughout the world. Perhaps the best known of these is the enactment of the passion and death of Christ which takes place every ten years in the little Upper Bavarian village of Oberammergau. As a way of expressing their gratitude to God for delivering them from the plague in 1633, the villagers undertook to act out the passion and death of Christ every decade. The event, which lasts six hours and involves about 700 people, is now a major tourist attraction. In the Philippines, the only Asian nation in which Christianity is the dominant religion, Good Friday is marked with particular fervor. In villages and towns throughout the nation, the crucifixion of Christ is re-enacted by young men who are willing to be nailed to crosses briefly as a sign of their commitment to the Christian faith.

Holy Saturday refers to the final day of Lent, immediately before Easter Day. Especially in the Eastern Orthodox churches, the day is marked by the "Paschal Vigil" – a late evening service, which leads directly into the following Easter Day, making extensive use of the imagery of light and darkness.

Easter

Easter Day marks the resurrection of Jesus, and is widely regarded as the most important festival of the Christian year. The religious importance of the festival is of fundamental importance. In the first place, it affirms the identity of Jesus as the risen Savior and Lord. In the Orthodox tradition, this point is often made through icons or pictures in churches, which show a triumphant and risen Christ (often referred to as *Christos pantocrator*, "Christ the all-powerful") as ruler over the universe as a result of his being raised from the dead. In the second place, it affirms the Christian hope – that is, the fundamental belief that Christians will be raised from the dead, and hence need fear death no more. Both these themes dominate Easter hymns and liturgies. A good example is provided by an early eighteenth-century collection of hymns known as the *Lyra Davidica*.

The *Lyra Davidica* on the Meaning of Easter

The *Lyra Davidica*, first published in 1708, includes a hymn which is widely used at Easter. The hymn consists of three stanzas, each of four lines. Each line ends with the word "Alleluia!" This has been omitted here, for the sake of clarity. Note the emphasis on Jesus enduring the pains of the cross for the salvation of the world, and the joy at the knowledge that Jesus is now risen from the grave.

> Jesus Christ is risen today,
> Our triumphant holy day;
> Who did once, upon the cross,
> Suffer to redeem our loss.
>
> Hymns of praise then let us sing,
> Unto Christ, our heavenly king;
> Who endured the cross and grave,
> Sinners to redeem and save.
>
> But the pains that he endured,
> Our salvation have procured;
> Now above the sky he's king,
> Where the angels ever sing!

STUDY PANEL 45

Similar themes to the hymn in Study Panel 45 are found in the poems of the Christian tradition. The words of the English poet George Herbert (1593–1633) illustrate this point well. For Herbert, Easter is about the believer's hope of rising with Christ:

> Rise, heart, thy Lord is risen. Sing his praise
> Without delays,
> Who takes thee by the hand, that thou likewise
> With him mayst rise.

In the Greek Orthodox church, the following traditional Easter greeting is widely used, and has become familiar within other Christian traditions during the present century:

Christos anestos ("Christ is risen").
Alethos anestos ("he is risen indeed").

Easter is marked in a wide variety of ways throughout the Christian world. In Catholic and Orthodox churches, particular emphasis is often

Table 15.1 Dates of Easter Sunday, 1995–2020

1995	16 April	2008	23 March
1996	7 April	2009	12 April
1997	30 March	2010	4 April
1998	12 April	2011	24 April
1999	4 April	2012	8 April
2000	23 April	2013	31 March
2001	15 April	2014	20 April
2002	31 March	2015	5 April
2003	20 April	2016	27 March
2004	11 April	2017	16 April
2005	27 March	2018	1 April
2006	16 April	2019	21 April
2007	8 April	2020	12 April

Once the date of Easter Day is established, the dates of all other related festivals can be established. Palm Sunday occurs one week earlier than Easter Day. Pentecost occurs seven weeks after Easter Day, and Trinity Sunday eight weeks later. Thus in the year 2000, the dates of these four festivals are as follows:

Palm Sunday	16 April
Easter Day	23 April
Pentecost	11 June
Trinity Sunday	18 June

placed on the importance of the symbolism of light and darkness. In the ancient church, baptisms took place on Easter Day, as a way of showing that the believers had passed from darkness to light, from death to life. The custom of giving Easter Eggs, widespread in western culture, seems to go back to the idea of an egg as a symbol of new life, pointing to the new life brought by the Christian gospel.

The liturgy and hymns of the Christian church are a particularly powerful witness to the importance of the message of the resurrection of Jesus Christ from the dead. The "Troparion of Easter" within the Byzantine Liturgy sets out clearly the significance of the Easter event for the world:

> Christ is risen from the dead!
> Dying, he conquered death!
> To the dead, he has given life!

Ascension

Ascension Day, which always falls on a Thursday, can be seen as completing the sequence of events celebrated at Easter. The feast recalls the final ascension of Christ after he had been raised from the dead, and recommissioned the disciples. Theologically, ascension marks the end of the period of appearances of the risen Christ to his disciples. These appearances, which are recorded in some detail in the gospels and hinted at in the letters of the New Testament, began immediately after the resurrection. The theme of "exaltation" is important at this point, in that Jesus is understood to have been exalted to the right hand of God.

Pentecost

Pentecost is the feast on which the church celebrates the gift of the Holy Spirit to the apostles, leading to the dramatic expansion of the church in its formative period. The Holy Spirit is of major importance to Christian thought and life. In recent times, the rise of the charismatic movement within the worldwide church has led to an increased awareness of the particular role of the Spirit. Pentecost falls on the fiftieth day after Easter. In the account of the death and resurrection of Jesus set out by Luke in his gospel and the Acts of the Apostles, there is a continuous sequence of events leading from the resurrection to the giving of the Spirit. After the resurrection, Jesus appears to his disciples on a number of occasions, to promise them the gift of the Holy Spirit. This is described as "the gift the Father promised," and is clearly linked with the theme of empowerment for evangelism and mission. John's gospel refers to Jesus promising the gift of the Spirit after he had been taken from his disciples. The basic theme is that the Spirit is given to the disciples after Jesus is no longer present with them physically, in order to remind them of his words and works. Note that the Spirit is referred to in John's gospel as the "Counselor." The Greek word *parakletos* could also be translated as "Comforter" or "Advocate."

New Testament References to the Gift of the Holy Spirit

John 14:16–17
And I will ask the Father, and he will give you another Counselor to be with you forever – the Spirit of truth. The world cannot accept him, because it neither sees him nor knows him. But you know him, for he lives with you and will be in you. I will not leave you as orphans; I will come to you.

John 14:25–6
All this I have spoken while still with you. But the Counselor, the Holy Spirit, whom the Father will send in my name, will teach you all things and will remind you of everything I have said to you.

STUDY PANEL 46

Study Panel 46 Continuted

John 16:13–15
I have much more to say to you, more than you can now bear. But when he, the Spirit of truth, comes, he will guide you into all truth. He will not speak on his own; he will speak only what he hears, and he will tell you what is yet to come. He will bring glory to me by taking from what is mine and making it known to you. All that belongs to the Father is mine. That is why I said the Spirit will take from what is mine and make it known to you.

Acts 1:1–8
In my former book, Theophilus, I wrote about all that Jesus began to do and to teach until the day he was taken up to heaven, after giving instructions through the Holy Spirit to the apostles he had chosen. After his suffering, he showed himself to these men and gave many convincing proofs that he was alive. He appeared to them over a period of forty days and spoke about the kingdom of God. On one occasion, while he was eating with them, he gave them this command: "Do not leave Jerusalem, but wait for the gift my Father promised, which you have heard me speak about. For John baptized with water, but in a few days you will be baptized with the Holy Spirit." So when they met together, they asked him, "Lord, are you at this time going to restore the kingdom to Israel?" He said to them: "It is not for you to know the times or dates the Father has set by his own authority. But you will receive power when the Holy Spirit comes on you; and you will be my witnesses in Jerusalem, and in all Judea and Samaria, and to the ends of the earth."

The specific event which is commemorated at Pentecost is the coming of the Holy Spirit, which is described in the Acts of the Apostles. Luke relates how the disciples had gathered together, when they were filled with the Holy Spirit. Luke's description of the event focuses on the impact of the event: the disciples were empowered to preach the gospel, and to break down the barriers of language separating them and their audiences. Theologically, the coming of the Spirit thus occupies a significant role in the scheme of salvation, in that it can be seen as a reversal of the "tower of Babel" (Genesis 11:1–32).

Pentecost is a major feast in the Christian year. In many Christian traditions, it is seen as second in importance only to Easter itself. Pentecost is sometimes referred to in older English writings as "Whitsun" (literally, "white Sunday"), on account of the tradition of the clergy wearing white robes on this occasion.

The Coming of the Holy Spirit

Acts 2:1–8

When the day of Pentecost came, [the disciples] were all together in one place. Suddenly a sound like the blowing of a violent wind came from heaven and filled the whole house where they were sitting. They saw what seemed to be tongues of fire that separated and came to rest on each of them. All of them were filled with the Holy Spirit and began to speak in other tongues as the Spirit enabled them. Now there were staying in Jerusalem God-fearing Jews from every nation under heaven. When they heard this sound, a crowd came together in bewilderment, because each one heard them speaking in his own language. Utterly amazed, they asked: "Are not all these men who are speaking Galileans? Then how is it that each of us hears them in his own native language?"

STUDY PANEL 47

Trinity

The final major feast of the Christian year is Trinity Sunday, which follows immediately after Pentecost. This festival completes the Easter sequence of events by celebrating the distinctively Christian doctrine of the Trinity, in which God is understood to be revealed as Father, Son, and Holy Spirit. It is placed immediately after Pentecost, which celebrates the gift of the Holy Spirit. The early church did not regard the doctrine of the Trinity as making the occasion of a chuch festival. The Orthodox Christian year, for example, does not include any direct equivalent of this festival (see p. 376). The feast first became of major importance in the Middle Ages, and was eventually given official sanction by John XXII in 1334. Trinity Sunday is the last major festival in the Christian year. The remainder of the year is reckoned in terms of "Sundays after Trinity," until the cycle resumes again on Advent Sunday.

The Liturgical Colors

The Catholic church prescribes the use of certain colors as a way of marking the seasons of the Christian year. These colors are reflected in the clothes (or "vestments") used at the eucharist, as well as the altar hangings and other items. There are five colors used in the modern Catholic church; examples of their use include the following:

White
This color is used to mark any church festivals which focus on Jesus (except when they commemorate his suffering, as on Good Friday). It is also used on Trinity Sunday, on any festival relating to Mary, and a number of other occasions.

Red
This color is used for the festivals of apostles and martyrs, and to mark Pentecost.

Green
This color is used on Sundays between Epiphany and Lent, and between Trinity Sunday and Advent.

Purple
This color is used to symbolize penitence, and is hence worn during the seasons of Advent and Lent.

Black
This color is used at funerals and other occasions which commemorate the dead.

Christianity and Culture

Christianity possesses the potential to change culture. This can be seen in both the ancient and the modern world. In the late third century, many Romans were convinced that the diminishing prosperity and influence of Rome were directly due to the rise of Christianity. The old religious cults were being abandoned in favor of Christianity. There is no doubt that one of the most significant contributing causes to the slow and inexorable death of classical pagan culture was the rise of Christianity. The same pattern can be seen in modern Chinese culture, where there is a widespread interest in Christianity amongst the younger generation. Traditional Chinese customs, such as "grave-sweeping" (in which children are regarded as being under an obligation to honor their ancestors by tidying their graves), are regarded with suspicion by younger Chinese Christians, who feel that the practice is linked with a set of beliefs which are not Christian. This traditional Chinese custom is being eroded, due to the growth of Christianity. Countless other examples could be given of cultural changes resulting from the growth of Christianity, including the decline of traditional religious beliefs and their associated practices in Africa and south-east Asia.

It must, however, also be appreciated that Christianity exists in a mutual relationship with culture. As the history of Christian expansion makes clear, Christians did not impose a uniform culture on peoples who had chosen to accept the Christian faith. It is quite clear that Christianity fostered an attitude of tolerance toward traditional cultural beliefs and norms, where these were not seen as having a direct relevance to the Christian faith. The wide range of cultural diversity within Christianity is perhaps one of the most striking differences between Christianity and Islam.

A wide range of traditional cultural customs and practices thus finds its way into Christianity. Some of these have achieved almost universal acceptance. Two examples will illustrate this. The traditional color associated with Christian bishops is purple. This was a sign of social status in the classical world, and was adopted by Christians as a means of designating the importance of bishops within the Christian community and beyond. Had Christianity had its origins in China, it is entirely possible that bishops might have worn yellow (the traditional Chinese color for royalty). This aspect of classical culture was regarded as acceptable by Christians, and thus eventually found its way within the church. A second example is the Christian practice (now widespread within western culture) of placing a wedding ring on the fourth finger of the bride's left hand. This reflects a traditional Roman custom, which Christians found perfectly acceptable – and thus incorporated into their marriage customs.

A further area of interest concerns the need for a supply of wine in order to comply with the explicit commandment of Jesus that this followers should use bread and wine to remember him. The great medieval monasteries in Spain, France, and Italy soon fell into the habit of establishing vineyards, in order to ensure a regular supply of communion wine. It was a monk – one Dom Perignon – who discovered how wine could be preserved by the use of the bark of the Portuguese cork oak.

In what follows, we shall explore two of the ways in which Christianity has influenced – and continues to influence – culture. It must be made clear that the restriction of the subject in this way is entirely due to lack of space. What follows must be regarded as illustrative of the way in which Christianity interacted with culture; in no way can this brief analysis be considered to be definitive!

Christian Symbolism: the Cross

We have already seen how the figure of Jesus Christ dominates the Christian faith. In particular, we noted how the death of Jesus on the cross is understood by Christians to be the foundation of the salvation of humanity. The cross is thus a symbol of salvation. It is also a symbol of the Christian hope, in that it affirms that death which has been defeated through the resurrection of Jesus. The cross – an instrument of execution – thus became a sign of the hope and transformation which are fundamental to Christianity.

The cross has been the universally acknowledged symbol of the Christian faith from a very early period, probably as early as the late second century. Indeed, it is fair to suggest that there is no symbol other than the cross which carries such weight, authority, or recognition within the Christian faith. Christians are baptized with the sign of the cross. Churches and other Christian places of meeting do not merely include a cross; they are often built in the shape of a cross. The Christian emphasis on the cross has had considerable implications for the design of churches. Indeed, it is probably at this point that Christian theology has had its most profound impact on western culture. To walk around a great medieval cathedral or church is to view theology embodied in stone.

Many Christians find it helpful to make the sign of the cross in times of danger or anxiety. The graves of Christians – whether Catholic, Orthodox, or Protestant – are marked with crosses. Careful studies of the origins and development of Christian symbolism have made it clear that the cross was seen as the symbol of the Christian gospel from the earliest of times. Even in the earliest writings of the New Testament, the phase "the message of the cross" is used as a shorthand summary of the Christian gospel (see 1 Corinthians 1:18–25). Two second-century writers bring out the importance of the cross with particular clarity: for Tertullian, Christians are "those who believe in the cross"; for Clement of Alexandria, the cross is "the supreme sign of the Lord." There is an anti-Christian graffito which has been preserved from ancient Rome, which depicts a man adoring a crucified man with the head of an ass. The inscription reads: "Anexamenos worships his god."

The final stage in the global acceptance of the cross as the supreme symbol of the Christian faith is generally regarded as having been the conversion of the Roman emperor Constantine (see pp. 253–4). At some point shortly before or after the decisive battle of the Milvian Bridge (312), Constantine saw a vision of a cross, which ordered him to place the sign on his soldiers' shields. During the reign of Constantine, crosses of various types were erected in Rome, and began to appear on Roman coinage. Crucifixion had continued as a means of execution under previous Roman emperors. Constantine outlawed the practice, and directed that the scaffolds used for execution would no longer be referred to as "crosses (*cruces*)" but as "patibula."

Early Christian writers regarded the cross as a teaching aid for the great themes of the Christian faith. Not only did it affirm the reality of salvation and hope in a world of death; it also affirmed the full humanity of Jesus. Early Christian writers were also prepared to read more ambitious ideas into the cross. As Justin Martyr argued, was there not a direct parallel between the Christian cross and the Platonic cosmic symbol of the Greek letter *chi* (which is cross-shaped: "X")? For an early writer, usually referred to as "pseudo-Hippolytus," the cross was like a tree rising from the earth to the heavens, around which the entire cosmos turned.

Pseudo-Hippolytus on the Cosmic Dimensions of the Cross

The means by which the death of Christ on the cross enabled humanity to be redeemed was the subject of considerable speculation in the early patristic period. This writing, which cannot be dated with certainty, views the cross against a cosmic background, arguing that the redemption achieved by Christ affected every aspect of the universe. The term "pseudo-Hippolytus" designates the unknown writer of this piece, who has clearly modeled his style on those of Hippolytus. Note in particular the way in which the cross is seen as of central importance to the well-being of the cosmos.

> This tree is for me a plant of eternal salvation. By it I am nourished, by it I am fed. By its roots, I am firmly planted. By its branches, I am spread out, its perfume is a delight to me, and its spirit refreshes me like a delightful wind. I have pitched my tent in its shadow, and during the heat I find it to be a haven full of perfume . . . This tree of heavenly proportions rises up from the earth to heaven. It is fixed, as an eternal growth, at the midpoint of heaven and earth. It sustains all things, the support of the universe, the base of the whole inhabited world, and the axis of the earth. Established by the invisible pegs of the Spirit, it holds together the various aspects of human nature in such a way that, divinely guided, its nature may never again become separated from God. By its peak which touches the height of the heavens, by its base which supports the earth, and by its immense arms subduing the many spirits of the air on every side, it exists in its totality in every thing and in every place.

STUDY PANEL 49

There is evidence that Christians in the first century were reluctant to portray the crucifixion of Jesus. However, it was one thing to make the sign of the cross; it was quite another to depict Jesus on the cross of Calvary, especially on account of the issues of taste and decency involved in portraying Jesus naked. However, these inhibitions were gradually overcome. Christian art, both in the east and west, began to focus on the crucifixion for devotional purposes. In response to the view that Jesus was purely divine, lacking any real human nature, Christian leaders encouraged artists to produce depictions of the crucifixion of Jesus as a way of emphasizing his full humanity. What better way of stressing the suffering and death of Jesus than to portray him on the cross? The implications of these considerations are considerable, and help us to understand the importance attached by many Christian writers to the devotional depiction of the crucifixion.

By the later Renaissance, the same attention once paid to the crucifixion was being devoted to other religious subjects. Renaissance artists regarded many incidents in the life of Jesus as of potential importance. Particular attention was paid to the Annunciation (that is, to the scene in Luke's gospel in which Gabriel informs Mary that she is to bear a son), the baptism of

The crucifixion of Jesus, as depicted by the celebrated fourteenth-century Italian artist Giotto in the lower church in the Italian town of Assisi, noted for its associations with St Francis. Sonia Halliday Photographs.

The Annunciation, by Malo
Vincenzo (1623–56). Christie's
Images.

Jesus, and the resurrection. Particularly important examples of works
depicting such scenes include Botticelli's *Annunciation* (1493) and
Grünewald's *Crucifixion* (1515–16). The appearance of the risen Jesus
to Mary Magdalene (John 20:17) was also the subject of many classic
works, including Fra Angelico's fresco *noli me tangere* ("do not touch
me"), painted over the period 1440–1 in the convent of San Marco in
Florence.

However, the cross remained of fundamental importance. This point
underlines the widespread use of crosses in Christian worship, both public
and private. Many churches are built in the shape of crosses, and display
crosses prominently within them. Of particular importance to many Christians is the *crucifix* – that is, a wooden carving of Jesus stretched out on the
cross, with the inscription "INRI" above his head (these letters spell out the

Latin words *Iesus Nazarenus Rex Iudaeorum*, which are to be translated as "Jesus of Nazareth, King of the Jews." See John 19:1–16 for the background). The crucifix is intended to remind Christians of the sufferings of Jesus, and thus emphasize the costliness and reality of the salvation which resulted from his death on the cross.

The cross has found its way into the symbolism of nations whose history has been steeped in the Christian faith. For example, the "Union Flag" of the United Kingdom consists of three different crosses – the crosses of St George (England), St Patrick (Ireland) and St Andrew (Scotland) – combined into a single design. Celtic crosses – that is, crosses with a circle embracing their four arms – are a particular feature of the Irish landscape. Other forms of the cross with particular national or regional associations include the "cross of Lorraine" and the "Maltese Cross." The background to the incorporation of this Christian symbol into national flags can probably be traced back to the second century. Justin Martyr and others then drew a parallel between the way in which conquering Roman armies marched behind their "banners and trophies (*vexilla et tropaia*)." In the same way, such writers argued, Christians marched behind the banner of the cross, which bore the trophy of a defeated death. This theme is brought out particularly clearly in the great processional hymn of Bishop Venantius Fortunatus (*c*.530–*c*.610), entitled *Vexilla Regis prodeunt* ("The banners of the king go forth").

Bishop Venantius Fortunatus on the Cross as a Banner

STUDY PANEL 50

In this processional hymn, Venantius Fortunatus compares the cross to a banner in a great triumphant procession. The cross symbolizes the reality of the victory gained by the death of Jesus on the cross. What follows is a selection of stanzas of the hymn, based on the translation by J. M. Neale. Note the emphasis in the first stanza on the fact that Christ is both the creator and redeemer of humanity.

> The royal banners forward go,
> The cross shines forth its mystic glow;
> Where he in flesh, our flesh, who made,
> Our sentence bore, our ransom paid.
>
> Upon its arms, like balance true,
> He weighed the price for sinners due;
> The price which none but he could pay,
> And spoiled the spoiler of his prey.

Although the cross dominates Christian symbols, it is important to note that other symbols were of importance in early Christianity. One of these may be noted. A fish was used as a symbol of Christian identity, on account of its potential as a teaching aid. The Greek term for fish is *ichthus*. The five letters of the Greek word for fish are ΙΧΘΥΣ ("i-ch-th-u-s"); these letters act as an acronym, spelling out the central Christian beliefs concerning the identity and significance of Jesus.

Greek letter	Greek word	English translation
Ι (iota)	Iesous	Jesus
Χ (chi)	Christos	Christ
Θ (theta)	Theou	of God
Υ (upsilon)	huios	Son
Σ (sigma)	soter	savior

The word *ichthus* thus spells out the Christological affirmation: "Jesus Christ, Son of God, Savior." References to "the fish" can be found in a number of early Christian writings, particularly on tombs. The Greek word *ichthus* and the symbol of a fish are both still widely used by Christians. If the automobile in front of you has a symbol of a fish on its bumper, it is probably owned by a Christian. If an organization or an Internet uniform resource locator (URL) has the word "ichthus" in it, you can be fairly certain it has something to do with Christianity.

Christian Music

The richness of Christian worship inevitably led to the adoption of all kinds of musical styles in the life of the Christian church. Although early Christian writers were hesitant over the use of music in worship, fearing that it would paganize what was a thoroughly Christian occasion, the value of music as an aid to Christian devotion was soon realized.

The most important early use of music can be traced back to the use of certain set forms of words, usually derived from the Bible, for monastic services (often known as "offices") – for example, the *Magnificat* ("My soul magnifies the Lord") at the early evening office of Vespers, and the *Nunc Dimittis* ("Lord, now allow your servant to depart in peace"), set for the late evening office of Compline. Each of these set pieces is known by its opening words in Latin. It was not long before Plainsong was introduced as a means of permitting these central texts to be sung, rather than just recited. The form of chanting which is probably best known in the modern world is "Gregorian chant," which is readily available in high quality modern recordings, these recordings often having been made in monastic settings.

Gradually, the patterns became more complex and ornate, with increasingly complex musical forms being used to express the various emotions associated with the biblical passages being sung in this way. Among the most important hymns set to music in this way, the following should be noted:

Te lucis ante terminum ("To you before the ending of the day"), a hymn sung at Compline, in which believers commit themselves to the care of God during the hours of darkness.

Pange lingua gloriosa ("Now, my tongue, the glorious mystery proclaiming"), a medieval hymn, often ascribed to Thomas Aquinas, which explains the meaning of the communion service. It was often used on Maundy Thursday (see pp. 380–1).

Puer natus ("A boy is born"), a short hymn sung at the entry of the choir, celebrating the birth of Jesus.

With the Reformation, controversy developed over the role of music. Zwingli and Calvin did not regard music as having a proper place in Christian worship. In other Protestant traditions, however, music continued to play an important role. Martin Luther composed settings for a number of traditional hymns, as well as writing hymns of his own. The most famous of these is *Ein feste Burg ist unsere Gott* ("A safe stronghold is our God"), which remains widely used in modern Protestant church life, particlarly in Lutheranism. The Church of England encouraged the setting of the Psalms and other canticles as chants.

The most dynamic form of musical development within Protestantism was due to the rise of Methodism, with John and Charles Wesley both recognizing the enormous potential of hymns to convey Christian teachings. Charles Wesley pioneered the use of "borrowing" secular tunes for Christian purposes. For example, the English composer Henry Purcell had written a superb tune to accompany John Dryden's text praising England, entitled "Fairest isle, all isles excelling." Wesley altered the words to reflect Christian interests, but retained Purcell's operatic tune, resulting in the well-known hymn: "Love divine, all loves excelling." Perhaps the most well-known of all Protestant musical pieces is Handel's *Messiah*, which sets to music a series of biblical texts, focusing on the coming of Jesus, and his subsequent glorification.

The most important musical developments within western Christianity, however, are linked with Catholicism. The great cathedrals of Europe demanded increasingly sophisticated and prestigious musical settings of standard Catholic liturgical texts. Of these, the most important were the text of the Mass and the Requiem. Virtually every major European composer contributed to the development of church music. Monteverdi, Haydn,

Mozart, Beethoven, Rossini, and Verdi are all examples of composers who made major contributions in this sphere. The Catholic church was without question one of the most important patrons of musical developments, and a major stimulus to the development of the western musical tradition.

Music continues to be an integral part of modern Christian life. The classics of the past continue to find service in modern Christian worship. However, it is clear that more popular styles of music are having an increasing influence on Christian worship, especially in evangelical and charismatic congregations.

Having explored some aspects of Christian life, we may now turn to look at the three main styles of Christianity found in the modern world: Catholicism, Orthodoxy and Protestantism.

1 What do Christians celebrate in the following festivals: Christmas; Easter; Pentecost?
2 Explain the importance of the following days in the Christian calendar: Maundy Thursday; Good Friday.
3 Why do some Christians not baptize infants?
4 Explain what Christians understand to be the importance of the ceremony involving bread and wine. What names are given to this? And what are the main understandings of the connection between this ceremony and Jesus himself?
5 Why is the cross such a central symbol for Christians?

STUDY QUESTIONS

16

CHAPTER

Modern Christianity:
an Overview of its Forms

In general terms, it is possible to divide modern Christianity into three broad categories, resulting from two major divisions within Christian history. The first such division, which is usually dated to 1054, saw the formal separation of the Latin-speaking western churches from the Greek-speaking eastern churches. The second division is associated with the European Reformation of the sixteenth century, and saw western Christianity split into two streams, usually referred to as "Catholicism" and "Protestantism." As a result of a complex series of differing political and social considerations, and subsequent internal divisions, a number of groups emerged within Protestantism. These groups are sometimes referred to as "denominations," such as Lutheranism, Episcopalianism, Methodism, and Presbyterianism.

However, the situation is more complex than this simple analysis might suggest. A number of churches do not really fit into this classification. An obvious example would be the Mar Thoma church, an indigenous church with its numerical center of strength in the south-east Indian state of Kerala. There is also considerable diversity within Protestantism, making it quite difficult to generalize concerning this movement. In what follows, an attempt will be made to sketch the distinctive ethos of each major constituent element of modern Christianity, as well as identifying those regions of the world in which it has a significant numerical presence. Further reading will be provided for those wishing to take their studies further.

A major feature of Christian life since the Second World War has been the ecumenical movement. This movement, which takes its name from the Greek word *oecumene* ("the whole world"), has aimed to work toward the cause of Christian unity, breaking down at least some of the barriers between the various Christian denominations. The movement has been hindered by a series of unrealistic expectations, such as the goal of visible unity between the churches. Nevertheless, it is clear that there has been a considerable improvement between various Christian groupings since 1945, both at the institutional and grass-roots level. In particular, there have been several significant dialogues between the major Christian denominations, allowing a better mutual understanding to result. It is now clear that there is no great enthusiasm for a merger between Catholics, Orthodox, and Protestants; for this reason, we shall consider the different characteristics of each of these movements, given that they will continue to be part of modern Christian life for the foreseeable future.

It must, however, be stressed that it is virtually impossible to convey the distinctive characteristics of the various styles of Christianity in writing. The reader who wants to understand Anglicanism, Catholicism, or any other form of Christianity will need to experience its regular worship and prayer life, and get to know those who have chosen to adopt this form of Christianity. Outsiders' perspectives have limited value; to understand any form of Christianity, you will need to get involved in it.

Catholicism

Catholicism (still sometimes referred to as "Roman Catholicism" by some) is at present by far the largest form of Christianity in the world. It has a particularly strong presence in western and central Europe. Several European nations, such as Ireland, Italy, and Poland have a strong sense of national identity which is closely linked with the Catholic church. As a result of the colonial expansion of Spain and Portugal in the sixteenth century, and Belgium and France in the nineteenth, there are particularly strong Catholic communities in North America, South America, southern Africa, and the Philippines. Parts of southern India, particularly the region of Goa, are also strongly Catholic. The former Portuguese colony of East Timor, annexed by Indonesia in the 1980s, remains a stronghold of Catholicism in a largely Islamic region of southeast Asia.

The distinctive ethos of Catholicism is difficult to summarize, on account of the complexity of the movement. However, the following points are important.

- The Catholic church has traditionally had a strongly hierarchical understanding of church government, focusing on the Pope, cardinals and bishops. The Pope has considerable influence over the appointment of bishops throughout the Catholic world. The College of Cardinals meets in secret sessions following the death of a pope, in order to elect his successor. A Cardinal is a priest or bishop, nominated by the Pope, who is entrusted with special administrative responsibilities.

- Partly on account of the importance of the Pope, the city of Rome has a particularly significant place within the Catholic ethos. The term "Roman Catholic," often used by Protestants to refer to this church, reflects the importance of Rome as a center for the movement. The Vatican City is widely regarded as the spiritual epicenter of Catholicism, and served as the venue for the two most recent councils: Vatican I (1869–70) and Vatican II (1962–5). Many Catholics will make a pilgrimage to Rome, on account of its strong historical associations with early Christianity (the apostles Paul and Peter being widely believed to have been martyred and buried in the city).
- The church is generally seen as a visible divine institution, whose structures are grounded in divine reality. Although this view of the church was modified slightly by Vatican II, it remains of importance for modern Catholicism. Particular importance is attached to the role of the teaching office of the church (usually referred to as the *magisterium*). The Council of Trent affirmed that no one was free to interpret Scripture "contrary to the sense in which Holy Mother Church, who is to judge the true sense and interpretation of the Holy Scriptures, has held and does hold."

Pope John Paul II on a visit to the English city of Coventry in May 1982. Popperfoto.

Lying behind this is a strongly corporate conception of the Christian life and of authority within the church, contrasting sharply with the individualism which has become characteristic of modern western culture during the twentieth century.

- The Catholic clergy are of major local importance in everyday Catholic life. Catholic clergy are not permitted to marry. This is one of the most noticeable practical differences between Catholicism and other forms of Christianity. Orthodoxy and Protestantism permit their priests (or ministers) to marry. Catholic priests are exclusively male. Although women are permitted to undertake some pastoral and liturgical responsibilities (the precise details of which vary from place to place), the Catholic church currently remains committed to an exclusively male priesthood.

- Catholicism is strongly liturgical. In other words, the forms of worship used by the church are fixed and laid down centrally, reflecting the conviction that the way in which the church prays and worships is inextricably linked to what the church believes (a point sometimes made using the Latin slogan *lex orandi, lex credendi*). The liturgy is seen as a public statement of the beliefs and values of the church, and a means by which continuity with the apostolic tradition is maintained. Until the Second Vatican Council, the language of the liturgy was Latin; the use of native languages is now permitted, although considerable care is taken to ensure that vernacular translations accurately reflect the sense of the original Latin versions of the liturgy.

- Catholicism is strongly sacramental, placing considerable emphasis on the "sacramental economy" (that is, the view that the benefits of Christ, which result from his death and resurrection, are communicated to the church through the sacraments). The Catholic church recognizes seven sacraments (whereas Protestants recognize only two). In terms of the regular liturgical life of the church, the most important sacrament is the Mass, which is understood to make present the body and blood of Christ.

- The monastic life continues to be of importance to shaping and articulating the Catholic ethos. Although there has been a decline in the traditional religious orders, they nevertheless continue to play a major role, such as acting as retreat centers for laity. Growing popular interest in Ignatian spirituality is of particular interest in this respect. The role of the religious orders in establishing and maintaining educational centers at every level should also be noted.

- Catholicism places an emphasis on the role of the saints in general, and the Virgin Mary in particular. The saints and Mary are understood to act as intercessors for both the living and the dead. The doctrine of the immaculate conception of Mary states that Mary was conceived without her sharing in the common human condition of original sin, thus providing a theological formalization for the high place of Mary in Catholic life and devotion. Nevertheless, Catholic writers are careful to draw attention to the distinction between the *veneration* due to Mary (which is honorific), and the *worship* which is due to God and to Jesus Christ as the Son of God.

Anyone wishing to gain a fuller understanding of the fundamental beliefs and practices of Catholicism is strongly recommended to study the 1994 *Catechism of the Catholic Church*, which sets out clearly and at length the basics of the Catholic faith.

Orthodoxy

Orthodoxy, whether in its Greek or Russian forms, represents a form of Christianity which retains a strong degree of continuity with the early Greek church, and traces its liturgy and doctrines directly back to the early church. Orthodoxy is numerically strongest in eastern Europe, particularly in Russia and Greece, where it has had a major influence in shaping a sense of national identity. However, it has also established a major presence in North America and Australia through emigration. The Australian city of Melbourne, for example, is home to one of the largest Greek Orthodox communities in the world.

Any attempt of describe the distinctive ethos of Orthodoxy would include the following elements.

- A very strong sense of historical continuity with the early church. Orthodoxy is thus strongly orientated towards the idea of *paradosis* ("tradition"), particularly the writings of the Greek fathers. Writers such as Gregory of Nyssa, Maximus the Confessor, and the writer who adopted the pseudonym "Dionysius the Areopagite" are of particular importance in this respect. Tradition is seen as a living entity, which remains essentially unchanged while being capable of meeting the new challenges of each succeeding age. This is reflected in the fixed liturgical forms used within Orthodoxy. Russian Orthodoxy places importance on the use of Old Slavonic in the liturgy, stressing both the theological and linguistic continuity with previous generations.
- Orthodoxy recognizes only seven Ecumenical Councils, and does not accept any council after the Second Council of Nicea (787) as having binding authority. Although local councils meet to deal with various matters, these are not understood to have the same authority as these earlier councils.

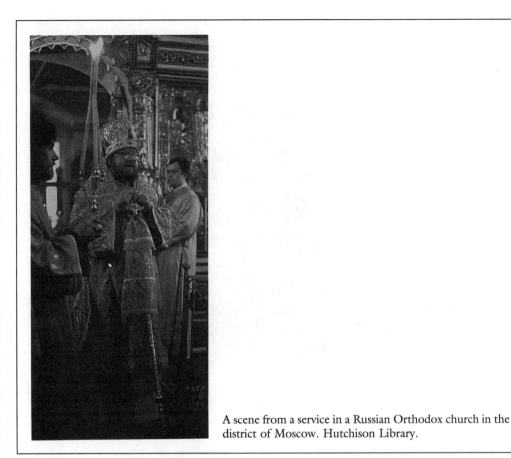

A scene from a service in a Russian Orthodox church in the district of Moscow. Hutchison Library.

- Orthodoxy has been very resistant to the ideas of authority which emerged within western Catholicism. In the twentieth century, increasing attention has also been paid by western theologians to the notions of "catholicity" which have been dominant in the Orthodox churches. This is often expressed using the Russian word *Sobornost*, which has no exact equivalent in other languages. While the term denotes the general idea of "universality," it also expresses the unity of believers within the fellowship of the church. The idea, which is developed most fully in the writings of Sergei Bulgakov and A. S. Khomiakoff, attempts to do justice to both the distinctiveness of the individual members of the church, and the overall harmony of its corporate life. This is linked with the notion of "conciliarity" (the Russian word *sobor* means "a council" or "an assembly"), by which the life of the church is governed in such a way

An icon from the Central Russian School, depicting the annuncia- tion, in which the angel Gabriel tells Mary she is to bear the Son of God. Christie's Images.

that authority is dispersed among all the faithful, rather that centralized and concentrated in any single quasi-papal figure.

- Theologically distinctive ideas include an insistence that the Holy Spirit proceeds from the Father alone (rather than, as in western churches, from the Father and the Son: see pp. 197–200), and the understanding of salvation as "deification." "God became human, in order that humans might become God." This theological refrain may be discerned as underlying much of the soteriological reflections of the eastern Christian tradition, both during the patristic period and in the modern Greek and Russian Orthodox theological traditions. As the citation suggests, there is an especially strong link between the doctrine of the incarnation and this understanding of salvation. For Athanasius, salvation consists in the human participation in the being of God. The divine Logos is imparted to humanity through the incarnation. On the basis of the assumption of a universal human nature, Athanasius concluded that the Logos did not merely assume the specific human existence of Jesus Christ, but human nature in general. As a consequence, all human beings are able to share in the deification which results from the incarnation. Human nature was created with the object of sharing in the being of God; through the descent of the Logos, this capacity is finally realized.

- The Orthodox use of icons – that is, pictures of Jesus Christ, Mary, or some other religious figure – is of particular importance. The strong emphasis on the incarnation of the Son of God is understood to have consequences for prayer and spirituality. Icons are "windows of perception," through which the believer may catch a glimpse of the divine reality.
- Monasteries continue to play a critically important role in the articulation and defense of the Orthodox ethos. Perhaps the most important monastic center remains Mount Athos, a peninsula stretching into the Aegean Sea. Most bishops are drawn from monasteries.
- Orthodox clergy are permitted to marry (providing they do so before ordination), unlike their Catholic counterparts. Bishops, however, are generally unmarried, on account of their predominantly monastic backgrounds. Orthodoxy insists that only males can be ordained, and rejects the possibility of female priests, largely on the basis of continuity with tradition on this matter.

Protestantism

The term "Protestantism" is widely used to refer to those churches which trace their historical origins back to the European Reformation of the sixteenth century. The term is potentially misleading, in that most Protestant churches stress their historical and theological continuity with the early church. It must be stressed that the term "Protestant" is not in tension with the idea of being "catholic." The orthographical distinction between "catholic" and "Catholic" is of critical importance! To be "Catholic" is to be "catholic" *in a particular way*, which Protestants reject. Anglican and Lutheran writers, for example, place particular stress on their continuity with the life and thought of the early church, and affirm their "catholic" credentials. Similarly, in 1536 John Calvin, the reformer of the city of Geneva, vigorously defended the Reformation against the charge that it had no place for the patristic heritage. In what follows, we shall follow the general convention of using the term "Protestant" to refer to those churches whose historical origins are to be traced back to the divisions which opened up in the sixteenth century.

Protestant churches have had particularly close links with the state in a number of areas of Europe. Lutheranism, for example, has had close links with the state in Scandinavia, just as various forms of Presbyterianism have been influential in Scotland and the Netherlands, and Anglicanism in England. Partly on account of those links, and more generally through their continuity with the mainline Reformation, these churches offer baptism to infants who are too young to confess the Christian faith. This serves to distinguish the Baptists, who insist that baptism should be administered only to those who are believing Christians (see p. 369).

The term "denomination" is often used to refer to specific Protestant churches, such as Lutheranism or Methodism. A number of trends have developed within Protestant denominations in recent times, of which two are of particular importance. Evangelicalism (see pp. 331–3) is now a major influence within most mainline Protestant denominations in the English-speaking west, although its influence has been, until relatively recently, significantly lesser in continental Europe. A number of independent churches have now sprung up with a distinctively evangelical ethos, especially in South America and southern Africa. The charismatic movement (see p. 334) has also been of significance in the life of many mainline Protestant churches, and its influence has also been felt within Catholicism. A number of specifically charismatic denominations (such as the Assemblies of God) are now of growing importance in global Protestantism. In what follows, we shall focus on five major Protestant denominations; it must be appreciated that the rapid growth of evangelicalism and the charismatic movement means that numerical growth within Protestantism is now increasingly likely to happen outside the mainline denominations.

All Protestant denominations permit their ministers to marry. In recent years, most – but not, it must be stressed, all – Protestant denominations have permitted women to be ordained to full-time ministry within the church. Other means by which Protestants can be distinguished from Catholics include the following:

- The authority of the pope is rejected. While some Protestants treat the Pope with respect, he is not regarded as carrying any moral or doctrinal weight for Protestants.
- Protestantism recognizes only two sacraments (see p. 367), and administers communion in both kinds (see p. 293). In other words, the laity are permitted to receive both bread and wine at communion. However, it should be noted that Methodism has traditionally insisted that unfermented grape juice, rather than wine, should be used at communion.
- A cluster of characteristic Catholic beliefs are rejected, or treated as strictly optional private beliefs for individuals rather than the official teaching of the denomination. These include: purgatory (see p. 228); the intercession of the saints, and any form of devotion to the Virgin Mary.

- Until the Second Vatican Council, the liturgy of the Catholic church was required to be read in Latin. This contrasted with the views of the reformers, who argued that all forms of public worship had to be in a language which the common people could understand.

Readers interested in following up on some of these historical and theological points are recommended to read works that deal with the history and theology of the Reformation, which will provide considerably more detailed explanations of these points, as well as expanding on them.

Anglicanism

"Anglicanism" is the term usually employed to denote the distinctive features of the *ecclesia Anglicana* – the national church of England, as it emerged from the sixteenth-century Reformation. The worldwide expansion of English influence, initially through the annexation of Ireland and Scotland, and subsequently through the colonization of North America in the seventeenth century, the Indian subcontinent in the late eighteenth century, and sub-Saharan Africa in the nineteenth, brought with it a significant enlargement of the sphere of influence of Anglicanism. The parody of Anglicanism as "the British empire at prayer" contains at least an element of truth; Anglicanism has exercised relatively little influence outside those realms once subject to British presence or rule.

The main features of Anglicanism are the following:

- Anglicanism is an episcopal church, which sees the episcopacy as a means of demonstrating historical continuity with the early church. This is of particular importance to the more catholic sections of the Anglican church.
- Particular importance is attached to the English city of Canterbury. The Archbishop of Canterbury is seen as the spiritual head of Anglicanism, although he lacks the powers invested in a pope. All the bishops of the Anglican churches are invited to Canterbury every ten years for the Lambeth Conference, which aims to review the directions taken by Anglicanism in the last decade, and plan for the future.
- Anglicanism is defined and distinguished theologically by the Thirty-Nine Articles.
- Anglicanism is a strongly liturgical church, which originally found one of its central foci on the Book of Common Prayer (1662), which embodied the "spirit of Anglicanism" in a fixed liturgical form. Anglical churches throughout the world have this in common, along with a common ecclesiastical structure. Yet the process of liturgical revision, which became of major importance in the 1970s, resulted in the Anglican churches in England, Canada, the United States, and Australia adopting

Salisbury Cathedral, seen from the south-west. The Anglican diocese and cathedral of Salisbury have often found their way into literary representations of the Church of England, including Anthony Trollope's celebrated portrayal of nineteenth-century Anglicanism in his *Barchester Chronicles*. Sonia Halliday Photographs.

different liturgical forms, thus severely weakening the theological convergence of the movement.

- The growing trend toward decentralization, linked with an increasing concern on the part of nations such as Australia and Canada to shake off their "colonial" image, has led to a new concern to develop distinctively national or ethnic approaches to Anglican identity. In its traditional forms, Anglicanism has been perceived as too "English" or "colonial" to maintain its credibility in the post-colonial era. As a result, Anglicanism has become increasingly diverse, reflecting its local concerns and resources. This trend gives every indication of continuing in the years ahead.
- Anglicanism is predominantly an English-language church, although there are small Anglican presences outside Anglophone contexts (such as Francophone Africa).

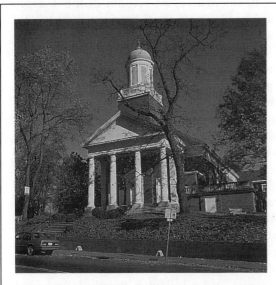

The Episcopal Church of the University of Virginia, Charlottesville, Virginia. Note the colonial style, typical of many buildings of this period. Hutchison Library.

The Baptists

The origins of the Baptist churches are to be found in the seventeenth century. The more radical sections of the Reformation had always insisted that the church was to be a pure society of believers, rather than a mixed body. During the seventeenth century, particularly in England, there was growing support not only for the idea that congregations should consist only of those who explicitly and publicly affirmed their faith, but for the related idea that baptism should be reserved only for those who affirmed their faith in this way. This contrasted with the Church of England, which permitted infants to be baptized (see p. 369).

The movement gained momentum in England during the nineteenth century, with great preachers such as C. H. Spurgeon drawing huge audiences for his sermons. The foundation of the Baptist Missionary Society (1792) by William Carey led to considerable effort being invested in mission. Baptist congregations were established in North America, where the movement has grown to have considerable influence in public life in the United States of America. The Southern Baptist Convention is one of the most important forces in modern American Christianity; its six seminaries have been of major importance in shaping the distinctive ethos of the denomination. Perhaps the best-known Protestant Christian of the twentieth century – Billy Graham – is a Baptist.

The Baptist ethos is difficult to summarize, on account of the diversity within the denomination worldwide. However, the following will be helpful in gaining something of an understanding of the movement.

- Baptists insist that baptism should be reserved for believers. Infant baptism is regarded as unjustified. This is probably one of the most distinctive aspects of the Baptist ethos.
- Baptists tend to be theologically conservative, placing a high value on the role of the Bible. The use of the term "the Bible Belt" to refer to the southern states of the USA reflects the importance of the Bible in Baptist church life, especially in preaching. Although the term "evangelicalism" is sometimes regarded with suspicion (it is seen as a "Yankee" – i.e., northern – word), it is clear that the southern Baptists are increasingly becoming evangelical in orientation.
- Baptist churches deliberately avoid the traditional form of church architecture, by which the altar is central and the pulpit to one side. This is seen as having the effect of focusing the attention of the congregation on the sacrament of the eucharist. Instead, Baptist church designs tend to place the pulpit at the center of things, to stress that the public reading of the Bible and the subsequent sermon preached on the biblical text are of central importance.
- Baptists have tended to be critical of fixed liturgies, seeing in them an unhealthy tendency toward a purely formal expression of faith, and a suppression of extempore prayer on the part of both minister and congregation.
- Baptist clergy are referred to as "ministers" (from the Latin word for "servant") or "pastors" (from the Latin word for "shepherd"). The term "priest" is completely avoided. The episcopal system of church government is rejected.

Lutheranism

Lutheranism is the form of Protestantism which derives directly from Luther's reformation of the German church in the 1520s. Lutheranism was initially restricted to parts of north-eastern Germany; however, by a gradual process of expansion, the movement established itself in Scandinavia and the Baltic states. Although there were early indications that Lutheranism might establish itself as the dominant form of Christianity in England during the late 1530s, it never gained the influence which some expected it to. The movement was active in missionary work, especially in India. However, the movement's greatest expansion came about through the emigration of Lutheran communities from Scandinavia and Germany to North America. The settlement of Swedish communities in Minnesota is a particularly good example of this phenomenon. Lutheran communities also settled in Australia through a similar process. As a result, Lutheranism today is to be found chiefly in Germany, Scandinavia, the Baltic states, and especially the northern states of the USA. North American and European Lutheranism have tended to pursue somewhat different agendas during the past century, reflecting their different contexts. However, the formation of the Lutheran World Federation has gone some considerable way toward giving Lutherans a common sense of identity and purpose.

The Lutheran ethos reflects, to some degree, the central themes of Luther's personal program of reformation, which stressed continuity with the medieval church while at the same time introducing doctrinal and other changes where these were regarded as necessary.

- Lutheranism is a strongly liturgical church, seeing the liturgy as a means of ensuring historical continuity with the past, and of maintaining doctrinal orthodoxy.
- Lutheranism is defined theologically by both the Augsburg Confession (1530) and the Formula of Concord (1577). As a result, the words "Augsburg" and "Concord" are frequently incorporated into the titles of Lutheran seminaries and publishing houses.
- Lutheranism retains a sacramental emphasis, going back to Luther, which is absent from many other Protestant denominations. It adopts a causative approach to baptism, arguing that baptism is "necessary and effectual to salvation." This contrasts with the view of other Protestant denominations (particlarly the Baptists), who tend to regard baptism as a sign of grace, rather than as something which is necessary before that grace can be given.

Methodism

Methodism was a movement within the Church of England, which subsequently gave birth to Methodism as a denomination in its own right. Its origins are especially associated with John Wesley (1703–91), a founder and early leader of the Methodist movement. Contrary to the intentions of Wesley, Methodism broke away from the Church of England, and became a distinct denomination. The distinctive emphasis of the early Methodists was the need for personal holiness. The term "Methodist" was originally a nickname, based on the methodical nature of the devotions and disciplines of the Wesleys and their circle. In general terms, Methodism has tended to be found primarily in English-speaking regions of the world, showing a parallelism with Anglicanism in this respect. As result of various union schemes, Methodism has ceased to exist as a distinct denomination in various parts of the world, including Canada and Australia. The formation of the World Methodist Council has gone some way toward maintaining Methodism as a distinct entity within global Christianity.

- Since its inception, Methodism has placed particular emphasis on the role of the laity. The office of the "lay preacher" illustrates this emphasis, which can also be illustrated in aspects of Methodist church government.
- Methodism has taken considerable trouble to attempt to integrate personal faith and social action, seeing the gospel as involving both personal and social transformation.
- Since the time of the Wesleys, Methodism has been characterized by a theological stance best described as "an optimism of grace." This contrasts with the more Calvinist approach to this issue adopted by Reformed churches.

The Reformed Churches

If the Lutheran churches owed their historical origins to Luther, the Reformed churches owed theirs to Calvin. Reformed versions of Christianity were soon established in western Europe, from where they spread to North America. In Europe, Scotland, and the Netherlands were soon established as particularly important centers of Reformed thought. In England, the two major Reformed traditions have been referred to traditionally as "Presbyterianism" and "Congregationalism," reflecting two different systems of church government. As a result of Dutch colonial policy during the nineteenth century, forms of Reformed Christianity were established in South Africa, the north-eastern parts of South America, and parts of south-east Asia. In the United States, Princeton Theological Seminary was established as a leading center of Presbyterian thought and practice. In recent years, South Korea has become a leading centre of Reformed church life, as a result of the very rapid growth of Christianity in that region. The World Alliance of Reformed Churches, constituted in its present form in 1970 (although tracing its origins back to 1875), provides a means of allowing the various Reformed churches to maintain their common identity.

The diversity within Reformed churches is such that it is difficult to generalize concerning them. However, the following aspects of the Reformed ethos are of importance.

- Reformed churches are generally governed by "presbyters" or "elders." (The word "Presbyterianism" derives from this practice.) Some Reformed churches regard the elders as ministers in their own right, with pastoral or teaching responsibilities; others see them as assistants, with specific responsibilities in relation to the administration and government of the church. The term "minister" is used.

- Reformed worship traditionally places considerable emphasis upon the reading and preaching of the Word of God. Holy Communion is celebrated regularly but infrequently. This emphasis upon preaching, rather than the sacraments, is especially evident from the regular Sunday worship of the Reformed churches.
- In the English-speaking west, and regions influenced by it, the Reformed faith is defined theologically by the Westminster Confession (1647). As a result, the word "Westminster" is frequently incorporated into the titles of Reformed seminaries and publishing houses.
- Most Reformed churches place an emphasis upon the sovereignty of God in predestination, which contrasts with the more "optimistic" view associated with Wesleyan Methodism.

Evangelicalism

As noted earlier, evangelicalism has become of major importance in the mainline Protestant churches since 1945 (see pp. 331–4). Although some new Protestant denominations have been formed which are explicitly evangelical in orientation, the general pattern which has emerged is that evangelicalism is a movement within the mainline denominations. Hence evangelicals within the Reformed churches retain much of the ethos of those churches (including its church structures), while supplementing these with at least some of the characteristics of evangelicalism, noted below. Similarly, evangelicals within Anglicanism adopt many of the characteristics of the latter (such as the episcopal system of church government, and the use of a fixed liturgy), while retaining an evangelical ethos within this church.

The four main distinctive features of the evangelical ethos are the following:

- Evangelicalism is strongly biblical in its emphasis. This is especially evident in the styles of preaching found within the movement. This emphasis is carried over into other aspects of evangelical life, including the importance attached to small Bible study groups within the life of the church, and to the regular reading of the Bible in personal devotion.
- Evangelicalism places a particular emphasis on the cross of Jesus. Although Jesus is of central importance to evangelicalism, its emphasis has tended to fall upon the saving death of Jesus on the cross. This is especially reflected in evangelical hymns and songs.
- Evangelicalism stresses the need for personal conversion. Considerable emphasis is placed on the dangers of "nominalism," meaning by this "a

purely formal or external acceptance of Christian teachings, without any personal transformation in consequence." Evangelical preaching often stresses the need for Christians to be "born again" (see John 3:1–16).

- Evangelical churches and individual evangelicals have a deep commitment to evangelism – that is, to converting others to the Christian faith. Billy Graham is a good example of a twentieth-century evangelical who has become well known on account of this emphasis. It should be noted that the words "evangelicalism" and "evangelism" are often confused, on account of their similar spelling. The former refers to a movement; the latter to an activity – but an activity which is especially associated with this specific movement.

The Charismatic Movement

The charismatic movement has grown dramatically during the twentieth century. Although there are some specifically charismatic denominations, such as the "Assembly of God," the charismatic movement (like evangelicalism) often takes the form of a trend within mainline denominations. It is also a growing presence within the Catholic church. The distinctive charismatic emphasis on the power and activity of the Holy Spirit is perhaps best seen in charismatic worship, which is generally characterized by its informality and exuberance, and the raising of hands upward as a sign of praise.

Among the distinctive features of a charismatic ethos, the following should be noted:

- Charismatic worship has evolved a distinctive approach to worship, which makes extensive use of reflective choruses and songs. These have been taken up by many non-charismatic churches. While all generalizations are dangerous, it is fair to suggest that charismatic worship songs often stress the positive feelings of believers toward God, Jesus or the Holy Spirit, and enhance these feelings by the repetition of key phrases or ideas.
- The idea of direct personal revelation through the Holy Spirit finds its expression in charismatic congregational life, with "words of knowledge" or "prophecy" being seen as ways in which God guides individuals or churches. The idea of some form of direct personal revelation often places charismatic Christians in conflict with evangelical Christians, who tend to stress that God's revelation and guidance is specifically contained in or channeled through the Bible.
- Charismatic worship is often characterized by the phenomenon known as "speaking in tongues." This phenomenon, which seems to be known to New Testament writers, generally takes the form of an ecstatic out-

pouring of feeling or emotion using words which appear unintelligible to outsiders. This phenomenon is particularly associated with classic Pentecostalism, which saw it as a major evangelistic tool. Although most charismatics would now question this, "speaking in tongues" remains an important aspect of much charismatic worship.

- The charismatic movement in general regards the events recorded in the history of the early church as being capable of being replicated today. Where some Christian writers argue that miracles (such as healings) were appropriate to the first phase of Christian expansion, but are no longer to be expected (a position often referred to as "cessationism"), charismatics generally argue that such miracles should be part of the ministry of the church. As a result, charismatic worship or other meetings may include healings or deliverances.

This brief survey of the major forms of Christianity in today's world brings to an end this introduction to Christianity. Restrictions on space have severely limited the amount of material which has been presented. However, it is hoped that what has been included will enable you to gain a deeper understanding and appreciation of the most influential religious movement in today's world. If this Introduction has left you feeling that you would like to know more, it will have served its purpose.

1 What practices or beliefs would allow you to identify a Catholic church, if you were to visit one?
2 Which Christian tradition places a considerable emphasis on icons? What role are they understood to play?
3 In what mays might you expect to distinguish an Anglican and a Baptist church?
4 Summarize the main points of difference between Catholicism and Protestantism.
5 How would you distinguish between an evangelical and a charismatic?

STUDY QUESTIONS

Christian Resources on the Internet

The World Wide Web (or WWW) is now a major resource for exploration of modern and classic Christianity, allowing access to an enormous variety of texts, debates, contemporary developments within different Christian traditions, and conferences via the Internet. It has now become of such importance that it is unthinkable for any book dealing with Christianity to ignore it. The present section aims to identify some of the key web site addresses which will be of interest to users of this textbook. They have been broken down into two general categories: subject indexes, which give access to a wide variety of resources; and selected sites, which provide access to more specific resources, usually grouped around a central theme or interest.

It should be noted that web site addresses are liable to change without notice. For this reason, the list of resources noted here will be updated regularly. Readers wishing to have access to an updated list should consult the Alister E. McGrath Home Page on the Oxford University Gandalf Starmaster network: http://users.ox.ac.uk/~mcgrath.

For those who are still not familiar with using the Internet, this section opens with a basic introduction to its terminology, and a guide to logging in to a Web site. Once you have mastered this, you will be able to cope on your own. Experienced surfers should skip this section.

An Introduction to the World Wide Web (WWW)

The World Wide Web (WWW) is a networked information retrieval system which works on the basis of *clients* and *servers*. A "server" is a delivery system, involving both a computer and the necessary software, which allows the system to offer a service to others. A "client" is a software application which allows the user to extract a service from a server at another location on the network. A "service provider" is an organization, such as Compuserve, which provides connections between your computer and other computers by the Internet. The Web is based on *hypertext*. This is a language which allows links to be established to other locations within the document which you are currently exploring (acting rather like bookmarks), or to completely different documents on another server. As a result, many servers now provide details of large numbers of Web sites of importance, grouped by subject, to which access can be had simply by clicking on the hypertext link. A typical browser, such as Netscape, displays hypertext in blue; additionally, the mouse pointer symbol will change from an arrow to a hand when it is placed over hypertext. To activate the link, simply click the mouse once over the link you wish to follow. The rest happens automatically.

Accessing the Internet

Each Web site has a specific address, referred to as the "uniform resource locator" (URL). The location typically identifies the type of service being offered (the prefix "http://www." means something like "a hypertext file on the World Wide Web"); the server (identifying the host computer); and the file reference (identifying the specific files you wish to access on this computer). You should enter the location exactly as it is printed. Please pay especial attention to the occasional use of upper-case letters and the "underline" (_) and "tilde" (~) characters. Above all, make sure that you use the forward slash "/" (to the bottom right of a typical AT keyboard) rather than the backward slash "\" (to the bottom left of a typical AT keyboard) when entering locations.

To help you get this right, you should practice logging on to a Web site. You should begin by following the instructions given by your service provider (Compuserve, America Online, Unipalm Pipex, etc.) for logging on to their networks. Follow their instructions for gaining access to the Internet. You will use a browser to explore the resources; the instructions which follow refer to Netscape, the most widely used browser. Other browsers use similar approaches, and you should be able to adapt these instructions with your own browser in mind.

With the mouse, click on the "File" item on the upper left hand side of the screen. A pop-down menu will appear. Click on "Open Location." A window will appear, with a space for your to enter the location. Place the mouse pointer at the right-hand side of the space, click it, and enter the name of the location. Try entering the following:

http://www.bakerbooks.com/ccc/

Make sure that you type the slashes correctly, and note that this location terminates with the slash. Then either hit the "Entry" key, or click on "Open." The browser will indicate that it is establishing the connection; shortly, your screen will display the opening page of Jason D. Baker's invaluable resource *The Christian Cyberspace Companion*, which is published by Baker Book House of Grand Rapids, Michigan. You will notice that a number of options are set out in hypertext. Click on any of them, and follow the links through.

Sometimes servers are out of action for brief periods, due to faults or updating sessions. If you are having difficulty with this site, try the following. Again, follow the same procedure, and follow up on some links until you feel at home. Remember that you can go backwards by clicking on the "Back" button, if you want to return to something you explored earlier.

> http://www.yahoo.com/Society_and_Culture/Religion/
> Christianity/

Again, note that this ends with a slash. Make sure you type that slash, and that it is the right kind of slash!

Now that you have got used to this procedure, you are ready to surf the Internet, and track down the fascinating resources at your disposal. These have been grouped by subject; many contain links to other resources. Enjoy – and learn!

General Christian Resources

The best guides here are the following. All have extensive hypertext links, sometimes with powerful search engines, allowing direct access to a wide range of important resources:

> http://www.bakerbooks.com/ccc/
> http://www.iclnet.org/pub/resources/christian-resources.html
> http://www.yahoo.com/Society_and_Culture/Religion/
> Christianity/
> http://galaxy.einet.net/galaxy/Humanities/Religion.html

Due to the rapid change in many Web site locations, you are recommended to make use of these sites to navigate your way around Christian cyberspace. However, what follows is a list of more specific resources which you will find of interest.

Christian Denominations: Basic Locations

Catholicism

The best place to start your explorations is the excellent Home Page at the following location:

> http://www.cs.cmu.edu/Web/People/spok/catholic.html

The following subdirectories should also be explored:

> http://www.cs.cmu.edu/Web/People/spok/catholic/
>   teaching.html
> http://www.cs.cmu.edu/Web/People/spok/catholic/worship.html

This is one of the most useful resources for the study of modern Catholicism.

Among the various matters which you could explore, the following are of interest:

The Vatican

> http://www.christusrex.org/

One of the most popular sites on the Web, offering access to tours of the Sistine Chapel, and an enormous range of images from the Vatican Art Collection. Related material can be accessed at:

> http:/sunsite.unc.edu/expo.vatican.exhibit/Vatican.exhibit.html

Texts of the Mass

> http://www.uccla.org/uccla/UCC/mass.html

Notre Dame Center for Pastoral Liturgy

> http://www.nd.edu/~ndcpl/

Catholic Prayer Page

> http://www.webdesk.com/catholic/prayers/index.html

Baltimore Catechism

www.Catholic.netRCC/Catechism/Catechism.html

Text of Second Vatican Council

http://www.christusrex.org/www1/CDHN/v1.html

Text of Recent Papal Addresses

http://www.vatican.va/

Catholic Answers (Apologetic resources particularly aimed at Catholic users)

http://www.catholic.com/~answers/

Catholic Apologetics on the Internet

http://www.cwo.com/~pentrack/catholic/apolo.html

Catholic Doctrinal Concordance

http://www.infpage.com/concorda.htm

Orthodoxy

The Orthodox Page

http://www.ocf.org:80/OrthodoxPage/liturgy/liturgy.html

There are also specialist pages available on:

http://www.ocf.org:80/OrthodoxPage/liturgy/liturgy.html
http://www.ocf.org:80/OrthodoxPage/icons/icons.html
http://www.ocf.org:80/OrthodoxPage/readings/readings.html
http://www.ocf.org:80/OrthodoxPage/news/news.html

Coptic Orthodox Liturgy

http://www.frugal.com/~stmary/liturgy.html

Coptic Church Home Page

    http://cs-www.bu.edu/faculty/best/pub/cn/Home.html

Details on the history and present life of the Coptic Church.

Protestantism

1 Anglicanism
The Church of England Home Page contains details of Anglicanism in England, and of Anglican Communion in general. It also features links to the Archbishop of Canterbury.

    http://www.churchnet.org.uk/churchnet/home/church_house/

Anglicans Online:

    http://www.infomatch.com/~haibeck/anglican.html

Excellent starting point for information relating to Anglicanism in North America, although with some information relating to England.

For direct access to news items relating to the United States, go to:

    http://www.infomatch.com/~haibeck/anglican/usa.htm

For access to the Episcopal News Service, which provides up to date information on the Episcopal Church of the United States of America, see:

    http://www.intac.com/~rollins/ens.html

For news of Anglicanism worldwide, see:

    http://www.infomatch.com/~haibeck/anglican/world.htm

All Saints Anglican Church, Burnaby, BC, Canada:

    http://www.wsi.ca/~allsaints

Lists readings from Book of Alternative Services of the Anglican Church of Canada, and provides other useful information.

Episcopal Church Home Page:

    http://www.ai.mit.edu/people/mit/anglican/anglical.html

Unofficial home page of the Episcopal Church of the United States of America.

2   Baptists

http://oscar.teclink.net/~tgeorge/bapt_cov.html

Useful resource with links to items relating to Baptist history and identity.

The Spurgeon Archive:

http://www.gty.org/~philo/Spurgeon.html

The Quiet Page:

http://www.grfn.org/~mr_bill/Quiet.html

Collection of Baptist devotional material.

3   Lutherans
Consult the index at

http://www.bakerbooks.com/ccc/cid/
Churches_and_Denominations/Lutheran/index.html

for an excellent overview of some important resources.

Evangelical Lutheran Church of America Home Page:

http://www.ecla.org/

A useful resource for accessing details of this major Lutheran denomination.

Documents of the Missouri Synod:

http://www.iclnet.org/pub/resources/text/wittenberg/
wittenberg-msynod.html

This collection of documents will be of interest to any concerned with this major component of modern American Lutheranism.

Project Wittenberg:

http://www.iclnet.org/pub/resources/text/wittenberg/
wittenberg-home.html

A collection of documents of particular importance to Lutheran history and theology, in their original languages and English translation.

A good selection of Lutheran material may be found using the gopher located at the Concordia University, River Forest Illinois.

gopher://crf.cuis.edu/

4   Reformed and Presbyterian
Center for Reformed Theology and Apologetics:

http://www.erc.msstate.edu/~barlow/reformed.html

A useful resource for those interested in Reformed theology.

Christian Reformed Church Home Page:

http://www.grfn.org/religion/crc/crc.html

Details of the history and beliefs of this American denomination.

Calvin College Gopher:

gopher://gopher.calvin.edu/

A major resource for searching for historical and theological material relating to the Reformed tradition.

Presbyterian Church of America News Service:

http://www.pacifier.com/~bordwine/pca/affirm.html

A useful guide to news and views within the PCA. The unofficial Home Page is also worth a visit, at:

http://www.wavefront.com/~contra_m/pca.html

Orthodox Presbyterian Church Home Page:

http://www.opc.org/

A useful introduction to the history and theology of this relatively small American denomination.

Presbyterian Church (USA) Home Page:

http://pcusa.org/

Useful links with various resources relating to this major Presbyterian denomination.

A Glossary of Technical Christian Terms

What follows is a brief discussion of a series of technical terms relating to Christianity that the reader is likely to encounter in the course of reading. The following work is particularly recommended to those wishing to gain more detailed understanding of Christian terms:

E. A. Livingstone (ed.), *The Oxford Dictionary of the Christian Church* (Oxford: Oxford University Press, 1990).

Adoptionism   The heretical view that Jesus was "adopted" as the Son of God at some point during his ministry (usually his baptism), as opposed to the orthodox teaching that Jesus was Son of God by nature from the moment of his conception.

Advent   The opening period of the Christian year, which immediately precedes Christmas. The term derives from the Latin term *adventus* ("coming" or "arrival"), and refers to the coming of Jesus Christ (see p. 376).

Alexandrian School   A patristic school of thought, especially associated with the city of Alexandria in Egypt, noted for its Christology (which placed emphasis upon the divinity of Christ) and its method of biblical interpretation (which employed allegorical methods of exegesis). A rival approach in both areas was associated with Antioch.

Anabaptism   A term derived from the Greek word for "re-baptizer," and used to refer to the radical wing of the sixteenth-century Reformation, based on thinkers such as Menno Simons or Balthasar Hubmaier.

Analogy of being (*analogia entis*)   The theory, especially associated with Thomas Aquinas, that there exists a correspondence or analogy between the created order and God, as a result of the divine creatorship. The idea gives theoretical justification to the practice of drawing conclusions from the known objects and relationships of the natural order concerning God.

Analogy of faith (*analogia fidei*)   The theory, especially associated with Karl Barth, which holds that any correspondence between the created order and God is only established on the basis of the self-revelation of God.

Anthropomorphism   The tendency to ascribe human features (such as hands or arms) or other human characteristics to God.

Antiochene School A patristic school of thought, especially associated with the city of Antioch in modern-day Turkey, noted for its Christology (which placed emphasis upon the humanity of Christ) and its method of biblical interpretation (which employed literal methods of exegesis). A rival approach in both areas was associated with Alexandria.

Anti-Pelagian writings The writings of Augustine relating to the Pelagian controversy, in which he defended his views on grace and justification. See *Pelagianism*.

Apocalyptic A type of writing or religious outlook in general which focuses on the last things and the end of the world, often taking the form of visions with complex symbolism. The book of Daniel (Old Testament) and Revelation (New Testament) are examples of this type of writing.

Apologetics The area of Christian theology which focuses on the defense of the Christian faith, particularly through the rational justification of Christian belief and doctrines.

Apophatic A term used to refer to a particular style of theology, which stressed that God cannot be known in terms of human categories. "Apophatic" (which derives from the Greek *apophasis*, "negation" or "denial") approaches to theology are especially associated with the monastic tradition of the Eastern Orthodox church.

Apostolic era The period of the Christian church, regarded as definitive by many, bounded by the resurrection of Jesus Christ (*c.* AD 35) and the death of the last apostle (*c.* AD 90?). The ideas and practices of this period were widely regarded as normative, at least in some sense or to some degree, in many church circles.

Appropriation A term relating to the doctrine of the Trinity, which affirms that while all three persons of the Trinity are active in all the outward actions of the Trinity, it is appropriate to think of those actions as being the particular work of one of the persons. Thus it is appropriate to think of creation as the work of the Father, or redemption as the work of the Son, despite the fact that all three persons are present and active in both these works.

Arianism A major early Christological heresy, which treated Jesus Christ as the supreme of God's creatures, and denied his divine status. The Arian controversy was of major importance in the development of Christology during the fourth century.

Atonement An English term originally coined by William Tyndale to translate the Latin term *reconciliatio*, which has since come to have the developed meaning of "the work of Christ" or "the benefits of Christ gained for believers by his death and resurrection."

Barthian An adjective used to describe the theological outlook of the Swiss theologian Karl Barth (1886–1968), and noted chiefly for its emphasis upon the priority of revelation and its focus upon Jesus Christ. The terms "neo-Orthodoxy" and "dialectical theology" are also used in this connection.

Beatific vision A term used, especially in Roman Catholic theology, to refer to the full vision of God, which is allowed only to the elect after death. However, some writers, including Thomas Aquinas, taught that certain favored individuals – such as Moses and Paul – were allowed this vision in the present life.

Calvinism An ambiguous term, used with two quite distinct meanings. First, it refers to the religious ideas of religious bodies (such as the Reformed church) and individuals (such as Theodore Beza) who were profoundly influenced by John Calvin, or by documents written by him. Second, it refers to the religious ideas of

John Calvin himself. Although the first sense is by far the more common, there is a growing recognition that the term is misleading.

Cappadocian Fathers   A term used to refer collectively to three major Greek-speaking writers of the patristic period: Basil of Caesarea, Gregory of Nazianzen and Gregory of Nyssa, all of whom date from the late fourth century. "Cappadocia" designates an area in Asia Minor (modern-day Turkey) in which these writers were based.

Cartesianism   The philosophical outlook especially associated with René Descartes (1596–1650), particularly in relation to its emphasis on the separation of the knower from the known, and its insistence that the existence of the individual thinking self is the proper starting point for philosophical reflection.

Catechism   A popular manual of Christian doctrine, usually in the form of question and answer, intended for religious instruction.

Catholic   An adjective which is used both to refer to the universality of the church in space and time, and also to a particular church body (sometime also known as the Roman Catholic Church) which lays emphasis upon this point.

Chalcedonian definition   The formal declaration at the Council of Chalcedon that Jesus Christ was to be regarded as having two natures, one human and one divine.

Charisma, charismatic   A set of terms especially associated with the gifts of the Holy Spirit. In medieval theology, the term "charisma" is used to designate a spiritual gift, conferred upon individuals by the grace of God. Since the early twentieth century, the term "charismatic" has come to refer to styles of theology and worship which place particular emphasis upon the immediate presence and experience of the Holy Spirit.

Christology   The section of Christian theology dealing with the identity of Jesus Christ, particularly the question of the relation of his human and divine natures.

Circumincession   See *Perichoresis*.

Conciliarism   An understanding of ecclesiastical or theological authority which places an emphasis on the role of ecumenical councils.

Confession   Although the term refers primarily to the admission to sin, it acquired a rather different technical sense in the sixteenth century – that of a document which embodies the principles of faith of a Protestant church, such as the Lutheran Augsburg Confession (1530) or the Reformed First embodies the ideas of early Lutheranism, and the Reformed First Helvetic Confession (1536).

Consubstantial   A Latin term, deriving from the Greek term *homoousios*, literally meaning "of the same substance." The term is used to affirm the full divinity of Jesus Christ, particularly in opposition to Arianism.

Consubstantiation   A term used to refer to the theory of the real presence, especially associated with Martin Luther, which holds that the substance of the eucharistic bread and wine are given together with the substance of the body and blood of Christ.

Creed   A formal definition or summary of the Christian faith, held in common by all Christians. The most important are those generally known as the Apostles' Creed and the Nicene Creed.

Deism   A term used to refer to the views of a group of English writers, especially during the seventeenth century, the rationalism of which anticipated many of the ideas of the Enlightenment. The term is often used to refer to a view of God which recognizes the divine creatorship, yet which rejects the notion of a continuing divine involvement with the world.

Dialectical theology A term used to refer to the early views of the Swiss theologian Karl Barth (1886–1968), which emphasized the "dialectic" between God and humanity.

Docetism An early Christological heresy, which treated Jesus Christ as a purely divine being who only had the "appearance" of being human.

Donatism A movement, centering upon Roman north Africa in the fourth century, which developed a rigorist view of the church and sacraments.

Doxology A form of praise, usually especially associated with formal Christian worship. A "doxological" approach to theology stresses the importance of praise and worship in theological reflection.

Easter Probably the most important festival of the Christian year, which celebrates the resurrection of Jesus Christ (see pp. 382–4).

Ebionitism An early Christological heresy, which treated Jesus Christ as a purely human figure, although recognizing that he was endowed with particular charismatic gifts which distinguished him from other humans.

Ecclesiology The section of Christian theology dealing with the theory of the church.

Enlightenment, the A term used since the nineteenth century to refer to the emphasis upon human reason and autonomy, characteristic of much of western European and North American thought during the eighteenth century.

Epiphany The section of the Christian year which focuses on the making known of Jesus Christ to the world. The feast of Epiphany itself relates to the visit of the "wise men" (or "magi") to the new-born Jesus (see p. 378).

Eschatology The section of Christian theology dealing with the "end things," especially the ideas of resurrection, hell, and eternal life.

Eucharist The term used in the present volume to refer to the sacrament variously known as "the mass," "the Lord's Supper," and "holy communion."

Evangelical A term initially used to refer to reforming movements, especially in Germany and Switzerland, in the 1510s and 1520s, but now used of a the movement, especially in English-language theology, which places especial emphasis upon the supreme authority of Scripture and the atoning death of Christ.

Exegesis The science of textual interpretation, usually referring specifically to the Bible. The term "biblical exegesis" basically means "the process of interpreting the Bible." The specific techniques employed in the exegesis of Scripture are usually referred to as "hermeneutics."

Exemplarism A particular approach to the atonement, which stresses the moral or religious example set to belivers by Jesus Christ.

Fathers An alternative term for "patristic writers."

Feminism A movement in western theology since the 1960s, which lays particular emphasis upon the importance of "women's experience," and has directed criticism against the patriarchalism of Christianity.

Fideism An understanding of Christian theology which refuses to accept the need for (or sometimes the possibility of) criticism or evaluation from sources outside the Christian faith itself.

Five Ways, the A standard term for the five "arguments for the existence of God" associated with Thomas Aquinas.

Fourth Gospel A term used to refer to the Gospel according to John. The term highlights the distinctive literary and theological character of this gospel, which sets it apart from the common structures of the first three gospels, usually known as the "Synoptic Gospels."

Fundamentalism A form of American Protestant Christianity, which lays especial emphasis upon the authority of an inerrant Bible.

Hermeneutics The principles underlying the interpretation, or exegesis, of a text, particularly of Scripture, particularly in relation to its present-day application.

Hesychasm A tradition, especially associated with the eastern church, which places considerable emphasis upon the idea of "inner quietness" (Greek: *hesychia*) as a means of achieving a vision of God. It is particularly associated with writers such as Simeon the New Theologian and Gregory Palamas.

Historical Jesus A term used, especially during the nineteenth century, to refer to the historical person of Jesus of Nazareth, as opposed to the Christian interpretation of that person, especially as presented in the New Testament and the creeds.

Historico-Critical Method An approach to historical texts, including the Bible, which argues that only proper meaning must be determined on the basis of the specific historical conditions under which it was written.

History of Religions School The approach to religious history, and Christian origins in particular, which treats Old and New Testament developments as responses to encounters with other religions, such as Gnosticism.

Homoousion A Greek term, literally meaning "of the same substance," which came to be used extensively during the fourth century to designate the mainline Christological belief that Jesus Christ was "of the same substance of God." The term was polemical, beign directed against the Arian view that Christ was "of similar substance (*homoiousios*)" to God. See also *Consubstantial.*

Humanism In the strict sense of the word, an intellectual movement linked with the European Renaissance. At the heart of the movement lay, not (as the modern sense of the word might suggest) a set of secular or secularizing ideas, but a new interest in the cultural achievements of antiquity. These were seen as a major resource for the renewal of European culture and Christianity during the period of the Renaissance.

Hypostatic union The doctrine of the union of divine and human natures in Jesus Christ, without confusion of their respective substances.

Ideology A group of beliefs and values, usually secular, which govern the actions and outlooks of a society or group of people.

Incarnation An term used to refer to the assumption of human nature by God, in the person of Jesus Christ. The term "incarnationalism" is often used to refer to theological approaches which lay especial emphasis upon God's becoming human.

Justification by faith, doctrine of The section of Christian theology dealing with how the individual sinner is able to enter into fellowship with God. The doctrine was to prove to be of major significance at the time of the Reformation.

Kenoticism A form of Christology which lays emphasis upon Christ's "laying aside" of certain divine attributes in the incarnation, or his "emptying himself" of at least some divine attributes, especially omniscience or omnipotence.

Kerygma A term used, especially by Rudolf Bultmann (1884–1976) and his followers, to refer to the essential message or proclamation of the New Testament concerning the significance of Jesus Christ.

Lent The period of the Christian year which immediately precedes Easter, widely observed throughout the Christian world as a time of fasting or meditation. Lent opens with Ash Wednesday (see pp. 378–82).

Liberal Protestantism A movement, especially associated with nineteenth-century Germany, which stressed the continuity between religion and culture, flourishing between the time of F. D. E. Schleiermacher and Paul Tillich.

Liberation Theology Although this term designates any theological movement laying emphasis upon the liberating impact of the gospel, the term has come to refer to a movement which developed in Latin America in the late 1960s, which stressed the role of political action and orientated itself towards the goal of political liberation from poverty and oppression.

Liturgy The written text of public services, especially of the eucharist.

Logos A Greek term meaning "word," which played a crucial role in the development of patristic Christology. Jesus Christ was recognized as the "word of God"; the question concerned the implications of this recognition, and especially the way in which the divine "logos" in Jesus Christ related to his human nature.

Lutheranism The religious ideas associated with Martin Luther, particularly as expressed in the Lesser Catechism (1529) and the Augsburg Confession (1530).

Manicheism A strongly fatalist position associated with the Manichees, to which Augustine of Hippo attached himself during his early period. A distinction is drawn between two different divinities, one of which is regarded as evil, and the other good. Evil is thus seen as the direct result of the influnece of the evil god.

Modalism A Trinitarian heresy, which treats the three persons of the Trinity as different "modes" of the Godhead. A typical modalist approach is to regard God as active as Father in creation, as Son in redemption, and as Spirit in sanctification.

Monophysitism The doctrine that there is only one nature in Christ, which is divine (from the Greek words *monos*, "only one," and *physis*, "nature"). This view differed from the orthodox view, upheld by the Council of Chalcedon (451), that Christ had two natures, one divine and one human.

Neo-Orthodoxy A term used to designate the general position of Karl Barth (1886–1968), especially the manner in which he drew upon the theological concerns of the period of Reformed Orthodoxy.

Ontological argument A term used to refer to the type of argument for the existence of God especially associated with the scholastic theologian Anselm of Canterbury.

Orthodoxy A term used in a number of senses, of which the following are the most important: Orthodoxy in the sense of "right belief," as opposed to heresy; Orthodoxy in the sense of the forms of Christianity which are dominant in Russia and Greece; Orthodoxy in the sense of a movement within Protestantism, especially in the late sixteenth and early seventeenth century, which laid emphasis upon need for doctrinal definition.

Parousia A Geek term, which literally means "coming" or "arrival," used to refer to the second coming of Christ. The notion of the *parousia* is an important aspect of Christian understandings of the "last things."

Patripassianism A theological heresy, which arose during the third century, associated with writers such as Noetus, Praxeas and Sabellius, focusing on the belief that the Father suffered as the Son. In other words, the suffering of Christ on the cross is to be regarded as the suffering of the Father. According to these writers, the only distinction within the Godhead was a succession of modes or operations, so that Father, Son, and Spirit were just different modes of being, or expressions, of the same basic divine entity.

Patristic An adjective used to refer to the first centuries in the history of the church, following the writing of the New Testament (the "patristic period"), or thinkers writing during this period (the "patristic writers"). For many writers, the period thus designated seems to be *c.*100–451 (in other words, the period between the completion of the last of the New Testament writings and the landmark Council of Chalcedon).

Pelagianism An understanding of how humans are able to merit their salvation which is diametrically opposed to that of Augustine of Hippo, placing considerable emphasis upon the role of human works and playing down the idea of divine grace.

Pentecost The feast which celebrates the coming of the Holy Spirit on the Day of Pentecost (see p. 385).

Perichoresis A term relating to the doctrine of the Trinity, often also referred to by the Latin term *circumincessio*. The basic notion is that all three persons of the Trinity mutually share in the life of the others, so that none is isolated or detached from the actions of the others.

Pietism An approach to Christianity, especially associated with German writers in the seventeenth century, which places an emphasis upon the personal appropriation of faith, and the need for holiness in Christian living. The movement is perhaps best known within English-language world in the form of Methodism.

Postliberalism A theological movement, especially associated with Duke University and Yale Divinity School in the 1980s, which criticized the liberal reliance upon human experience, and reclaimed the notion of community tradition as a controlling influence in theology.

Postmodernism A general cultural development, especially in North America, which resulted from the general collapse in confidence of the universal rational principles of the Enlightenment.

Praxis A Greek term, literally meaning "action," adopted by Karl Marx to emphasize the importance of action in relation to thinking. This emphasis on "praxis" has had considerable impact within Latin American liberation theology.

Protestantism A term used in the aftermath of the Diet of Speyer (1529) to designate those who "protested" against the practices and beliefs of the Roman Catholic church. Prior to 1529, such individuals and groups had referred to themselves as "evangelicals."

Quadriga The Latin term used to refer to the "four-fold" interpretation of Scripture according to its literal, allegorical, tropological moral, and analogical senses.

Radical Reformation A term used with increasing frequency to refer to the Anabaptist movement – in other words, the wing of the Reformation which went beyond what Luther and Zwingli envisaged, particularly in relation to the doctrine of the church.

Reformed A term used to refer to a tradition of theology which draws inspiration from the writings of John Calvin (1510–64) and his successors. The term is now generally used in preference to "Calvinist."

Sabellianism An early trinitarian heresy, which treated the three persons of the Trinity as different historical manifestations of the one God. It is generally regarded as a form of modalism.

Sacrament In purely historical terms, a church service or rite which was held to have been instituted by Jesus Christ himself. Although Roman Catholic theology and church practice recognize seven such sacraments (baptism, confirmation, eucharist, marriage, ordination, penance, and unction), Protestant theologians generally argue that only two (baptism and eucharist) were to be found in the New Testament itself.

Schism   A deliberate break with the unity of the church, condemned vigorously by influential writers of the early church, such as Cyprian and Augustine.

Scholasticism   A particular approach to Christian theology, associated especially with the Middle Ages, which lays emphasis upon the rational justification and systematic presentation of Christian theology.

Scripture principle   The theory, especially associated with Reformed theologians, that the practices and beliefs of the church should be grounded in Scripture. Nothing that could not be demonstrated to be grounded in Scripture could be regarded as binding upon the believer. The phrase *sola scriptura*, "by Scripture alone," summarizes this principle.

Soteriology   The section of Christian theology dealing with the doctrine of salvation (Greek: *soteria*).

Synoptic Gospels   A term used to refer to the first three gospels (Matthew, Mark and Luke). The term (derived from the Greek word *synopsis*, "summary") refers to the way in which the three gospels can be seen as providing similar "summaries" of the life, death, and resurrection of Jesus Christ.

Synoptic Problem   The scholarly question of how the three Synoptic Gospels relate to each other. Perhaps the most common approach to the relation of the three Synoptic Gospels is the "Two Source" theory, which claims that Matthew and Luke used Mark as a source, while also drawing upon a second source (usually known as "Q"). Other possibilities exist: for example, the Grisebach hypothesis, which treats Matthew as having been written first, followed by Luke and then Mark.

Theodicy   A term coined by Leibniz to refer to a theoretical justification of the goodness of God in the face of the presence of evil in the world.

Theopaschitism   A disputed teaching, regarded by some as a heresy, which arose during the sixth century, associated with writers such as John Maxentius and the slogan "one of the Trinity was crucified." The formula can be interpreted in a perfectly orthodox sense and was defended as such by Leontius of Byzantium. However, it was regarded as potentially misleading and confusing by more cautious writers, including Pope Hormisdas (died 523), and the formula gradually fell into disuse.

Theotokos   Literally, "the bearer of God." A Greek term used to refer to Mary, the mother of Jesus Christ, with the intention of reinforcing the central insight of the doctrine of the incarnation – that is, that Jesus Christ is none other than God. The term was extensively used by writers of the eastern church, especially around the time of the Nestorian controversy, to articulate both the divinity of Christ and the reality of the incarnation.

Transubstantiation   The doctrine according to which the bread and the wine are transformed into the body and blood of Christ in the eucharist, while retaining their outward appearance.

Trinity   The distinctively Christian doctrine of God, which reflects the complexity of the Christian experience of God. The doctrine is usually summarized in maxims such as "three persons, one God."

Two natures, doctrine of   A term generally used to refer to the doctrine of the two natures, human and divine, of Jesus Christ. Related terms include "Chalcedonian definition" and "hypostatic union."

Vulgate   The Latin translation of the Bible, largely deriving from Jerome, upon which medieval theology was largely based.

Zwinglianism The term is used generally to refer to the thought of Huldrych Zwingli, but is often used to refer specifically to his views on the sacraments, especially on the "real presence" (which for Zwingli was more of a "real absence").

Further Reading

The present work has introduced a wide range of historical, theological, and practical issues relating to Christianity. What follows is a brief listing of some books for further reading which will allow you to follow up these introductory sections in much greater depth.

Part I Jesus of Nazareth: the Founder and the Sources

The Bible

D. A. Carson, Douglas J. Moo and Leon Morris, *An Introduction to the New Testament* (Grand Rapids: Zondervan, 1994).

Bruce Chilton, *Beginning New Testament Study* (London: SPCK, 1986).

R. E. Clements, *The World of Ancient Israel* (Cambridge: Cambridge University Press, 1995).

James D. G. Dunn, *Unity and Diversity in the New Testament*, 2nd edn (London: SCM Press, 1990).

Robert H. Gundry, *A Survey of the New Testament* (Grand Rapids: Zondervan, 1994).

Luke T. Johnson, *The Writings of the New Testament: An Interpretation* (Philadelphia: Fortress Press, 1986).

Otto Kaiser, *Introduction to the Old Testament* (Oxford: Blackwell, 1975).

Bruce M. Metzger, *The New Testament: Its Background, Growth and Content* (Nashville, TN: Abingdon, 1983).

——, and Michael D. Coogan, *The Oxford Companion to the Bible* (Oxford: Oxford University Press, 1994).

J. R. Porter, *The Illustrated Guide to the Bible* (Oxford: Oxford University Press, 1995).

Jesus

William Barclay, *Jesus as They Saw Him* (London: SCM Press, 1962).

R. Bauckham, R. T. France, M. Maggay, J. Stamoolis, and C. P. Thiede, *Jesus 2000: A Major Investigation into History's Most Intriguing Figure* (Oxford: Lion, 1989).

R. E. Brown, *Jesus, God and Man: Modern Biblical Reflections* (Milwaukee: Bruce, 1967).

F. F. Bruce, *The Gospel of John* (Grand Rapids: Eerdmans, 1983).

Oscar Cullmann, *The Christology of the New Testament* (Philadelphia: Westminster Press, 1959).

Stephen T. Davis, *Risen Indeed: Making Sense of the Resurrection* (Grand Rapids: Eerdmans, 1993).

John Drane, *Jesus and the Four Gospels* (Oxford: Lion, 1984).

James D. G. Dunn, *Christology in the Making* (London: SCM Press, 1980).

James D. G. Dunn, *The Evidence for Jesus* (London: SCM Press, 1986).

Richard T. France, *Jesus and the Old Testament* (Downers Grove, IL: InterVarsity Press, 1971).

——, *The Evidence for Jesus* (London: Hodder & Stoughton, and Downers Grove, IL: InterVarsity Press, 1987).

Michael Green, *Who is this Jesus?* (London: Hodder & Stoughton, 1990).

Aloys Grillmeier, *Christ in Christian Tradition*, 2nd edn (London: Mowbrays, 1976).

Murray J. Harris, *Jesus as God: The New Testament Use of Theos in Reference to Jesus* (Grand Rapids: Baker, 1992).

Morna D. Hooker, "Interchange in Christ," *Journal of Theological Studies* 22 (1971), pp. 349–61.

Ernst Käsemann, "The Saving Significance of the Death of Jesus in Paul," in *Perspectives on Paul* (Philadelphia: Fortress Press, 1971), pp. 32–59.

J. Macquarrie, *Jesus Christ in Modern Thought* (London: SCM Press, 1990).

I. H. Marshall, *The Origins of New Testament Christology* (Downers Grove, IL: InterVarsity Press, 1976).

L. Morris, *The Apostolic Preaching of the Cross*, 3rd edn (Leicester: Inter-Varsity Press, 1975).

C. F. D. Moule, *The Origin of Christology* (Cambridge: Cambridge University Press, 1977).

G. O'Collins, *Jesus Risen* (London: Darton, Longman and Todd, 1987).

W. Pannenberg, *Jesus – God and Man* (London: SCM Press, and Westminster: Philadelphia, 1968).

A. J. Saldarini, *Pharisees, Scribes and Sadducees in Palestinian Society* (Edinburgh: Clark, 1989).

J. R. W. Stott, *The Cross of Christ* (Leicester: Inter Varsity Press, 1986).

G. Theissen, *The Shadow of the Galilean* (London: SCM Press, 1987).

C. P. Thiede, *Jesus – Life or Legend* (Oxford: Lion, 1990).

D. F. Wells, *The Person of Christ: A Biblical and Historical Analysis of the Incarnation* (Westchester, IL: Crossway, 1984).

N. T. Wright, *Who was Jesus?* (London: SPCK and Grand Rapids: Eerdmans, 1992).

Part II The Teachings of Christianity

The most widely used introduction to Christian theology is:

Alister E. McGrath, *Christian Theology: An Introduction* 2nd edn (Oxford/Cambridge, MA: Blackwell Publishing, 1996).

This book can be used in conjunction with a collection of nearly 300 primary texts, gathered together in:

Alister E. McGrath (ed.), *The Christian Theology Reader* (Oxford/Cambridge, MA: Blackwell Publishing, 1995).

The following are also useful as introductions to this general field, and are all worth exploring. The annotations indicate the kind of approach adopted by their authors.

C. E. Braaten and R. W. Jenson (eds), *Christian Dogmatics*, 2 vols (Philadelphia: Fortress Press, 1984). Very demanding, and written from an explicitly Lutheran perspective; however, it is worth the trouble to read, especially its essays relating to revelation and the doctrine of God.

Millard J. Erickson, *Christian Theology* (Grand Rapids: Baker, 1992). Written from a broadly Baptist and evangelical perspective.

Francis F. Fiorenza and John P. Galvin, *Systematic Theology: Roman Catholic Perspectives*, 2 vols (Minneapolis: Fortress Press, 1991); also published as single-volume edition (Dublin: Gill and Macmillan, 1992). An excellent overview of the leading themes of systematic theology from a Roman Catholic perspective.

Stanley J. Grenz, *Theology for the Community of God* (Nashville, TN: Broadman & Holman, 1994). A stimulating overview of the whole field of Christian theology, written from a Baptist perspective.

P. Hodgson and R. King (eds), *Christian Theology* (Philadelphia: Fortress Press, 1982); also available in an expanded edition, with two extra essays on theological method and the sacraments respectively. Written from a generally liberal perspective; stronger on more recent discussions of classic questions.

Daniel E. Migliore, *Faith Seeking Understanding* (Grand Rapids: Eerdmans, 1991). A useful overview of all the main areas of theology from a generally Reformed perspective by a highly stimulating and engaging writer.

Part III The History of Christianity

Paul

B. R. Gaventa, *From Darkness to Light: Aspects of Paul's Conversion in the New Testament* (Philadelphia: Fortress Press, 1986).

E. P. Sanders, *Paul and Palestinian Judaism* (Philadelphia: Fortress Press, 1977).

A. F. Segal, *Paul the Convert: The Apostolate and Apostasy of Saul the Pharisee* (New Haven: Yale University Press, 1990).

K. Stendahl, *Paul among Jews and Gentiles* (Philadelphia: Fortress Press, 1976).

The Patristic Period

Henry Bettenson, *Documents of the Christian Church* 2nd edn (Oxford: Oxford University Press, 1963).

Henry Chadwick, *The Early Church* (London/New York: Pelican, 1964).

Jean Comby, *How to read Church History*, vol. 1 (London: SCM Press, 1985).

Jean Daniélou and Henri Marrou, *The Christian Centuries*, vol. 1 (London: Darton, Longman and Todd, 1964).

W. H. C. Frend, *The Rise of Christianity* (Philadelphia: Fortress Press, 1984).

Ian Hazlett (ed.), *Early Christianity: Origins and Evolution to A.D. 600* (London: SPCK, 1991).

Herbert Jedin and John Dolan (eds), *A Handbook of Church History* vol. 1 (London: Burns & Oates, 1965).

J. N. D. Kelly, *Early Christian Doctrines*, 4th edn (London: A. & C. Black, 1968).

F. van der Meer and Christine Mohrmann, *Atlas of the Early Christian World* (London: Nelson, 1959).

J. Stevenson, *A New Eusebius: Documents Illustrating the History of the Church to A.D. 337*, rev. edn (London: SPCK, 1987).

——, *Creeds, Councils and Controversies: Documents Illustrating the History of the Church, 337–461*, rev. edn (London: SPCK, 1987).

Frances M. Young, *From Nicea to Chalcedon* (London: SCM Press, 1983).

Women in Early Christianity

Mary Hayter, *The New Eve in Christ* (London: SPCK, 1987).

Morna Hooker, "Authority on Her Head: An Examination of 1 Corinthians 11:10," *New Testament Studies* 10 (1964), pp. 410–16.

W. D. Thomas, "The Place of Women in the Church at Philippi," *Expository Times* 83 (1971), pp. 117–20.

Ben Witherington III, *Women in the Ministry of Jesus* (Cambridge: Cambridge University Press, 1984).

——, *Women in the Earliest Churches* (Cambridge: Cambridge University Press, 1988).

Celtic Christianity

Louis Gougaud, *Christianity in Celtic Lands* (London: Batsford, 1981).

Richard T. Hanson, *Saint Patrick: His Origins and Career* (Oxford: Oxford University Press, 1968).

James P. Mackey (ed.), *An Introduction to Celtic Christianity* (Edinburgh: T. & T. Clarke, 1989).

Douglas Simpson, *The Celtic Church in Scotland* (Aberdeen: Aberdeen University Press, 1935).

The Middle Ages

Peter Burke, *The Italian Renaissance: Culture and Society in Italy*, rev. edn (Oxford: Polity Press, 1986).

Frederick Coplestone, *A History of Christian Philosophy in the Middle Ages* (London: Sheed & Ward, 1978).

Robert O. Crummey, *The Formation of Muscovy, 1304–1613* (London: Longman, 1987), pp. 116–42.

Manfred P. Fleischer (ed.), *The Harvest of Humanism in Central Europe* (St Louis, MO: Concordia Publishing House, 1992).

Etienne Gilson, *The Spirit of Medieval Philosophy* (London: Sheed & Ward, 1936).

Judith Herrin, *The Formation of Christendom* (Princeton: Princeton University Press, 1987).

David Knowles, *The Evolution of Medieval Thought*, 2nd edn (London/New York, 1988).

Alister E. McGrath, *The Intellectual Origins of the*

European Reformation (Oxford: Blackwell, 1987), pp. 32–121.

John Meyendorff, *Byzantine Theology: Historical Trends and Doctrinal Themes*, 2nd edn (New York: Fordham University Press, 1983).

Heiko A. Oberman, *Masters of the Reformation* (Cambridge: Cambridge University Press, 1981).

John W. O'Malley, Thomas M. Izbicki, and Gerald Christianson (eds), *Humanity and Divinity in Renaissance and Reformation* (Leiden: Brill, 1993).

J. H. Overfeld, *Humanism and Scholasticism in Late Medieval Germany* (Princeton, NJ: Princeton University Press, 1984).

Steven E. Ozment, *The Age of Reform 1250–1550: An Intellectual and Religious History of Late Medieval and Reformation Europe* (New Haven: Yale University Press, 1973).

Josef Pieper, *Scholasticism: Personalities and Problems of Medieval Philosophy* (London: Faber & Faber, 1961).

Roy Porter, and Mikuláš Teich (eds), *The Renaissance in National Context* (Cambridge: Cambridge University Press, 1992).

B. B. Price, *Medieval Thought: An Introduction* (Oxford/Cambridge, MA: Blackwell, 1992).

Lewis W. Spitz, *The Religious Renaissance of the German Humanists* (Cambridge, MA: Harvard University Press, 1963).

Individual Theologians of the Middle Ages

Frederick Coplestone, *Aquinas* (London: Pelican, 1975).

Brian Davies, *The Thought of Thomas Aquinas* (Oxford: Clarendon Press, 1992).

Leo Elders, *The Philosophical Theology of St Thomas Aquinas* (Leiden: Brill, 1990).

Gillian R. Evans, *Anselm* (London: Geoffrey Chapman, 1989).

Gordon Leff, *William of Ockham* (Manchester: Manchester University Press, 1975).

Andrew Louth, *Denys the Areopagite* (London: Geoffrey Chapman, 1989).

John Meyendorff, *A Study of Gregory Palamas*, 2nd edn (Crestwood, NY: St Vladimir Seminary Press, 1974).

James A. Weisheipl, *Friar Thomas d'Aquino: His Life, Thought and Work* (Garden City, NY: Doubleday, 1972).

Allan B. Wolter and Marilyn McCord Adams (eds), *The Philosophical Theology of John Duns Scotus* (Ithaca, NY: Cornell University Press, 1990).

The Reformation and Post-Reformation Periods

John Bossy, *Christianity in the West* (Oxford: Oxford University Press, 1985).

Euan Cameron, *The European Reformation* (Oxford: Oxford University Press, 1991).

Owen Chadwick, *The Reformation* (London/New York: Pelican, 1976).

G. R. Elton (ed.), *The Reformation 1520–1559*, 2nd edn (Cambridge: Cambridge University Press, 1990).

Timothy George, *The Theology of the Reformers* (Nashville, TN: Abingdon, 1988).

Alister E. McGrath, *Reformation Thought: An Introduction*, 2nd edn (Oxford/Cambridge, MA: Blackwell, 1993).

Richard A. Muller, *Post-Reformation Reformed Dogmatics* (Grand Rapids: Baker, 1987).

Mark A. Noll, *Confessions and Catechisms of the Reformation* (Grand Rapids: Eerdmans, 1991).

John W. O'Malley, Thomas M. Izbicki, and Gerald Christianson (eds), *Humanity and Divinity in Renaissance and Reformation* (Leiden: Brill, 1993).

B. M. G. Reardon, *Religious Thought in the Reformation* (London: Longman, 1981).

Robert P. Scharlemann, *Thomas Aquinas and John Gerhard* (New Haven: Yale University Press, 1964).

Lewis W. Spitz, *The Protestant Reformation 1517–1559* (New York: Scribners, 1986).

Individual Theologians of the Reformation Period

Roland H. Bainton, *Here I Stand: A Life of Martin Luther* (New York: Mentor Books, 1955).

W. J. Bouwsma, *John Calvin: A Sixteenth-Century Portrait* (New York: Oxford University Press, 1988).

E. J. Furcha and H. W. Pipkin (eds), *Prophet, Pastor, Protestant: The Work of Huldrych Zwingli* (Allison Park, PA: Pickwick Publications, 1984).

Further Reading

Alexandre Ganoczy, *The Young Calvin* (Edinburgh: T. & T. Clark, 1988).

James M. Kittelson, *Luther the Reformer: The Story of the Man and His Career* (Leicester: Inter-Varsity Press, 1989).

Walter von Loewenich, *Martin Luther: The Man and His Work* (Minneapolis: Augsburg, 1986).

Bernard Lohse, *Martin Luther: An Introduction to His Life and Work* (Philadelphia: Fortress Press, 1986).

James McConica, *Erasmus* (Oxford: Oxford University Press, 1991).

Alister E. McGrath, *Luther's Theology of the Cross: Martin Luther's Theological Breakthrough* (Oxford: Blackwell, 1985).

——, *A Life of John Calvin* (Oxford/Cambridge, MA: Blackwell, 1990).

Perry Millar, *Jonathan Edwards* (New York: Sloane Associates, 1949).

T. H. L. Parker, *John Calvin* (London: Dent, 1975).

Hugo Rahner, *Ignatius the Theologian* (London: Chapman, 1990).

R. J. Schoeck, *Erasmus of Europe: The Making of a Humanist 1467–1500* (Edinburgh: Edinburgh University Press, 1990).

Harold P. Simonson, *Jonathan Edwards: Theology of the Heart* (Grand Rapids: Eerdmans, 1974).

John E. Smith, *Jonathan Edwards: Puritan, Preacher, Philosopher* (London: Chapman, 1993).

W. P. Stephens, *The Theology of Huldrych Zwingli* (Oxford: Oxford University Press, 1986).

François Wendel, *Calvin* (New York: Harper & Row, 1963).

Rowan Williams, *Teresa of Avila* (London: Chapman, 1991).

D. F. Wright (ed.), *Martin Bucer: Reforming Church and Community* (Cambridge: Cambridge University Press, 1994).

The Modern Period

Sydney E. Ahlstrom, *A Religious History of the American People* (New Haven, CT: Yale University Press, 1972).

Owen Chadwick, *The Victorian Church*, 2 vols (London: Black, 1966–70).

David F. Edwards, *The Futures of Christianity* (London: Hodder & Stoughton, 1987).

Edwin S. Gaustad, *A Documentary History of Religion in America*, 2 vols (Grand Rapids: Eerdmans, 1993).

Adrian Hastings, *A History of English Christianity 1920–1985* (London: Collins, 1986).

Hubert Jedin, *The Church in the Modern World* (New York: Crossroad, 1993).

Kenneth S. Latourette, *Christianity in a Revolutionary Age*, 5 vols (New York: Harper, 1958–62).

John McManners, *Church and State in France 1870–1914* (London: SPCK, 1972).

Sydney E. Mead, *The Lively Experiment: The Shaping of Christianity in America* (New York: Harper & Row, 1963).

Edward R. Norman, *Church and Society in England, 1770–1970* (Oxford: Clarendon Press, 1976).

Individual Theologians of the Modern Period

There are numerous study aids available for those wishing to pursue details of individual theologians during the modern period. The following works are of fundamental importance.

For a survey of Christian thought and thinkers since the Enlightenment, see:

Alister E. McGrath (ed.), *Blackwell Encyclopaedia of Modern Christian Thought* (Oxford/Cambridge, MA: Blackwell, 1993).

For specialist studies of nineteenth-century Christian theology and theologians, see:

Ninian Smart, John Clayton, Patrick Sherry and Steven T. Katz (eds), *Nineteenth-Century Religious Thought in the West*, 3 vols (Cambridge: Cambridge University Press, 1985).

Claude Welch, *Protestant Thought in the Nineteenth Century*, 2 vols (New Haven: Yale University Press, 1972–85).

For valuable surveys of twentieth-century writers, see:

David F. Ford (ed.), *The Modern Theologians* (Oxford/Cambridge, MA: Blackwell Publishers, 2nd edn, 1996).

Stanley J. Grenz and Roger E. Olson, *Twentieth-*

Century Theology: God and the World in a Transitional Age (Downers Grove, IL: InterVarsity Press, 1992).

For further details of many theologians active in the nineteenth and twentieth centuries, see Martin E. Marty and Dean G. Peerman, *A Handbook of Christian Theologians* (Nashville: Abingdon Press, 1984).

Christianity in the Developing World

Kofi Appiah-Kubi and Sergio Torres (eds), *African Theology en route* (Maryknoll, NY: Orbis Books, 1979).

Robin S. H. Boyd, *Introduction to Indian Christian Theology*, 2nd edn (Madras: CLT, 1974).

William A. Dryness, *Learning about Theology from the Third World* (Grand Rapids: Zondervan, 1992).

—— (ed.), *Emerging Voices in Global Theology* (Grand Rapids: Zondervan, 1995).

Elizabeth Isichei, *A History of Christianity in Africa* (London: SPCK, 1995).

Kosuke Koyama, "Asian Theology," in D. F. Ford (ed.), *The Modern Theologians*, 2 vols (Oxford/Cambridge, MA: Blackwell Publishing, 1990), vol. 2, pp. 217–34.

Jung Young Lee, "Korean Christian Thought," in A. E. McGrath (ed.), *The Blackwell Encyclopaedia of Modern Christian Thought* (Oxford/Cambridge, MA: Blackwell, 1993), pp. 308–13.

Stephen Charles Neill, *A History of Christianity in India*, 2 vols (Cambridge: Cambridge University Press, 1984–1985).

John Parratt (ed.), *A Reader in African Christian Theology* (London: SPCK, 1987).

C. S. Song, *Third-Eye Theology: Theology in Formation in Asian Settings* rev. edn (Maryknoll, NY: Orbis, 1990).

R. S. Sugirtharajah and C. Hargreaves (eds), *Readings in Indian Christian Theology* (London: SPCK, 1993).

Shunici Takayanagi, "Japanese Christian Thought," in A. E. McGrath (ed.), *The Blackwell Encyclopaedia of Modern Christian Thought* (Oxford/Cambridge, MA: Blackwell, 1993), pp. 280–4.

Carver T. Yu, "Chinese Christian Thought," in A. E. McGrath (ed.), *The Blackwell Encyclopaedia of Modern Christian Thought* (Oxford/Cambridge, MA: Blackwell, 1993), pp. 71–7.

Part IV The Christian Way

The Christian Life

Jane Dillenberger, *Style and Content in Christian Art* (London: SCM Press, 1986).

Louis Duchesne, *Christian Worship: Its Origins and Evolution* (London: SPCK, 1949).

Thomas S. Garrett, *Christian Worship: An Introductory Outline* (Oxford: Oxford University Press, 1963).

René Guéron, *The Symbolism of the Cross* (London: Luzac, 1958).

H. A. L. Jefferson, *Hymns in Christian Worship* (London: Rockliff, 1950).

Norman Laliberté and Edward N. West, *The History of the Cross* (New York: Macmillan, 1960).

Allen A. McArthur, *The Evolution of the Christian Year* (London: SCM Press, 1953).

E. Panofsky, *Gothic Architecture and Scholasticism* (London: Thames & Hudson, 1948).

Gertrud Schiller, *Iconography of Christian Art*, 2 vols (London: Lund Humphries, 1971).

David Self, *High Days and Holidays: Celebrating the Christian Year* (Oxford: Lion, 1993).

James F. White, *A Brief History of Christian Worship* (Nashville, TN: Abingdon, 1993).

Modern Christianity

Robert A. Baker (ed.), *A Baptist Source Book* (Nashville, TN: Broadman, 1966).

Henry Bett, *The Spirit of Methodism* (London: Epworth Press, 1937).

Emory S. Bucke, *The History of American Methodism* (New York: Abingdon, 1964).

Ian Bunting (ed.), *Celebrating the Anglican Way* (London: Hodder & Stoughton, 1996).

Rupert E. Davies, *Methodism* (London: Epworth Press, 1976).

Werner Elert, *The Structure of Lutheranism* (St Louis, MO: Concordia, 1962).

Timothy George and David S. Dockery, *Baptist Theologians* (Nashville, TN: Broadman, 1990).

John H. Leith, *Introduction to the Reformed Tradition* (Atlanta, GA: John Knox Press, 1981).

Further Reading

H. Leon McBeth, *The Baptist Heritage* (Nashville, TN: Broadman, 1987).

Alister E. McGrath, *Evangelicalism and the Future of Christianity* (Downers Grove, IL: InterVarsity Press, 1995).

Elsie Anne McKee and Brian G. Armstrong, *Probing the Reformed Tradition* (Louisville, KY: Westminster/John Knox Press, 1989).

Donald K. McKim (ed.), *Major Themes in the Reformed Tradition* (Grand Rapids, MI: Eredmans, 1992).

David Martin, *Tongues of Fire: The Explosion of Protestantism in Latin America* (Oxford: Blackwell, 1990).

John Meyendorff, *The Orthodox Church*, 3rd edn (Crestwood, NY: St Vladimir's Seminary Press, 1981).

Richard Quebedeaux, *The New Charismatics: The Origins: Developments and Significance of Neo-Pentecostalism* (New York: Doubleday, 1976).

Wade Clark Roof and William McKinney, *American Mainline Religion: Its Changing Shape and Future* (Princeton: Rutgers University Press, 1987).

Vinay Samuel and Christopher Sugden, *Lambeth: A View from the Two Thirds World* (London: SPCK, 1989).

David Stoll, *Is Latin America Turning Protestant?* (Berkeley: University of California Press, 1991).

Stephen W. Sykes and John Booty (eds.), *The Study of Anglicanism* (London; SPCK, 1988).

C. Peter Wagner, *The Third Wave of the Holy Spirit: Encountering the Power of Signs and Wonders Today* (Ann Arbor, MI: Servant, 1988).

Software Packages Relating to the Study of Christianity

A large range of computer software is now available for those wishing to study Christianity in more depth. Most focus on the Bible, often making available the original Hebrew and Greek texts of the Old and New Testaments, as well as a wide range of English translations (including the King James Version, the Revised Standard Version, and the New International Version). Many are available in DOS, Windows and Macintosh versions, often on CD-ROM. Many also offer important classical Christian texts in English translation, grammatical aids, Bible atlases, and reference notes or commentaries.

The following are illustrative of the types of material available. In each case, the name of the software package is provided, along with the address of the electronic publishing house responsible for its production or distribution.

Bible Source
Zondervan Publishing House, 5300 Patterson Avenue SE, Grand Rapids, MI 49530.

Logos Bible Software
Logos Research Systems, 2117 200 Ave W., Oak Harbor, WA 98277.

PC Study Bible
BibleSoft, 22014 7th Ave S., #201, Seattle, WA 98198.

The Bible on Disk for Catholics
Ligouri Faithware, One Ligouri Dr, Ligouri, MO 63057.

Thompson Chain HyperBible
Kirkbride Technology, 335 W. 9th St, Indianapolis, IN 46202.

The Lion CD-ROM of the Bible and Christianity
The Lion PS History of Christianity
IVP New Bible Dictionary of the Bible
IVP New Bible Atlas
All available from Lion Publishing, Peter's Way, Sandy Lane West, Oxford OX4 5BR, United Kingdom.

Index